The Cornerstone:

Classroom Management That Makes Teaching More Effective, Efficient, and Enjoyable

The Cornerstone:

Classroom Management That Makes Teaching More Effective, Efficient, and Enjoyable

Angela Powell

due season PRESS

The Cornerstone:
Classroom Management That Makes Teaching More Effective, Efficient, and Enjoyable
by Angela Powell

Printed in the United States of America

ISBN 978-0-9823127-0-4

www.due-season-press.com

Dedication

All glory, honor, and praise unto the Creator for constantly guiding and inspiring me.
He is the true Cornerstone, the foundation of everything I have accomplished, and the Author of all that is to come.

It's all for His glory!

Acknowledgements

Mom and Dad, you have always recognized God's plan for me in teaching, and have supported my educational pursuits at great personal sacrifice. You were the earliest fans of my writing and the first to suggest that I pursue my talents professionally. Thank you for loving me, no matter what, and for never giving up on me. I love the Lord like I do because of your example.

Curtis, you have kept me focused on the big picture and God's vision for our lives since day one. You are the moon reflecting onto me the beauty and light that emanate from the Son alone. I shine brighter because of you. Your encouragement has been unceasing, and your unconditional love continues to astound me. Thank you for being there every step of the way, for teaching me to never limit myself or God, and for your faith that His plan will be exceedingly, abundantly above all we could ask, think, or imagine.

About The Cornerstone

This book is about solutions. It is about what's worked in my classroom and what I know will work in yours. I wrote this book for the same reason I created my website (http://www.TheCornerstoneForTeachers.com): to share tools for overcoming discipline issues, disorganization, paperwork overload, and the regimented, boring curriculums that drive so many teachers from the classroom each year.

My advice is based on a tremendous amount of research that I have studied, modified, and implemented in various classrooms over the years. My experience has been with second and third graders, as well as preschoolers in Head Start and severely autistic students in an early childhood special education center. I've worked in eight schools, public and private, in three different school districts in two different states (just over the Washington, D.C. border in Maryland, and later in Miami and Fort Lauderdale, Florida). I've taught in an extremely affluent suburban community and in some of the most challenging urban areas in the country. This book is the summation of what I've learned through it all.

I've included photographs and sample forms wherever possible to help illustrate my points and make my suggestions easier to implement. Unfortunately, the cost of this book would have been prohibitively high if the photos were colorized, so in order to provide a reasonably-priced resource for teachers, I've kept everything in black and white. The good news is that you can view all the photos from this book and countless others in an enlarged and full-color format on the website. There's also a blank version of every form in this book available for free download. All the documents are in Word format so you can type in any changes you want to fit your own needs. You'll also find on the site hundreds of other forms that I didn't have room for here.

All of the photos and ideas in this book are from my own classroom, so another great advantage of the website is that you can access other teachers' ideas. I've collected a massive amount of links to free printable resources and more in-depth information on almost every classroom management topic imaginable. These links are changed and updated all the time, so if there's an idea in this book you'd like to learn more about, chances are good that my website will direct you to additional current resources.

Effective classroom practice is all about trying new ideas, reinventing old ones, and experimenting with whatever it takes to help kids learn. I don't believe there's one right way to manage a classroom, especially since there's no one teaching method or strategy that will reach all students. Only YOU can determine what will work best in your classroom—but you need to be highly knowledgeable about best practice in order to make those decisions. I hope this book and the accompanying website will be two of many resources you use to help determine the most effective methods for your teaching context and philosophy.

Each time you open this book, I hope that you will find a practical suggestion for improving your classroom management, and each time you close it, I want you to feel inspired, rejuvenated, and full of confidence that you can handle every task that's set before you. My aspiration is to make your teaching life as effective, efficient, and ENJOYABLE as possible!

Angela Powell

Table of Contents

PART SIX: IMPLEMENTING INSTRUCTION EFFECTIVELY

PART SEVEN: PARTNERING WITH PARENTS, COLLEAGUES, AND ADMINISTRATION

PART EIGHT: LEARNING AND ADAPTING TO THE REALITIES OF TEACHING

Part One:
Beginning the Year With Confidence

Chapter 1: Classroom Arrangement
Setting up an environment that is conducive to learning

Whether you're a new teacher or a veteran, the experience of walking into your classroom for the time in August always involves a unique juxtaposition of emotions. You feel both optimistic and anxious, enthusiastic yet overwhelmed, excited about the fresh start and saddened by the end of a long summer vacation. Personally, I love to have a clean slate at the start of every school year. I enjoy wiping away the dust of the summer from shelves and setting up new classroom materials and workbooks. I like picking out new bulletin board paper and borders (although I never look forward to putting them up!). And I especially enjoy rearranging my classroom.

The possibilities for classroom set-up are broad and varied, and I like to switch things around at least a little bit every year. It's one of the most important things I do in August, because my classroom is where I'll be spending at least 40 hours a week. I want it to be comfortable, inviting, and functional for me and the children. During the week of teacher planning before school starts, I often spend hours shifting things around in the classroom and taking photographs, then carefully examining the photos at home and sketching out alternatives to try the following day. I keep making changes until I feel like I've found an arrangement that will truly support the instruction I've planned and make it as easy as possible for the students and myself to stay organized.

The first step in effective classroom management is setting up a physical classroom layout that will facilitate your routines and procedures. You should view your arrangement as a work in progress that will probably be changed multiple times throughout the year as you adjust things for your students' evolving needs. That means you don't have to have everything perfect right away.

There are several basic components of an elementary classroom that you will probably need to plan for:

1) **student desks**
2) **instructional area in the front of the room**
3) **your desk area**
4) **computers**
5) **group work areas (tables), including space for small group instruction**
6) **classroom library**
7) **whole class meeting area on a rug or carpet (optional)**
8) **centers (optional)**

I've listed each space in the order I think is most important. For example, your student desk area should be considered first, because desks take up the most amount of space and their placement will either enhance or detract from instruction. Your own desk area is critical because in order for you to stay organized, you have to provide yourself with easily accessible storage space around your desk. While computers are not a central component of whole-class instruction, you should consider their placement before determining your layout for other elements, because you will probably be limited by the distribution of outlets and Internet jacks in your classroom.

Once those elements are in place, you can plan an area for the children to sit on a rug or carpet, if that's a management strategy you like to use. (I highly recommend it, because the rug can be a great place to read a story, have a class problem solving meeting, or teach a lesson in which you don't want students distracted by materials in their desks.) If your students will be completing partner and group work activities, it's also helpful to have tables and open floor space around the room for them to meet with each other. This also prevents students from having to sit in the same seat all day long.

If you have a large collection of children's books, then a library area is important to consider. The idea of a cozy reading area with a rug and bean bags is appealing but not really necessary unless you plan a structured time and method for students to utilize it. The library may be part of your center areas, if you choose to include these in your room. Centers are an option that you may want to begin using later in the year and you can plan space for them. However, most teachers do not have extra room in their classroom for separate and distinct center areas, and if they are not an integral part of your curriculum, it's not necessary to design your room that way.

The rest of this chapter will provide a description of the areas listed, as well as ideas for setting them up. Each explanation is accompanied by photographs from classrooms I've taught in over the years. There are innumerable effective ways to set up a classroom, and it's nearly impossible to copy someone else's ideas unless you have the exact same materials and classroom layout, so please don't feel like there is one right set-up that you have to discover. The process of arranging a classroom is closely related to your own intuition and creativity. Try drawing a few arrangements on paper first and see what works for your needs. My ideas are presented here only to help you remember to plan for each necessary element of your classroom, and to assist you in thinking ahead about how your arrangement will facilitate procedures and routines.

Arranging Student Desks

Once you're comfortable with the way you have arranged your desks, all your other areas will begin falling into place. Like everything else in your room, desk arrangement doesn't have to be permanent, and you can change the set-up as often as needed. With some groups of children, I used one arrangement all year; with others, I tried new set-ups every few weeks. There are several basic desk arrangements that I rotate between:

- Rows (Straight or Angled)
- Modified U (or Horseshoe)
- Groups (or Teams)
- Combination (desks in various positions)

Rows: Straight or Angled

Pros: *Enables the teacher to see what every child is doing, gives all students a clear view of the front of the room, can take up less floor space than other arrangements.*
Cons: *Does not work well with a large number of desks because students will be too far away, less effective in terms of management when more than two rows are used.*

I like having desks in rows (straight or angled) because all the kids are facing me. This helps me see if they're on-task and makes it easier for them to concentrate. Row arrangements also make it easy to move around the room. Another benefit is that students can work with partners without having to move their desks because they are sitting right alongside one another.

The advantage of angled over straight-facing rows is that the angle makes it easier for students to see and leaves space in the front of the room for a rug, open area, overhead projector cart, podium, table, and so on. The photo to the right shows the angled style in a different classroom, this time with a projector cart in the middle instead of a rug and the desks pulled much closer to the front of the room.

Modified U/Horseshoe

Pros: *Allows you to fit many desks into a small space, students talk less when they are further apart from their friends.*
Cons: *Spreads children out considerably so that it can be hard to address them all.*

As shown on the left, I began one particular school year with 22 desks in a modified horseshoe shape, leaving a small break in the middle and sides of the desk arrangement to use as walk-through spaces. This created a large center space that I could stand in to see each student's work.

The photo to the right shows what the same arrangement looked like the following year when I took away the front part of the horseshoe and started adding desks to the center in clusters. This arrangement had 27 desks. It looks a bit crowded in the picture, but it worked well because I could see everyone's face and move around to help them easily.

The modified U was one of the few ways I could have that many desks and still provide room for all the areas I like to leave in the back of the room (tables, classroom library, etc.). This set-up also provided a large space in the front of the room for kids to sit on the rug while I taught.

The two pictures on the next page show a modified U in a different classroom with only 20 desks. The photo on the left was taken from the entrance, and the one on the right was taken from the opposite corner in the back of the room. The U-shape was perfect for the end of the year when I was doing less direct instruction and the kids were working more independently (with their desks that far away from one another, it can be hard to teach everyone at the same time). Students do tend to talk less when they are this spread out. Having the table and rug in the center was also helpful, because I could move students to these areas during instruction if they needed to see better or if they were playing around at their desks. I was able to utilize the space against the walls and windows for tables and group work areas.

Groups/Teams

Pros: *Can save floor space even with many desks, supports cooperative work.*
Cons: *Promotes off-task behavior, distracting for many students.*

This was an arrangement I wasn't able to use when I had close to 30 kids in my class, because when children were facing one another at their desks, it was just too much work to keep them from talking during instruction and independent work times. However, I have found that there are some smaller classes of children who can handle sitting in groups. This arrangement shows 3 groups of 5, with 2 kids who could not handle the groups sitting by themselves off to the side. I loved having the groups angled like this because all the kids could see the board and I could stand in one spot and see everyone's face and work area.

The arrangement in the photo to the right was designed to have 4 groups of 4 with one child sitting alone. A new student enrolled and one of the groups then had 5, for a total of 18 kids. The desks are not set on an angle so there would be space in the middle of the groups for my overhead projector cart.

Combination Arrangements

Pros: Provides for each individual student's needs; extremely flexible.
Cons: Requires special procedures for passing out and collecting papers/supplies.

When I taught second grade in the inner-city, most of my class had an extremely difficult time demonstrating self-control and appropriate social behaviors. The best desk arrangement for those children didn't fit any standard set-up. Instead, I had the kids who needed to sit alone in separated desks (shown on the left), usually with a chart stand separating them into two rows so they couldn't see the person next to them. In the picture on the right, you can see two desks pressed together: one was for a girl with behavior problems and the other was for a very quiet boy that worked exceptionally well with her. I had four kids who were capable of sitting in a group, so their desks were pushed together. Other children could better handle sitting in a row. The close proximity helped them because they could tell what they were supposed to be doing by looking at their neighbors, but they didn't have anyone directly facing them. Another child's behavioral outbursts were so severe that his desk was placed in the very back of the classroom where he would be less likely to hurt other students. As you can see, this 'non-arrangement' actually looks very nice and contributed to positive classroom management. So, you don't have to limit yourself to one particular set-up if a variety of arrangements will work best for you and your students.

Arrangements I Have Not Used (And Why)

- **Pairs:** This is a very effective arrangement in terms of minimizing talking and ensuring that the teacher can see everyone, but takes up a tremendous amount of floor space.

- **Desks completed separated:** Although this set-up makes it difficult for children to talk and play around, it also makes it difficult for them to work together. In addition, having all the desks apart is the most space-consuming arrangement.

A Note About Children Who Need to Sit Alone

It is absolutely fine to have certain children sit apart from their peers. Nearly every teacher I know has at least one student whose desk must be in an isolated area. When I set up my desks at the beginning of the year, I try to leave space for one or two desks to be apart from the class, and move children there as needed. I let the kids know that everyone will get the chance to make good choices and stay with the group, but there is a place for them if they can't handle it.

Some children need to sit alone as a consequence for poor behavior. Others simply work better when there's no one nearby to distract or talk to them. Explain to students that you are seating them alone in order to help and not punish them, and provide lots of encouragement when they stay on-task in their isolated spots. They can have a chance to move back with the rest of the class if they make good choices. Some kids are in and out of 'isolation' all year, while others only need to be set apart for a few days or weeks.

The way you handle this situation is up to your professional discretion; my advice is to prepare for the eventuality that some children will work better by themselves and leave space in your room arrangement to accommodate their needs.

Determining Where to Place Particular Students' Desks

One of the most important considerations in positioning each particular student is personality. Alternating boys and girls usually helps cut down on off-task behavior. I try to place students away from their close friends but near people they get along with to avoid constant petty arguments. Talkative and easily distracted students are usually placed on the sides of the room so there are less people around them. Another consideration is for children who have vision impairments or other disabilities and need to be placed up front.

If you like to try different room arrangements or move students' desks around a lot, you know it takes a lot of forethought in terms of matching up personalities and abilities, considering proximity to the front of the room, and so on. Laminate two index cards and then cut them into little rectangles, writing a student's name on each one. Add Velcro to the back and keep the rectangles on a piece of felt. Then you can play with various set-ups throughout the year without having to physically move desks until you know you've got the right arrangement.

Setting Up Your Instructional Space(s)

If you plan to do all of your whole-class instruction with students at their desks, then you only need to plan one space where you will keep instructional posters/

displays and the materials you need to teach. If you also want a whole-class meeting area on a rug or carpet, you will need to plan two instructional spaces. Consider the function of each as your arrange your classroom: what will you be teaching when students are in each place, and what materials will you most likely need to have nearby? I like to keep certain supplies in my main instructional space in

front of students' desks as well as in my secondary instructional space by the rug. Sticky notes, pens, markers, timers, scissors, and so on are kept in two or sometimes three spots around the room for easy access.

While it's not advisable to hang things on the walls until you've got your furniture where you want it, you should plan ahead for certain materials that need to be displayed prominently in your classroom. When setting up your whole-group meeting area, you may want to consider the placement of a calendar and the accompanying activities you will do with your class, a daily schedule display, maps, class behavior plan posters and reminders, etc.

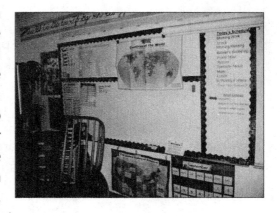

In one school, I used a large white bookshelf as my 'podium' to hold the materials I needed to access when I was in front of the class. I kept my teacher's guides, worksheets for the day, reading group supplies, and even a trashcan inside! It was slightly off-center in the front of the room so that it wouldn't block the kids' view when they sat on the rug.

Many upper elementary teachers like to have a table in the front of the room to hold the materials they use when teaching. I tried this one year but disliked standing behind the table when writing on the board. However, I did like being able to sit down at the front of the room while the kids were working independently, rather than sitting at my desk.

(Left) I prefer to use bookshelves and various carts to hold my instructional materials. (Right) I keep a lot of things on my overhead projector cart: the middle shelf holds individual dry erase boards, felt erasers, and markers, and the bottom shelf of the overhead cart holds all of my transparencies. The organizer that fits around the overhead projector holds timers, equity sticks, math manipulatives, and more.

I also make good use of every square inch on my television cart! I keep extra scissors and glue sticks in containers next to the VCR/DVD player so helpers can

pass them out when needed. Behind those are the videos and DVDs I own. I also have plastic drawers on the shelf, in which I keep various teaching resources. Other materials that are kept on the television cart include a cassette/CD player, a drawer for extra class work papers (so that anyone who is missing a paper or needs another copy can find what they need), and art supplies for kids to access during projects.

Setting Up the Teacher's Desk Area

Desk Placement

Traditionally teachers have placed their desks front and center in the classroom. However, most elementary teachers no longer find much time to sit at their desks during the instructional day, and now place their desks to the side or even in the back of the classroom. I have put my desk in every imaginable place, and the spot I always preferred was in the front, off to the side. This way I could sit at my desk and still keep an eye on the kids, without having it in my way when I was

trying to teach. If you do plan to sit at your desk or a table while students are in the classroom, I recommend placing your more mischievous kids near where you'll be sitting and the more trustworthy ones on the furthest end of the room.

You may want to consider where most of your shelving and storage is, and place your desk near that area so that everything can be kept in one easily accessible location. I try to utilize every bit of space around my desk and leave very few materials on the desk itself so that I have a neat space in which to work.

You should also think about the placement of your desk relative to the door. You may not want your desk area to be visible from the doorway, yet having it on the

opposite side of the room from the entrance can be a big hassle when you need to run back in to get something. If you keep a computer or laptop on your desk and don't have wireless Internet access in your classroom, you will need to consider the location of Internet jacks in the room. Buying an inexpensive cordless phone can prevent you from having to keep your desk near a phone jack.

Setting Up Computers

Designing a functional, attractive space for computers is one of the biggest headaches for teachers as they set up their rooms because of the jumble of wires, cords, and outdated materials. Many schools are now getting wireless carts which hold class sets of laptops. The good news for those who don't have the latest technology is that you can place all of your computers in one spot even if your Internet jacks are spread out around the room by spending about twenty dollars on an Internet router. The router functions a lot like a power strip, in which you plug it into one Internet jack and then plug the Internet cords for the rest of your computers directly into the router. On the other hand, it can be helpful to have your computers spread out around the room, because students are less likely to talk to each other while they're supposed to be working on a program. I always prefer to have my computers behind student desks so that the kids are not looking at what's on the screens while they're at their seats.

One year, I used a horseshoe table for computers and I loved the way it kept all the equipment together in one location, yet provided space between each monitor so the students were not distracted by what others were doing.

I color-code each monitor, keyboard, mouse, outlet, and Internet jack with sticky dots to keep track of which items go with each machine. The half hour I spend at the beginning of the school year to untangle, set up, and color-code all of the equipment is well spent.

Since every computer is already color-coded, I use the same system to set up a computer schedule that shows each child which computer to use at each time during the day, along with particular programs that I want them to use. The schedule can be modified at any time, and then slid into the page protector which has the sticky dots on it.

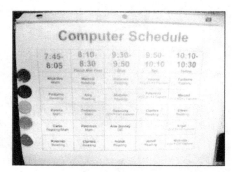

Setting Up Group Work Areas (Tables and/or Centers)

Having places in your classroom for students to complete partner and group work can be very helpful, especially if their desks are not in clusters and it is difficult for them to work together at their seats. Being able to 'sit around the room' is a big treat for kids because it allows them to move away from their regular seating areas and work with different people.

I try to have enough group work areas so that if I were to have all of the kids pair up, each set of partners would have a separate place to work. For a class of twenty, that means having ten group work areas. This is not as impossible as it sounds, because not all students will choose to work at tables. Some kids like sprawling out on small area rugs or carpet scraps with clipboards. They also love using TV trays. In a pinch, I'll allow two groups of students to sit at the same table, but I typically like to have the class spread out so they don't distract or copy each other.

In the classroom shown on the left, there are five tables (four of which are pictured), but nine group work areas because there are four spaces on the floor in various parts of the room. The photograph on the right shows ten group work areas, several of which double as center areas (Social Studies, Science, Language Arts, Reading, and Math). Students used the areas during our reading block to complete centers, and during the rest of the day, they were free to choose any one of the spots for group work. This classroom is actually quite a bit smaller than the one shown in the first photo, but I was able to fit in all the areas because most are small (accommodating only 2-3 students).

Setting Up Your Reading Group Area

The intricacies of setting up your materials for small group reading instruction are explained in depth in Chapter 20 of this book. Since your reading groups won't begin until several weeks into the school year, you don't need to spend a lot of time on this area before school starts. However, you will need to choose a space in which to teach.

The table you use should be in close proximity to wherever you have your students do their independent work while you work with groups. For management purposes, you should be able to see all of your students easily from your reading group table.

Placing your table near a board or easel (or leaving room for a small portable board) is also helpful. Additionally, you should include a shelf, cabinet, rolling cart, or other storage place to hold all of your reading group supplies.

This is my favorite reading group table, because it's a U shape. When I sat in the middle, I was able to see all of my students easily and was in arm's reach of everyone. I placed the table in front of a chalkboard, and I used a small whiteboard as well. The little black cart hidden behind the table held my supplies, and was on wheels so I could push it out of the way as needed.

In another classroom, I had a rectangular table for reading instruction. I had one blue chair and all the others burgundy so that students would know which seat not to sit in. The cabinets, shelves, and crates held my reading group supplies.

Setting Up the Classroom Library

This is an older photo, taken back when the fire marshal still allowed us to have throw rugs, couches, and lamps! This was a very comfortable area that the students looked forward to reading in. I even held parent conferences there.

While it's ideal to have your library set up in a cozy corner, the most important factor to consider when placing your book area is shelf space. If students will be spending the majority of time reading at their desks, then having your library in the middle of a classroom wall (as pictured here) will work fine. Spread out the space as much as possible so that students will not be bumping into one another when choosing books. Also, if you place book bins too high, too low, or in a hard-to-reach spot, students will be less inclined to put them away neatly.

Windowsills can be a great location for book bins if you have a limited number of shelves. The windowsill shown here holds students' individual book boxes. (More details about this concept and organizing a class library can be found in Chapter 7, Maintaining a Class Library.)

This photo shows the labels for my book bins that indicate genre. Under each bin, the shelf has a matching label so that children can put the bins back correctly if they take them off the shelf to look through. Also, each book has a sticky dot on it with a genre abbreviation so students can return books to the correct bin.

Hanging pocket charts can hold nonfiction reading materials such as menus, maps, magazines, atlases, and so on. Two spinning book racks were obtained for free when a local craft store went out of business. I use them to hold the books that students can take home. Having a separate area for take-home books prevents the kids from accidentally borrowing books from our classroom library.

Inexpensive Ideas for Decorating Your Classroom

- **Don't change bulletin boards frequently and keep them generic.** There's no law that says you have to have new bulletin board displays for every holiday. Pick bulletin board paper that will work all year long and change the border only if you must. (For example, red paper is nice for fall leaves and apples, then for Christmas, later for Valentine's Day, and finally for a general or thematic display towards the end of the year.) I buy one versatile set of borders for each bulletin board I have and leave them up. I have frogs, planets, paintbrushes, designs, plain colors, and other themes not associated with any particular time of year. Also, remember that your border does not have to correlate with the material that's on the board, as long as the colors and styles complement one another. A bulletin board about transportation does not have to have a train border: a plain blue one will work just fine.

♦ **Display a minimum of seasonal decorations.** I try to pick borders that don't need to be changed—I don't want to worry about having snowflakes still displayed in April! In fact, I rarely hang up kids' seasonal work, focusing on thematic displays or things that look good all year, such as "Our Best Work." When I do hang seasonal work, I try to do it at least a month before the occasion so it can stay up as long as possible.

♦ **Focus on useful displays.** A pretty poster is just taking up wall space unless it's helping the kids learn, retain, and utilize their skills. Hang up your text connections poster, tricks for remembering multiplication facts, directions for long division, the correct writing format, a calendar with important dates and events for your students clearly marked, and so on. Refer to the posters often and your kids will, too. You'll find that once you've filled your room with useful materials, you'll have very little space that must be 'decorated'.

♦ **Make (simple) things.** Craft stores sell special markers that let you draw on windows—these can be used to create innumerable seasonal displays and instructional aides. If your school has one, use the die cutter to cut out shapes to spruce up wall displays. Use what you have, what your school provides, and the things other teachers are willing to share to make your classroom beautiful. Don't get fooled into thinking that things have to be fancy or store-bought.

♦ **Have students make decorations.** My kids have made posters explaining how to solve math problems, displays of different geometric shapes in the classroom, a 'quilt' of their favorite books, etc. Also, large paintings done by children always look beautiful. Use student's work rather than store-bought posters. It's more meaningful to the kids, and tells visitors more about what's happening in your classroom.

♦ **Look for free posters.** There are often free pull-out posters in teacher magazines. If your college, public library, or school media center subscribes, ask if you can take the posters out of older issues. The teacher's guides for student's science and current event magazines often have posters in them as well, so if the school pays for your class' subscription to a magazine, you will automatically receive new displays for your classroom walls almost every week.

Chapter 2: Planning for the First Weeks of School
Making preparations and starting the year off right

If it's any consolation to a stressed-out teacher in August, let me assure you that the start of school is definitely the hardest time, and things WILL get easier as the school year progresses! There are days in the beginning of the year in which you want to collapse by noon because you are so exhausted. That's totally normal, even for veteran teachers! So if you're close to having a nervous breakdown and school hasn't even begun yet, be encouraged. There will be other stressful points in the year, certainly—but by the end of September, you'll be over the first and biggest hurdle. There is light at the end of the tunnel!

Two Common Misperceptions

When preparing for their first job, new teachers often make two mistakes in their thinking:

1) The most important task is planning what to do on the first day
2) Having fun back-to-school activities is essential

The first day of school is certainly critical, but it's only one aspect of the big picture of classroom management. Creating, introducing, modeling, and reinforcing your procedures and routines is the most crucial task you will accomplish in the beginning of the year and must be viewed as a long-term plan. You will be setting the tone for your class throughout the first several weeks of school. You will be constantly reinforcing your rules and routines because you can't teach all of your procedures on the first day, and students need lots of modeling and practice. Plan ahead—what will you do on the SECOND day of school? It's important to think out how you will reinforce your routines the following week, and the week after that. (Don't worry, I'll walk you through every step!)

The second misperception comes from the wealth of resources about what to "do" with the kids on the first day of school. You teach them, that's what! Rules, routines, procedures, and then academics as soon as possible. You don't need a bunch of cutesy get-to-know-you games mixed with "curriculum light"—in fact, many principals are cracking down on this tradition and insisting that grade level curriculum be taught on the first day of school. Whether you think that's too extreme or not, the best teachers do get procedures in place quickly so they can get down to business right away. You only have your children for ten months— you cannot afford to waste a week or two on back-to-school activities. The exception to this is when those activities are educational, but that is seldom the case—the purpose is generally to get kids acclimated and ready to learn. If students know your expectations and procedures, and your classroom tone is safe and inviting, students will adjust easily within your regular curriculum and routines.

Preparing for Classroom and Behavior Management

Planning When and How to Teach Routines and Procedures

The most important thing you can do is plan out your routines (the regular procedures). All of them. Pencil sharpening, bathroom privileges, passing in papers, even stacking chairs on desks at the end of the day. Figure out exactly what you want kids to do, and how to communicate those expectations to them. The more specific you are, the less room there will be for students to misinterpret or push the limits of what is acceptable. Write down the procedures you plan in case you forget or if you are put on the spot, and leave the list for substitutes so they can reference it when needed. Don't worry, you can always change things later. It's better to say to students, "You know? I don't think this way is working, let's try this" than to let the classroom be a free-for-all until you have it all figured out. (By the way, even after many years in the classroom, you won't EVER have it all figured out. I still try new procedures and routines every year, looking for the optimal way to make my classroom run smoothly. That's part of the art of teaching, so enjoy the possibilities!)

You can't teach it all the first day. You have to prioritize which routines must be taught first thing, which can be taught later in the day, and which can wait for later in the week. How to move about in the classroom (no running), where to hang coats and backpacks, and hand-raising policies are things you will probably cover as the situations arise naturally within the first half hour of children entering the room. Later, you can practice hallway behavior, bathroom expectations, pencil sharpening routines, and rules/conflict resolution. (With my Pre-Kindergarten children, I would talk about friendship and respect as soon as the class was settled down, so that I could begin to model problem solving, rather than spend the day intervening in conflicts. With elementary-aged kids, I generally wait until the afternoon or the second day because they already have some knowledge of what is appropriate and what isn't in school.) In the afternoon, you can teach students about heading papers, homework procedures, and dismissal routines. On the second day, you will explicitly reinforce what you have already taught, and add things such as how to pass in papers, distribute supplies, and participate in teaching techniques you plan to use (think-pair-share, partner reading, noise level monitoring devices, the 3 Before Me rule, etc.).

Sample Lesson Plans for the First Week of School

First Day Procedures

- **What students should do when they walk in the room on the first day**
- **What to do with school supplies they've brought (for now)**
    (Students do Morning Work while teacher takes attendance, finds out how students are getting home after school)
- **Quiet signals (clicker, hand signal, bell, etc.)**
- **What students are to do when they want your attention**
- **What to do when the bell rings/announcements/the pledge begins**
- **Bathroom/hand washing/getting a tissue/drinks procedures**
- **What to do with trash (when to throw away and where)**
- **Pencil sharpening procedures**
- **Friday Folders/Works in progress (put Morning Work inside)**
- **How to pass out papers (for the next activity)**
- **What to do if you don't get a paper or have extras**
    (Getting to Know You activity such as Name Scavenger Hunt)
- **How to pass in papers (from last activity) and where completed papers go**
- **How to move from desks to rug and how to sit on rug**
- **Intro class rules/behavior system/rewards and consequences**
- **Intro procedures for 'following along' during instruction**
    (Teach a short interactive lesson, such as Daily Language Review, to break up procedural information)
- **Go through school supplies (put in desks/collect extras)**
- **Teach desk organization**

-Explain and choose class jobs
-Discuss lining up and hallway expectations, how to hold door
   (Specials Classes)
-Procedures for staying 'on-task' during independent work
   (Inventory test/baseline assessment for math)
-Introduce agendas, homework routines, Home-School Folders
-Review lining up, hallway procedures
-Lunch procedures
   (Lunch)
-Teach playground rules
   (Recess)
-Intro forms to be signed and put in Home-School Folder
-Dismissal procedures and keeping quiet when the loudspeaker comes on

Second Day Procedures

-Review what students should do when they walk in the room on the first day
   (Students do Morning Work while teacher takes attendance and attends to misc. tasks)
-Review what to do when the bell rings/announcements/the pledge begins
-Review quiet signals (clicker, hand signal, bell, etc.)
-Review bathroom/hand washing/getting a tissue/drinks procedures
-Review pencil sharpening procedures
-Discuss tardy procedures
-Where to find assignments if students have been absent
-Review procedures for 'following along'
   (Teach short reading lesson: explain how students are to show that they understand something, choral response, individual response)
-Watch Code of Conduct video and discuss
-Read a book about making good choices and discuss
-Review class rules/behavior system
   (Spelling lesson)
-Review lining up/hallway procedures
   (Specials)
-Intro math warm-up procedures
-Review procedures for 'following along'
   (Math lesson)
-How to head papers
-Procedures for staying 'on-task' during independent work
   (Baseline writing assessment)
-Review how to pass in papers
-Review lunch procedures
   (Lunch)
-Review recess rules
   (Recess)

-Review procedures for 'following along'
   (Science lesson)
-Review dismissal procedures

<u>Third Day Procedures:</u>

-Continue with procedures already put in place with continual modeling and reinforcement
-Intro class library
-Intro writing workshop format, practice independent writing, what to do with journals
-Review respect and intro 'supportiveness' in preparation for cooperative learning

<u>Fourth Day Procedures:</u>

-Continue modeling/reinforcement for routines and play procedures game (see Chapter 9)
-What to do during emergency drills
-Intro regular academic routines such as Mountain Math and mad minute fact drills
-Intro procedures for 'working together' and give a partner assignment at desks

<u>Fifth Day Procedures:</u>

-Continue modeling/reinforcement for routines and play procedures game
-Review behavior plan and Friday reward
-Review 'working together' and do another lesson that includes cooperative work (pairs)

<u>As Needed:</u>
Going to the office (nurse)
Finding directions for each assignment
Getting materials without disturbing others
When visitors are in the classroom
If the teacher is out of the classroom
Saying 'Excuse me'
If a student is suddenly ill and what constitutes an emergency
Social expectations and manners (i.e., saying thank you, not interrupting conversations)

Rules vs. Procedures

Many new teachers are very concerned about how to create and enforce classroom rules. Let's clarify what purpose rules serve and how they differ from routines. ***Rules set the tone for the learning environment and provide broad guidelines about what should and should not be happening as a whole in the classroom. Procedures and routines are specific steps that kids are supposed to take in particular scenarios.*** Therefore, your focus as a teacher should be to prevent rule violations by pro-actively planning routines and procedures.

A possible analogy for this difference can be made using our speed limit laws. The *rule* on a particular road may be for cars to go no more than 55 miles per hour. But the *procedure* is to keep an eye on your speedometer. The *procedure* is to keep both hands on the wheel and stay focused on the road ahead of you, not talking on a cell phone or listening to really loud music that will distract you from monitoring your speed.

The procedure tells you how to be successful at keeping the rule. The procedure is practiced over and over until it is automatic. If the procedure is practiced diligently, the rule will be broken and consequences will need to be enforced far less often.

Similarly, you will get better results with practicing how to line up quietly (over and over and over in August) than with saying, "Stop running! That's against the rules!" (over and over and over all year long). Rules are what help set the general tone for your classroom, but routines are what keep your classroom running smoothly.

You will need rules so that students have a framework for the routines you set up. Children should follow the routines for keeping their desks neat because that's part of the rule about being a responsible student. They should follow the routines for passing in papers without disrupting others because that's part of the rule about respecting other people. They should follow the routines for raising their hands because that's part of the rule about respecting the teacher.

Instead of Rules, Create Goals

Another way to think about and explain rules is to set them as goals (i.e., Goal #1: Respect Yourself, Goal #2: Respect Others). The routines and procedures help children meet those goals successfully. If you phrase things this way with the children, the corrective statement "Hitting is against the rules" changes to, "Our class goal is to be respectful to our friends. Hitting does not help us meet our goal." Following the 'rules' then becomes a team effort to meet the goals that children agreed upon from the beginning of the year.

Setting Rules/Goals

Some teachers like to make rules as a class. I've also found that to be effective, but you've probably figured out by now that I like to do things differently with each group of children I have. In recent years, I have usually had the rules already made up. Normally I select three rules that pretty much cover everything from talking to fighting to writing on desks:

1. Respect yourself.
2. Respect others.
3. Respect the school [you could include "and everything in it"].

What does RESPECT....	
Look like? [picture of eye]	Sound like? [picture of ear]

On the first day of school, we talk about the meaning of the word 'respect' using a chart like the one shown. Students describe what a respectful classroom looks and sounds like, and we refer to the chart as needed during the first few weeks of school to analyze whether certain actions are respectful or disrespectful. Respect is usually a 30 minute lesson broken up into two days (15 minutes each day) but I have taught classes for which only one lesson was needed because most students came from homes in which parents had already instilled this value in their children.

If I feel like my class needs to explore the concept further, on the second day I put scenarios on scraps of paper, have students draw them out of a box and read them, and we discuss. I try to choose situations that are 'gray areas' and not obvious to encourage critical thinking, moral reasoning, and lots of group discussion! It gives me a good idea of who has higher-order thinking skills in place and what students' value systems are. We also talk about disrespect (a term that most of them are familiar with from home, music, etc.). They can easily name all the disrespectful behaviors that take place in the classroom, but need help brainstorming a list of alternative actions.

I taught at a school that had an awesome set of five "Rules of Respect" that I thought were perfectly phrased, so I created the posters above. They can serve as powerful classroom goals:

1. I will reflect RESPECT.
2. I will be a RESPONSIBLE student.
3. I will display GOOD MANNERS.
4. I will practice acts of KINDNESS.
5. I will promise to ALWAYS DO MY BEST!

Working With District Guidelines

Some schools already have a system of rules and consequences that they will expect you to use (such as checkmarks or tallies) which track misbehavior and enforce punishments such as time-outs, filling out problem solving sheets, missing recess, phone calls home, suspension, and so on. For legal and accountability purposes, I think these decisions are best made with your grade level team and administration, if they are not already mapped out by your school system. Some districts have general guidelines, which each grade level in the school modifies as appropriate. The rules and consequences are then signed by the principal, parents, and students, so that if problems arise, everyone already knows the expectations and consequences.

Choosing Logical Consequences

In general, consequences should be logical and related to the offense. It is typically more effective to tie a misbehavior to a natural consequence than a teacher-derived one. For example, if a student loses his crayons, he can't color his paper. If a student continually disrupts the children around her, she should have to sit in a place where she can't bother others. Logical consequences make sense to children, especially when explained calmly to them and enforced consistently. In a young child's mind, pushing someone during reading groups is totally unrelated to missing recess at one o'clock. It would make more sense to have that child talk about what happened, and then move his chair apart from the group to keep the other children safe.

Punitive and Rewards-Based Behavior Management Systems

If you choose to have a punitive system, make sure you have also set up a simple but effective behavior management plan that rewards positive behavior, and explain it the first day. You may be able to tie it into your punitive system, but if the reward system is set up properly, you can rely on that much more heavily, rather than focusing on misbehavior. This does not have to be complicated or time-consuming. I have created a token system and a bead system which I and many other teachers have used successfully, so if you would like some ideas to modify for your own classroom, please see Chapter 16, Whole-Class Reinforcement Systems.

Preparing Activities and Lessons

Guidelines for Choosing Back-to-School Activities

Remember, the purpose of your back-to-school activities is to set up an environment conducive to learning and reinforce procedures and rules so that you can begin to teach the curriculum as soon as possible. If an activity does not contribute to that goal, why use it? You can find links to free online activities and resources that follow these guidelines by visiting my website, www.TheCornerstoneForTeachers.com.

 ♦ **If you are a beginning teacher (or a veteran who gets easily stressed out), keep it very, very simple.** You can always try those elaborate ideas later in the year, or next school year.

♦ **Pick activities that use few materials and require very little prep work.** You don't want to be in the middle of a project and realize you don't have paper bags or pipe cleaners, because your students will require your constant and full attention on the first days of school. Also, the kids won't have mastered your routines for passing, sharing, and throwing away materials yet, so getting too many things out can be chaotic.

♦ **Choose several activities which your students can do independently.** Even a simple word search or coloring page will work. You may not plan to use these activities, but if an urgent issue comes up, you need to have something to engage the students. You may also need a few minutes of 'down time' for yourself, so prepare some easy dittos just in case.

When to Introduce Academic Concepts

You can introduce academic concepts on the first day if you and your students are ready, the second day at the latest. Your activities could be as simple as a Mad Minute addition drill, a spelling game, or map activities. You don't have to get into the textbooks immediately, but do start working. The children are there to learn, not to get to know each other—after the second day, let that part happen naturally.

Procedures and routines can be built right into academic lessons. For example, plan a shorter than normal writing prompt so you can spend fifteen minutes teaching how to head papers. Plan a brief math lesson using manipulatives so you can introduce the items to students and practice using them correctly first.

When and How to Start Reading Group and Center Routines

This will depend on your comfort level, how well you have established routines, how mature your group is, and of course, the requirements of your administration. Usually, between the third and fourth weeks of school is about right. However, this is a slow process. It's a critical part of two of the most important tasks you will tackle this year: maintaining order in your classroom and teaching your students to read. It takes considerable time and attention at the beginning of the year to make the process run smoothly. I would advise you not to worry about reading groups before school starts, because you've got more immediate matters to attend to. Later on, when you're ready, you can reference Chapter 20, Managing Reading Groups, and Chapter 21, Rethinking Centers.

Frequently Asked Questions

▶ **What if I've forgotten to plan for a procedure or routine?**

While it's important to plan things out in advance, it just isn't possible to prepare for every eventuality. The good news, whether you realize it or not yet, is that teachers are good at thinking on their feet! Handle new situations as they arise— it's better to have to change a procedure than to not introduce one at all and let the kids run the show however they want. Just remember that your students will have to un-learn any routines you create (or don't create, and therefore don't enforce) once you know what you want them to do.

▶ **How do I prepare when I don't have a classroom or can't access it yet?**

Sometimes you won't be able to do much until the last minute because you don't know which school or grade level you'll be in, or you can't access your room for some reason. (One year my school was being painted and the contractors were behind schedule. The estimated completion date was August 16th—the students' first day of school!)

In those situations, the best thing to do is gather your ideas and plan your routines. That year, I used my summer to do lots of research on word walls and morning messages, plus I made centers that I knew second graders would need no matter what the curriculum looked like (since I didn't have the documents yet). Try to get in contact with other teachers in your district who can explain things to you. You can also go to your school and school system's website. Take a look at your union contract (which is probably available online) and take some time to get to know the district expectations—and your rights. If you read your contract, you can most likely find out how many hours your workday is, how much planning time you are entitled to, how many mandatory meetings can be held, and other info that is important to keep up with. You won't have time to read that once school starts, so it's a good thing to do early on. There's no point in stressing out or worrying, so take a deep breath and try to relax!

► **Help! I'm panicking! There is no way I'm going to get this all done before the first day of school!**

I think every new teacher (and most veterans!) feel this way at the start of the year. Teachers always go around asking each other, "Are you ready? Are you ready?" and we all roll our eyes and say, "No, even if I had another week I would still have a million more things to do." The good news is, not everything has to be done before the first day of school.

Remember: You don't have to grade anything right away. Don't stay after school the first week marking papers—get your room and lessons together! It's important not to let things pile up, but prioritize. You have eight more weeks before grades are due.

► **What are the things that I HAVE to get done before the first day?**

If you're able to get into your classroom before the planning week, I recommend doing so. I typically work one extra day unpaid, usually the week prior to planning week so that I still get a break for a few more days. The exception is when I'm in a new school, in which case I like to have three days (one to unpack and clean, one to organize, and one to put up bulletin boards and hang things).

The things that absolutely MUST be done before the kids walk in the door depend on you and your school. For me, the priorities are having:

1) Student's names memorized. I like to go down my class list the night before school starts (not earlier, because even if I'm lucky to have it further in advance, the list changes often). I practice saying difficult names (using hints from the previous year's teachers) and if there's a school yearbook for me to reference, I try to visualize each child in my mind while saying his or her name. It's much easier to manage a classroom when you know the names of the kids in it, so the sooner this task is accomplished, the easier your life will be.

2) Student nametags ready. This way you can call on kids by name before you have memorized them all. Just scribble first names quickly on plain sticky labels—you don't have to be fancy. When the kids enter the classroom for the first time, introduce yourself to the children individually and hand out their nametags, showing them where you want the tags to be worn. You may want to have students stick the nametags on their shirts themselves so that you are not touching their chests. Sometimes I also have kids wear nametags on their backs in case I am behind them and need their attention quickly. Emphasize that nametags should not be removed and replaced because they will lose their stickiness.

3) Student desk tags labeled. These will show kids where to sit and you'll know who should be where. You can find tags for free on the Internet through a search engine or buy them at office and teacher supply stores, as well as dollar stores. I often write mine on colorful chart strips and use packaging tape to affix them to desks without laminating. It's not necessary to have expensive desk tags that display the alphabet, numbers, and so on.

4) Cubbies, folders, and textbooks labeled with student numbers. I try not to put student names on very many things because I have to redo them every August and again anytime a child transfers in or out of the class. I give children their 'special numbers' (also called personal identification or PINs) sometime during the first day of school and explain to them all the ways their numbers will be used, and why. It's a good idea to wait to assign student numbers until your planning/lunch break on the first day of school, or even the second day if possible, because your class list will likely change as parents register their kids that very morning. Don't get too attached to having everyone in alphabetical order, because new students always register and enrolled students don't show up. If you have to assign 'Bernard Brown' to #21 in your classroom because he enrolled on the twelfth day of school, that's just a fact of life! To prevent confusion, don't change a student's number once you assign it.

5) A list of students' names hanging on the door so children know if they have come to the right room. Type it because there will be lots of changes, even during the first week of school, and you'll want a name list many times throughout the year—just enlarge the font for your sign and print.

6) A rough plan written for EVERYTHING you will be teaching the first two days, if not the first week. You will not follow it exactly or get to everything, but you should know approximately what you want accomplished each day.

7) An outline completed of ALL of your routines and procedures. This solidifies them in your mind and provides a reference if needed.

8) All materials gathered for the first day. You will probably not be doing reading groups, centers, and computer activities right away so these things do NOT have to be in place yet. If you want your kids to use the class library, get your system together for that, but otherwise, don't worry about it. You can stay after school later on and organize; kids can choose books from selected book baskets until your library is up and running.

9) The office supplies on your desk organized (papers, pens, paper clips, etc.). It will be too distracting to have to search for these things on the first day of school—your area should be ready to go. If you have time, set up your filing system, but if you don't, at least get all extraneous papers in a filing cabinet. Supplies and materials you haven't sorted through yet can be placed in boxes or containers in a closet or even a corner of the room. The idea is to get clutter out of the way—if you need a safety pin, rubber band, or red marker at any point on the first day of school, being able to grab for it automatically will be a relief. Also, when you finally get to sit down at your desk to de-stress, you won't have a ton of materials in your way.

10) A system in place for kids' school supplies. When students bring in their materials, where should they put them? A back table? In or on their desks? What about large items like tissue boxes? During your planning and/or lunch times, you can move things to where you want them and teach the kids in the afternoon how to use their supplies properly and put them away.

11) Anything mandated by administration. You will have at least one staff meeting before school starts (probably many meetings!) and your principal will spell everything out for you. Even if a task doesn't seem important or pressing to you, when administration requires it, get it done right away.

NOTE: Bulletin boards and cute displays are NOT included on this list. It is tempting to want to do your displays early on to make it look like you have accomplished something and actually have a 'real room', but they are extremely time-consuming (I've spent HOURS on them in August). You definitely don't want to hang things when you're not sure where you want your furniture. When you are stressed out, pressed for time, and feeling overwhelmed, bulletin boards should not be your priority. Children can learn without them in place for a few days. If your room is neat, clean, and organized, children will feel relaxed and welcome. You may even be able to elicit their help in making things for the walls. Additionally, you will want to leave a lot of room for student work and for 'growing' displays (such as a word wall or timeline, which will probably start off blank).

► **What do I need to buy for my classroom?**

Need to buy? Nothing! Could buy? The list is endless! You have no obligation, however, to spend any money on your classroom, especially when you haven't begun setting it up and don't know what you already have. Most schools provide furniture, office supplies (scissors, staples, folders. etc.), bulletin board paper, textbooks, and manipulatives. However, this varies WIDELY from school to school and district to district—so check first before buying anything! It would be helpful if you bought the following items (but you DON'T have to):

- **Bulletin board borders:** These can be purchased for about three to six dollars, and can sometimes even be found in dollar stores. Schools usually provide bulletin board paper but not the borders (go figure). Choose ones that can be left up all year if you don't want to keep redoing your boards.

- **Organizers for your supplies:** The school will probably give you a bunch of pens but nothing to put them in.

- **A calendar to "do" with your kids**: Be sure the last teacher in your room didn't leave you one—these can be expensive.

- **More unusual office supplies your school cannot provide (ask FIRST):** Examples are sticky-tack, masking tape, magnets for holding things to the board, ink pads, a dry erase board, dry erase markers, and so on. Due to budget cuts, a school may provide these things one year but not the next, so make no assumptions.

- **Children's books:** These are never a waste of money if you get a range of reading levels so any child you teach has a selection. Some schools provide class libraries but don't expect to have one.

- **A pocket chart:** These are always useful, especially in the primary grades.

- **Stamps for grading student work:** Smiley faces and 'Good Job' stamps are useful, but I'm referring specifically to stamps that will keep you from having to write the same message out repeatedly, such as 'Completed together in class' or 'Please go back and check your work'.

▶ **Are there things I shouldn't buy if I have a limited budget?**

- **Decorative posters:** Use kid's artwork, word walls, time lines, class-made charts and other things kids can actually use. Even educational posters can be handmade or printed free from the Internet. Commercial displays are okay, but if money is tight, skip them.

- **Fancy center materials**: You can download center materials for free online, borrow reproducible books from other teachers, and so on, AFTER you know what type of activities you want your kids to do. Most likely you won't be using centers for a few weeks anyway.

- **Stickers, pencils, candy, and other tangible rewards**: If you're on a budget, buy things for your classroom that will last and have a direct impact on student learning for years to come.

▶ **What do I do with the supplies students send in?**

Children come in on the first day of school with all kinds of cool supplies, half of which weren't on your list. They'll also continue to bring in supplies during the first few weeks of school, especially in impoverished communities in which parents wait to shop until the payday after school starts. Have notebook paper and pencils ready to loan to those who come to school with nothing in their backpacks and decide how you will handle returning supplies you've lent out and the possibility of borrowing from other students. To handle the materials that kids do bring in, I have children complete a checklist, send home reminder notes when supplies still need to be sent, and follow up with thank-you notes for parents after the process is complete. These forms can be downloaded for you to modify at TheCornerstoneForTeachers.com.

▶ **What if school is starting and I feel like my classroom still isn't set up or organized the way I want it?**

That's okay! Everything doesn't have to be in place right away. Setting up takes awhile, and you'll want to change things as you figure out how you want to use materials and space. I like to rearrange all year long. It takes the pressure off me in August because I know nothing is permanent, and I get to adapt things to accommodate the children's changing needs.

▶ **Is it normal to develop an eye twitch because I'm on complete information overload?**

YES. Even veteran teachers who have been at the same school teaching the same grade for years feel this way every August—if you don't believe me, ask them! Teachers have a TON of information thrown at them during the fall, and between technology glitches, curriculum gaps, and procedural omissions and misinformation, EVERYONE feels like they're getting way more information than they could ever possibly retain. Take good notes and keep your handouts organized and easily accessible (try taking your notebook and teaching guides home at night to review). It won't be like this forever, I promise! Usually by the second week, I feel like I'm in my groove, and most new teachers begin feeling this way sometime during the first quarter. There is an end in sight!

The beginning of the year is the most physically and intellectually draining for everyone, but you won't be falling into bed exhausted EVERY night for the entire year. Be prepared to work extra hard now and you will reap the benefits quickly. And whatever you do, remember that feeling overwhelmed is completely normal, and that even if other teachers aren't showing it, they're experiencing beginning-of-the-year stress, too. You're not an idiot because you're unable to process everything the first time you hear it. It's okay to do things wrong the first time, make lots of inadvertent mistakes, ask questions that have already been answered, have people repeat themselves, and get them to remind you of their names 'one more time'. ☺

Chapter 3: Open House
Hosting an informative, stress-free event for families

Open House (or Back-To-School Night) can be a source of great stress for teachers who hate speaking in front of a group of adults. It's natural to be nervous and concerned about creating a good impression on the families you will have to partner with for an entire school year. One of the most important elements of a successful Open House is letting your personality shine through so that parents can make a real connection with you as a person who cares about their children. The following guidelines will help you feel calm and prepared so that you can let parents see the real you: a person who loves their kids and wants to help them succeed.

Prior to Open House: Creating a Parent Letter

It's helpful to send a letter to families to introduce yourself, provide an overview of the school year, and inform parents of rules and procedures. If you send these letters out before Open House, you won't have to go into as much detail in your presentation because parents will have already had a chance to familiarize themselves with how your classroom is run. You can also use your letter (or a class handbook that you provide in advance) as the basis for your presentation.

You can download several examples of parent letters and my class handbook at www.TheCornerstoneForTeachers.com. All documents are available for free in Microsoft Word format so you can modify them as you see fit.

PARENT-TEACHER CONTRACT

You can expect the following from me this school year:

1. Regular communication about your child's behavior and work habits as needed.
2. Frequent communication throughout the year about your child's academic progress through conferences, phone calls, progress reports, and notes home.
3. A comfortable, structured, and fun learning environment in which your child is respected as an individual with unique challenges and talents, and receives instruction that is tailored for those needs.

I expect the following from the families of the children in my class:

1. Nightly review of the student agenda and Home-School Folder, initializing the agenda each Thursday.
2. Assistance with weekly homework assignments as needed.
3. Timely return of forms sent home for signature.
4. Students sent to school *on time* EVERY day prepared to learn, with all needed school supplies.
5. Respectful communication about any questions or concerns about what is happening in the classroom. (Please call to schedule a convenient time to see me about any problems.)

That's it!! If we are both committed to these things, your child will have the support that's needed to be successful this school year! This is going to be a fantastic year for your family.

Please contact me with ANY questions you have during the year. Additionally, Open House will be on Wed., August 29th (details forthcoming) and we'll go over basic classroom information and cover your questions at that time. I'm looking forward to getting to know your children better and meeting each one of you on the 29th. See you then!

☺ **Ms. Powell**

-------------------------------------CUT AND RETURN--

I have received and agree to the expectations above and in the attached Parent-Teacher contract. I have read and agree to the policies on behavior, grading, homework, parties, school supplies, and snacks in the attached parent letter.

_____   _____   _____
Parent/Guardian Signature   Email Address   Date

What is Back-to-School Night?

The purpose of Open House or Back-to-School Night is to provide a time for parents to meet the teacher and review expectations. It is NOT a time for individual conferences, and you'll need to make that clear to parents. Open House is usually held in the early evening and lasts between 30 and 90 minutes, depending on the format that your school uses. In some schools, the teacher will need to present for as long as 45 minutes; in others, the teachers are lucky to get 15 minutes. Ask your colleagues what Open House is normally like at your school.

How Do I Organize the Event?

There are several components of the typical Open House. Some schools have parents go to the cafeteria or auditorium first for a general welcome, then to individual classrooms. No matter how your school sets it up, you should expect to have families trickling in for a good 30-45 minutes, if not longer: some will be very early, and others will come in when it's nearly over, especially if they had to visit siblings' classrooms first. The younger the children you teach, the higher the priority parents will give to your classroom. Pre-K and kindergarten classrooms often get the best turnout in the school and parents will visit them before going to their older children's classrooms. Some schools have two 30-minute sessions so parents with more than one child can visit multiple teachers without missing a lot of information.

After most people arrive, you will give a short presentation about your class. However, because of the trickle-in effect, you will need productive activities for your families to do while they wait for you to begin. Talking with you will not be an option as you attend to a million other things that seem to pop up. Open House is not always the best time to have parents fill out forms because they are often rushed and distracted. You can, however, have volunteer sign-up sheets for them and handouts to peruse.

Have a self-running sign-in system that you don't have to operate yourself. Right inside my classroom door I have a desk with nametags, a sign-in sheet, and a packet of materials that I will be reviewing that night. (If you place the desk in the hallway, you won't be able to ensure that all parents have signed in.) Some teachers like to offer a small bowl of candy or treats, as well. My sign-in sheet asks for the parent's name and the child's name, as well as a daytime phone number, so that when conferences come, I don't have to rack my brain wondering, "Did I meet her before? Didn't she come to Back-to-School night, or was it dad that came?" I have introduced myself to the same parent several times, only to have them say, "Yes, I remember...we met at Back-To-School night." Whoops! There will be dozens of people in and out of your room and family situations can be complicated, so it's very hard to keep track of everyone.

Make notes to yourself in the margin afterwards (woman with red hair, had infant with her, grandma came along, didn't speak much English, etc.) to help you place the name with the face later on.

Make it clear where parents should sit—normally, at their child's desk. Some teachers like to have work samples or other materials out; I have done this in the past and found that papers wind up on the floor or somewhere else they don't belong in all the hustle and bustle. Have extra chairs available for families to sit together. You may want to have all the children sit on the floor in the front or back of the room if space is limited.

What Should I Include in My Presentation?

Your school will probably give you guidelines on the material they want you to cover. There is no one right way to do this, but I have found the following format effective:

1) Tell a little about yourself (name, where you went to school, teaching experience, and family/hobby information if you like).

If it's your first year teaching, don't feel obligated to announce that, but definitely don't lie, either! At my first Open House, I said, "This is my first year teaching this grade level," and left it at that. Some teachers show their family photos, which can be very endearing and encourages parents to view you as an approachable, real person. I like to tell why I chose the grade level I did and what I think is special about it. This is a good transition into the presentation and if someone comes in late, they're able to catch up easily.

2) Give an overview of the most exciting things you have planned for the year to get parents enthusiastic about what's happening in the classroom.

I spend just a minute or two telling them that their children will be choosing community outreach and charity projects to get involved with, doing a home and school fitness plan, and so on. Be sure to mention anything out of the ordinary that you plan to do (specific field trips, etc.) that sets your class apart.

3) Use your daily schedule to introduce parents to the way their children will be learning.

This is the 'meat' of your presentation. Without burdening them with too much detail, walk your families through the children's day, from Morning Work to dismissal procedures. Each time you mention a specific subject area, explain how it will be taught. For example, you might mention small group reading instruction, centers or centerjobs, integration of content areas (such as using social studies to teach reading comprehension strategies, etc.). Use photos of the kids working or actual materials as props to keep everyone focused. I like to also call on kids who are in attendance to explain things ("Would one of our class members tell how we use the math games?"). This gives parents a break from listening to me talk and it's always entertaining to hear the kids' explanations.

4) Spend no more than a minute or two discussing standardized tests.

You can also mention your grading system or scale if necessary, but in the primary grades, this shouldn't be a big deal. Do NOT get bogged down with state standards and outcomes—you can provide these in a handout and parents can read them later. If your grade level doesn't give any standardized tests, you could even skip this altogether.

Let parents know that all of your instruction and assessment is aligned with state standards, and in plain English that means you design all of your lessons to meet state requirements in order to prepare students for the tests and for the next grade level. Tell them that you will be providing handouts, conferences, benchmark tests results, workshops, etc., throughout the year to help them understand the testing expectations, and that your communication with them will be routine and ongoing. Promise that there will be no surprises and that they will have an indication if their child may have difficulty passing long before the actual test date arrives.

5) Outline your approach to behavior management and class rules.

Make your expectations clear now so parents know what to expect! For example, if you never accept late homework or papers without names on them, are a stickler about tardies and make-up work, or don't let kids call home when they forget a book or agenda, explain your philosophy up front. I wouldn't run down a list of no-no's, but I do explain that I make class rules and consequences collaboratively with the students, and send them home in writing for parents and students to sign. (By Open House, this is usually done, anyway.) I tell them that after a grace period, which usually ends around October, I enforce the rules without exception in order to be fair and to teach the students responsibility and accountability. For example, one year I decided that all no-name papers would have one letter grade taken off beginning in November. When a parent called to complain once, I reminded her of the written notice and announcement of that policy at Open House. If you can't discuss these things at Open House due to time constraints, be sure to have them in writing so anyone with concerns can bring them to you before they become a problem. End this portion on a positive note by explaining the reward systems and fun activities you have planned for the students (Fun Friday, etc.).

6) Close with the methods of communication you will use (newsletters, email lists, class webpage, daily agendas, and so on).

If parents are welcome to volunteer in your classroom, briefly explain the procedures for this as well. If you want them to sign up for volunteer opportunities or specific classroom tasks, tell them where the sign-up sheet will be and encourage them to add their names to the list after the presentation. Be sure to thank them for coming out and urge them to call, email, etc., anytime they have a question or concern. Let them know that due to time constraints, you've been specifically instructed not to discuss any individual students during Open House, but that you have a conference sign-up sheet available for that purpose.

7) Explain how you will handle parent questions.

One year, things were very calm and settled and I took questions and answered them in front of the group for about five minutes. Another year, things were very hectic and I asked parents to either approach me individually with questions or write them down and I would call them the following day. You may begin taking questions and realize that parents are asking things that only pertain to their child or a small percentage of the class; you can always give a general response and tell the parent you will follow up with them later on (give a specific time and method of communication).

If you notice that a lot of side conversations begin and the whole group isn't listening anymore, they've probably had enough 'lecturing' for the evening and you can end it! With some groups, I can literally see how tired they are from working all day long and then rushing to the school and sitting through lengthy presentations, knowing they still have to get home and bathe the kids, do homework, get everyone ready for bed...and then get up again in a few hours for another work day! Make it brief for those groups. You can also help by not assigning homework on Open House night, or excusing it for the students of parents who attend (that's always a great motivator for kids to get their families to show up!).

What Are Some Fun Ways I Can Make the Night Special?

It's not necessary to create a lot of elaborate things for families to do at Open House. However, if you're looking for easy-to-implement, high-interest activities, here are a few ideas. I have included parts of the activities below, and the full versions are available as free Word document downloads at TheCornerstoneForTeachers.com.

- **Scavenger Hunt:** Families can complete this activity while they wait for you to begin the presentation, and/or afterwards while they wait to talk to you. One parent sent me an email afterwards saying how much she enjoyed it because she had a purpose in walking around the room and knew what she was looking at. The scavenger hunt can end with the parent at the child's desk, waiting for you to begin talking.

Back-to-School Scavenger Hunt

While you wait, see if you can find and check off the following things in our classroom.

1. **Our "Welcome" bulletin board** (There's a place for the lunch menu, Box Tops, Did You Knows, which are the school's weekly newsletters, and more information for parents to use.)
2. **A computer with our class web page pulled up** (Take a moment to check it out!)
3. **Our job chart** (We change jobs monthly, and we get to choose which ones we want.)
4. **Our word wall, with words that we often forget how to spell** (We are responsible for always writing/copying these words correctly in class.)
5. **Our reading area** (We have twenty minutes of independent reading each day.)
6. **Our cursive alphabet** (We'll start learning this in January.)
7. **Your child's desk** (Have a seat!)
8. **Your child's journals** (You may have noticed that few assignments written on notebook paper are sent home. Look inside the black and white composition notebooks to see what we have been doing during class time.)
9. **Your child's math book** (We just started chapter 2, and are learning about place value. Flip through the table of contents in the front of the book to see what topics we'll cover this year.)

- **How Well Do You Know Me? Fun Survey:** Parents can complete this at anytime during the evening—it's waiting for them on the child's desk. The kids get to grade it for the parents the next day, which they love! Note: Have something enjoyable to do the next day for the kids whose parents couldn't come so they don't feel left out while the others read the surveys.

☺ **How Well Do You Know Me?** ☺

Dear Family: Please answer the following questions. I will grade your paper for you tomorrow and bring it home in my binder so you can see how you did.

1. What's my favorite food? _____
2. What's my favorite color? _____
3. What's my favorite T.V. show? _____
4. What's my favorite song? _____
5. What's my favorite subject in school? _____
6. Who is my best friend? _____
7. What's my favorite holiday? _____
8. What's the first thing I do after school? _____
9. What's my favorite season? _____
10. What's my favorite animal? _____

- **Shared Journal Entry:** The kids write on a topic such as "The Hardest Part/Best Part of Being a Kid." They then set up the page across from that page with the title, "The Hardest Part/Best Part of Being a Parent." The families complete the journal entry at Back-To-School night and children read them in the morning. (Have another morning warm-up for kids whose parents did not come.) This is a good activity if you use journals and workbooks a lot: it lets parents see how much work the child is doing in class, even though it may not all come home because it's not on loose-leaf paper. Be aware that some parents may not feel comfortable with their own reading or writing skills or may be preoccupied with their young children or the papers you have handed them, and may not take part. I have had moderate success with this activity in that regard, but the parents who did do the journal entry absolutely raved about it.

Any Tips for Making This Run More Smoothly?

☑ **Set up an area for children so parents can be undisturbed.**

One school I taught at did not allow children to attend...but I told my families I would rather they come with little ones than not show up at all! I arrange my reading area so that children can sit in the back of the room and read with their siblings. Not all kids will want to separate from mom and dad but I have found that this helps. If it gets noisy, I don't hesitate to stop what I'm saying and kindly but firmly remind the children that I'm speaking with adults and I need them to lower their voices. I speak to the kids exactly as I would if their parents were not in the room, and I think families enjoy hearing and seeing how we interact.

☑ **Send home your class rules and routines ahead of time and then provide a second copy at the Open House.**

Parents should have already had a chance to familiarize themselves with your expectations so they can be ready with questions at Open House. This will also save you from having to cover everything in a short amount of time.

☑ **Don't plan to talk for long.**

In many communities, there will be lots of children (and crying babies), and parents will come late and leave early as they attempt to make the rounds to all of their children's classrooms. That means your fantasy of a quiet classroom with parents ready in their seats and hanging on your every word is just that—a fantasy! If I'm allotted 30 minutes, I plan to speak for 15. I have never had 'extra' time. If I did, I would just take more parent questions or end a few minutes early.

☑ **Use a Power Point presentation to hold the audience's attention.**

Print out the slides for parents' reference and to send home the next day with children whose parents weren't able to attend. If you don't have access to the technology needed, simple overheads can help focus the parents on what you're saying. It also takes the pressure off of you—you can work from the overhead rather than from notes (which looks kind of stilted) and people will look at the visuals instead of at you!

☑ **When you first begin your presentation, ask parents to write down any questions they have.**

If you run out of time for questions, they can always hand them in and you can write a response the next day or call later. You may want to provide sticky notes or scratch paper for this purpose, as well as for note-taking.

☑ **Don't go crazy trying to organize time-consuming projects in order to impress parents.**

There's no point in having elaborate activities if you are too frazzled to genuinely greet each person and you mismanage your time so that you have to stop your presentation halfway through. You can always try new things the following year.

What Parents REALLY Want From an Open House

In my experience, what family members expect is relatively simple:

1) A clean and organized classroom that their child takes ownership of
2) A warm and friendly teacher who welcomes them
3) A light-hearted, enjoyable, and easy-to-understand presentation that gives them a good sense of what the year will be like

Parents have no idea what to expect from a teacher their children have never had before. Most of them are not worried about how often you'll be giving science tests or what materials you'll use to teach addition. They want to know:

> ➢ Does the teacher like my child?
> ➢ Does the teacher care about the kids and enjoy teaching?
> ➢ Does the teacher want to support me and my child?
> ➢ Is the teacher going to be fair and easy to work with?

These things are communicated through the energy you put out and the environment you create in the classroom. Some of it can be communicated verbally, but most of is conveyed in your demeanor. Smile! Smile! Smile! Act relaxed even though you're not. Listen attentively to parents and treat their questions and concerns seriously. They are not your superiors there to observe you, so don't be intimidated. They are your equals, so treat them with kindness and respect and don't worry about what they're thinking. Most of them are extremely grateful to have you in their children's lives, and want to support you in having a successful Open House and school year.

Making a Personal Connection With Each Family

Ideally, you should be able to connect with parents and make them feel valued and appreciated in the same way you treat your students as unique individuals. That can be difficult to do during Open House when you're short on time, but I try to always say something specific and positive to each parent as we meet. ("Oh, you're Edward's dad! I am so glad to meet you! He is such an awesome kid; he always has some fact to share with the class! Just the other day, he said..." or "Brianna's mom! Great to see you again! Brianna is the sweetest child; I can always count on her to help her friends and to be a peacemaker. I'm so glad she's in our class!") No matter how awful a child has been in class, it's possible to find some good attribute to comment on so that the first feedback a parent hears is a compliment. The type of quotes above could easily be used for challenging students: Edward, for instance, could be a child who talks non-stop in class about totally random information, and Brianna may be a busy-body who's always telling the other kids what to do. Look through to each child's heart and intentions, and you'll be able to come up with something good to say about all of your students. Plan it out in advance for certain children if you need to.

You Can't Fit It All Into One Presentation

There's a lot of pressure on teachers to say everything they need to about behavioral expectations, homework, testing, grading systems, key skills and concepts, and how to support learning at home...all in one night! It's just not possible. Parents, like kids, need time to digest information and make it their own, and hands-on experiences are the best way to do that. I hold a parent workshop each month, but I know teachers who hold only one a year or one a quarter. Start with whatever you are comfortable with and use parental feedback to determine what to do the following school year. I hold a variety of festivities, some of which are just opportunities for families to socialize with one another and build a sense of community. After each event, there is an evaluation form for parents to fill out to help me revise for next year. See Chapter 30, Creative Family Outreach, for details and more ideas.

Part Two:
Organizing the Classroom

Chapter 4: Avoiding the Paper Trap
Creating <u>one</u> place for <u>each</u> paper that you come across

Organizing the mounds of papers we encounter everyday is not as difficult as it seems. In fact, you can set up a system in a very short amount of time that will provide a place for every single paper! You've heard the old adage: *A place for everything, and everything in its place.* It really is that simple!

**It doesn't matter what type of containers you use,
as long as you have a designated spot for each type of paper.**

You can use baskets, crates, magazine file boxes, metal organizers, plastic trays, or any combination of resources that are on hand. I'll show you photos here of a variety of organizers that have worked for me over the years. I've changed systems many times. But the idea is always the same: there is ONE place for EVERY paper.

You MUST choose containers that make it easy to put papers where they belong. If it's too much trouble to put them away, you won't do it.

I hear a lot of overwhelmed teachers say they don't know where to start when it comes to tackling the massive amounts of paper in the classroom. So I divided the organizational process into steps which I've listed in order of priority. If you do one or two steps a week, you'll be completely and permanently organized in about a month's time. *You can do it!* These are easily sustainable systems that can be taken with you to any grade level and any school you teach in for the rest of your career.

Gather all the containers and organizers you have, and then choose among them for each category of papers, one step at a time. If you don't have anything suitable, list the types of containers you'd like to buy, and then make an investment in your own sanity by heading out to a discount store to purchase them. You'll be glad you did once everything's in place.

Step 1) Temporary Places for Incoming Papers
Step 2) Binder for Lessons, Grades, and Reference
Step 3) Frequently-Referenced Forms and Papers
Step 4) Student Papers
Step 5) Activities and Worksheets You're Using Now
Step 6) Teaching Resources for All Skills Taught
Step 7) General Files

STEP 1) TEMPORARY PLACES FOR INCOMING PAPERS

The concept for step one is having a designated spot for any paper that an adult or child gives you until you have a spare moment to handle it. These are TEMPORARY places that should be emptied throughout the day whenever you have time. I know what you're thinking! But, once you have a set place for all your papers, clearing out temporary spaces will be very easy and they will be empty almost all the time. The photograph to the left shows what my desk looks like on a typical day—it CAN be done!

Incoming Papers From Students (Not Class Work/Homework)

The black tray shown is called my in-box. Students use it for notes from their parents, signed forms they are returning, tardy slips, field trip money, etc.—anything they need to give me that is not class work or homework.

To the right of my desk, on top of a rolling cart, is a large gray basket. This is where I toss papers that I just brought in from the office: class sets of photocopies that need to be paper-clipped and put away and other papers to read and sort through. Using this basket keeps me from laying the papers on my desk and therefore creating clutter (which I don't allow on my work surface even for a short period of time). If I have even one thing that I can't put in the correct spot immediately, I put it in the gray basket. Once I have the kids settled into an activity, I'll pull the papers from the basket and stick them in their designated place.

To Read/Do/Keep/File

This system works like a traditional in-box's more organized cousin. Instead of just piling papers in a huge stack, have a spot for each action that you need to take:

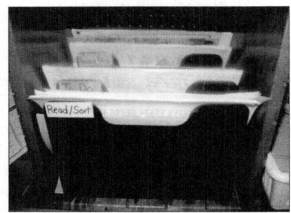

- **To Read/Sort:** This slot is for things that you need to read through before you can throw them out or sort them into a more permanent place (e.g., newsletters, district publications). Remove things from this slot about once per week when you can make time to concentrate on reading and properly placing them.

- **To Do Immediately:** This is the next slot, and it's for items that require you to complete some sort of action THAT DAY, like a parent request for a phone call, or a form that has to be completed for an afternoon meeting.

- **To Do ASAP:** Place items here that require an action from you but aren't your top priority (e.g., child study paperwork that needs to be finished by Thursday, a field trip head-count that's due next Monday). These papers should be completed as soon as possible, so try to make sure this is empty at least every other day.

- **To Keep On Hand:** This slot is for forms you need to reference in the upcoming weeks and don't want to put into a more permanent place for that reason.

- **To File:** These are papers you need to keep but probably won't need to access in the foreseeable future (paystubs, receipts, warranties, completed sub plans, notes from your supervisor). Once a month or so, put these papers into the proper place in your file cabinet (which will be set up in the last step). Of course, if you have the self-discipline to file each paper as you encounter it, that's even better!

To Take to the Office or Other School Locations

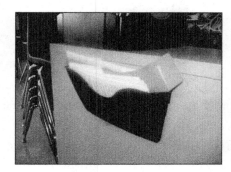
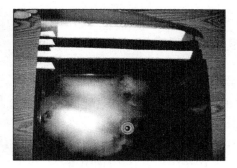

Anything that you want to bring with you the next time you leave the classroom should go into one easily-accessible spot. You can use a container like the one shown on the left or a sectioned folder like the one on the right (which has slots for photocopies, PTA, office, and other teachers). When you take the kids to specials or lunch, grab whatever's in this spot and bring it with you. If you use a folder, then anything that you pick up in the office can be carried back to the classroom in the same way. Remember to put the papers you bring back to the room in your Incoming Papers spot right away.

Ongoing Projects

You'll also need a place for things that you're trying to complete but need more time with—mine is the white basket shown here. Examples of projects are: laminating that needs to be cut out, math manipulatives you're making, papers that need to be hole-punched and organized into a binder, and items that need to be colored. These things are too large to fit in a small tray and may need to stay in one place for a few days or even weeks. If you have a large basket or container that's out of the way, you can just pull it out when you're ready to work.

STEP 2) BINDER FOR LESSONS, GRADES, AND REFERENCE

I like to keep a binder with all of the papers I need during the day. The most important components are my lesson plans and grade book. In the very front, I usually keep a school supply organizer to hold a calculator, pens, pencils, etc. Then I use dividers to create some variation of the following basic sections:

> ➤ to-do lists
> ➤ current lesson plans (old ones are filed away about every other month)
> ➤ grade book
> ➤ one section for each subject area (for pacing guides and reference)
> ➤ class reference (student lists, pull-out class rosters, birthday info)
> ➤ school reference (sub lists, staff phone numbers)
> ➤ meeting notes (kept in chronological order)
> ➤ sections for reading and math data, plus a section for testing results
> ➤ schedules and calendars (for reading groups, computer usage, cafeteria)

I encourage you to CONSOLIDATE and copy as much information as possible into the forms and papers already in your binder so you don't have to keep every new paper that you are given. For example, if you get a notice about an upcoming child study meeting, write the time onto the appropriate day in your lesson plans or your to-do list for the week, and throw the paper out! There is nothing magical about the paper a notice is written on—copy the useful information in an easily-referenced place, then toss the memo itself. Also, when you get updated class lists and schedules, don't just add them to your binder—throw away anything obsolete.

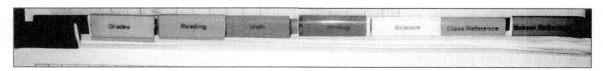

STEP 3) FREQUENTLY-REFERENCED FORMS AND PAPERS

Emergency Cards and Other Small Pieces of Paper

Keep parent contact cards in an accessible place, along with student data cards that the previous year's teachers filled out (if your school district uses these). Since you will need an organizer that works well for little cards and pieces of paper, you can keep other small materials in this location as well, such as attendance cards, photocopy request forms, school nurse passes, half slips of paper you use for individual behavior plans, and so on.

Papers You Need to Look at Daily

As you may surmise, these get hung on bulletin boards or magnetic surfaces such as your refrigerator or the side of a file cabinet. Be strict with yourself here! If you're not constantly referencing a paper (at least once per day), hole-punch it and put it in your lesson plan binder where it will still be easy to find. The only things I have hanging in my room are the  list of room numbers and phone extensions for the school and a class list with student's names and I.D. numbers.

Blank Forms and Papers You Need to Keep for Easy Reference

You may have separate places for reference papers and blank forms, but I use one pocket chart for both. A simple accordion file would work well, too.

In the chart (or accordion file), keep the papers that you would want to hang on a bulletin board if you had room for all of them. These are papers you will need to access frequently, such as: technology user guides, older lesson plans, TV schedules for district broadcasts, and older school newsletters. I don't need these often enough to keep them in my lesson plan binder, but I do need them at my fingertips and don't want to have to dig through a file cabinet.

Blank forms that I need to access quickly are kept in the same pocket chart: clinic passes, guidance counselor requests, child study packets, maintenance requests, blank lesson plan pages and grade book pages, office referral forms, and so on.

Notes and Handouts from Meetings

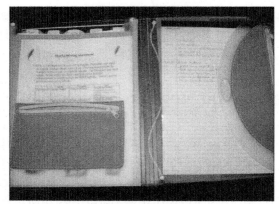

You could keep things very simple by just hole-punching meeting agendas and notes and storing them in your lesson plan binder. Or, if you have a lot of meetings and plenty of papers you're supposed to bring, you could have a separate organizer. This way, everything you need for meetings is kept in one spot so that you can just grab the notebook and go without having to lug a big binder around. The organizer shown here cost me about $3 at a discount store and has a pocket for pens and sticky notes, a legal pad, and five separate folders. I labeled each folder with the name of a committee or team that I served on and placed all the notes inside.

Extra Copies of Papers That Were Passed Out to Students (For In-Class and to Go Home)

After passing out worksheets to students, you may find that you have one or two leftover copies. Teach students to put extra papers in a designated place (mine is the basket pictured in the center). You can empty the basket every few weeks when it's full. Do the same thing for PTA notes, newsletters, etc., that you send home for parents: my designated place for extras is in the basket shown on the far left. (The basket on the far right is where I keep papers and fliers that I plan to send home that day.)

Sets of Blank Papers

This photo shows the blank papers my students and I frequently need (graph, grid, cursive, copier, construction, and notebook paper). I got the organizer for free from a craft store that was going out of business. I keep this in a place where the kids can use it, but these papers can be kept in a cabinet if you don't have an appropriate container.

The organizer shown here is actually a wooden puzzle-holder that a retiring kindergarten teacher gave me. I use it to hold papers I need frequently but that my kids don't access, such as blank transparencies, interims, and parent conference forms. These could be kept in the same place as the other blank papers, depending on your storage options.

STEP 4) STUDENT PAPERS

Artwork and Letters from Students

Young children often like to draw things for their teachers, but finding a place for all of their artwork is a job in itself! Make sure your kids are trained to use your in-box (see Step One) and then you can move artwork to a bulletin board. I taught my kids to put their artwork directly on the board using tacks, thereby skipping the in-box, but you'll have to decide if you can trust your kids to use tacks independently.

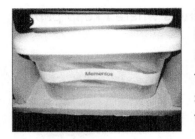

Every now and then I discreetly "clean up" the bulletin board and tell the kids I had to make room for all of the beautiful new pictures they will draw! For those items that have great sentimental value, I do have a medium-sized plastic bin with a lid where I keep little mementos from over the years.

Forms and Money You Collect from Students

Occasionally, teachers collect picture or field trip money, book orders, signed report cards, and various forms from parents. Have children put these in your in-box (as explained in Step One). Then you can transfer them to the place you keep form/money collections. My place is the small wooden organizer shown to the right. Usually I keep a blank manila folder there and just stuff the papers in until I have them all, at which point I organize and place them where they belong permanently, which is usually either in students' files or with the school secretary.

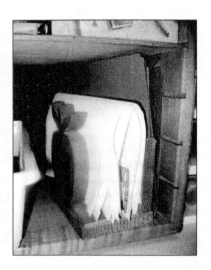

Work to Be Graded

In the past, I have had one tray shelf for each subject area, but I've also tried having my Paper Collectors put student work on any empty shelf they see. ALL work to be graded gets turned in here and is never just laid on my desk or

someplace else where it can get mixed up. When all the shelves are full, I know I better start going through them! After papers are graded or stamped, I put them directly into the place for papers to go home.

Graded Work to Be Sent Home

There are many options for organizing student work that you're ready to send home. This process is explained more fully in Chapter 11 (Tips and Tricks for Procedures), but the information that follows will help you choose containers as you set up your organizational systems.

Large Basket: One way is to put graded papers and fliers that are ready to be sent home in a big basket and have student helpers pass them out once a week. This takes about ten minutes for kids to do and it's very simple.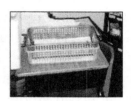

 **Crate with hanging files:** Another way is shown in the photo to the left. Put papers in a hanging folder that says "To Be Filed" and have student helpers file them (each child is assigned a number and his papers are kept in the file with the corresponding number). This works well if your kids have time to file for you (while waiting for their buses to be called or during Fun Friday). Then, once a week, the helpers take the papers out of the files and either put them on the students' desks or into Home-School folders.

Mailboxes: If you have a 'mailbox' system, every child can have his own slot for Mailbox Helpers to place papers in. These can be obtained from office and teacher supply stores. Special pocket charts can also be used.

Student Files (Portfolios)

Each child in my class has a hanging file folder in the crate shown here for work samples and test results. (I prefer crates to file cabinet drawers because they're easier for me and the kids to access.) The file folders are labeled with numbers rather than student names so that I don't have to redo them every year, and I glue a list of student names/numbers on the front of the crate for reference. The very first hanging file in the crate is labeled "To Be Filed". Normally I put students' papers in their corresponding folders as I go, but if I have a whole stack of student work or forms, I'll put them in that front folder and have a student file them for me.

Right behind the "To Be Filed" folder is a folder of interim/progress reports, parent conference forms, and report cards. I use one folder for the entire class, because keeping everyone's official forms together in one folder helps me keep track of conferences I've held and makes filing papers in students' cumulative records easier at the end of the year.

Book Order Forms

In the very back of the crate I use for student files, I also keep Scholastic Book orders, one folder for each month. I put a colored paper clip on the folders to indicate whether I'm still collecting student money (red), waiting for the book order to arrive (white), or if the items have arrived and the order is closed (green).

Parent Correspondence

This accordion file is numbered to create one slot for each child. Inside, I keep all notes from parents, absence/tardy excuses, conference requests, informal notes, etc. This is solely to cover myself in case I need documentation. I keep all the papers inside until the first week of

school the following year and then I empty the whole thing into the trash. (Anything that would go into students' permanent records such as conference forms and interims reports would have been in their student files.)

STEP 5) ACTIVITIES/WORKSHEETS YOU'RE USING NOW

Class Sets of Photocopies and Other Materials for Current Lessons

This is a cool organizer I got from an office supply store that holds hanging files and has slots for books and office supplies, but you can use a crate and hanging files just as easily. There is a file for each day of the week, plus files that say 'Sometime This Week,' 'Next Week,' and 'Next Few Weeks.' I have green folders and tabs for reading, blue for math, and red for everything else (I don't use many photocopies for the other subjects). Any materials you will be using to teach lessons in the near future can be kept here—the reading test you want to give on Wednesday, the math worksheets you will use on Thursday or Friday, and the book you want to read aloud next week. Check these files regularly to make sure you didn't accidentally leave something in there!

Each subject area also has a laminated two-pocket folder inside a hanging folder, in which I keep extra class sets of papers that could be used at any time. These sets of papers are usually fun worksheets or miscellaneous activities that I can pull out when I have a substitute or a few extra minutes at the end of a lesson.

Materials for Today's Lessons

The day before you teach your lessons (or the morning of, depending on when you like to prepare), pull papers out of the files described above and put them in an organized place that you can easily reach from the front of the classroom.

Things that could go here include a sample project you want to show, tests the class will correct together, and worksheets to be completed. To keep this organizer functional, you'll need to empty it at the end of every day (unless you're going to use the same materials two days in a row). Reserve it ONLY for today's things.

STEP 6) TEACHING RESOURCES FOR ALL SKILLS TAUGHT

Lesson Materials and Papers for All Subject Areas

Keeping materials organized for lesson plans is a big and important task, and I've described my ideas in detail as part of Chapter 5, Finding and Filing Instructional Resources. Basically, original copies of papers are kept in a folder, which are then put inside a file box or drawer along with class sets of photocopies, read-alouds, activities, and other related materials. Whenever I come across a paper for a particular concept, I place it in the related folder. Then right before I teach the unit, I go through and organize all the papers the file box or drawer contains and pull out the materials I want.

Transparencies

I keep all of my transparencies in a container on the bottom shelf of my overhead projector cart. They are organized into binders, with an additional box of blank transparencies.

STEP 7) GENERAL FILES

As you know from reading this chapter, I detest file cabinets and only use them to store papers that I know I will not need to access on a regular basis. There are several types of files that I do keep in my file cabinets:

Lesson materials I'm not using: There are certain materials I've collected over the years that I don't want to let go of, even though I'm not currently teaching with them. For example, I have a fantastic unit on severe weather that isn't in my current curriculum but I may use again at some point in my career. The unit has excellent resources that I couldn't just pull from the Internet or books if needed, so I decided to file them. In my file cabinet, there is a hanging file folder for each subject and each quarter, filled if needed with manila file folders that are labeled with more specific topics or skills.

Seasonal materials: I have a hanging folder for each month of the school year, with file dividers inside that are labeled with the respective holidays and special

occasions. Those sections hold resources and lesson ideas that I may or may not use each year, depending on the day of the week the holiday falls and how well I can tie it into our curriculum. I don't usually do a lot of holiday-related activities because they tend to get kids hyper and unfocused, and also because students often do a variation of the same thing every year (do they really need to hear about the Pilgrims every single November for thirteen years of schooling?). That's my own personal preference, but if you choose to do a lot of holiday activities, make sure your seasonal files are in an accessible place.

Older files from previous school years: I also have personnel records from previous school systems, test scores from former classes, work samples and lesson plans from my first year of teaching, and so on that I don't want to throw away for various reasons. I have less than one full drawer devoted to all of these things and I clean it out every other June.

Chapter 5: Finding & Filing Instructional Resources
How to locate any teaching material quickly and easily

Organizing the materials you use for instruction is critical for good classroom management—nothing slows down the momentum of an exciting lesson more than having to dig around for worksheets and materials. Designing easily accessible storage places for your lesson materials and photocopies is a matter of having appropriate, easily accessible containers. Here are some different ways to utilize drawers, cubbies, and magazine file boxes to organize materials for each subject area.

Reading and Language Arts

I purchased enough three-drawer plastic organizers to have one for each story in our reading series. (That's twelve containers at about $6 each, so $72 total.) Not cheap. But considering you can reuse these versatile organizers for years to come, I think it's a worthwhile investment. Buying these containers has solved the never-ending filing problem for me because I don't have to dig through file cabinets to put things away properly. Anything associated with a story in our series goes into the corresponding drawer, such as spelling tests, worksheets, activities, student work samples (to show the kids the following year as models), games, transparencies, CDs, and DVDs.

Since my instruction is very tightly aligned with state standards, I also keep a magazine file holder for each of the state's eight reading strands (such as Author's Purpose, Plot and Conflict, and Cause/Effect). There are a lot of activities

I do with the kids that focus on one particular strand, but aren't associated with any specific story in our reading series, so I keep those materials separate from the drawers and use the magazine file boxes. These were purchased for less than a dollar each. There is a laminated two-pocket folder inside each box to hold original copies of all the papers. Behind the folders, I keep class sets (photocopies) of the originals that I plan to use in the upcoming weeks.

There is also a manila folder in each box to hold the mini-assessments our school district gives for each strand. Additionally, because 'Vocabulary' is such a broad strand, I have a three-ring binder, pictured on the far right side of the photo, that has dividers for each sub-skill (e.g., homophones, multiple meaning words, context clues, and root words).

Social Studies and Science

I purchased slightly bigger drawers for social studies to hold artifacts and props, and large drawers for science that can accommodate materials for experiments. Each drawer has a laminated legal size folder for each chapter in the unit. The

folders hold original copies, and photocopied class sets are just stacked in the drawers. The key element here is that the containers are drawers, not regular bins, because if I had to unstack them and take the lids off every time I needed to put something away, I know I would be too lazy to do it! With this system, if I come across something I might like to use for a later science or social studies unit, I can just open the appropriate drawer and toss it in, then sort everything out when it's time to teach the unit.

Math

I don't use drawers for my math papers because they would need to be large enough to hold all of the manipulatives and games. With thirty chapters, each covering multiple skills, I would go broke trying to organize them all! Instead, I've arranged my lesson materials for math in two different ways, depending on the type of storage I had in a particular classroom.

Option 1): All papers, manipulatives, and materials together

One year, I had two large shelves with adjustable cubby sections, and I set up one compartment for each math chapter.

The photos show how I organized each compartment: I kept materials for each skill in the chapter, plus center activities and a folder for all the lessons, worksheets, and activities that I used. Right before I was ready to teach the chapter, I pulled out the folder and had copies made of all the papers inside. This system kept all of my materials together and worked wonderfully, although it was a little more difficult to put away papers since the file folders were so spread out. One year I pulled the folders for the current and proceeding chapters and kept them in an organizer near my desk so I could easily refile items after use.

Option 2): Papers in one place, larger materials in another

When I moved to a new school and didn't have the shelves anymore, I switched to a more compact system which keeps all of the file folders together in sturdy, colorful magazine file boxes. There is one for each of the thirteen major concepts we study (e.g., measurement, time, money,

multiplication). I kept the same folders from the cubbies that were explained above, with multiple folders in each file box (so the folders for Customary Units and Metric Units were both stored inside the Measurement file box). Any class sets of papers were also kept in the magazine box, but not inside the folder (which was only for originals). This system worked extremely well—anytime I needed to put a paper away, I just stuck it in a file box.

Since math materials are obviously too large to be kept in magazine file boxes, I stored them in this large black rolling cart. Each drawer is labeled with a concept. Any class sets of manipulatives and games for the unit were in the corresponding drawer, so I had Math Helpers pass the items out at the beginning of a lesson and return them to the drawer at the end. This method was convenient enough for me to put the materials back even if I would need them again the very next day, because all I had to do was open the drawer.

Whether I have cubby shelves or magazine file boxes, I always keep math fact test and practice papers in a separate place, since I use so many of them over the course of a school year. All of the fact practice worksheets are kept together in a magazine file holder that is slightly more open than the traditional design. I laminated pieces of construction paper to use as dividers, so there is one section for addition fact practice papers, one for subtraction, and one for division. (We don't do much fact practice for these operations in third grade, so I only need one section for each. The sections hold mixed fact practice paper-clipped together.) There is a separate section for each multiplication table (0, 1, 2, 3, etc., up to 10) because students are quizzed on these tables individually. In the back are mixed multiplication fact practice papers and a section for the original copies to make class sets from.

Chapter 6: Organizing Classroom Materials
How to create a functional space that facilitates routines

Having a clear and easy-to-maintain organizational system for classroom materials not only sets the precedence and framework for students to be organized themselves, but lays a foundation for the procedures and routines that make instruction possible.

Children will only be able to follow pencil sharpening routines if they can easily access the sharpeners (without having to ask where they are located that particular day, or wait in a long line of playful and impatient children, or crowd around each other in a too-small area). If this provision isn't made, kids won't be prepared to write and your instruction will be compromised. Similarly, students can only pass their papers in to be graded if there's a consistent and appropriate space for the Paper Collector to place them (without having to ask where papers go, or what happened to the paperclips, or what to do with the other stacks of graded work). If the classroom is not organized in a way that facilitates such routines and procedures, time will be taken away from learning as you scramble around to handle materials.

In this way, a lack of classroom organization contributes to a downward spiral, in which routines and procedures can't be followed, behavioral problems result, and less time is spent on-task. The end result? An exhausted, overwhelmed teacher and students who aren't making learning gains the way they should.

Student must understand where all needed materials are kept, how they should be accessed, and how they should be returned. Your job is to set students up for success by providing clearly organized spaces that facilitate predictable routines. Your classroom materials are the conduit for learning, the resources that enhance and support students' understanding, and their usage is therefore tied directly to achievement.

Setting Up Classroom Supplies and Children's Materials

What Will Students Be Accessing?

One of the most important organizational tips I can offer is to think carefully about which supplies you want the kids to access and which ones you don't. Anything they need to be able to get to should be in VERY sturdy containers that are easy for children to keep neat (nothing too elaborate) and in convenient, low-traffic areas.

For example, I want my Paper Passers to distribute various types of blank paper from time to time, so I keep it on an open shelf at the children's waist level so that I don't have to get the paper down from a cabinet to give to the Paper Passer. I also want children to be able to access art supplies, but I need to keep an eye on what they're taking and how they are returning things, so I keep the art supplies in the front of the classroom. This way I can observe them without having to stop a lesson if I'm teaching or get up from my desk if I'm not.

Conversely, the things that the kids don't need to access are hidden away. Most children are respectful of off-limit areas, so my main motivation in putting things away is not to prevent children from touching them. Rather, it's because kid-friendly, accessible shelf space is at a premium, and I don't like to waste it with things the kids will never be using. Extra textbooks, vats of soap, office supplies, posters, etc., are hidden away in cabinets so that the open shelves and containers around the room can be filled with the supplies I want kids to access.

Storing Infrequently-Used Texts and Workbooks

Usually there will be too many textbooks, workbooks, and school supplies to fit into a child's desk neatly, so you will need a place for less-frequently used materials. I keep magnetized signs on my board that show kids what books they should have in their desks, because the materials are rotated all the time. The year this photo was taken, the school provided students with over 20 different resources, so having a management system was critical! (The sign is only for books—the same classroom supplies are always

kept in students' desks, as explained further on in this chapter.) There are several options for storing extra texts and workbooks for students:

Option 1) Individual cubbies or shelving areas

Organizing is simplest if you have access to shelving that provides an individual space for each child in your classroom. When I'm assigned to a classroom that provides this storage, I label each shelf section with a number (rather than a child's name, which would have to be changed each year). Students then keep the majority of their workbooks and texts, along with extra school supplies, in their cubbies. To have students get materials from their cubbies without pushing or shoving, call half the class at once (I put #1-10 on the top row and #11-20 on the bottom, and called children according to number).

Option 2) One shelving area for the whole class, with all like materials stored together

If you don't have cubbies to hold workbooks and textbooks that you don't use very often, you can keep things on standard bookshelves in an easily accessible place. This photo shows an organization of all like workbooks together. When using this arrangement, I have two helpers get the workbooks from the shelves and pass them out to the class as needed.

Option 3) One shelving area for the whole class, with each child's materials stored together

In this set-up, each child's workbooks are in one place (all books for student #1 together, all books for student #2 together, and so on). There is an index

card on the shelf above which tells the order the books should go in (blue, purple, green, yellow) so the shelf looks neater and the materials are easier to find. An added benefit of this system is that you can tell at a glance which students are hoarding things in their desks instead of returning them to the shelf. For upkeep with this arrangement, I have to give the class a few procedural reminders during the year, and every other week during Fun Friday, I have helpers straighten the shelves. When students need to get their workbooks, I either call them by teams or by even/odd numbers to make sure there are only a few kids at the shelf at a time.

Storing Shared Classroom Materials

If children have too many supplies in their desks, items will get misplaced, used up for non-academic purposes, or become distractions during instruction. Additionally, things will be constantly falling out of students' overcrowded desks and children will have a difficult time staying organized.

The only school supplies my students keep in their desks are those that are used daily and are not easily consumed. (Sticky notes, for example, have a tendency to 'disappear' when students are allowed to keep a stack of them.) The supplies they keep are pencils, a blue pen (for making corrections to their work), a highlighter, eraser, crayons, scissors, and a glue stick. Some groups of children

cannot handle keeping scissors and glue and will play around with them constantly, so if you don't use those materials on a regular basis, store them someplace other than in student desks. If you explain, practice, and reinforce keeping ALL school supplies except pencils and erasers in a supply bag/box, most children will be able to handle the responsibility.

The materials that I don't allow students to keep in their desks are stored in various containers, and I have my Supply Helpers pass out and collect them as needed.

You can also have students keep extra materials in one central location for each group or team of students. A helper from each team can distribute and collect supplies from his team's container.

Sharing Individual Materials

I do not allow students to share their personal school supplies for several reasons which we discuss the first week of school (and again throughout the year as needed). The main reason is because it disrupts instruction: an unprepared student has to interrupt other children to ask about borrowing things. Sharing crayons, colored pencils, and markers is the worst—students meander around the room trying to find just the right shade of purple in someone's box, or lean over and bump people to reach what they need, and so on.

Another reason I don't allow supply sharing is because some children use their possessions to control and manipulate other students. Inevitably, someone will decide that only certain people can use her pink gel pen and there are hurt feelings and long arguments in the middle of instruction.

Yet another reason not to allow supply sharing is that the child who is prepared for school has to do without materials. It's extremely unfair, in my opinion, for a child to give away notebook paper because another child chose to draw on all of his during recess, or for a child to stop cutting in order to let someone who lost her own scissors borrow them. If parents don't provide basic supplies for their children, I do, so there is no reason for anyone to be without unless they have been irresponsible.

I have no idea how students lose items that never go beyond two feet of their desks, but it always happens! Many children try to take their materials home, and I am adamantly against that—they're called *school supplies* because they belong at *school*. If a child needs a ruler or something at home, I tell them to let their parents know, and if no one buys it, I will "see what I can do to take care of it."

Communal Supplies

One year I used only communal supplies: I collected all of students' crayons, pencils, notebooks, etc., and kept them in one place for everyone to share. I know teachers who love this method because it ensures that all children have the things they need, but in my experience, children like to use the pencils, notebooks, etc., that they picked out at the store. Most of the children in my class did not like this method, and a few parents complained, so I didn't try it again.

Making the Most of Student's School Supply Lists

If your administration allows you to choose materials to be included on student's school supply lists, I recommend requesting as many things as you believe the class will need. I like to have a list of 'recommended' or 'required' supplies (pencils, crayons, etc.) and a list of 'optional' contributions such as hand sanitizer, sticky notes, plastic baggies, and dry erase markers. These things are needed in my classroom but are just too expensive for me to continually buy. Even if only five kids bring them in, it saves me a tremendous amount of money!

Many times I only have to ask for certain supplies every other year. For example, two years ago, I had so much glue and so many rulers left over, I didn't ask parents to purchase them the next year. Now for the coming year, I need those things again, but I have tons of left-over sticky notes and bags, so I won't request those. I also send home requests before winter and spring break asking for donations. Most parents don't send anything, but the ones who do really make a difference. It's worth asking, if you can. (Some school districts prohibit teachers from asking for supplies in general, or have banned particular supply requests, so make sure you check with your administration.)

There is also a trend in some schools for teachers to ask parents for $20-$35 and the teachers purchase all the school supplies. This way they can get bulk discounts and make sure every child has the right materials. Leftover funds can go towards additional classroom supplies. This method may be more costly for bargain-shopping parents who generally spend far less than that amount, even if it is easier on them time-wise, so be sure to think about your demographics and get your principal's permission before trying this.

Inexpensive Ways to Get Classroom Materials

You don't have to spend a ton of money out of your own pocket to have a well-equipped classroom! Set an annual budget that you will not go over (mine is $100). The best teachers make do with what they have! Borrow or make things that you feel like you can't live without. Scour yard sales and flea markets if you 'must' buy something. Don't spend your hard-earned money on cutesy bulletin board borders—your kids *will* learn without them! Ask parents, local businesses, friends, relatives, your significant other's co-workers, and other community members for items you need. I have gotten everything from free children's books to furniture to file folders and art supplies just by asking! Here are some resources for inexpensive and free materials that you may find helpful:

- **Highlights Magazine:** This is a great source for stickers, organizers, CDs, and more! You send home a slip asking parents to subscribe. They check yes or no, and every slip returned to you gives you a point towards free merchandise, regardless of whether the parent subscribes or not! I have gotten an organizer for my overhead projector, carbon-copy notes, sticky tack, colorful magazine file boxes, two huge and sturdy pocket charts, stickers, a set of classical music CDs, and much more. The best part is, the quality of the products is excellent and the materials are extremely durable. Highlights also publishes Puzzle Mania and Math Mania, offering the same merchandise deal for those publications**.**

- **Yard Sales:** You can find books, toys, games, and much more at yard sales. And don't forget flea markets, silent auctions, church auctions, and garage sales...check the newspapers to see what's going on near you.

- **Trade with other teachers:** Each year in June when you clean out your room, make a stack of all the things you could consider parting with (I know, it's hard!) and get together with co-workers and teacher friends from other schools. This is an especially tempting idea for those who are switching grade levels or schools—be sure to personally invite them. Swap your materials and ideas, and walk away with new stuff, less junk, and money still in your pocket!

- **Free Stuff for Educators**: Do an Internet search using those terms or 'teacher freebies'. There are an amazing number of promotional materials available at no or low cost for teachers.

Chapter 7: Maintaining a Class Library
Teaching kids to organize and utilize books effectively

Your classroom library is a powerful tool for improving students' literacy skills. Like any collection, your classroom library will take years to develop and is always an ongoing process. This chapter will not only help you set up and maintain a functional library, but show you how to give kids ownership of it. You will learn how to select and organize your books and how to teach children to care for and utilize them. The library you'll create will not just store books: it will motivate kids to read more and further their learning and interest in the world around them.

Obtaining Reading Materials

Choosing Books for Your Collection

When selecting books for your library, keep in mind two facts: 90% of the reading we do as adults is non-fiction, and children often prefer non-fiction to fiction texts. Since we know that students need to be familiar with strategies for reading non-fiction texts in preparation for real life and that they enjoy exploring such books, we need to be careful not to fill our class libraries primarily with fairytales and made-up stories. Having lots of nonfiction books will provide an additional bonus to you as a teacher, because you'll be able to use them to supplement your science and social studies instruction as read-alouds.

I also encourage you to ASK YOUR STUDENTS WHAT THEY WANT TO READ before you select more books for your library. I guarantee you will be surprised by the responses! Your students will probably be interested in authors, series, or topics that you are completely unfamiliar with. Have your kids fill out a survey, or talk to them individually during your silent reading time. You can graph the responses and analyze them as a class. Remember that children are more likely to read when they have materials they are interested in, so everyone benefits when you ask for student input before selecting new materials.

Sources for Affordable Books

- **Your local library:** Sign up to be notified by email or phone when the library cleans out the children's section, or check regularly to see what books they have put up for sale. Books can go for as low as $0.25 and are usually hardcover! Also ask if teachers can check out books for extended periods of time. Some libraries will allow educators to keep books for 3-12 weeks, which is long enough to utilize the resources throughout an entire thematic unit. Don't forget to check out audio books for your listening center, as well as the selection of children's music and movies.

- **Online auction sites:** A few years ago, I purchased fifty children's books for $34—including shipping and handling! Books are shipped using media mail rates, which are very, very low. Many teachers sell books when they switch grade levels, move, or retire, and this is a great way to build a classroom library cheaply!

- **Book Fairs:** These are regular events held throughout the country. They sell new books that were over-printed, out of print, etc. I recently got thirty-five books for $29! Check your local newspaper listings or go online to see what book fairs come to your area.

- **Scholastic book orders:** This is by far the best deal anywhere for teachers. You get points towards free books every time you or one of your families buy books, and prices start from $0.50.

- **Secondhand Shops:** The stores for charitable organizations are a great source of used books, and the money you spend goes toward a good cause.

- **Corporate Donations:** Many companies have literacy outreach programs in which they donate books to schools. A phone company used to send a representative each year to one of my former schools to read to all of the third grade classes. Their company was associated with the First Book Program, which provides reading materials to low-income children, and they donated at least one book for every student. I kept many of the books in the classroom so all the children could read them. Over the course of two years, I obtained about 100 books from corporate donations. Go to companies' websites or call them, and ask friends who work for big corporations to look into sponsorship for you.

- **Printouts from the Internet:** There are online sites where you can print children's books for free. Students can then color, fold, and staple them to create little readers. Do an Internet search for 'free printable books' and see what you can find!

Organizing Your Library

Categorizing Your Collection By Genre

Like most teachers, I group the books in my class library by genre. Some kindergarten and first grade teachers simplify genres and group their books topically or thematically (e.g., dinosaurs, careers). There is no one right way: choose whatever system makes sense to you. You can even have the kids help you come up with an organizational system and decide which categories they would like to have: this gives them more ownership over the library and makes it easier for them to locate books and keep the library neat. Whatever you decide to do, I would advise you to think long-term so that you don't have to completely redo your system in a few years when you have a lot more books or when you switch to another grade.

Leveling Books

Putting a reading level on a book is called leveling, and it's a practice that is becoming less emphasized among educators. There are researchers, including the well-respected Patricia Cunningham, who advocate leveling as an appropriate tool for helping kids choose books. However, there is an increasing body of research that indicates students need to learn how to choose suitable books without the aid of a leveling system. Personally, I dislike leveling because it limits kids—they often feel 'stuck' on their level, afraid to try more challenging texts, or become stigmatized by continually having to read books that are clearly marked for younger students. Also, leveling an entire classroom library takes a long time for the teacher to complete, so I don't recommend it unless your district requires you to do so.

You can, however, give kids a heads-up on the difficulty of a book through a simpler form of 'leveling'. When I first began teaching, I used sticky dots to 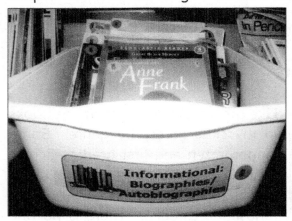 indicate the genre of books so students would know where to return them, e.g., 'RF' for Realistic Fiction and 'Sci-Fi' for Science Fiction. I used green dots for the easiest books in my collection, yellow for the medium, and red for the hardest books I had. In my experience, students did not restrict themselves to one color, especially when reading conferences were held to monitor book choices and encourage students to be more adventurous in their selections. One year I did not explain the color-coding system at all to the class, leaving them to rely solely on strategies such as the 5 Finger Test to determine if a book was right for them, and they managed fine. Overall, I have found the sticky dot system easy to maintain, and a helpful guide for students without being a crutch that they depend on.

Book Bins and Baskets

Teachers sometimes store books on the shelves of their class libraries with the spines facing out, instead of using book bins. This is normally done to save space and money, since teachers generally have limited shelving areas and have to buy their own containers.

You may wonder if it's really necessary to have book bins. I'll give you several reasons why they're important. First of all, containers help children keep the library looking neat and organized. Secondly, they help kids select books because the covers can be seen (this is especially critical for emerging readers, who can't quickly peruse titles on the spines). And finally, consumer report studies have proven that books displayed with the covers facing out in bookstores outsell by huge margins the books that are shelved with only their spines visible. This is an important marketing strategy that we should make use of in the classroom to encourage students to read important and challenging texts.

If we want kids to read books, we need to make them look appealing and keep them easily accessible. Think about what is inviting to you in a bookstore, and try to recreate that in your classroom library, placing emphasis on the books you most want your students to choose.

Book Check-Out Systems for Children

Using Individual Book Boxes

If your kids spend twenty minutes looking for a book to read and thirty seconds reading it, you may want to consider using book boxes. These are containers that students keep their reading materials in and utilize whenever they are given time to read independently. I purchased mine from a teaching catalog for about $3 each, so that's a bit expensive for a class set. However, I viewed them as a multi-year investment in classroom management and in my students' independent reading skills. If you can't afford to buy book boxes, you can use cheaper plastic baskets or containers from the dollar store. I also tried using cereal boxes which students took home and decorated  with pictures of things they like to read about (see the photo on page 278). These only lasted a few months, though, sometimes less if students chose large or heavy books.

Twice a week, I allow my kids to pick up to five new books from our classroom library to keep in their book boxes. Later in the year I give a variety of guidelines to help children vary their choices and take risks: *at least one book in your book box must be a chapter book, you must have at least two non-fiction books, try a genre that you didn't have in your book box last week,* and so on. I also give additional restrictions for children who tend to pick books that are too easy or all of the same genre.

I sometimes provided leveled books such as the little readers that go with our reading curriculum and had children choose two 'little books' in addition to the five regular books. This ensured that students were continually reading materials that were appropriate for their reading levels.

The problem of reshelving books from the book boxes is solved by assigning the job of Class Librarian to two students in the class. When kids get new books for their book boxes, they stack the old ones neatly on a table. The librarians later reshelve the books to make sure they are put away correctly and neatly.

Borrowing Books for Classroom Use

A lot of teachers glue library pockets in the back of their books and have kids check out books out that way. However, I have hundreds of books and that's too daunting of a project for me, so I just stamp the inside of each with my name! I did use a check-out system my first year of teaching third grade: the kids filled out a class log indicating which book they had, the date they checked it out, and the date they returned it. This system was incredibly simple and worked well. However, I didn't see the need for it in later years. I figured the advantages of not having to keep track of my books outweighed the possibility of having a few books lost or stolen, so I stopped having any check-out system at all.

Over the years, I have 'lost' only a handful of books to stealing, even when I was teaching in the toughest of neighborhoods. So my advice to you is: concentrate more on teaching kids to properly handle books and don't worry about a check-out system, unless you can do it in a way that is simple and requires little management. Just make sure kids don't keep your books in their desks, because they're likely to become damaged or misplaced. It's far more likely that your books will get torn up or stained because of improper care than lost altogether because you had no check-out system.

Taking Books Home

Some teachers allow this practice, but I really want to keep all of my resources intact and available for myself and the kids to reference. I have never let students take home the books from our classroom library because I paid for them with my own money and consider them my personal property. However, when I taught at a school that provided about 250 trade books for the classroom, I kept my personal collection of books for the kids to read in class and began allowing children to take the school's books home. The school also provided small canvas bags for students to use when transporting the books back and forth.

The photograph here shows the books that my students were allowed to take home (from the spinning racks). They were separate from the books in bins so students clearly understood which books were for home. Also, my personal books that I paid for had my name on the inside, and the other books were stamped with the school stamp.

Since the books were leaving the classroom, it was important to keep track of the materials each student borrowed. Each morning I called two teams at a time to check out new books for home. At the beginning of the year, I was closely involved with the checkout process, but after the first two weeks, I allowed students to get books independently. Each child held up his old book for me to see, then returned it to the spinning rack and chose a new book.

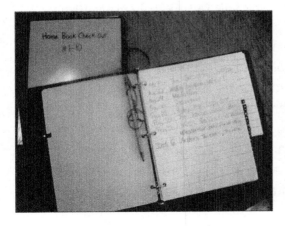

This photo shows the home book checkout system I used. There were two binders (one for the first half of the class, one for the second half) because many of the kids wrote slowly and this kept others from having to wait as long for their chance to sign in. The binders had numbered tabs so that each child had his or her own section. The form students filled out was simple: book title and date checked out.

Every other week, I looked through the binders and followed up with kids who hadn't checked out books recently—I asked if they were still reading the same title (and if it wasn't a chapter book, why). If a student lost her book, I sent home a note (or had the student write a note in her agenda) to remind her family to look for it. If two weeks passed and I saw from the check-out log that the book was still not returned, I spoke with the child about responsibility and allowed her to get a new book. I made it clear that I would only excuse a lost book once during the school year. I never had a child lose two books, but I would have taken away check-out privileges if the situation arose.

Teaching Kids How to Use Your Classroom Library

If you don't model your expectations, your classroom library will soon look like a tornado hit. Introducing your library is a process that takes several days and can begin on the first day of school if you want to get kids reading authentic materials right away. Each lesson should be about 5-20 minutes (depending on students' attention span) and should be followed by time for guided student practice.

Day One- How to Handle Books Appropriately

Show the class your library and get them excited about the prospect of exploring all of the different materials therein! Most children will be enthusiastic, but if students aren't responding, select a few book covers to show them and get a discussion going about the titles students have read and are interested in trying. Explain that the library is very special and very expensive, so the class will need to take a few days to learn how to use it before they can begin choosing books.

You can brainstorm guidelines together as a class, writing them on chart paper. Your list should focus on how to handle books. In addition to obvious rules such as not writing on, throwing, or tearing books, kids should be guided towards rules such as: don't fold pages (use bookmarks), don't hold books by their pages (hold by the spine), and don't press the pages down flat because it weakens the binding. Model the correct way to hold and read a book, and have students practice. Use the same reinforcement narration and performance feedback techniques as you do for the introduction of all new routines (see Chapter 9).

Day Two- Pretending to Read vs. Real Reading

If your students are functional readers, you can follow up by demonstrating the difference between real reading and pretending to read. Tell the kids you're going to read a book and have them watch to see what you do wrong. Hold the book upside down and flip through the pages in three seconds. Start at the end of the book and go backwards. Start at the beginning and only look at the pictures. Start reading and then skip pages. Guide children to understand what REAL reading is, and set the expectation that they should not just be previewing or taking picture walks with the books in their book boxes, they should be doing real reading.

Explain that the only way to get good at something is to practice. If you want to become a better basketball player, you have to play basketball. If you want to become a better reader, you have to *read*. Book boxes and independent reading time are for REAL reading. End the discussion by having guided practice in which children demonstrate their skills with 'real reading' as you provide feedback.

Day Three- Introduction to Genre and the Organizational System

This can be a multiple day lesson if you want to really go in depth, and it could be an ongoing lesson (each time you explore a new genre in your reading series, you can talk more about it, showing further examples from the class library to get kids excited about the genre). Or, you can just tell kids about the difference between fiction and non-fiction and show the different types of each in your library.

The idea is to get kids to understand that books are organized in a way that will help them find things they are interested in. Ask students to name things they like to read and see if volunteers can determine where in the classroom library they could find related titles. For example, if a child likes Dr. Seuss or books about dinosaurs, discuss the genres those books would be part of and where they could be found. At first, there will be a lot of discussion, but as children get the hang of it, "Find That Book!" can be used as a fun, quick activity throughout the year to refresh kids' memories and help them use the library effectively.

Day Four- Selecting and Returning Books from the Class Library

If you're using individual book boxes for kids to hold their reading materials, this is the time to introduce that routine. Regardless of whether students will have book boxes or not, the lesson should focus on how to take and put books back appropriately. Model non-examples of how to take care of the library, then have students model the appropriate ways. Narrate what the children do as the class watches, then give every individual a chance to try as the others read silently.

You can also warn students that if they continually misuse your library, you will shut it down for a week or so, review procedures, and try again. Repeated problems with the whole class indicate that you should consider changing your organizational system: if it's not child-friendly, the kids won't be able to keep it neat. You may want to allow only trained classroom 'librarians' to reshelve books and have the other children place their books neatly in a large container when they are finished reading them.

If you plan to let children take books home, tell them they must first prove their responsibility with books in the classroom. After several weeks of showing you that they can handle books appropriately, tell the class you're going to be entrusting them with a huge privilege, and discuss your procedures for home book check-out. If certain students are misusing books in the classroom, you can speak with them privately and review the expectations they must meet before they can be allowed to take books home.

Creative Ways to Give Kids Ownership Over the Library

- **Favorite Author Displays:** Create an arrangement of a particular author's books, print-outs from his website, and book reviews (from newspapers, the Internet, and students). Change the display every few weeks as students' interests develop. This can be a student-led project with older children.

- **Book Talks**: A guaranteed way to get children interested in specific books is to do weekly Book Talks, also called 'The Blessing of the Book'. Choose a book you want kids to get excited about, perhaps from a genre you've been studying, or a non-fiction text related to your social studies or science unit. Read an excerpt, and keep multiple copies of the book available if possible for students to read. I can tell you from experience that any book 'blessed' by the teacher will be a class favorite for the rest of the year ("Look what I'm reading! Remember when you read this to us?").

- **Student-Led Book Reviews:** Put kids in charge of your book talks or book reviews! The reviews can be compiled into a class notebook that is saved from year to year for students to reference. They can see which books were popular years ago, and if you have students' siblings, they can see what older sisters and brothers enjoyed reading when they were in your class!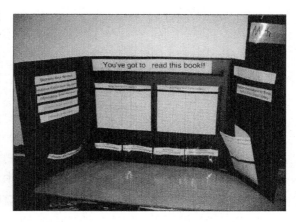

- **Book Picks (Peer Book Recommendations):** Another way to get students interested in reading books from your class library is to have an area displaying their favorite choices. You can have the class vote on their favorite titles and display the children's 'Top Ten' or 'Best-Sellers'. You can also have students take turns creating a display of their favorite titles, the way libraries, bookstores, and video rental stores sometimes do (i.e., 'John's Picks').

- **Student-Authored Books:** Books which students have made and class-created books are always popular and great for motivating students to read.

- **Book Awards**: Decide on several categories as a class, such as Best Illustrations, Best Series, Best Historical Fiction, Most Humorous, etc. You can vote on which books get the awards or form committees to select the winners. Students can design awards (similar to the Newberry Medal or Caldecott icons) and place them on the cover of the books. This gets kids to think critically about what they read and encourages them to read a wider variety of books, both to discover new books for an award and to see what's so great about a book that was already awarded. This strategy is also fantastic for getting kids to distinguish between genres, and analyze the features of quality literature as they determine criteria for an award. You can incorporate persuasive writing, having kids make commercials or ads for the books they want to win, or discuss point of view and perspective. Give the book award idea to kids and see where they take it!

Chapter 8: Cleaning, Packing, and Moving
What to keep, what to toss, and where to put it so you can find it

There are lots of teachers who move to new classrooms or schools, and I've had many ask how I decide what to keep and what to get rid of when I change teaching assignments. (I've had enough experience—nine rooms in eight schools in three districts across two states!) I created this chapter to share the ideas I've amassed for cleaning out classrooms, packing and moving them, and creating portable storage that's easy to access.

Guidelines for 'Spring Cleaning' (Or Fall, or Winter)

☑ **Clean and organize only when you're in a purging mood**.

If you're feeling sentimental or stingy, don't waste your time—you'll end up keeping everything and then wondering how you accumulated so much junk!

☑ **Spend a week slowly cleaning out your files and papers.**

Any unused class sets of copies can be put on a table for your coworkers to pick through. If you haven't used an activity in the past two years, it's trash. (The exception is if you're changing grade levels, but be realistic: are you REALLY going to want that worksheet from 1992?). When you look at a paper, you should think, "This is great. If I were teaching this unit right now I would go run the photocopies immediately. I can't wait to use this next year—the kids are going to get so much out of this!" If your thoughts are more similar to, "Hmm, this is pretty good. I would probably use it. Well, I think I'd like to see if there was anything better first...," then be ruthless.

☑ **Remember, with the Internet, pretty much any written resource is at your fingertips instantly.**

There's just no need to hang onto a stack of timed math quizzes or synonym worksheets just in case you need 'extra practice'. If the materials your district provides aren't enough (and really, don't we all have more resources than we could ever have time to actually implement?), you can type what you need into a search engine and print out something of quality in minutes. And chances are good that your paper-hoarding coworkers have a ton of books and worksheets you could borrow if you ever needed to. So eliminate those files!! Keep a single copy of everything you actually use and that's it.

☑ **Plan to stay late ONE day (no more than two) and clean out your cabinets**.

If this becomes a multi-day job, you're over-thinking things. Do you use it or not? Be merciless, and if you can't, get someone to help you. Non-teacher spouses and friends tend to be excellent about putting things in perspective, since they marvel at how much stuff teachers accumulate, anyway, and tend to shame us into getting rid of things. Most teachers do Fun Friday or something similar at the end of the week, so that's an excellent day to finish closet and cabinet cleaning. Use your planning time and lunch to clear everything out, and then while the class works independently, you can...

☑ **Make a pile of everything you want to give away and have student volunteers carry it all into the hallway.**

Make an announcement via intra-school email or the intercom that you've got give-aways outside your door. Teachers are notorious pack-rats and nearly everything of value will be gone within the hour.

☑ **As you watch your things being snatched up, console yourself with this thought: everything that you won't get to keep will be treasured and utilized by someone else, so kids will continue to benefit from it.**

Wasn't that the whole purpose of creating those centers and buying those resource books? You're not 'getting rid' of your precious things, you're redistributing them for the greater good. By letting go of older things with lesser value, you're also clearing space for newer and better things to come.

☑ **Instruct the custodian to throw out anything left in the hall after 24 hours.**

The old adage, *better to have it and not need it than to need it and not have it* doesn't apply when you're purging. It's better to throw something out than to drag your same old mess into a new room. It can be comforting to know that you have something familiar to use 'just in case'. However, you must stay focused on the satisfaction that will come from having a streamlined and organized classroom. That feeling is far superior to being surrounded by ancient clutter.

Packing and Moving Tips

Moving a classroom is almost as difficult as moving a home, in my experience, especially since my classroom has almost always been larger than the apartment or condo I lived in! Hopefully you will have completed the process of cleaning so that you don't have to transport boxes of junk that haven't even been sorted through. Make sure you know what's in your classroom—and that it's quality stuff—before you start packing.

- ◆ **If you have your job lined up and you know where your new classroom will be, don't be afraid to ask the principal how soon you can move your things in!** Hopefully you will be able to take boxes from one classroom directly to the other. One year I couldn't do this and had to bring everything home, which I hated doing because almost every school has bugs and I was paranoid about bringing roaches in! Plus, I had to move everything home and then back out again. I had a basement then so it was okay, but in later moves when I was in a one-bedroom condo, moving everything straight into the school was the only feasible option.

- ◆ **Enlist your students (or kids from the older grades, if yours are too young) to help organize.** My third graders sorted all of my bulletin board trimmers and filed them in a box, took down all of my posters (removing sticky tack and staples) and placed them in a super-size plastic bag, cleaned out my classroom library and ensured all books were in the right place, etc.

◆ **After you remove everything you don't want from your room, begin piling all of your personal belongings into one corner of the room.** This will help you keep things separate, and if you're moving to a new school, you'll have an idea of what kind of vehicle(s) you will need based on how much room your things take up.

Keeping everything piled in one place in the room is also a good idea once you move things into your new classroom. That way, you have space to arrange your furniture and take inventory of what's already in the room before you start unpacking. Also, if you move your things in during the summer, custodians can clean around your belongings more easily when they're altogether.

◆ **If you have big/heavy/extensive amounts of items, consider renting a moving truck to save yourself a lot of trips.** Because I have shelves, 1,500 children's books, a frig, a microwave, a copier, and tons of plastic drawers (all of which I utilize daily and won't get rid of), I just rent a truck when I move. People laugh at me but I don't care—it's the least time-consuming way to get everything where it's going! The truck is only about $20 for the day (it's mileage that's so expensive) so if your two schools are close together, you've got a pretty good deal. When I moved from Washington, D.C. to Florida, I actually hired a moving team to pack and unpack my room. Because they were already moving my household goods, adding an extra stop at the school was very cost-effective.

◆ **If your materials are already kept in boxes, drawers, or plastic tubs, moving is simple.** Even though I had enough things to fill a twenty-foot moving truck, I only needed three large boxes to hold all of my miscellaneous things because everything else was already in organizers! One caveat: this does take up more space when moving. For example, if I shoved dividers and page protectors in a box, they would have taken up a fraction of the space that my drawers did (see photo). But unpacking was

so easy—I just picked a shelf to stick the drawers on, and everything was already in its place! Cardboard file boxes (available from office supply stores) are cheap yet sturdy ways to store materials if you don't want to invest in plastic tubs.

♦ **Some people like to label boxes or use color-coded sticky dots to indicate box contents**. I didn't do that last time I moved because almost everything was already in clearly-labeled organizers. For me, labels are only necessary when I have a whole bunch of different things that aren't normally together in one box, because otherwise, the contents become pretty clear as soon as you peek inside.

♦ **Fill one box with things you know you want to access immediately in your new room.** Label it 'Open First." I include pens, post-its, paperclips, cleaning supplies, and other things I want to take out right away.

Unpacking and Organizing Your New Room

Basic Steps for Setting Up a New Room

Step 1- Give it a thorough cleaning
Step 2- Plan the room arrangement on paper and put the furniture in place
Step 3- Move personal belongings into the room
Step 4- Set up each area of the classroom with your materials

1   2   3   4

Pacing Yourself So You Don't Get Overwhelmed

Hopefully, you will be able to see your room prior to the beginning of the school year so you can make plans early. Taking photos of the room will help you do this. When I accepted the position at my latest school and the administration showed me my new classroom, I quickly snapped a few shots of the previous teacher's set-up (see photo on left). A little embarrassing to do, yes, but well worth it! The sketches that I did over the summer while waiting to work in my room were just rough ideas, but deciding where to place my desk and which direction to have student desks face was something I wanted to have figured out ahead of time.

When you first arrive, place your purse and all of your personal materials in one spot in the room so that those things are safely out of the way. Here's what my latest classroom looked like when I first went in, a few days before teacher planning week in August. Obviously the former teacher's things were gone and the custodians had cleaned out the room during June and July.

Next, give the room a thorough cleaning and arrange the furniture roughly how you want it. I always end up moving things a few more times as I refine my plans, and continue to adapt the space to our needs throughout the year, but it's good to have things basically in place. I didn't want to start dragging my own belongings out and then have to shove them out of the way so I could rearrange furniture.

Also, many of the shelves and cabinets were dusty and dirty and I wanted them to be clean before I put my things there. Most classrooms need a deep cleaning at the start of the school year, and if the teacher before you left a lot behind, you'll need large trash bags for cleaning out old materials. I filled four gigantic boxes with ancient reading series and textbooks, and then notified the office so they could send the boxes to the district book depository. (If you're new to the school system or grade level, you will probably want someone to look over the materials you're tossing out to make sure you won't need any of them.) There were still some things I wasn't sure if I needed or not so I stacked them neatly in the closet until I could have my team leader let me know what I could toss.

After the furniture is set up the way you want it, begin unpacking your things. I like to place items in the general area of the room that I want them in, then organize one area at a time. For example, I piled all of my book boxes, children's magazines, and children's literature over the in the far left corner where I knew I would keep my class library, but didn't organize or unpack the boxes there until I was ready to set up that area. I also kept extra boxes and plastic  tubs in one area of the room so I could pick through them any time I needed a container to organize something. Posters, things to hang on the walls, plants, and decorative items stayed together in one spot, as well, for me to put up last.

I put any textbooks/workbooks that I knew I wanted kids to keep in their desks on a designated table so that I could put them in individual student desks right before school started. (I didn't want to do this yet so the desks would be light enough to move around as needed, and also because I wasn't ready to assign  book numbers to students yet.) Textbooks that I knew we wouldn't use often were stored on cubby shelves. I made sure to leave room for consumable workbooks that hadn't yet been distributed for the new school year. At this point, the room was looking pretty messy, way worse than before I started unpacking! I left it like this at the end of the second (ten-hour) day.

I continued to organize and arrange materials slowly for several weeks. Even my bulletin boards weren't completely in place when school started. Setting up a new room is a lot like setting up a new home—allow yourself time to go slowly, and don't feel pressured to have things look 'done' right away.

Part Three:
Developing Procedures and Routines

Chapter 9: How to Teach Any Procedure
Making your classroom management expectations a reality

The steps are essentially the same when teaching any new concept or skill to students. You determine your expectations and goals, plan how to teach towards them, explain the material to students, and model how to apply the skill. Then you guide students through their own practice repeatedly while reinforcing accuracy and redirecting errors, reviewing the skill over time.

When we assume procedures don't need to be taught, or can be mentioned once or twice before mastery, we're forgetting about how the learning process works. It is no different from assuming that you don't have to teach subtraction if the kids already learned it last year. This is faulty thinking because your expectations are higher in the next grade level. Students are capable of learning and doing more. You have to teach the newer, more challenging content. What children did last year just laid the foundation for what you're going to teach this year.

Teach Procedures Like Any New Skill

The Importance of Ongoing (Distributed) Practice

You would never introduce the concept of subtraction and then expect mastery the following day: *I just told you that 32-15=17! Don't you know that? How many times do I have to show you how to regroup?* You know that for students to truly demonstrate mastery, they're going to need ongoing practice in a variety of situations, with lots of modeling and reinforcing. So why would children magically understand procedures upon the first introduction?

Similarly, you wouldn't expect students to remember everything about subtraction when it's been four months since the last time you mentioned the concept. The only way to ensure that students retain information is through distributed practice (revisiting the same concepts and skills over and over throughout the year). Even if your current math focus is measurement, you would still give subtraction practice through warm-ups, math games, homework practice, and test reviews. One of the few advantages of our test-obsessed teaching culture is that school districts are finally planning opportunities for students to review and apply knowledge throughout the year. Just as you don't want students to be out of practice and 'forget' how to regroup on a state test, neither do you want them to 'forget' how to follow procedures. You MUST plan distributed practice for procedures.

Some students will grasp the concept of two-digit subtraction within a few lessons, maybe even after the first. Most of the class will need a little more practice. And some students still won't have a clue in June. But you don't give up. You keep providing more opportunities for practice and reinforcement. Even the most challenging students make progress. Your instruction in procedures and routines works the same way.

Precise Expectations

What Exactly Do You Want?

Specificity is crucial in regard to procedures, because if you don't know what you want and teach for it, you'll never get it. It is not enough to think, *I want students to line up quietly.* What does quietly mean? Is talking okay? What if it's whispering? Can they shuffle their feet? What if they hum or tap? And by line up, do you mean that students need to be in a straight line? What does straight look like?

Many times teachers think they have been clear with their expectations and are mystified as to why students are not meeting them. The answer often lies in the exactitude of instruction. If you taught your class to form a straight line but never specified how far from the wall they should walk, the line won't stay straight for long. If you don't specify how to leave an appropriate amount of space behind each child, you'll have clumps of students in some places and huge gaps elsewhere in the line. If these are the sort of problems you're having with your students, recognize that they are not your students' problems. There has been a miscommunication, a gap between your expectations and theirs. You cannot punish children for their inability to read your mind.

What Not to Do

Telling children what not to do is like telling a dog, "No!" when he jumps up on you. The dog gets frightened, but hasn't a clue what he should be doing, so he tries the same thing over and over again or cowers in a corner. If you've ever trained a puppy, you know that the more effective command is "Off!" or "Down!" because these are specific actions that the dog can take to correct the behavior.

This is part of the reason why classroom rules are supposed to be phrased positively (instead of "No hitting" the teacher should say, "Keep your hands to yourself"). The first phrase requires a small child to independently determine a more appropriate action, while the second phrase gives her a concrete step to take and crystallizes the teacher's expectations. If the child hears your warning and begins shoving her neighbor, technically she is obeying the "no hitting" rule—you haven't told her not to push! But if you've said, "Keep your hands to yourself," then you've specifically stated what the child needs to do with her hands instead of using them to harm others.

Assume that if children don't do what you ask, it's because they don't know how. A child may know WHAT to do, but not HOW to do it.

This is not unlike the teacher's situation—she knows WHAT procedures to teach but not HOW to teach them. The teacher is not purposefully being negligent in her procedures instruction. Most of the time, the kids aren't being purposely negligent in following them. Both the student and the teacher need to learn HOW to do their respective jobs.

A Caution Against Misusing "*We*"

It took me many years to figure out the dangers of including myself in a statement that was actually directed towards students. I was trained in college to use "we" whenever possible: *We need to get quiet. We need to put our pencils down. When we're ready to line up, we'll go to lunch.* The theory is that using this pronoun connotes a team effort, in which 'we' work together to follow procedures and get work done.

This can send the wrong message to children when used to discuss responsibilities and expectations. Your job as a teacher and theirs as students are very different. You are not waiting for yourself to be quiet, you are waiting for them. *When you're ready to line up, I can take you to lunch. When you are quiet, I can show you our activity. When you put your pencil down, I can explain the next direction.* These statements show children the powerful connection between their behavior and how the classroom is run (see Chapter 14). Students will learn that their choices influence your decisions and the outcome of the school day.

In this way, differentiating between *you* and *I* empowers and motivates students to follow routines. It also confers a great authority to the teacher that is sacrificed when the word 'we' is used. "We worked really hard today, so maybe we'll get to play outside a little longer!" sends a completely different message than, "You all worked really hard today and were so on-task! I will give you those five minutes you saved to play outside."

Saying "we" is very effective when you truly do need to work together to accomplish a goal. I use the term a lot in my classroom when the students and I are in a joint position ("We'll finish our science lesson tomorrow" or "We'll go out to the playground after this"). Just be cautious not to say "we" when your actions are separate from those you expect from students.

Using Signals

Having something other than the sound of your voice as a signal during routines can sharpen students' focus and instill automatic responses. You can use timers, bells, rain sticks, chimes, and so on. I especially like little clickers (as seen in the center of the photo). These can be purchased in pet stores and are great for when you need a sound that's softer and quicker than a bell. Teach students not to

begin until they hear a particular signal, and to freeze whenever they hear it again. More information about using signals when giving directions is provided in Chapter 26, Making the Most of Every Moment.

Reinforcement Narration and Performance Feedback

These are some fancy-sounding terms I chose to concisely describe a process I'll be referencing throughout this book.

Reinforcement narration is the act of talking students through a procedure or routine to draw attention to what they're doing correctly or incorrectly, e.g., *Let's watch team one line up. Oh, look, Maria and John remembered to push their chairs in. And now Isaiah's doing it, too. None of them are talking to each other. See how silent they are as they walk over to their places? Isaiah is facing straight ahead. Maria is checking to make sure she is one arm's length behind him. The entire team has gotten in line and is waiting quietly for the other children to get behind them. I'm going to call team two next, and I want you to notice how team one stays quiet even while the second group is getting in line behind them.* You simply narrate what you see or give a synopsis to reinforce behaviors.

Performance feedback is your evaluation of how well students are meeting your expectations. You can give some of the feedback yourself and elicit student input part of the time to keep the children actively involved in the process. *How did this last team do when you were watching them line up? Did they get in place without talking or making noises? Are they standing an arm's length apart from each other? Something is happening with the back of the line there—what needs to be fixed? Okay, so someone needs to put his hands down at his sides. How does it look now? Alright, we've got everyone in line—I'm looking to see how well you all have followed our guidelines. I see everyone standing on the third tile, which means the line is straight. I don't hear anyone making noise with their bodies, so the line is quiet. This is exactly the way you should be standing in line. This is what I expect to see every time we line up. You can do it. This is excellent.*

Steps for Teaching ANY Procedure or Routine

I've dedicated the entire third section of this book to procedures and routines, because there are specific hints, tips, and guidelines for managing each one. But the teaching process is very simple, and once you understand it, you can apply the steps to any procedure you want. Knowing how to teach procedures means you can modify and adapt your routines continually throughout the year without confusing children or creating chaos. Once you understand this, you will have complete control over the way your classroom is run and total freedom to create needed change.

Staying focused on your own expectations is the key to teaching routines. The entire process is about what you do with expectations: determine, plan how to teach, explain, model, guide, reinforce, and review/adapt through ongoing practice.

1. Clearly *determine* your own expectations.

Figure out what you want ahead of time. You should record your expectations as you plan. Your list will be a great reference for future years when you wonder, "What exactly WAS my procedure for that?"

2. *Plan how you will teach* your expectations.

Next, design the lesson that will present your expectations. Decide what you will say, examples and non-examples you want to give, how much student input you will elicit, how you will model, and how you will manage student practice. I suggest standing in your classroom before school and saying the words out loud to get comfortable with the phrasing and help you anticipate issues that will arise during the lesson.

3. *Explain* your expectations and the reasons for them.

As an introduction to your lesson, you will need to explain why you feel the need for a particular procedure. ***Students need to understand that there is a***

problem and you have a solution. For your initial introduction to basic procedures, this may be general: "What would happen if everyone moved down the hall in any way they wanted? Why do we need hallway rules?" However, the more specific you can be about an actual problem, the more students will buy into your solution. "I tripped over two backpacks this morning. I also saw someone get their pencil stepped on and broken because it was on the floor. This tells me that we have a problem with messy desk areas. It is becoming unsafe and supplies are getting broken and lost. We need to fix that. I'm going to show you how to keep a neat desk so that you will know where all of your supplies are and nothing will happen to them."

As you teach each criterion of your expectations, make sure the reasons are clear to students. "Whenever you pass in papers, you'll hand them to the person on your right. *That way no one gets confused about which direction to pass.* Only the person on the end of your row will put the papers into a neat stack. *If every person in the row tries to line the papers up perfectly, it will take forever to get the papers in.* You can demonstrate your reasoning as appropriate. "Here, I'll show you. Team one, I want you to pass your papers in, and as you get the stack on your desk, fix it up so everything's exactly even... See how long this is taking? We'll be late for lunch every single day! No one will get to finish their dessert! Team one, try it again and this time, just pass the stack gently and quickly to the person to your right, and the person on the end will fix them. There, see how fast that was? This is the reason why only one person will straighten the stack of papers."

4. *Model* your expectations.

You will be the first to demonstrate your expectations because only you truly understand them. Use reinforcement narration so students pick up on the things you are doing and understand how your actions contribute to the overall goals of the procedure. "Watch as I show you how to head your paper just like the poster shows. I'm putting the title in the big top part. That's called the top margin. Notice how I don't use up the entire space. Now I'm going to put my name on the first line. Am I

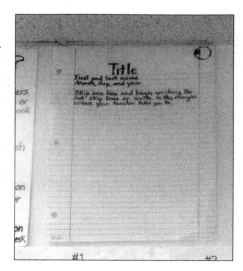

skipping a line now? Right. Watch what I put on the second line. The date, exactly! See how I am writing first the day, then the month, then the year. Oops, I made a mistake! Am I bunching up my paper and starting all over? No way, I'm not going to waste it. I'm going to gently erase...."

Sometimes students are fascinated by this sort of demonstration and will hang in there with you for in-depth modeling, and you should take advantage of their interest! But in general, teacher modeling should be kept brief and involve students as much as possible to keep them attentive. Their guided practice will be an opportunity for you to reinforce in more detail what you've modeled.

5. *Guide students through practice* using reinforcement narration.

Have several groups of children 'try out' what you just showed them. The rest of the class should watch and prepare to give feedback afterwards. "Now it's your turn to try returning workbooks to the shelf correctly. Let's start with group three. Right now the rest of you are going to watch them and give feedback— that means let them know how well they followed the procedure. Group three, come show us how it's done." Telling children that they will be asked to evaluate and later replicate what the other kids are doing will keep the whole class motivated to follow along.

Use reinforcement narration to help children make sense of what they're seeing. "Kylie is walking quietly up to the shelf. She's found her number and is putting her science book right next to it. Hmm, I see Rhea putting her book on a different shelf than the one I showed you all. Rhea, look to see what Kylie did. Exactly. Now Rhea's putting her book next to Kylie's..."

6. *Give performance feedback* about student practice.

"Some people were confused about where to put their books, but they watched their friends, and they fixed their mistakes. That was a smart strategy. We decided there would be no talking when returning the books to the shelves. Did you hear any noise? Neither did I. "

Student input may also lead to clarification of criteria. "Wait, Tom has his hand up, yes, Tom, did you hear noise?... Okay, so Tom is thinking that when Melanie dropped her book, that was making noise. Good point. We should definitely not be dropping any books on purpose. Did Melanie choose to drop her book? So it was an accident? Accidents will happen sometimes. Melanie handled it by picking up her book without saying a word. She didn't yell out. No one else started talking to her about it, or laughed at her. How did the group handle the accident? Okay, so that's what we should do, then. This group followed the guidelines."

The feedback can also set the expectation for improvement the next time. "It did take a little long, though. Let's see if the next group can do this faster, without having to dig through all the books for the right place to return them. This group will still walk and not push each other, but they'll try to be just a bit quicker."

7. *Review* your expectations as many times as needed with ongoing practice, constantly at first and periodically throughout the entire school year.

Practice your procedures and routines as often as possible during the first few weeks of school. You will get tired of it before students demonstrate mastery, so prepare yourself to be exceptionally patient! Remember that the time you are investing now will result in fewer reminders throughout the year. You will notice that things run significantly smoother in your classroom in a very short time.

After kids have practiced a routine several times, they can start to self-evaluate. Ask questions such as, *How did we do with the pledge of allegiance this morning? Were most people standing straight with their right hands over their hearts? Did you hear more people reciting the pledge today than yesterday? What happened when it was time to sit down? What should we do differently tomorrow during the pledge?*

As you plan situations for guiding students, keep in mind that distributed training and practice will be more effective than massed practice, meaning that students will retain more when opportunities for practice are spread out over time. Distributed practice allows time for information to consolidate and sink in, and helps transfer learning from short-term to long-term memory.

One way I plan for ongoing reinforcement throughout the year is to play the 'Procedure Review Game' with my kids. When I was student teaching, I got the idea to write procedural questions on slips of paper and have children take turns drawing them out of a bag and calling on peers to answer them. The game was so popular that I've used it every year I've taught, and recently transferred the questions to a Power Point presentation in which the questions flash up on the screen with sound effects. (The answers aren't provided, because I want to be able to revise my procedures without having to update the game every time.) We play the game a lot in the beginning of the year, and the kids never seem to get tired of it! I reintroduce it around holidays, the last month of school, and other chaotic times of the year, as well as when a new student enrolls, to ensure that expectations are firmly established. You can download the game and modify it to fit your needs by visiting TheCornerstoneForTeachers.com.

Revising Expectations and Criteria

You will probably come up with additional criteria as you model for students or guide them through practice, and that's okay. If the children are not successful because you didn't address certain criteria or explain it clearly enough, you can add new information. "I'm noticing that some people are standing at the water fountain for a very long time. This is causing the people behind them to get impatient. Let's try a solution to fix that problem. I'll have the drink monitor count to five while each person gets water, and then that person's turn will be up. Jessica, will you try that for us? Let's watch and see how that works..."

If children are following the procedure exactly as you showed them yet things aren't working because your design is flawed, you can address that, too. "Hmm, five seconds doesn't seem to be quite long enough. Everyone is very thirsty from being outside. Jessica, would you please try counting to eight instead? Great... okay, that seems to be better. Let's make eight our magic number at the water fountain for now."

As you develop a rapport with your kids, they will begin making their own suggestions ("It's really hot today, do you think we should make the magic number ten?"). I require students to raise their hands before submitting any questions or comments to me, and if they have a lot to say, I'll ask them to wait until a specified time to give me their ideas, so student suggestions are always presented in an orderly and respectful way. Many times my students come up with more effective procedures than I do! They know I value their input and am always looking for a better way to do things.

Children don't need to believe you are perfect and all knowing. They should understand that accruing knowledge is a flexible and ongoing process, and that you are a learner, as well. Students will respect you more for addressing flaws and weaknesses than if you pretend they do not exist and stick with ineffective procedures and routines. You will not lose control of the class if you continue to present a calm, assertive demeanor. Your tone and word choice will either indicate, *Uh-oh, this isn't working—now what?* or *Hmm, this isn't working. I'm going to figure out a solution right now with my class because I am in charge and capable of handling every situation.*

When Students Don't Meet Your Expectations

Repeat the Practice, Not the Command

If your students heard you the first time you asked them to do something, don't repeat yourself. Ask them questions instead to encourage problem solving. "What should you be doing right now?" is one of my favorite redirection responses. Sometimes the child will automatically self-correct, and I thank them, and sometimes the child will answer my question outright, and I say, "You know it! Good."

If a child can't respond to my question about what she should be doing, I know I need to give a refresher course in the procedure. I typically have a handful of students who need extra time to process expectations. I sometimes have to walk them through procedures even at the end of the school year. "What should you be doing in line? Right, standing quietly. What's the second thing you need to remember to do? Good. What else? Which one of those things are you not doing? When you've got all three things down, we can go to art."

Nagging, pleading, and begging students does not communicate that you are in control of the situation. When you're tempted to repeat your command, give performance feedback instead. "Please have a seat... I see three teams sitting down and one team still playing. Good, now we're waiting for just one person to follow the directions. I see all hands folded on top of desks. That means we're ready now to begin. Oh wait, there's someone standing up again... Okay, great. Let's start."

If the performance feedback is taking longer than what's described in the previous paragraph, you may want to start from scratch and take a firmer, less upbeat tone. "Wait. I don't like the way this is going. We're wasting too much time. Let's all try that again. When you hear the signal, everyone is going to sit down in their chairs immediately and fold their hands on their desks. I believe every person will be successful this time."

Keep practicing until students are meeting your expectations exactly. Do not settle for anything less than what they are developmentally capable of doing. Give students frequent opportunities to practice procedures that are being done sloppily. Remind them of the criteria before you give the direction: "When you hear the signal, I'm going to ask you to put away your books. You will not move until you hear the signal. Remind your friends what to do—your book will be placed in a neat? [Stack] Inside your desk. You will stay? [Seated] You will fold your hands on top of your? [Desk] Will your mouth be moving at all? Wonderful—you know how to put away your books. Here comes the signal." Use reinforcement narration as students complete the task and performance feedback afterwards.

"Go Back and Try It Again"

When you see students make any deviation from the routine, call attention to the situation immediately ("Two people haven't pushed their chairs in" or "I hear talking at the end of the line, and we can't move forward until it stops"). Sometimes this will need to be done for the entire class, and sometimes for individual children.

The consequence for an incorrectly followed procedure is not punishment. It's additional practice. Say, "I'm still noticing that chair problem we just talked about. Let's have a seat and try it again. I will call you to line up once more and this time we'll see if everyone can remember to push their chairs in." This is done very calmly and in a matter-of-fact tone. You should not get angry or express any emotion at all: students have chosen a behavior, and you are following up with a logical consequence to make sure your expectations are met. As soon as children do the right thing, re-enforce the appropriate behavior. "Team one has pushed in their chairs. Thanks. Team two, you can line up again. They've got their chairs in, also. Great... I knew you all could do it! *Now* we can leave."

Students should be expected to redo the procedure without complaint or showing any outward signs of disrespect. More details about gaining students' cooperation in redoing procedures can be found in Chapter 11, Tips and Tricks for Difficult Procedures.

Students With Special Needs

You may have a child who simply isn't able to function on the same level as the rest of the class in terms of procedures. This child will need additional structure and reinforcement through an individual behavior plan. If you implement it consistently, you will see progress. Sometimes other children will question why the rules seem different for another child. Chapter 17 explains in detail how to communicate with the class about why you differentiate for students' individual needs.

Avoiding a Slow Descent Into Laziness

When expectations have been taught effectively, students will start to successfully meet them with little reinforcement. Following the procedure becomes the norm. The teacher relaxes because she doesn't have to be constantly on top of the kids, and then the kids start to relax. That's when you may see a slow, almost imperceptible decline in the way students perform routines. Children do this when they think you don't care anymore or have stopped watching.

This problem can be averted by giving performance feedback every now and then. When the class does something exactly to your expectations (even if it's after five sloppier executions), a simple compliment can make a huge difference. "Wow, did you notice how quiet it was in here when the dismissal announcements came on? Not a single person was talking! I love when that happens because we can hear everything being said and we know whose bus was called." You can also compliment individuals: "Hey, that was exactly the right way to return your books to the class library! The smallest books are in the front of the bin, and they're all facing out. Thank you for being so responsible with our books." This statement is not made to manipulate or guilt-trip those children who followed the procedure incorrectly—it's a genuine compliment meant to reward appropriate behavior.

Call attention to general problems so students know you're paying attention. Because the procedure has already been taught, your reminder will take less than thirty seconds. "Our class this year has been doing a great job with stacking chairs at the end of the day. But I've noticed that a lot of people have been forgetting this week. I keep having to remind individual children and I think we should address the problem as a class. Someone remind us why we need to stack chairs? Thank you. So let's make sure we handle that when we line up." The next time children leave the room, give performance feedback: either, "Thanks for remembering—it will be so much easier for the custodian to clean our floors now" or "Let's try that again and get it right."

Choosing Related Rewards and Incentives

You can reward students for completing procedures correctly, but that should not be the incentive or students will become dependent on extrinsic reinforcers. Any rewards you provide should be occasional and unexpected, and tied directly to students' behavior. For example, you could say, "I didn't have to stop this lesson one time because people were talking! Everyone was following along. We actually finished a few minutes early! I think I'll let you have those extra minutes to play with the manipulatives before we clean them up. Thanks for being so respectful of our time." Or, "You all used the dry erase boards just the right way today. I didn't see anyone drawing and everyone erased only when I gave the signal. You've shown me that you can be responsible, and that makes me want to give you more privileges. I'm going to plan another dry erase board activity for tomorrow. The more you follow my directions, the more fun things I'll trust you to handle."

In general, I want students to do the right thing because they see the benefits of doing so, not to earn a prize or gain recognition. However, an occasional, unexpected reward accompanied by verbal reinforcement can provide the additional incentive needed during procedures that require a lot of effort or self-control. So, I do occasionally use our class reward system (beads or tokens—see Chapter 16, Whole Class Reinforcement Systems) in conjunction with procedure practice, especially at the beginning of the year.

Rewards show students that the teacher is paying attention and still values a procedure that may not be mentioned on a regular basis anymore. For example, I usually don't say anything about heading papers after November because I expect students to do it correctly without reminders. So, every few weeks in the winter and spring I'll walk around with beads and say, "Wow, look at all the people who still remember to write their FULL name and put the date in the right place! I'm so impressed."

Interestingly, kids respond just as well to the compliment alone as they do when I pass out beads. I tell the students that I consider beads in this scenario to be a thank-you gift, and a gift must be given from the heart—it cannot be requested or expected. "I don't always give beads for this behavior, because I expect you to do it automatically. But I appreciate not having to remind you all about it. It makes me happy to see that you are so independent. Your behavior is making it fun and easy for me to teach. Sometimes I thank you with my words, and sometimes I want to give you something to let you know I appreciate you and your hard work."

I also use written compliments to let children know I appreciate their cooperation with procedures and routine expectations. I spent ten minutes one day typing up single-sentence thank you notes (such as "Thanks for keeping your desk clean,

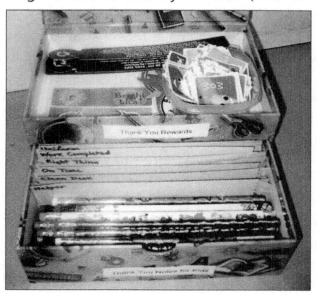

even when no one is looking"), copied and pasted each sentence repeatedly on a page, and printed out several copies on colorful paper. I cut the slips apart and keep them filed in the box shown, along with stickers, pencils, and bookmarks. Occasionally I will place one of these items on selected students' desks along with thank you notes (or just the note by itself), so when kids enter the classroom, they see a token of my appreciation. This is an easy way to recognize children's efforts to be on time for school, wear their uniforms, return papers, and demonstrate general responsibility. Small gestures like this require very little effort on the teacher's part, and can work wonders in motivating children and gaining their cooperation.

Chapter 10: Predictable Daily Routines
Structuring transitions that set kids up for success

Establishing predictable routines is one of the foundational elements of good classroom management. That's because children need structure, and most respond well to highly detailed systems. Kids are known for asking outlandish 'what if' questions ("What if lightning struck the school and broke the ovens in the cafeteria—would we still get to eat?"). Children like to know that there's a plan in place for every eventuality. It makes them feel safe and confident because they know how they should respond...and how YOU, their fearless leader, will handle any problems that arise.

This chapter will describe in detail the major routines for your daily schedule that need to be established, and provide suggestions for creating procedures that meet the needs of you and your students. Remember that routines can and should be modified throughout the year, so nothing is ever set in stone. Decide on something you think will work, teach it to your students, and adapt it as needed, taking the time to explain to children why you are making changes and showing them exactly what you'd like them to do differently. The possibilities for classroom structure are varied, and you have a great deal of freedom to try new things when you know how to teach procedures effectively.

Arrival at School

When students first enter the classroom each morning, they should expect a predictable set of tasks to be awaiting them. This will set the tone for the entire day and communicate to children, "Welcome back. This is a safe, familiar place for you. You know exactly what to do, and you will be successful at meeting the expectations." The morning should be a calm, quiet time (assuming that's your preference) for you and the students to gear up for the school day.

The precise tasks you require of your students will depend on your school's arrival system for students. One of the most influential factors is whether children will be slowly trickling in for fifteen to thirty minutes, or whether most will arrive all at once. If students come in slowly, you will need to have open-ended and 'early finisher' activities planned for students who have completed their tasks before other students even enter the room. This can be handled quite simply by having early arrivers read books quietly or get on the computers. If students come in all at once, you will need to design procedures to prevent chaos when students are unpacking, getting their chairs, and sharpening pencils. If your children line up outside your door in the morning, you can let five in at a time when the bell rings, and spend a moment greeting and talking with the others.

Regardless of your situation, you will still have many routine tasks you want students to complete: unstacking chairs, unpacking book bags, taking out homework and papers from home, using the bathroom, sharpening pencils, and so on. You will need to explain these things on the first day of school. I usually review them at the end of every day during the first week ("So, when you arrive in the classroom tomorrow morning, what are the things you will need to do?"). I also include them on my Morning Work list written on the board until students are able to recall and complete them routinely.

Morning Work

After settling in, students should have some sort of Morning Work to complete. Also called Bell Work or Warm-Ups, Morning Work is the assignment(s) on the board when students enter the room that will get them quiet and focused. Morning Work usually takes 5-20 minutes but can be designed to take longer. For example, one year I had students trickling into my room for 25 minutes before the tardy bell would ring, so the Morning Work was substantially longer. Morning Work can be journaling, math practice, independent reading, centers, or any other task that reinforces targeted skills. I typically don't grade Morning Work because it's for practice, but we do usually review the work together, either right afterwards, or during the subject area the Morning Work was reinforcing (during math time if the students completed math tasks, etc.).

In the beginning of the year, Morning Work should be as simple as possible. It's preferable to have the Morning Work assignments be similar each day. Have students do a page in the same workbook, or write in the same notebook. You can change the type of assignment periodically, but in general, the longer you use the same task, the more automatic it will become for students. Even if it seems a bit monotonous for you, most students appreciate the structure and predictability of having the same tasks each morning.

Whichever assignments you choose, make sure you have them consistently written in an easily visible spot. I write mine in red marker, so students always know to look on the board for the red writing that says 'MW' for 'Morning Work'.

Returning to the Classroom From Lunch and Special Classes

Whenever students enter the classroom, they should be able to count on a predictable routine. That routine will depend on whether you want students to complete a task right away, or listen for your specific directions. You could have different procedures for specific times of the day: for example, when returning from specials, students may need to sit and wait for you to give directions for the science lesson, but when you return from lunch, you may want the class to take out their journals and immediately begin writing. Decide ahead of time what you want students to do each time they return to the classroom. Then explain, model, practice, and reinforce your procedures.

❖ **If you want students to do a warm-up (or need a few minutes for yourself before instruction begins), teach kids to look at the board for directions when they enter the classroom.**

Students shouldn't sit down in their seats and start talking or playing around while they wait for you to get your things together, nor should you expect yourself to always be ready to teach the moment you walk in the door. After recess, I sometimes need a minute to speak to individuals about playground problems, examine cut knees, give permission to retrieve forgotten coats, etc. Students know to sit down and begin their math warm-up immediately when entering the room, freeing me to handle other duties.

❖ **If you don't want kids to do a warm-up, insist on total silence while they wait for your directions.**

I've taught my kids to go straight to their desks after lunch, sit quietly, and be looking at me for instructions so we can start our science activity without wasting any time. Because I don't use a warm-up at this time of day, I like instruction to begin within seconds of entering the classroom, because 'down time' makes it harder to get kids focused. I communicate this expectation outright: "I need you to be completely silent when you come in so I can explain what you need to do." If kids are noisy, I say, "How will you know what's about to happen if you're talking?" or "You don't know what's going on yet. There's nothing to talk about right now." And of course, I reinforce appropriate behavior with, "Thank you so much for coming in quietly. I can tell you all about the review game we're going to play now and I don't even have to wait for the talking to stop." Entering the classroom silently becomes so routine that when someone does talk, the other students will shush them while I stare silently ("Shh! She's waiting for you!").

❖ **Have students go directly to their seats, regardless of what you what them to do afterwards.**

If you need students to be out of their seats for some reason when they first come in (to get drinks or materials), I recommend having them sit first and then calling them in groups to complete the task. They will sit down faster if you call the groups in the order in which they're ready. Also, make sure you have a task for students to do while waiting for their turn, and afterwards while waiting for everyone else to finish. This can be a warm-up activity or a simple direction to take out materials (write them on the board since there will be some commotion as kids get up and down).

End of the School Day

Dismissal can be one of the most chaotic times of day, especially if students are dismissed slowly by their means of transportation home (bus riders, then daycare students, then car riders, and so on). That's unfortunate, because a hectic and stressful dismissal can leave the teacher feeling exhausted and unproductive, even if the majority of the day went well. Here are a few ideas for making the last transition of the day a smooth one:

☑ **Have structured routines so things don't end on a crazy note.**

In my classroom, homework is handled during Morning Work and I only pass out papers to go home two or three times per week, so most of the time, my instruction continues until one minute before dismissal begins. Obviously I allow about ten minutes in the beginning of the school year because I'm still teaching routines, but after a week or two, I try to make the dismissal process as brief as possible. In my experience, the more time kids are given to 'pack up', the more they dawdle and the harder it becomes to maintain order. When there's only about a minute left until dismissal, I ask students to put away their materials and get their backpacks on, then wait silently to be dismissed. If they are talking, they know I will hold them after the bell to practice the procedure, so they're pretty good about being quiet. All bus riders go first and car riders sit at their seats (they are dismissed 5-7 minutes later). I stand at the door and say goodbye to the children on their way out.

After the bus students are gone, I have the car riders stack chairs and do dismissal jobs, which range from changing the calendar to erasing the board to doing filing. It's the same job for each kid every day so the routine goes smoothly—they change jobs once a month or so. Whenever students finish, they either go on the computers or sit on the rug and talk quietly until the final bell rings and they are allowed to leave.

In some schools, I have had to walk car riders out to the front of the school and wait for them, and I handled the dismissal process the same way as described here. Every teacher I know dismisses kids a little differently, but the important thing is to make sure the kids aren't running wild in your room and that they have a chance to say goodbye to you on their way home. Your smile may be the last one they see that day if there's no one at home that cares, and the kids love to end the school day with a personal connection.

☑ **Insist on absolute silence when dismissal announcements come over the loudspeaker.**

Whatever students are doing, they must freeze and get silent anytime they hear the loudspeaker. I tell the class, "If you're talking, we can't hear. They could be making a very important announcement. They could be calling YOU to the office. We have to be listening so we know what to do. Even if you think you know what they're going to say next, you still need to listen, because there are always exceptions." For the first few weeks of school, right before dismissal starts, I remind the kids, "Remember, you must get completely silent when you hear the loudspeaker. If you want to go home, you have to listen so you'll know when you can leave." When an important or unusual announcement is made, I reinforce the procedure with a comment such as, "See, it was a good thing you all were so quiet. We wouldn't have heard them say we're under lightning watch and car riders need to stay in the classroom. I'm so glad I can count on you to do the right thing."

If talking during dismissal announcements is repeatedly a problem, and it always is at the beginning of the year, I have the whole class put their heads down during the entire dismissal time. This is not presented as a punishment—it's an additional form of structure that helps kids exercise self-control until they can be silent with the distraction of their peers looking at them. Having them put their heads down shows the kids that I mean business and am going to be vigilant in enforcing the procedure. Very few teachers insist on silence during dismissal announcements because of the amount of initial reinforcement needed, and your students will probably not be used to it. However, with patience and persistence on your part, dismissal will become far less hectic and you'll always be able to hear who has been dismissed.

☑ **Have a visual reminder so students know which buses have been called.**

I used to teach in a school that had many bus riders and many different routes. I used the display pictured as a visual accompaniment to the verbal announcements. When each bus was called, a student helper displayed it in the pocket chart.

☑ Keep a record of how students have been dismissed for the day.

A dismissal schedule is required in most schools, and is extremely useful for the teacher, substitutes, and panicked parents who call the school asking where their child went after school (this happens more often than you might think!).

When students have consistent schedules, you can post a more permanent sign like the one shown to the left. I recommend laminating the sign first then writing the names with permanent marker, because your writing can be erased from the lamination's plastic coating when students transfer schools or have a change in dismissal schedules.

At another school, I had few students riding the bus but many who had complex schedules (living with mom three days a week and with dad four, or went to karate practice right after school on Wednesdays and to grandma's on Tuesdays, etc.). I could never keep track of who was going where each day, so I typed up all of the dismissal options and wrote each child's name on a clothespin. I taught students the procedure of 'moving their clip' as part of their Morning Work so I always knew how students would be going home.

Chapter 11: Tips and Tricks for Difficult Procedures
Ideas for lining up, getting drinks, passing papers, and more

While it's impossible to have a plan for everything, there are many events that students can count on happening every day: entering the classroom, using the bathroom, retrieving materials and supplies, and so on. If kids know that these procedures are going to be done the same way each time, the routines will become automatic and almost effortless. You will also have a tremendous amount of freedom in your instruction to try new activities and ways of doing things, because students know the overarching routines that tie these things together.

****The classroom structure and routines you've already taught
are the glue that holds instruction together and prevents it from
becoming overwhelming to students, and therefore, to the teacher.****

For example, you can easily do an intricate collage project when students know the procedures for getting supplies, passing out papers, throwing away their scraps, and cleaning up their desk areas when finished. If these procedures have been explicitly taught, modeled, and reinforced consistently, kids won't get out of control during the project, because they already know what to do during each step. This chapter will provide tips and tricks for managing some of the most difficult classroom routines and procedures so that you can focus on delivering effective instruction.

Bathroom Procedures

Conveying Responsibilities and Privileges

The bathroom may take first place on your list of Annoying Inevitabilities In The Classroom. Children have no idea what they put their teachers through in this area. So, I tell them! On the first day of school, I just lay it on the line and explain why bathroom routines are such a hassle for other teachers and why I don't want to have those same problems. I tell horror stories about my former students peeing on the walls and kids in other classes overflowing the toilets with paper towels (being careful not to give them too many ideas!). I tell them how some teachers have to regulate every single child who goes in and out of the bathroom. The kids love to chime in with stories of their own ("My last year teacher only let us go after reading groups and we had to have a bathroom monitor check the bathroom afterwards every single time!"). I nod sadly and say, "Isn't that a shame when students behave so poorly that teachers have to treat them like little babies?"

I then let kids know that OUR classroom this year will be different. I won't have the problems with them that I had with prior classes. And they will behave better for me than they did for their teachers last year. In OUR room this year, everyone's going to be responsible, independent, and mature about using the bathroom.

Assuming the facilities are in the classroom or close by in the hallway, I explain that students will be allowed to go whenever they need to [pause for dramatic effect], as often as they need to [another long pause], and without a sign-in sheet [pause while kids ooh and ahh excitedly]. But that's under the condition that they do not abuse my policy and recognize it as the privilege it is. If people start going five times a day, hanging out in the bathroom for ten minutes, leaving a huge mess...I'll have to limit their trips and make them sign in and out. Sometimes this needs to be done only for certain individuals until they can prove they are responsible, and sometimes the problem is so big that the whole class has to suffer. We make an oral agreement to be responsible with the bathroom, I teach and enforce the procedures, and students are expected to follow them.

Some classes can't handle this freedom, but I would rather give them the benefit of the doubt because it's so much easier on me than having a tightly-regulated system. I have used a sign-in sheet in the past (a column for the morning and one for the afternoon) and each child could sign in once for each column. I've had classroom meetings and bathroom monitors and rules about checking the sign-in sheet to find the person who went in before you so she can go back and clean up messes. But I have found in general that the more rules and discussions we have about bathroom procedures, the worse things get. When I stay focused on instruction, the kids are typically more independent and responsible.

Signals to Indicate When Students Can Use the Bathroom

If you want students to ask for permission before they use the bathroom, you can teach them to give a special hand signal, such as two fingers in the air. Let them know that you will respond with a nod or with one finger in a 'wait-a-minute' gesture, in which case they shouldn't go until you tell them.

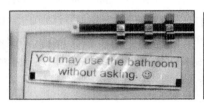 

If the primary reason you have students ask for permission to use the bathroom is so that they don't go at inopportune times (such as during instruction), you can consider using a bathroom sign instead. I keep mine posted all the time and use it as my sole indication of when students can excuse themselves. On one side of the sign, it says in green writing, "You may use the bathroom" and it says, "Please wait to use the bathroom. If you have an emergency, please hold up 2 fingers" in red on the other side. I affixed two small magnets to each side and flip the sign to indicate whether students can go freely. If the sign is on red and students have an emergency, they can hold up two fingers and I will allow them to go. (An emergency means that if you wait more than a few minutes, you will probably have an accident.) It takes several weeks for students to adapt to this system and they will ask to use the bathroom from time to time, but all you have to do is point to the sign and smile.

Never Deny Bathroom Permission!

Always allow a child to use the bathroom when he asks to go. Most school systems require this now, but when I started teaching, it wasn't a rule, and there were several accidents when I told kids they couldn't go because I thought they were just trying to get out of working. Yikes! If you have a child who is, in your opinion, going too frequently, say, "I've noticed that you're using the bathroom many times during the day [staying in the bathroom for more than five minutes at a time, etc.]. Is there something I should know?" Sometimes the child will offer more information than you want to hear! If so, just say, "Okay, so it sounds like you have a temporary situation that will get better soon. That's fine." If the child doesn't provide a valid reason, explain that you are concerned about him missing instruction and that if the problem doesn't improve, you will need to ask the parent to make a doctor's appointment and ensure everything's okay. The mention of this consequence is almost always enough to fix the problem of dawdling and playing around in the bathroom!

Do contact the parents if the issue persists. Keep things very non-accusatory ("I've noticed that Leanna has been using the bathroom four or five times a day and is staying in there for several minutes each time. Have you seen this happen at home? Is there anything I should know about?") I've done this a few times and it solved the problem. And once I had a parent tell me, "Oh, she has a serious bladder condition—I forgot to send in the doctor's note!"

Using the Bathroom During Recess

Sometimes students need to use the bathroom when we're outside on the playground, which is a no-no for supervisory reasons. I explain that to my kids and tell them to only ask to use the bathroom if it's an emergency (which would be the equivalent of putting two fingers up when the sign's on red in the classroom). Usually when children ask about the bathroom at recess, I inquire whether they can wait for a few minutes until we get back to the room—most of the time, they can. If a child continually asks and I suspect she is up to something, I'll give a choice: "You can go, but it's going to cost you five minutes of recess when you get back. Is it worth it?" This procedure is highly effective in weeding out those students who really need to use the bathroom and those who want to roam the hallways alone.

Teaching Toilet and Sink Expectations

The amount of detail you will need to include during your bathroom discussions will depend on the age of your students. I only spend two minutes on this with my third graders, and ask them to provide the majority of information: What do you do when you close the bathroom door behind you? (Use the toilet. Nothing else. No playing around.) How much toilet paper should you use? (About four squares.) What do you do after you finish using the toilet? (Flush! Please!)

The after-bathroom and sink procedures will need to be spelled out in a little more detail. Discuss how to walk quietly over to the sink, get ONE pump of soap, scrub your hands while you count silently to eight (shorter periods of time won't kill all the germs), take ONE paper towel and dry your hands, then use the paper towel to turn the water off. (The purpose of using the paper towel to turn the water off is because the water spigot is dirty from when you just touched it before washing your hands, so you don't want to touch it again with clean hands.) Talk about this at the front of the classroom, miming each action as you do it, then actually model it (go into the bathroom, flush the toilet, and come right back out while the whole class watches, talking them through the process ("Okay, I got my soap. Now what? Count with me...1...2..."). For management purposes, during guided practice you may want to have students just mime the action at their seats. Once the class is settled into an independent activity, you can call them by groups to practice hand washing.

If kids laugh or get embarrassed during the discussion, stay nonchalant and tell them that the things you are talking about are not funny, dirty, or bad. They're just part of life. We all use the bathroom and since we all have to share one at school, we need to agree on some rules about what's appropriate.

Managing Whole-Class Bathroom Trips

Not having a toilet in your classroom can actually be a good thing! You don't have to deal with students constantly coming in and out of the bathroom, getting distracted by flushing, making faces at smells, and so on! If you have 'gang bathrooms' (facilities with multiple toilets/urinals), you can take the entire class at one time and get the whole process over with.

I had gang bathrooms for two years and took my third graders as a class three times per day. If there was an emergency, students were allowed to go at other times, but I really stressed the importance of going with the group. I found that when my lessons were engaging and interactive, the kids didn't think about going to the bathroom and I had very few 'emergencies' during the school day.

You will need to teach students how to use the bathroom appropriately, as described previously (toilet paper usage, flushing, washing hands). Then you can explain procedures for using gang bathrooms. Be specific about inappropriate behaviors that will not be tolerated, e.g., crawling under and writing on stalls, throwing trash on the floor, and splashing water at the sink. Be quite firm in your discussion about these actions. Explain what the bathroom monitor will do and what you expect from students in the hall. Use reinforcement narration and performance feedback as students practice. Here are a few tips:

☑ **Have two Bathroom Monitors, one for the girls and one for the boys.**

This person goes inside the bathroom and ensures things are orderly while you wait in the hall with the rest of the class. The monitor can make sure there are a set number of people in the bathroom at any given time and lean out the door to call in the next person when someone exits.

☑ **Teach children to sit at the end of the line when they finish using the bathroom.**

This way, the only kids who are standing are the ones waiting to be called in. This makes the entire process easier to manage and keeps kids from getting too silly, since they're not expected to stand still for an extended period of time.

☑ **Read aloud to students or play a game while they wait.**

You won't be able to do this until bathroom procedures are firmly in place, because you'll need to focus your attention on reinforcement narration and performance feedback, as well as handle incidents as they arise. Tell the children what you plan to do with them later and explain that the fun will start as soon as they've proven they are responsible enough to use the bathroom without your constant supervision. When they're ready, you can read aloud a high-interest book with lots of big pictures that your students will hurry out of the bathroom to see. You could also review math facts, or play a guessing game. The idea is to have something more interesting for students to do than splashing at the sink or peeking under the stalls.

☑ **If the whole class seems to be dawdling, set a time limit and/or use a timer**.

This can be made into a game (can everyone get in and out in five minutes?). Or, keep track of the time it takes for the entire class to be finished and have them try to beat their record each day until the efficiency becomes automatic.

Water Fountain Procedures

Your routines for getting drinks will depend on whether you have a water fountain in the classroom or need to use one in the hallway. For both scenarios, I highly recommend training a Drink Monitor who can assist you in keeping the class orderly while they get drinks. The monitor can count slowly to five while kids get drinks, and make sure no one is splashing.

Using Hallway Water Fountains

If you don't have a water fountain in your classroom (or if the kids don't like it because the water's warm), you'll probably need to take the entire class to get drinks once or twice per day. The drink monitor can help keep things calm. If there's any place in your school that has multiple fountains side by side, it's probably worth the walk because the process of getting drinks will be so much faster and easier to manage.

A fun way to keep kids from getting too carried away while waiting in a long line for a drink is to have each child answer a math fact. Go right down the line, and as soon as a child answers, he can get a drink. Afterwards, the child should go to the end of the line. Stand towards the middle of the class for proximity control. If your kids get too excited by this, play a game to see who can be Hallway King or Hallway Queen (the child with the best hallway behavior). You can have your Hall Monitor choose for you if you want, so that you're free to supervise behavior at the water fountain. The reward could just be the title of king or queen, or you could tie it into your classroom reward system (i.e., give a bead or token). I don't recommend extrinsic rewards as a long-term strategy for procedure reinforcement, but it can be helpful when students are having difficulty developing routines or have had a chaotic change in schedule (holiday events, after an assembly, when there's a substitute, etc.).

Another option for those who don't have water fountains in the classroom is for the teacher to stay in the room with the majority of the class while several students at a time leave to get water. Have the Drink Monitor stand by the fountain, the Hallway Helper stand in the hall, and the Door Helper (or other helper, if you don't have someone for the door) stand in the doorway. You can then call students a few at a time to get drinks. If any of the helpers have to speak to a child two days in a row about behavior problems, the child can lose the privilege of getting a drink the following day. Stress to the children that only those kids who can be trusted to go in the hallway without a teacher will get drinks this way, and the others will have to be personally escorted by you.

Obviously, you will need to model this procedure and watch students very closely at first. I would recommend getting drinks together as a whole class for the first week or two of school, and slowly introduce this method. You should stand in the doorway the entire time while students practice the procedure. Even after students have the routine down, you should still plan to poke your head out in the hallway at least once every time you do this process. The rest of the class should be engaged in some kind of warm-up or independent task, which will free you to oversee things and keep kids on-task while they wait for everyone to get drinks.

Using a Water Fountain in the Classroom

If your water fountain is built into a sink in the classroom, train students to get drinks at specified times of the day. I allow my students to get drinks without permission during Morning Work, right before specials and lunch, and after health (which is usually recess). There is a sign posted by the water fountain in case anyone forgets when they are allowed to drink. Students can get drinks freely at the posted times, except after recess when I know almost everyone will want water (I have students go to their seats when they enter the room and take out their writing journals, then get called by teams to get drinks.) As with all routines, water fountain usage should be done at regular, predictable intervals throughout the day so that kids know what to expect and don't keep asking for permission to get up during instruction. If students ask to get a drink during other times of the day, I always say no unless they are coughing or have the hiccups. In my experience, if you have pity on a thirsty child one time, you will end up with the entire class asking you daily to let them make a trip to the water fountain!

The Water Bottle Solution

Since I like to have a water bottle on my desk all day long, I always feel a bit mean by regulating how often kids can drink water. I especially dislike the practice of counting while kids drink, as if three seconds or even five seconds is enough when someone is really thirsty. For management purposes, I do insist on counting, unless we're at an outdoor water fountain right after recess and the kids can talk and be a little bit noisy while they wait for everyone to drink as much as they want.

So to make sure kids are well hydrated, I allow them to keep water bottles at their desks. Anytime they're thirsty, so they have water available without getting out of their seats. Yes, there are spills at times, but water bottles are far less distracting than I thought they would be when I first started encouraging the kids to keep them. In low-income areas, it is helpful to provide a small bottle of water to students a few times throughout the year if their families do not buy bottled water. Some students will refill bottles from juice or sports drinks.

Passing Out Worksheets and Materials

How often do you hear, "I didn't get one!" or "You gave me two by mistake!" But when you're ready to teach the lesson, you don't have extras for those who need them, nor do you want to be handed the leftovers.

Teach students that all extra papers are kept in a special drawer or basket labeled 'Extra Class Work Papers'. Children can simply walk over to the designated place and take (or put back) papers as needed without ever making you aware of the situation. When a student says, "I didn't

get a paper!" shrug and say, "I don't have them, either," while pointing to the basket. I like using a deep container because I don't clean it out often. You would be surprised how many times either a child or I need a paper that was passed out weeks ago. Every few months, I'll take out the oldest papers from the bottom and let kids complete them during Fun Friday if they want to.

There are a variety of ways you can distribute papers and related instructional materials to students. You may need to try several different methods to see which best fits your needs:

❖ **The teacher can hand materials to one person in each group or row.**

With this method, you will have to personally count out the materials for each group. However, this can be quicker than having student helpers do it. I like to do this with heavier or awkward materials, such as individual dry erase boards, and have student helpers distribute the markers and erasers. I usually pass out papers this way, also, because it saves time.

Student's responsibilities will need to be explicitly modeled and practiced, just like any other procedure. They will need to learn how to pass to the person next to them. When your desks are in rows, make sure you teach kids to pass to the person beside them rather than in front of them. Passing across rather than forward/backwards cuts down on how often kids 'accidentally' bump each other or drop the papers, because the next person can see the stack coming.

You may have problems with children fumbling with papers or sitting there totally oblivious to a stack on their desk waiting to be passed on. One possible solution is to try using plastic baskets from the dollar store to keep papers together while they are being passed. Teach students never to let the basket sit on their desks, not even for a second. They should immediately grab it, take one paper from the basket and pass it on. The last person to get the basket returns it to a designated place.

❖ **Helpers can hand materials to one person in each group or row.**

I have separate Paper Passers and Supply Passers, since I often need multiple things distributed at one time. If you change jobs daily, you may not want to include these tasks in your job rotation and instead assign them as monthly responsibilities. Having a new Passer every day will lengthen the amount of time it takes to distribute materials as new helpers learn the routine. Train your helpers where to get supplies and papers, how to circulate among the desks to make sure everyone gets what they need quickly, and where to return extras. Those two people can train the helpers for the following week or month.

❖ **Helpers can pass out materials to each individual child.**

Have helpers move in a set order around the room so they don't skip anyone or overlap each other. Young children have difficulty remembering which desks they've already been to and have a tendency to skip some students and give twice to others. They need you to provide a system to keep the process organized in their minds. Each helper could be assigned to one half of the room. You could also show them how to move from right to left across a row, or suggest a specific order to approach each of your teams or groups.

Collecting Student Work

Passing in Papers

Have one member of each group (or the last person in each row) be responsible for collecting all work for the team. This way you will never have students who 'forget' to turn in their work or 'lose' it immediately after finishing (which happens much more frequently than I ever would have imagined before I began teaching). This person may also be assigned the task of checking for names and handing papers back to anyone who hasn't used the correct heading.

Insist that students pass in papers so that they are all facing the same direction. We practice this a LOT at the beginning of the year, and if (more like WHEN) they get lazy about it during the year, I have the Paper Collector give all the papers back to their owners and they do it again, with reinforcement narration, until they get it right.

You may want to use baskets when kids pass in their papers. Some years I have a small class or fairly mature class that doesn't need them, but in general, I've found that papers are far less likely to be dropped, shuffled, or lost when kids pass a basket instead of a pile.

Placing Papers in a Designated Spot to Be Graded

After papers have been passed to one person in the group or row and that person has begun checking to see that all papers are headed correctly and facing the right way, a Paper Collector can take the stacks. My Paper Collector job is separate from my two Paper Passer jobs, because sometimes I need to have a set of materials distributed immediately after the old ones are collected.

The Paper Collector should have one consistent place to always put papers. The designated spot should NOT be on your desk! If you're like me, you've got enough stuff on your desk as it is—you don't need kids adding to the clutter. I use the top of a low file cabinet to hold trays for student work. In the past, I had a small student desk adjacent to my own where papers went. A shelf or windowsill would work just as well.

Your Paper Collector can put a paperclip on each stack of work, if you like. He could also put the work in alphabetical order if that makes it easier for you to record the grades. Simply assign each child a number and teach students to write it in the top right hand corner of their papers: the Paper Collector can then just put papers in number order. The process can take a minute or two to complete, but if you need it done, you may find it's worth training students to do it for you.

Sending Papers Home with Students

Organizing Graded Work and Parent Notices

When you first begun organizing your classroom in August, you should have set up a location for graded papers and fliers that need to be sent home. Chapter 4, Avoiding the Paper Trap, shows photographs of how a large basket, hanging file folders, or 'mailbox' system can be used. Papers for the entire class can be kept in one

basket or container and passed out at the end of the day or week. Or, you could have student helpers file the papers into individual hanging files for each student, and then distribute the file contents to students as often as you choose. A third method is to use 'mailboxes'.

Tips for Using 'Mailboxes' (Individual Slots for Student Papers)

If you want to send papers home daily (or as you grade them) along with fliers and notices, use a 'mailbox system'. Combination metal-and-plastic paper organizers like the one pictured on the left are ideal, but can cost close to $100 at office supply and educational stores. (I was fortunate to inherit mine from a retiring teacher.) Cardboard versions can be purchased fairly cheaply, but don't typically last longer than one or two school years, so I don't recommend them. However, cubbies, divided shelving systems, and even pocket charts could be utilized in the same manner.

When you have papers to be passed out, put the stack in one of two extra slots labeled 'Mailbox Helper 1' and 'Mailbox Helper 2' (I often have multiple fliers to go home so I give some fliers to one helper and different fliers to the other helper.) I usually keep the same mailbox helpers for several weeks. It's not part of the regular job rotation because it's too important to have random kids doing it all the time, so I just choose kids that I know will be responsible to handle it indefinitely. Each day right before dismissal, the mailbox helpers automatically check to see if there is anything in those slots and distribute them to each child's mailbox.

I then call the children to get their mail when they are ready (desk cleared, floor clean, sitting quietly, hands folded on desk). Everyone accesses the mailboxes in the same direction, walking towards the door and going around a nearby table and then walking away to the right so that traffic flows in a smooth line without anyone bumping into one another. Also, only one child is allowed to reach into a mailbox at a time; others must wait patiently behind the child standing in front of the mailboxes until that child walks away. This prevents anyone from being pushed, tripped, or mixing up their papers.

If you have extra mailbox slots, those can be used in many helpful ways. In my organizer, I created four slots that say 'Take One of Each'. Sometimes if I don't have time for the mailbox helpers to distribute papers, I put one set of papers to go home in each of the 'Take One' slots and when the kids check their individual mail, they also take from there. I also have two slots that say 'To Go Home Later' for book orders, fliers, and homework sheets that I want to send home the following day or later in the week. The rest of the slots say 'Extra Papers to Go Home' with one slot for each month. When the mailbox helpers finish passing out the papers, they put the extras in the 'extra paper' box for the month. Then, if someone loses a form or a parent requests another flier, I know exactly where to look for it. It's really helpful to have all the extra forms organized, especially when it's not taking up any space in my filing cabinet or on my desk!

A Consistent System for Papers to Go Home

If you want to send papers home weekly, choose one day and try to always send things home on that day so that parents know what to expect. Many teachers have Friday Folders; others do Monday Folders so that papers can be graded over the weekend (which I hope you aren't having to do on a regular basis). You can choose whichever day works best for you, but try to be consistent.

It's helpful to have a special folder for sending home papers that parents and kids instantly recognize. Laminated two-pocket folders will last throughout the entire year for most kids and cost around $0.10 each. Even manila envelopes or plain file folders will do. Ideas for ensuring student accountability for graded work are included in Chapter 31, Keeping Parents Informed.

Collecting Forms, Money, and Other Papers from Students

Students can be trained to always place items they have for you inside your in-box (a special container in a location on or near your desk). I collect forms first thing in the morning ONLY (8:00-8:20), giving one or two verbal reminders ("Anyone else have book order money? Last call!"). Students put the forms in my in-box and sit down. At 8:20, I sort through the forms all at once and erase the numbers off the board shown in the photograph.

While I prefer to handle everything right away each morning, I do make my in-box available at all times for students to turn in notes and other items. This prevents students from handing miscellaneous papers to me throughout the day, or leaving them in random places where they will get misplaced before I have a chance to examine and respond to them.

It's helpful to have a visual reminder for you and the kids to determine what materials are still outstanding. On a small whiteboard, I write the name of the item, the date it's due, and then the students' numbers (1-20 or whatever: this is easier than writing names and protects confidentiality, since visitors to the classroom won't be able to match kids with numbers).

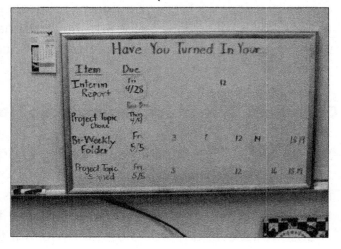

The children can erase their numbers themselves when they turn their papers in, but sometimes they erase the wrong thing, so you'll have to keep an eye on them. No number is erased until I have personally checked to make sure the form is there and filled out completely and correctly. When something is overdue, I circle it in yellow and indicate that on the board.

You can have a variety of consequences for past due forms: I usually take five minutes of recess or Fun Friday if it's something really important and more than a week late. I do think it's important to have some kind of consequence: kids need to get used to deadlines, including some inflexible ones. However, I always try to work with those children who aren't able to get forms returned in a timely manner because of problems in the home.

Lining Up and Hallway Expectations

Why It's Difficult for Kids to Move Quietly Around the School

Most teachers know what they're supposed to have kids do, and most kids understand the expectations pretty well even on the first day of school. The problem is that walking in a quiet line is difficult for children developmentally, and teachers are stuck in the midst of the ongoing battle, Kids vs. The Hallway. Sharpening pencils and passing in papers are quick procedures that are reinforced by the other routines in the classroom. Lining up and hallway expectations are designed solely to keep kids quiet and orderly...without the benefit of classroom structure.

In the hallway, children are excited to be out of the classroom and, in their minds, free from all its rules and restrictions. The teacher is busy greeting other adults and probably has her back to most of the class as she walks ahead of them. There's no academic task that students are supposed to be attending to, so that mean it's recess! Time to talk, skip, stretch, play...what else is there to do?

Most children who are playing around in the hallway aren't being intentionally 'bad' or disruptive... they're just taking advantage of the opportunity to talk and move their bodies, and sometimes, they push the limits. They're young. Plus, going to lunch and specials at school is the only time in their lives that they ever have to walk silently in single file with a group of their peers. They don't do this at the mall, the grocery store, or in their neighborhoods. What we're asking them to do—travel in complete silence to a common destination with familiar friends—is totally against our social human nature.

Now, that doesn't mean teachers should allow a free-for-all. There are good reasons why students have to form an orderly line, and having a large group of children together in a hallway requires a unique type of structure. But the reality of what you're asking children to do should always be kept in mind as you create, communicate, and reinforce your criteria for behavior in line. Students have to be set up for success, and if our expectations are inappropriate, the result will be ongoing frustration for everyone involved.

Creating a 'Line Order'

If you find that you are wasting a lot of time getting kids to line up ("He cut in front of me!", "I got there first!"), you may want to consider having a line order. This system helps eliminate the problem of students running for the door or squabbling over who gets to be first. One caveat: I tried this years ago with a larger class (27 kids) and found it took way too long for the kids to line up. But, I gave it another shot with a smaller class (21 kids) and I liked it so much that I've used it every year since.

I plan out my line order based on student personalities, placing the kids boy-girl whenever possible. You will need to teach students to remember who is in front of and behind them so that they can find their spots quickly, and how to leave space for people who belong in front of them but have not yet lined up. You can change the line order periodically as needed.

Every few weeks, I would make the 5th or 6th person first and send the ones who were in the front to the end. This would shift the ones who were previously at the end up to the middle, etc., so that no one was in the back of the line for long. I also tried having a child be the line leader for the day, then move to the back of the line, giving the next child a chance to head up the line the following day. This daily rotation was popular with the kids but often caused some disruption in the back half of the line as students adjusted to their new spots, and it was a bit confusing for some of the children. Giving every child one week to lead the line, then move to the back, seemed to be the best solution.

Line order provides an additional bit of structure to the otherwise volatile process of lining up 'first come, first served', and therefore helps tremendously with behavior management. The element of predictability is exactly why it works, so if you do a line order, use it consistently, even when students are walking a very short distance. The kids need to know they can count on this routine, or it's not worth doing: they'll spend their time arguing over whether they need to be in line order or not.

You can post a line order sign by the front door as a reminder for yourself, the kids, and substitutes. This can be done on a dry erase board or with vis-à-vis marker on a page protector so alterations can be made easily.

The Initial Lining Up/Hallway Discussion

About ten minutes before the class needs to line up for the first time, I tell the children where we'll be going and that we need to prepare to walk there together. I ask them to think about hallway rules they remember from previous years, and to help us decide what our rules should be now. I don't write anything down because the kids already know the expectations (unless they're kindergartners): walk, don't run, keep your hands to yourself, etc.

Then I ask the class why they think we have these rules—is it because teachers are mean and like to make kids do things for no reason? Usually someone suggests that we have to be quiet in the hall because other children are trying to learn, so we discuss times we've heard 'elephants' in the hallway and how it distracted us. We talk about how a straight line makes it easier for other classes and people to pass us. At that point, I suggest a way to help them follow the rule—stay on the third tile from the wall.

I also mention that a beautiful line impresses other adults in the school. It makes them think, "Wow, look how quiet and orderly her line is! Those kids must be really smart and well-behaved. That's a great class!" (Whenever we get a compliment from another teacher in the hall, I reinforce our discussion by saying, "See? I told you people would be impressed and realize how awesome our class is!") I also explain that the students' behavior in the hallway is a reflection on the teacher ("What do you think people would say about a teacher whose children are always running and screaming in the hallway?") and talk about how the kids' behavior is a sign to other people that I'm teaching my students all the right things about how to act. If the class has shown signs of being even a little rowdy, I usually get firmer at this point in the discussion and say, "I expect you to represent me and our class properly in the hallway. I will not be embarrassed by the way you act when I take you out in public—outside of the classroom—because I know you can do the right thing."

Since the kids know I am trusting them to behave in the hallway, I have them name some of the appropriate things that they could do with their hands while they walk, e.g., put them behind their backs, keep them at their sides, or hold one finger over their lips to indicate silence. I explain that they can make their own decision about what to do with their hands in the hallway as long as it isn't disruptive to anyone around them and they're not touching anything on the walls, which can leave dirty hand prints and destroy bulletin board displays.

The overall tone of this initial discussion is very low-key because the success of hallway procedures depends primarily on recurring practice and reinforcement. We end the talk by summing up expectations quickly and reiterating the purpose of appropriate hallway behavior—to allow other children to learn without interruption and to get where we are going safely and quietly.

Walking and Door Holding Practice

After the discussion, I ask each child to individually show us the right way to line up as I use reinforcement narration. ("Johnny's going to line up first. Let's watch as he pushes in his chair gently—go ahead, Johnny—and walks over to the line. Okay, now Susanna's going to do the same thing. Excellent. She didn't stop to talk to anyone, and she's standing behind Johnny without touching him or speaking to him at all." The process is very slow for the first few kids and speeds up towards the end ("Okay, let's have Tyrone, Ciera, and James try it... thank you for being so quiet... next will be...").

Once the whole class is lined up, I give performance feedback. "Everyone is now standing in line, facing front, with their hands to themselves. I don't hear any talking at all. This is exactly right. This is what I want you to do every time we line up. Now, we're ready to try walking to Music. Katie's leading the line, and she's going to walk on the third tile and stop at the door. We're going to do this slowly because it's our first time, and I'm going to go over everything I need you to do, so please don't rush or tell anyone to hurry. Practice is important. Alright, let's try walking in the hall."

I dislike having a Door Holder who has to run up to the front of the line to hold the next door before we get there (or bother with having two Door Holders for this purpose). I think the simplest solution is to teach students the common courtesy of holding onto a door until the person behind you grabs it. The kids like being entrusted to do things 'the grown-up way'.

If you are using a Door Holder system, then explain that on the way out the door ("Mary is going to hold the door for us, and then walk up to the front of the line again"). If you're having students hold the door for the person behind them, stand in the doorway and narrate everything. "Okay, Katie is first, she's going to place her hand right here on the door until Jerome puts his hand here. Okay, now Jerome did that, so Katie's going to keep walking, and Jerome's waiting for

Paul to hold the door. Good, now, Jerome's through, Paul's holding it for Jessica, there she goes, she's holding it for Leila" and so on. Use this type of narration the first few times you go somewhere, and then every fourth or fifth time until you're sure they've got it. Periodically throughout the year (maybe once every other week), you can narrate again to reinforce the procedure.

After everyone is through the doorway, turn your attention to the line and narrate what you see there, reinforcing appropriate behavior. When the line leader has stopped at the place you asked him to, praise what students have done so far and prepare them for the next part of the walk. "Now we're going to go down the steps. We're going to stay in a quiet line just like we have been, keeping to the right. Our right hand will be on the railing, our left hand will be to ourselves. Katie will stop at the bottom of the stairs. Okay, let's try it."

Ways to Call Kids to Line Up

The methods you use to call kids to get in line can be very flexible; you don't have to do thing the same way every time. I like to use three or four methods and switch them up for variety. Here are a few ideas:

☑ **Call students by teams to line up so the power of peer pressure works in your favor.**

Only call a team or row when ALL of the students in it are COMPLETELY ready. The faster kids on the team will help the pokier ones put away materials, tie their shoes, etc., so that everyone can get to lunch or recess faster. I have my kids fold their hands on top of their desks when they have everything they need to take with them, because I would often call a team for lunch and then discover that one kid still needed to grab a juice box from his backpack and the whole class would be lined up waiting for him. Now, I don't call teams until all hands are folded, and if their hands are folded, they know that they must go directly to the line when they are called and may not get anything else from their desks or backpacks.

☑ **Use quirky, fun categorizations to determine who lines up first.**

I don't do this often because it tends to get the children talking and laughing...

but laughter in the classroom is a good thing, and there are times when I know the kids need a break. You can call kids by the colors or type of shoes they're wearing, birthday month, food they're eating for lunch, number of siblings they have, and so on. The list is endless and it can be a great way to learn new things about your students and for them to find commonalities amongst each other.

☑ **Have students answer an academic question before lining up.**

This technique is best used when you have a few spare minutes. Pose an open-ended challenge to students and tell them to raise their hands when they have an answer. After a child responds correctly, she can line up. Example tasks are: name two words that rhyme, say a word that has a prefix, and name something that is in the shape of a rectangular prism. This can be a great way to check for student understanding, as well. One word of caution: pick the slower-thinking students first so they can give the more obvious answers, and higher-achieving kids can be left contemplating more unique responses. Also, if you have your quick-thinkers line up first, they'll end up playing around while you wait for the last few kids to figure out the answers. When most of the class is lined up, you may want to stand near the line while you pose the final questions to the others that are seated. Your proximity will ensure that everyone stays quiet.

☑ **Have a student call kids to line up so you can get your belongings together and tend to individual student concerns.**

If you need to gather materials or handle an issue before you go out the door, this is a great strategy to use. Teach kids to pick the quietest students first. I have also found it's best to have them pick boy-girl because most elementary kids pick everyone of their same gender first.

☑ **Use 'The Magic Touch' to line kids up.**

You can also use a technique that my third graders love as much as my Pre-Kindergarten kids did! It's called 'The Magic Touch'. The first few times you use this method, you should be the one to give the magic touch so you can model your expectations. Later on, you can choose a child to look for those who are sitting quietly, and that person walks around and gives them a *soft* pat (the magic touch) on their heads. It will be unbelievably silent in the room while the kids wait to be chosen. Make a rule that if someone gestures or says, "Pick me!," they cannot be chosen. You may need to stand by the door to reinforce the quiet line behavior of those kids who are already lined up, and if students start talking, they have to sit back down and wait for the magic touch again. Just knowing this is enough to keep most of them silent.

☑ **If students start playing around in line, have them sit back down.**

I like to do this a few times during the first week of school so students realize I'm serious. I call them to line up and give a reminder if they are talking. When I notice several kids still whispering or not standing straight in line, I make a disappointed face and say, "Oh, I guess we're not ready to go after all. Have a seat, and we'll try again." The first time the kids hear me say this, they look a little confused, so I repeat, "Go ahead. Everybody. Have a seat, we'll have to try again. I apologize to those of you who were doing the right thing, because I know not everyone was noisy. But you need to all work together as team to line up." They walk in stunned silence back to their seats and I pause for absolute quiet. Then I call them to line up again (usually by teams so it's quick) and reinforce the appropriate behavior with, "Thank you. Now you're showing me that you're ready to go to art." You can do this with individual students, as well. Say, "Valentina, that's not the way we line up. Have a seat please." After everyone else is in line, call the child to try it again and thank her for doing it the right way.

This can be repeated as many times as necessary, even if the class is late. "Wow, I still hear a lot of noise. Unfortunately we're going to be late to lunch because of all this talking. Have a seat, please." It won't take long at all for students to realize you mean business if you are consistent in your expectations. **_Don't settle for anything less than what you know students are capable of, even when you are in a rush._**

If students have already figured out not to back-talk, you won't have any problems when asking them to sit back down, but if someone sighs or mutters, say something sternly along the lines of, "I shouldn't hear anyone complaining. It was the class' decision to be noisy in line. You know that we can't leave the classroom until everyone lines up quietly. By choosing to play around in line, you choose to sit back down." Going back to the desks is never presented as a punishment inflicted on children by the teacher: it's a logical consequence that is tied to misbehavior. The teacher is just reminding the class of what they have to do as a result of their choices, and overseeing the process.

More Ideas to Prevent Hallway Behavior Problems

One of the easiest things teachers can do to prevent problems in the hallway is to walk near the end of the line instead of the front. The reasoning here is obvious—when your back is to three-fourths of your class, the kids will try to get away with things that they don't do under your watchful eye. Train your line leader where to stop (a good rule is at all corners, intersections, and doorways) so you can stay towards the back while the class walks.

Another smart thing to do is keep the line moving quickly. You'll need to go slow the first few times, but keep in mind that the longer students are in the hallway, the more energy-releasing behaviors you'll see. Waiting for others to get in line or catch up causes problems, as well. If a few individual students aren't getting it and need to try again, let the rest of the class start walking while you stay behind and supervise procedure practice.

Logically-related incentives for moving around the school quickly can also be helpful. Reminders such as, "Let's keep moving so that we have our full thirty minutes for lunch" or "If we are late, we won't have time to get drinks. If that's something you're interested in doing, please face forward and focus on getting back to the classroom."

When necessary, you can give incentives for good hallway behavior. I give kids an extra bead (from our class behavior system) whenever they get a compliment in the hallway from another adult. This REALLY gets them on their best behavior! Some teachers give 'compliment parties', keeping track with beans in a jar or paperclip chains of how may compliments the class has gotten, and when the jar is full or the chain is hanging all the way to the floor, the class gets to have a party. If you choose to do this, mention it to your kids after they've been in school for a few days and the 'newness' is wearing off. "You know what, you guys are doing such a great job in the hallway and so many people are complimenting you, I think we should have a reward system just for the way you behave when we're out of the classroom." You can include compliments the class receives from specials teachers during art, music, etc., if you want to ensure that students are well-behaved when they're with other teachers.

Ongoing Hallway Reinforcement (Without Losing Your Mind)

You'll need to do a LOT of reinforcement narration at the beginning of the school year, but each time you walk somewhere, you'll need to do less and less. If you start seeing problems, try narrating again.

Remember that kids are not robots and will never form a quiet straight line for the entire journey from your classroom to the cafeteria. If you're a control freak, you're going to have to learn to let go in this area. I will warn you now: lining up and hallway procedures will need to be frequently reinforced throughout the entire year, so don't get discouraged.

You should not have students wondering where to put papers or trying to sharpen a pencil in the middle of your math lesson in October, but it is perfectly normal for children to need reminders about hallway behavior all the way through June.

You are dealing with children who are learning to exercise self-control. They have probably been asked to sit still and work quietly for the majority of their day, and if they need to do some sort of exaggerated tip-toe motion or whisper silly-sounding words under their breath while walking, try to be understanding. You don't have to allow the behaviors, but you should correct students with empathy and not anger.

Normally to communicate that this type of energy-release behavior is not okay, I just make eye contact, smile, and shake my head 'no' quickly. Many times the child is not aware of any behaviors until he sees me looking, and usually he will then give an embarrassed smile and apologize. If children are talking out loud or being knowingly disruptive in the line, just say their names and shake your head. They know what they did wrong, so you don't need to lecture. If you're not certain that the child remembers the expectations AND the reasons, reiterating them *occasionally* can be helpful. "Remember that our hands are off the walls, because we don't want to get them dirty." Say these things in a positive, encouraging tone. A child touching the wall is not a huge deal in the grand scheme of things and not worth getting worked up about. I try to give brief corrections whenever possible: "Third tile, please. Hands to yourself. Walking. *Walking.* Thank you." Inhale, exhale, let it go.

Inevitably, someone will run in the stairwell, and I will ask them to go back and try it again while the rest of the class waits. This has to be done throughout the school year, too, as it is incredibly tempting to run down the steps. I know I do it whenever the kids aren't around!

Children absolutely hate having to go back to where they started in the hallway and walk again, or back up the stairs and come back down, and therefore it's an extremely effective consequence for running. Give your directive without anger so you don't get attitude back—"Mabelin, you were running. That's dangerous. Please go back and show me you know how to do it the right way. Thanks." Treat the whole scenario as an unfortunate occurrence and not a punishment— it's something that has to be done in order for everyone to move around the school safely.

In the beginning of the year, before students realize that I don't take any kind of back talk or mumbling, I usually have someone start muttering, sighing, or complaining when I have them go back and walk. I address the disrespect very firmly in front of the whole class so no one else tries it. "I don't know why you're giving *me* attitude, because I'm not the one who ran. If anyone should be upset, it's the other twenty-two kids who have to stand here and wait while you go down the stairs properly. Thank goodness they have manners and are polite enough to wait quietly without rolling their eyes or sighing. Thank you guys for doing the right thing and waiting while we get everyone together. [Cheerful tone] Okay, line leader, let's go." If the child shows any further attitude, I say simply and firmly, "I'm going to get our class to lunch right now. I will deal with your attitude later" and then follow-up as appropriate with the child. When the child does start walking quietly in line, I speak to her again in front of the whole class, and this time I make sure it's positive. "Great, Mabelin, now you've got it! I knew you could do it."

Chapter 12: Student Responsibility and Organization
Giving children ownership of their learning environment

I had an extraordinarily disorganized student one year. In April, he was *still* shoving books from our class library anywhere on the shelves. I knew he came from an upper-class family who bought lots of children's books, and I was so incredulous that I chided him one day, "These books are all facing different directions!! Is this how you put away books at home?!" He blinked and said, "No. I just shove them all under my bed!"

Don't assume kids have seen *any* sort of organization before! Some parents, just like some people in general, are more organized than others. Also, many parents baby their children and clean up after them constantly. **Either way, your classroom might be the first time a child is expected to stack something neatly or keep a desk tidy.** Even the teachers your students had previously may not have taught or enforced organizational skills.

Children NEED to learn to organize themselves, especially at school—why not be the one to instill in them that value? I once had a particularly messy little girl from an affluent but highly disorganized family who told me at the end of the year, "This was the first time I ever knew where anything was in my desk." I smiled and said, "Doesn't that feel good, to know that you are taking care of your things and you know how to find them?" She was beaming from ear to ear. Her natural tendency was still to leave things strewn everywhere, and that was reinforced by her home environment. But, she had experienced pride in keeping her belongings neat, and I truly believe that will inspire her for life.

IT IS WORTH EVERY MINUTE YOU SPEND TEACHING ORGANIZATION AND CLEANLINESS TO KIDS! Taking care of one's belongings may not be a skill on standardized tests, but is a critical component of being an efficient and productive adult.

Teaching Organizational Skills

What Does a Clean Desk Look Like?

Your criteria for a clean desk is probably very different from that of a seven-year-old! Clarity in expectations takes on an even greater importance when it comes to organization. Make a class list or diagram of what a clean desk looks like, or what the classroom looks and sounds like when children are cleaning up. Brainstorm qualities of a clean room together, and leave the poster up to serve as a benchmark for expectations. Be specific about what you want and teach for it.

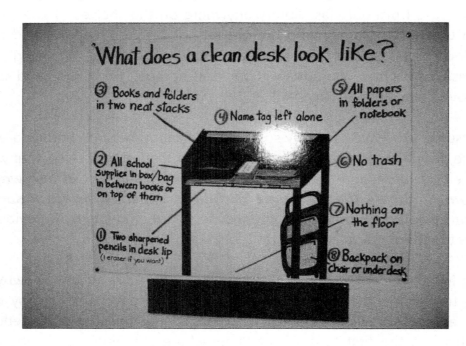

Do lots of modeling in the beginning of the year and throughout as needed. Have the class watch certain students "show us how to do it" and use reinforcement narration and performance feedback. Always compare their demonstration to the diagram or list of expectations.

Keeping the Appropriate Amount and Type of Supplies

Some supplies are used by students daily and are kept in their desks (such as pencils, notebook paper, and erasers). Sometimes a child has an entire pack of paper or 20 pencils, and I offer to keep them in a cabinet until the child needs them (putting a sticky note on top labeled with the child's name so I don't get confused).

Some years I kept paper and pencils as communal supplies so that every child would have enough. The simplest way to manage this was to pass out additional paper and pencils once a month or so to make sure everyone had plenty. Another option that I used for awhile was to have the kids fill out supply slips during Morning Work time. Then every other day (or once a week, depending on the class), a student helper filled the requests and filed away the slips. That way I had a record of how often the kids ran out of supplies. The slip also required the students to explain why they needed more supplies (e.g., ran out, used it up, lost it, took it home, or someone borrowed it), so if parents questioned why they needed to send in more, I had documentation from the child. Too-frequent requests were not filled.

If students have too many things in their desks, they won't be able to keep them neat. See Chapter 6, Organizing Classroom Materials, for more about managing school supplies.

Caring for School Supplies

Inevitably students will say things like, "I can't find my scissors" or "I took my crayons home." I shrug and say, "You are responsible for your school supplies. If you don't have them, you won't be able to do the activity." The student then has to improvise (I suggest another way to complete the assignment) or has to take it home for homework.

About once a quarter, I distribute replacement supplies to students for anything that is provided to me by the school (erasers, pens, crayons, etc.). I say, "I'm going to pass out supplies to make sure you have everything you need. If you do not have an eraser, please come see me now" and give erasers to anyone who comes over. I repeat this with all of the supplies I can give out, and finish by saying, "You should have everything you need now. I am giving these things to you because I care about you and want you to be prepared to learn. Please take good care of them. Do NOT take anything home. They are called school supplies because they belong at school. If you need something at home and your parents can't buy it for you, please let me know and I will try to help you out. But, everything I have given you must stay in your desk at all times."

Where Have All the Pencils Gone?

The pencil problem is one that sounds petty to anyone who isn't a teacher. But those who work in a classroom realize that pencil acquisition and sharpening will either drive you crazy or prove completely inconsequential, depending on whether you have established effective procedures.

Most kids function at one of two extremes. Either they have nothing to write with (ever), or they store fifty-seven pencils in their desk that come clattering out every time they try to remove materials. To fix this problem, I tell my students that they must keep two and only two pencils in their desks at all times (extra supplies are either in their cubbies or kept by me until students need them). At the end of each day, the 'Desk Inspector' randomly checks the desks of two children (or checks the whole class a few times per week), and if they have two pencils in their desks, they get a reward through whatever reward system I'm using that year (such as a bead or a token). This routine ensures that students always have something to write with without cluttering up their desks with an excessive amount of pencils.

If a pencil breaks and the others are lost or unsharpened, students can write with gray crayon, which they hate. Some teachers loan out little golf pencils, which are an equally effective deterrent. Another option is to let kids use pencils that have your name on them, which means they can't pass the pencils off as their own, but they may still lose them. I used to allow students to borrow pencils from each other, but then the responsible kids wouldn't have any left because they had loaned them all out. Also, I've had problems with cliques forming ("Cory gave me and her a sparkle pencil but you didn't get one, ha-ha!") so I put a stop to sharing materials years ago. Once my expectations are taught, I try to stay as uninvolved with pencil issues as possible and insist that children solve them independently.

Sharpening is another issue altogether. In my classroom, I allow pencils to be sharpened during Morning Work time only, and no sharpeners are kept in student desks. When a child is late to school, she can quickly use a silent hand-held sharpener that that I keep in a communal basket. This procedure includes colored pencils—I remind students in the morning that we will use those materials later in the day and expect them to prepare accordingly. This keeps students from hovering over sharpeners all day long and missing out on instruction.

<u>Teaching Students to Clean Up After Themselves</u>

Throwing Away Trash

Consider a class rule: no throwing away trash at ANY time without permission. Some kids will find a staple or paper scrap and walk the long way around the room to the furthest possible trash receptacle and then slowly wander back to their seats. Not only does this rule eliminate that problem, it also creates order when the entire class needs to throw away trash, such as after a cutting project.

In recent years I stopped using this rule because my class size is low, making it less disruptive for those kids who physically need to get up and move sometimes, but I do still use it during projects when we're all cutting at once. Then I call kids to the trash cans one row at a time, or boys then girls, so it doesn't get too chaotic. If you call one side of the room (or group) at a time to throw away trash, you can see who should and should not be at the trash can. You can also train students to automatically throw away trash when they line up to go to music or lunch, if those activities follow your lesson.

Routines for Cleaning Up

☑ **Teach kids to always clear their desks before leaving the room.**

If you need students to leave something out because they'll need it when you re-enter, insist that materials be stacked neatly on the upper right hand corner of their desks. Remember: administrators, parents, and district visitors can visit your room at any time. Have the kids keep it looking organized!

☑ **Don't line anyone up for lunch or recess until desks are clean.**

What better motivation for kids to clean up than the lure of food or free time outside? Once a day or every other day, I give my kids thirty seconds to clean up their areas (not just desks—the chair and floor, too), then send around the Inspectors. If any part of a child's area does not look like the clean desk diagram, the child has to fix it. At the beginning of the year, you should provide several minutes for cleaning and inspection: the time will lessen throughout the year.

☑ **Give a time frame for cleaning up, and, if needed, a consequence.**

"I need you to be ready for math in three minutes (or when this bell goes off)." If you want, you can add, "Anyone who is not ready will ___ (fill in a penalty)." Counting down from 10 to 0 also works well, especially with younger students because they can easily gauge how much time they have left (and you can count more slowly or quickly as needed). Be warned that if you hype the children up, they will act like it's a race—things will get done quickly, but also loudly and sloppily.

☑ **Have the 'Desk Fairy' do random inspections.**

I know primary grade teachers who pretend that there is actually such a creature that flies around to classrooms and leaves rewards for students whose desks are clean. I think it's a cute idea, but I don't like to give false information to my kids and I want them to know that I am the one who rewards them, so I just tell the class every now then when they come into the room from specials or lunch, "I played the Desk Fairy while you were gone...check if you have a bead [part of our class reward system] on your desk! If you don't, check the clean desk diagram and see if you can figure out what needs to be fixed." The kids never know when I'm going to do this, so it's a motivation for the messier kids and a reward for those who are consistently well-organized. Also, I have little strips of paper already printed and cut out that say, "Thank you for keeping a clean desk, even when you think no one is looking. ☺ Ms. Powell." I leave those on desks from time to time, sometimes with beads, to let the kids know I appreciate their efforts.

Teaching Kids to Rely on Routines and Procedures

When children ask obvious questions, it's often because they're forgetting your rules and procedures. Sometimes it's easier to give a quick answer than to require children to figure things out on their own. However, when you consistently expect kids to answer their own questions, they learn to do so without involving you.

By directing students back to the things they know are consistent about your classroom routines, you can help them problem solve independently. Notice how in each of the examples below, a child is asked to recall the procedure that's already been taught and follow it, rather than look to the teacher for reassurance.

When a student says...	Respond with...
"I looked everywhere for my crayons but they're gone."	"Well, what are your choices if you don't have your crayons?"
"My pencil broke—can I sharpen it?"	"Can you? What's the rule?"
"I'm finished, what do I do?"	[Point to the 'When Finished' sign on the board]
"Can I use the bathroom?"	[Point to the bathroom sign on the board]
"What page are we on?"	"That's a 3 Before Me question."
"What do I do with my paper when it's done?"	"Good question—what DO you do with a paper that's done?"
"Can I get a drink?"	"Is it time for us to go to specials yet? Okay, so the answer is... Right. Not yet."
"I found this on the floor."	"What should you do with it?"

The Importance of Classroom Jobs

Designing a Genuinely Useful Class Helper System

I would be lost without my classroom job system! My kids do dozens of routine tasks for me, and complete them automatically. When I miss a day of work and have to call a substitute, I know that the classroom will be maintained because students are aware of their responsibilities and anxious to complete them.

Sometimes I hear from teachers who dislike having classroom jobs, and feel like they're just a big hassle. Typically, these teachers are only assigning jobs because they want students to learn to be responsible for the classroom. However, that's not the job system's main function. Students learn responsibility everyday as they practice caring for their belongings and keeping their desk area well-organized and neat.

The primary purpose of classroom jobs is to transfer responsibility to students for keeping the classroom running smoothly, resulting in uninterrupted instruction.

If your classroom job system is effective, you will never again have five kids waving their arms and shouting, "Ooh! Ooh! Can I do it?" because your answer will always be the same: "Are you the helper for that?"

When meaningful tasks are assigned to students, and the kids understand and are capable of your expectations, classroom jobs become a fundamental part of your classroom, and your students can be a tremendous assistance. Here's how to make that happen...

Designing a Functional Classroom Job System

1) Make a list of ALL your routine tasks and assign them to students through a classroom job system.

Any regular classroom task which you want to be performed automatically without your direct supervision should be assigned. I usually add and delete jobs over the months as the needs in our classroom change. I like to have one job for each child in the class, partially so no one feels left out, but mostly because I have so many things that I need help with!

Paper Passers 1,2	Desk Inspector
Paper Collector	Windows/Blinds Monitor
Supply Passers 1,2	Media [TV, DVD, CD] Monitor
Plant Waterer	Cutters 1,2
Attendance Taker	Filers 1,2,
Floor Monitor	Breakfast Helper
Door Holder	Trash Monitor
Line Leader	Board Eraser
Line Ender	Calendar Helper

Pledge/Flag Helper
Computer Helper
Centers Monitor
Bulletin Board Helper
Dictionary Helper
Book Bin Helpers 1,2
Lamp Monitor
Lights Monitor
Door Monitor
Lunch Count Helper

Cubby/Coat Closet Monitor
Sink Monitor
Soap Helper
Weather Helper
Hall Monitor
Token Helper
Errand Runner
Drink Monitor
Recess Helper
Homework Helper

There are a few considerations you may want to keep in mind as you select jobs. You may want to:

♦ **Choose 'semi-permanent' or 'indefinite' jobs which you want students to do for a longer period of time.** For example, keeping my class library organized is a big job that only very mature, responsible kids can do, so I don't put that in my regular rotation. I show kids my list of indefinite jobs and tell them I'm going to choose students who demonstrate specific qualities that are needed for each job.

♦ **Allow certain jobs to be done only by students who leave the classroom last at the end of the day.** In addition to my regular job system, I give extra responsibilities to car riders (the students who are last to be dismissed). They straighten desks, change the calendar marker to the next day, erase the board, and so on. I work with the car riders to decide who will do each job, and they are responsible for completing them indefinitely (until there is a problem or they want to switch).

♦ **Assign some jobs to multiple students.** I have two Table Washers, two Recess Equipment Helpers, and so on. I just list them as Helper 1 and Helper 2 on the job chart, and both are equally responsible.

♦ **Have the job of 'Substitute' who takes over for anyone who's absent.** If a helper is out of the room or otherwise engaged, I have my Substitute complete tasks as needed.

♦ **Have one or two students take the job of 'Teacher's Helper' for those miscellaneous tasks that aren't specifically covered on the job chart.**

This comes in handy when an unexpected situation arises, such as the need for passing out extra napkins during a class party. You won't have to look around for kids who have been 'good' to help you out—just ask your Teacher's Helpers.

2) **Find a way to display your classroom job assignments.**

There are a million cute ways to do this, but I use a simple, functional, pocket chart. The most important thing is that your display is sturdy (since students will need to move their names around) and easily visible throughout the room (so that wherever you're at, you can call on the people you need).

3) **Decide how jobs will be assigned.**

Some teachers have a rotation system so that every child gets to do every job an equal number of times. I like to allow children to choose their jobs so that I know things will get done properly. Most of my kids don't want to refill the soap and paper towels in the bathroom, and if I assign that job to them, they won't do it to the best of their ability. However, there are always a few kids in the room who love this task, and if I allow them to volunteer for it, I can be sure it will be done routinely and to my standards.

I used to have my students choose in order of how well they did the previous week/month's job (those who did not need constant reminders were allowed to pick first—we discussed this as a class so they would understand my criteria and reasoning), or according to social skills grades on weekly evaluations (i.e. the most responsible students who followed class rules picked first). Both ways made sense to the children, but you could pick randomly if you prefer, and that method has worked well for some of my groups of children, too.

I typically put the name cards in the order I want them and have a student call the kids up to choose their jobs during Fun Friday or Monday's Morning Work to save me time and minimize interruptions to instruction. Sometimes I'll take the cards out of the pocket and have them lying on the table when students enter the classroom, listing 'Choose a new job' as one of the Morning Work tasks written on the board. Having kids pick jobs first thing in the morning also encourages them to be on time for school.

Students can choose a job they have already had, but not twice in a row (they will naturally keep track of this mentally for each other so you won't have to remember—trust me). If there are no jobs left that a student wants, she can opt not to have a job and someone else can take two. (This only happened once, but handling the issue this way gives the kids a sense of control and empowerment.)

4) Determine how long students will keep their jobs.

I like for my kids to keep the same jobs for at least a week. With some groups of children, I switch every other week or even monthly. The longer the student holds a job, the more automatic it becomes, and the better they do it. Also, it's easier for me to remember who has which job (in case it isn't done, or the student is absent). Switching jobs daily can lead to confusion and poorly done tasks, because the children forget what their jobs are and how to do them properly. Remember, the primary purpose of classroom jobs is not to teach students responsibility (they learn that principle daily in taking care of their own belongings); the main function is to keep the classroom running smoothly so that instruction is not interrupted.

<u>Introducing and Maintaining the Job System</u>

☑ **Explain the system *briefly* to students.**

Most children don't have the attention span or memory to recall one long explanation of how to do all the classroom jobs. Tell the kids on the first or second day of school that you would like their help in running the classroom, and you've selected some responsibilities that you'll be trusting them to handle. Explain how often jobs will be changed and how they'll be assigned. Read each job title to the students. If you've chosen simple titles, this will be pretty self-explanatory. For more complex jobs, give kids a one-sentence summary and tell them you'll go into more details later as you need the related tasks completed.

☑ **Teach students to do their jobs in whole-class modeling/practice sessions, as part of your introduction to routines and procedures.**

The first time you need any student to do a job, teach him in front of the entire class. If you're introducing jobs during the first week of school, this will be a natural part of your instruction in routines and procedures. In fact, when you teach your classroom helper routines this way, you actually have the opportunity to reinforce your other classroom expectations. For example, if you have a drink monitor, then when it's time for students to get drinks, say,

"I need my Drink Monitor to come up. Sarah, you're going to stand right here next to the water fountain. Does everyone see where Sarah is standing? You'll need to remember that, because one day soon you'll be the Drink Monitor. Sarah is going to wait here while I call teams to get drinks. She's going to count to 5 while you drink. When she says five, that's it, you have to stop drinking and walk away. Then she'll count for the next person. If Sarah sees you getting out of line, pushing, or being noisy, she's going to say, 'Please stop doing that.' If you listen to her, you will get your drink. If you don't listen to her, Sarah's going to let me know and I'll handle it. Does everyone understand?

"Okay, let's try it. Team One, come get drinks. Notice how this team is walking over to the water fountain. They're not pushing, they're not running, and they're very, very quiet. Oh, look, Karen was a little bit ahead of Andrew, and he just let her go ahead of him. He could have run a little bit so he could be in front, but he was patient. He knew he'd still get a drink. Thank you, Andrew. That was a very grown-up thing to do.

Now, let's listen while Sarah counts to 5 for Karen. Go ahead, Sarah. Great. Karen got her drink, and look, now she's walking back to her seat quietly. Andrew's up next, Sarah's going to count. Wonderful. Sarah, what would you

do if Natasha started splashing right now? Exactly—you'd ask her to stop. And if she didn't? Right. Good thing Natasha knows how to follow the rules, and I don't have to say anything to her. Great job, Natasha. Okay, let's see if Team Two is ready for drinks."

You can do the same thing for every job you assign to students: Paper Passer, Pledge Helper, Door Holder, and so on. Get the entire class actively involved in the process, and remind them that they'll be doing the other jobs soon so they need to know how to do them. Let students see their role in assisting the person assigned to a job, and how the entire class can work together to get things done efficiently.

☑ **After your job procedures are established, have students train and help one another as needed.**

With time, your classroom helper system will be solidly in place and the type of in-depth modeling and practice described in the example above will only be happening on an as-needed basis. The drawback is that students forget how to do the jobs they haven't held yet, or haven't held in awhile. You can have students who recently did a particular job train the next child how to do it.

If you keep jobs for a whole month, you can use the final two days of each month as your training days. The last person to have the job teaches the next person how to complete the task. That means you only have to teach each job in-depth one time (in August). After that, the kids teach one another. If children have a question, they are to ask the person who had the job before them. This makes the 'turnover' each month very smooth.

If your students change jobs more often, you can still have kids help each other. I find that my Paper Collectors often forget where to turn in papers, so when the new helper says, "Where do these go?" I say, "Peterson, you were Paper Collector last week, could you please show Eileen what to do with the papers?" Because I almost always say this about classroom job questions, students stop asking me after awhile, and I hear them saying to each other, "Hey, where am I supposed to put these? Peterson, weren't you the Paper Collector last week?"

☑ **Use your helper system *consistently*.**

If you have kids constantly asking if they can do something for you, you're not being unremitting about using your classroom helpers. Any deviation from the agreement about who is doing what job will undermine your system. When you're in a rush, it might be easier to just have the kid standing next to you pass out your papers, but it will disrupt the flow of the classroom. The child will wonder, *Why did she ask me to do that? I'm the Hallway Monitor! Is there something wrong with the person who's supposed to be passing out papers? Are we not doing classroom jobs anymore?* And that's not to mention the look of disappointment you'll get from the actual Paper Passer who wants to know why somebody else is doing her job! If you want tasks to be completed automatically, don't tamper with the system. Let it work for you.

☑ **Rearrange your system as often as needed, using student input as much as possible.**

You can add, modify, or take out jobs anytime you feel doing so would help your classroom run more smoothly. I regularly make changes based on my needs and the abilities of my children. Don't ever feel locked into doing something in a way that's not working, just because you don't want to 'confuse' the kids. Level with them by saying, "I don't think this is working, because I'm noticing __ and __. So instead, I want to try __." Seek the kids' input and value their opinions.

I once had a new student join the class and asked my kids to suggest another job for me to add to the job chart. Some of their ideas were tasks I would never have thought of, and they greatly improved the level of efficiency in our classroom! Keep kids involved in the process, and show them that's it's important to reflect on what's working and what's not in life, and make changes appropriately. This type of critical thinking will stay with children long after they leave your classroom.

Chapter 13: Teaching Work Habits
Clear expectations for following along, staying on-task, and more

Work habits are probably the most important procedure you'll need to teach. You will have to be very clear about what you want from students during instruction, independent work, and in cooperative groups. If you do not teach procedures for working, you will be constantly repeating yourself and nagging students to sit down, get to work, and pay attention. This chapter will teach you how to make abstract concepts concrete and explain your expectations so that students can practice them as regular routines.

Teaching Students What to Do During Instruction

When the Teacher Talks, the Students Listen

In order to maintain control of instruction and classroom discussions, you MUST set the expectation for students to stop talking the moment you open your mouth. Explain this on the first day of school and reinforce it frequently in the beginning by saying sternly to interrupters, "I should not ever hear someone trying to talk over me. It's my job to make sure everyone can hear each other and has a chance to participate, and I can't do my job when you interrupt me. When I talk, you listen. Period." Later I just say, "If I'm talking, you're listening."

Many teachers try to enforce this rule but aren't sure how to do it. The key is in having *predictable* procedure enforcement and an *unpredictable* teaching style. Students must count on FIRM, CONSISTENT correction of any 'no interrupting' rule violation, but also anticipate you saying unexpected, compelling things at unusual times.

If you want people to listen to you, then you have to be interesting! My kids (usually) hang onto my every word not just out of respect, but because they want to hear what I'm going to say. They never know when I'm going to make a joke, reference something in popular culture, or make an announcement that's out of the ordinary. I might suddenly lower my voice to a whisper, or start singing a direction. Because my regular routines and daily procedures are solidly in place, I can and do change things up at a moment's notice—kids know that if they're not paying attention, they're going to miss something good.

Teachers must convince their students that what they have to say is interesting, relevant, and important. In the middle of a dull but necessary lesson on rounding to the nearest hundred or identifying adverbs, you have to rely on tone, body language, and teaching techniques to keep students engaged (see Chapter 25, Teaching Techniques that Minimize Off-Task Behavior).

Once you've proven to your kids that what you say is worth listening to, don't tolerate any interruptions. This is the only expectation that I do NOT give friendly reminders about or say with a smile—correction always comes quickly and forcefully, usually in the form of a very cold stare. Sometimes I'll pause for effect, and sometimes I'll continue the lesson while shooting proverbial daggers at the talker. If I have to address the problem verbally, I usually raise my voice. The kids notice this marked departure from my normal reaction to procedural infractions and respond accordingly. They learn very quickly and remind each other if anyone ever talks over me ("Shh! She's trying to tell us something!").

What Does 'Follow Along' Mean?

Students must be told precisely what you expect them to do while you're teaching. Your expectations should be introduced, practiced, and reinforced like any other procedure. You can use the term 'following along' to describe the behaviors that you expect from your students while you are teaching, and then define the term in a way that fits your expectations.

My definition of following along during instruction is written on a poster that is displayed prominently in the front of the classroom. 'Following along' means students should:

1) Have all of and ONLY the specified materials on your desk
2) Look at and listen to the person who is speaking
3) Stay at the right place in any text we're using

4) Touch your materials only when directed
5) Talk to your neighbor only when directed
6) Use whispering for the 3 Before Me rule [see Chapter 15]
7) Participate whenever you have something helpful to say
8) Be respectful and supportive of other people

This is a rather lengthy list, but it's better to be precise in your criteria and reinforce it every time than to give students the freedom to interpret your routines any way they want. The expectations for following along are taught during the first week of school with all other procedures. I explain my expectations and the reasons for them, model what I want, have students practice, and use reinforcement narration and performance feedback (as described in Chapter 9, How To Teach Any Procedure) to help students develop the skill of following along. After we've practiced, I say at the start of most my lessons during the first weeks of school,

'FOLLOW ALONG' MEANS:

1) Have all of and ONLY the specified materials on your desk.
2) Look at and listen to the person who is speaking.
3) Stay at the right place in any text we're using.
4) Touch your materials only when directed.
5) Talk to your neighbor only when directed.
6) Use whispering for the 3 Before Me rule.
7) Participate whenever you have something helpful to say.
8) Be respectful and supportive of other people.

"We're going to begin our writing lesson now. You will need to follow along. Someone please remind the class what it means to follow along—what exactly should you be doing now?"

At the start of every lesson throughout the school year, I convey to students that I expect them to follow along by saying, "We're going to start on page 104. Please follow along" or "Today we're going to be doing some timeline activities. You will need to follow along as I show you what to do." When students deviate from the procedure, I may just point silently to the poster that specifies what following along means. I may also prompt the student with, "What should you be doing right now?" or "Which part of following along do you need to do?"

Almost every misbehavior during instruction can be addressed by referring to the procedure for following along. You can make comments and pose questions such as:

- "In order to follow along, what should be on your desk right now?"
- "Following along means looking at the person who's talking. Who should you be looking at right now?"

- "What page of the book should you be looking on to follow along?"
- "Where should your hands be if you're following along?"
- "If you are following along, you are not talking to anyone near you."
- "Those who are following along have their hands up to share ideas."
- "We have three people participating right now. If you're following along, please raise your hand and contribute to our discussion."

These questions and comments refer students back to your expectations during instruction. There is no need for repeated commands or nagging when students understand the procedure for following along. If multiple students are not meeting your expectations despite performance feedback, you should stop the process just like in any other routine. "We have too many students not following along, and I won't continue until everyone's ready. If you can tell us one of the eight things everyone should be doing right now, please raise your hand... Now that we all remember what following along means, let's try that again."

Expectations for Sitting

If you have a young group of students who can't sit still well, you will need to specify and practice your expectations. At desks, this is relatively simple: bottom on the seat, your back touching the back of the chair, feet resting on the floor if you can reach it.

If you have your students sit on a rug or carpet while you teach, you may want to say 'criss-cross applesauce' or something similar to indicate what you want children to do with their legs. I used to be strict about how kids sat on the rug but have since realized that if students are uncomfortable, it will be difficult for them to learn. I prefer to allow students to spread out as long as they are sitting up and not touching other people (lying down is allowed during videos only). If the rug is too small to accommodate this, I allow students to take turns sitting on beach chairs or bean bags. Some students would rather be in chairs and I usually allow them to pull up seats next to and behind the rug area. For me, trying to force 20 or 30 kids to sit perfectly in a tight space is not a battle that's worth fighting. Giving children space to be themselves—literally—makes my life and theirs so much more pleasant and comfortable and allows us to concentrate on what's really important: learning.

When teaching preschool, I gave students assigned seats on the carpet using pieces of tape labeled with their names. If your rug is divided into sections or has graphics that students can sit on, that works just as well. These visual aides help children learn how to stay in their own areas and not touch other people. If a student is perpetually whining that someone's shoe or hair or knee is touching him, I'll say, "If you can't concentrate here, you're welcome to pull up a chair and sit in the back. Your choice."

Teaching Students How to Work Independently

What Does 'On-Task' Look Like?

'On-task' is the term I use to describe what students should be doing during independent work. I created a poster with my expectations for this procedure and display it alongside the 'following along' poster:

1) Have all of and ONLY the specified materials on your desk
2) Complete your work doing your very best job
3) Talk to your neighbor only when directed
4) Use whispering for the 3 Before Me rule

This expectation is also explicitly taught. In the beginning, I model examples and non-examples of on-task work, pretending to be a student who displays typical behaviors and having the class discuss which part of on-task I'm not showing. Students learn that playing with a shoelace, flicking a pencil eraser, and staring into space are all quiet and probably non-disruptive behaviors, but are not acceptable because they're not part of the 'on-task' list.

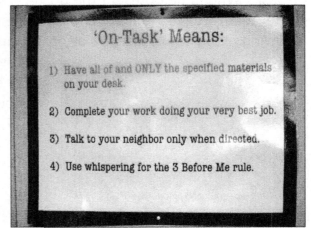

'On-Task' Means:

1) Have all of and ONLY the specified materials on your desk.

2) Complete your work doing your very best job.

3) Talk to your neighbor only when directed.

4) Use whispering for the 3 Before Me rule.

#2 is the critical expectation, because any playing around means you are not completing your work. 'Doing your very best job' is really a qualifier that respects children as individuals, because for some kids, a small amount of playing around IS their best and requires a tremendous amount of self-control. I try to praise all effort towards improving one's own best job.

When students understand the definition of on-task, they can easily recognize behaviors that are off-task. Talking to someone when you're not asking a 3 Before Me question is off-task. Following the teacher around the room is off-task. Digging through your backpack is off-task.

Teaching Students How to Work Cooperatively

What Does 'Work Together' Mean?

After students have successfully practiced staying on-task during independent work for increasing periods of time, I begin teaching them how to complete partner and group activities. The term for this is 'working together' and the corresponding poster lists these criteria:

1) Have all of and ONLY the specified materials in your work area
2) Look at and listen to the person who is speaking
3) Be respectful and supportive of other people
4) Complete your work doing your very best job

These expectations are a hodge-podge of those for following along and staying on-task. When I first present the poster, I ask students for their observations and guide them to the understanding that cooperative work is partially about following along with a partner or group, and partially about staying on-task with the work you are responsible for. More details about teaching kids to work cooperatively can be found in Chapter 27, Hands-On and Cooperative Learning.

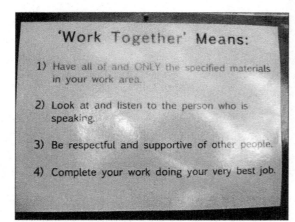

Teaching Students How to Stay Quiet

What is Quiet?

My definition of 'quiet' is making no unnecessary (or unneeded) noise. If a student needs to cough, that's necessary and is allowed during quiet times. If a student needs to whisper a 3 Before Me question, that's necessary and also allowed. Conversely, if a student wants to make loud burping sounds to make people laugh, that is unnecessary and not allowed. During quiet times, I expect to hear students rummaging around in their desks, walking back and forth to the bathroom, blowing their noses, and so on.

Once the term 'quiet' is defined, you can address the concept of doing things 'quietly'. If I ask children to work quietly, that's not an abstract term meaning my head hurts and I don't want to hear them talking. Working quietly means doing work with no unnecessary noise. A child may need to whisper, but she doesn't need to talk so loudly that everyone around her can hear. Walking quietly means walking with no unnecessary noise. If a child's shoes make a soft squeak on the concrete, that's okay, as long as the student isn't intentionally creating unnecessary noise by making the squeak as loud as possible.

Differentiating Between Silence and Quiet

When teaching expectations for quiet and silence, I distinguish between the two terms so students know exactly what I expect. The only times when I typically require total silence is during our moment of silent meditation after the pledge of allegiance, during standardized testing, when announcements come over the loudspeaker, and when I ring a bell or give another silence signal. During all other times, I request quiet.

Silence means absolutely no noise whatsoever (or 'at all'). With silence, there should be no movement in the classroom. No one should be whispering for any reason. If you practice this procedure by setting a timer for ten or twenty seconds, children should be able to stay totally silent the entire time. If someone breaks the silence, stop the timer and talk about why the behavior does not qualify as 'no noise whatsoever'.

Once students have been silent for the amount of time you set, explain that what they just did is what you will expect for certain times during the day. You will need to practice silence multiple times for students to get it. If you expect silence during announcements, review your expectations and practice right beforehand. ("In one minute, announcements will begin. You will need to be silent. That means what? Let's practice what you will do during announcements. I will set the timer for thirty seconds. We will not make any noise whatsoever. Ready, set, go... Great—there was noise at all, except when someone giggled one time. That can't happen during silence. Now announcements will begin. Let's try silence once more, this time with no noise—including giggling. You can do it!" Repeat this as often as needed until the habit becomes automatic.

Getting Quiet vs. Staying Quiet

If you have effectively taught 'quiet' as a procedure but are still having trouble getting your kids to work quietly, be sure you have properly taught and practiced your expectations for staying on-task ('talk to your neighbor only when directed'). You may also need to emphasize that getting quiet is not the same thing as staying quiet. You can't make any assumptions with young children, so if you announce, "It's too loud, you need to get quiet," be prepared to have a noisy class again very quickly! Students must understand that when you ask for quiet, you mean for them to stay quiet until you give a different direction ("Now you may discuss this with your partner" or "Thank you for completing your assignment quietly. Please take out your science book now").

It's easier for them to remember this when you word your directions more precisely and explain when the quiet will end. Try saying, "I need you to work quietly on this until the timer goes off. Then you'll clean up," or "Please walk quietly in the hall and then enter our room in silence while you wait for my directions." If students begin making unnecessary noise, you can follow up with, "We are staying quiet until everyone's in their seats and I have given you instructions for the next task."

Teaching Students to Whisper

If students must talk during quiet times to use the 3 Before Me rule, I require them to whisper. They also need to whisper during certain partner and group work activities. Like every other expectation for young children, this concept must be taught.

Every teacher has a different standard for whispering. You will need to tell students how loud they can talk, model it, and practice. I tell my kids that whispering means only the people whose desks are right next to theirs can hear. Emphasize that the person they want to whisper to MUST be close enough to hear—they cannot loudly say the name of someone further away and then try to whisper. I used to explain that only the person you are talking to should be able to hear, but I've found that to be an unrealistic expectation for most third graders.

Keep in mind that for young children, whispering may be developmentally inappropriate. When I taught Head Start, I recognized this right away and defined whispering as "your quietest indoor voice," which contrasted with an 'outdoor voice'. Some children's quietest voices were considerably louder than others, but I accepted the best they could do. Even for second graders, whispering can be too difficult. Unfortunately I discovered this firsthand and drove myself insane for several weeks before figuring it out. I stuck to the definition of 'no one except the people right next to you can hear', but I had to accept some students' best efforts toward this.

Even more nerve-wracking was the discovery that many second graders can't read silently. I kept asking, *Who is talking? Who is talking?* but not seeing anyone turned to someone near them. I finally realized that no one was talking—they were mumbling the words they were reading under their breath! For some students, drawing attention to this habit lessened the issue, and served as a springboard for discussion about whispering ('When you whisper, pretend like you are reading to yourself in your quietest voice'). Other students finished the year completely oblivious to the fact that they read aloud. My point is, be patient with young children and meet them where they're at. The vast majority will make great strides in learning how to whisper during the school year.

Part Four:
Approaching Behavior Management Pro-Actively

Chapter 14: Five Strategies for Preventing Behavior Problems

A pro-active approach to behavior modification

The key to maintaining order in your classroom has nothing to do with tangible rewards. You don't have to give food, toys, stickers, and pencils as rewards for children, or spend any money at all, in order to gain their cooperation. In fact, teacher control can and should be replaced whenever possible by student self-control. How is this possible? The key is preventing problems before they start:

1) Have a routine in place for EVERYTHING and practice procedures, not punishment.

2) Have a very SIMPLE, positive whole-class reinforcement system and use individual modification plans for kids with behavioral issues.

3) Have a low-maintenance method for regular communication with parents about behavior.

4) Make general rules and consequences that are related and logical, and enforce them in ways that are appropriate for individual children.

5) Show kids the power of their influence on how the classroom is run and make a clear connection between the way THEY behave and the way YOU behave.

1) Have a routine in place for EVERYTHING and practice procedures, not punishment.

Know all of your rules and procedures to the tiniest detail, and if a child stretches those rules even a tiny bit, call them on it. You can get a little more laid back as the year goes on, but make no exceptions for any class rules at the beginning of the school year. Not only do students have to learn your expectations, they have to UNLEARN those of their previous teachers, since everyone has different standards and routines.

It's important not to make any assumptions about what kids know how to do. When I moved down to second grade from third, I said to the kids on the first day of school, "Hold the door for the person behind you" and noticed that all day the kids held the door for the entire class. I thought they just wanted to hold the door for the fun of it, but on the second day I realized that they didn't understand what I meant. Unlike my third graders, they were used to having a door holder and did not know how to simply touch the door until the person behind them touched it, and then walk on. We had to practice for a week and do follow-up reviews throughout the year on how to 'hold for the person behind you'. So, take nothing for granted, and prepare for all situations.

Remember, when it comes to procedures, students need PRACTICE, NOT PUNISHMENT! It will take weeks to get your students to where you want them to be, and you will have to continually reinforce their behavior all the way through June. Sure, you would think that by the second or third (or twelfth!) grade kids would automatically put the correct heading on their papers or behave a certain way in the hall, but the fact is, they don't do it without positive reinforcement. Please don't get frustrated in September because your kids still ask where to turn their papers in—keep practicing! It's NORMAL. Don't ease up and allow kids to get sloppy. Having your procedures firmly in place will make teaching easier and more effective throughout the entire year.

It can be tempting to punish kids when they don't do what we expect, but many times if we had really ingrained in students what they are supposed to do, they would comply by default. Here's an example of choosing procedure practice over punishment. I once had my second graders doing word wall work in journals. It was the fifth week of school and we had practiced DAILY which page students were supposed to write on (the page that said 'Word Walls for Sept. 13-17'). They *should* have all known to use one page for the whole week and not start a new blank page every day because it wastes paper. But of course, I saw a child who had started on a new page just seconds after I reminded the kids where to write.

I wanted to scream, "What did I just say!?! We've gone over and over this for five weeks! Why don't you follow directions? LISTEN!!" Fortunately I was able to control myself because that obviously would have been embarrassing for the child and just plain ineffective because he still wouldn't have known what to do. I took a deep breath and reminded myself that he was not purposely disobeying. In fact, whether he was listening to my directions or not was irrelevant, because the child should have been able to follow the procedure without hearing my reminder. Clearly he needed more practice because the procedure had not yet become automatic. I decided that if he wasn't going to listen, maybe I could put him on auto-pilot for such a routine task! So I said, "Which page should you be doing this on? A new page? So where should you be doing it? Let's find it" and stood at his desk waiting until he got to the right place. For the next three days, I stood right next to him as he flipped to the correct page and verbally reinforced the routine. By the end of the week, the procedure had become automatic.

This is the life of a primary-grade teacher: repeating and rephrasing and reinforcing and reminding EVERY SINGLE DAY until the last day of school (and I assure you, kids will still need reminders in June about how to walk in the hallways and to turn in their homework everyday). The sooner you accept the fact that repetition of procedures and routines is part of your job duty and plan accordingly, the happier you and your students will be.

2) Have a very SIMPLE, positive, whole-class reinforcement system and use individual modification plans for kids with behavioral issues.

I believe that the most effective whole-class plans are based on positive reinforcement for appropriate behavior. This is in direct contrast to punitive systems that use the 'descending levels' model and provide increasing consequences or punishment for misbehavior.

Typically, a whole-class plan that provides incentives for good behavior is enough to motivate the majority of children in your class and creates a much more supportive learning environment. The needs of more challenging students can be met through individual behavior modification plans which provide additional structure.

I know I'm going to be stepping on a lot of toes here, but I need to be honest. One extremely popular consequence-based whole class management tool is the 'card-flipping' system, in which children stay on 'green' if they follow class rules, and each time they misbehave, they 'flip a card' (e.g., yellow=a warning, red=phone call home). The majority of kids stay on green all day long, and therefore get no reinforcement or reward for their appropriate behavior. The system serves very little purpose for them other than basic accountability (which could have been accomplished with verbal reinforcement or a note home in the daily agenda). The minority of the class who are frequently in trouble find themselves on red by 9:00 in the morning. Then what? Exactly how many times can you call home to say a child was out of his seat and talking again? The system isn't effective for those kids, either.

Some children may benefit from having the card system as a visual reminder of their behavior, and the dynamic of the system improves when teachers allow students to flip their cards back towards green as they follow the rules later in the day. However, cards and play money and stickers and treasure boxes often become just another headache for teachers who already have too many things to keep track of, and end up not truly meeting the needs of any of the children.

Most elementary school children will generally do what they are supposed to when the expectation is developmentally appropriate and consistently modeled, practiced, and reinforced.

Little ones can be trained to work effectively and efficiently with the smallest of motivators, such as being chosen to pass out glue or line up first. They will respond if you reinforce appropriate behavior with compliments and simple reward systems that are based on incentives for positive behavior rather than on punishment for misbehavior. Most kids WANT to behave and do well, and they are successful when provided with enjoyable, motivating lessons.

There are classes that have an inordinate amount of troubled students, and those groups will need a highly structured whole-class system in addition to individual plans. But I encourage you to determine whether the behavior management system you use is meeting the needs of YOUR class, or if you're just doing it because everyone else in your school uses it. Just because something is popular doesn't mean it constitutes best practice.

Here are some examples of positive whole-class management systems that reinforce appropriate behaviors. The World's Easiest Token System and the Bead System are my own creations and are explained in further detail in Chapter 16.

- **The World's Easiest Token System:** This management plan is tied into classroom jobs: kids love to help out in the classroom, so why not let them earn the privilege?

- **The Bead System:** This is something I started a few years ago and the kids LOVE it! The system is very simple and basically involves rewarding students for making good choices by giving them beads, which can be traded in at the end of the week for privileges and/or rewards.

- **Team Points and Privileges:** These can be used as your whole-class management system or in conjunction with other plans such as the token or bead system. Team points are a great supplement in the beginning of the year and around holidays when it is especially difficult for kids to follow the rules and an additional incentive for following procedures is needed. I use the top right-hand corner of my board and just scrawl the team numbers on the board quickly, making tally marks whenever 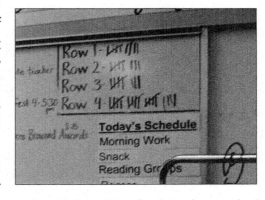 I give points. Groups can earn a point for being the first to have their materials ready, having everyone stay on-task during a lesson, etc. If I see one student doing something exceptional, I often give a point to the team on his behalf, which is a great boost for the child's self-confidence.

If the class is immature and needs regular incentives, I give a reward to the team with the most points at the end of the day. For more mature groups, I reward a team whenever they earn 20 points, which allows them to compete only against themselves since the point cycle is independent of all the other teams. Teams are allowed to select from a list of intangible rewards I created with student input (sitting on the couch during self-selected reading time, bringing a stuffed animal or something special from school to show the class and keep on their desks for a day, extra computer time, eating snack with me in the morning, etc.).

The rewards tied to team performance are always in addition to logical consequences and privileges. For example, the first team who is ready gets to line up first or pick a book bin first. Teams who talk and play around get called last. You can even allow the person on each team who has done the best job completing the task at hand (such as putting their materials put away quickly and quietly) to have a privilege when appropriate, such as passing papers out to their team or putting the manipulatives back on the shelf. All you have to say is, "I will be looking for someone from each team to..." and they will instantly sit up straight and tall with their hands folded!

3) Have a low-maintenance method for regular communication with parents about behavior.

If the majority of your class is well-behaved, you may not need an ongoing communication system with parents. When there is an incident that you feel a parent should know about, a great solution is to send home the child's own reflection on what happened. Filling out problem solving sheets will document misbehavior (which is important for conferences, office referrals, child study meetings, and so on), and more importantly, helps students reflect on their choices and responsibilities. Children can fill the out the sheets themselves or can dictate to you if they are unable to write independently. You can fit problem solving sheets into any behavior modification system you are using (whole class or individual): just add completing the sheet to the consequence for a certain type or level of misbehavior.

Problem Solving Sheet

Today I chose to_____

I made that choice because_____

Some better choices are _____

Next time I will _____

_____   _____   _____
Student Signature   Teacher Signature   Parent Signature

There are lots of strategies for communicating with parents about behavior in Chapter 31, but I'll share a synopsis here. One way I've communicated with parents is through daily reports, in which I signed off on children's agendas or notebooks each day. Another method is weekly evaluations, in which I tracked students' behavior throughout the week, marking off misbehavior and missing work as problems occurred, and then summarizing them on the weekly evaluation. Some years, I did those solely to document student behavior and work habits for my own purposes and to update parents. One year with a more difficult class, I also used it as a whole-class behavior management system, letting the kids know how many checks they had and giving rewards (Fun Friday) or consequences (missed recess) based on their performance. I really don't like using punitive systems anymore unless it's truly necessary, but I want to keep the details here as a resource for you, because only you can determine what is best for your class.

4) Make general rules and consequences that are related and logical, and enforce them in ways that are appropriate for individual children.

Behavior	Related Consequence
Playing around during group work	Finish assignment alone
Ripping up class materials	Not allowed to use them
Loses crayons	Can't color
Talking during instructions	Sit by yourself
Pushing at recess	Can't play that day
Name calling	Write an apology letter
Disrespecting teacher	Sent to another teacher's room for a short time*

Students should lose access to whatever they show disrespect towards, whether it's a place, thing, or person. It is a huge punishment for most kids to work in another classroom.

The chart shown here is NOT a list of hard-and-fast rules that should be hung up in the classroom. Every incident should be handled on a case-by-case basis, because each child and situation are different. However, there should be a common thread running throughout and all kids should see a clear connection between what they do and the resulting consequences. Taking away recess or centers isn't necessarily effective when the child wasn't having problems at recess or centers. I recommend tying the consequence directly to the child's action whenever possible.

5) Show kids the power of their influence on how the classroom is run and make a clear connection between the way THEY behave and the way YOU behave.

Students' cooperation or lack thereof has a remarkable effect on both the direction and outcome of a lesson. The problem is that children don't realize the power of their influence unless you point it out to them.

Students must be led to understand that when they follow the rules, you smile a lot, you give them privileges and additional freedom, and you trust them with fun activities. Similarly, they must learn that when they don't contribute to an orderly classroom, you have no choice but to pull in the reins. This must be taught EXPLICITLY at first—students do not automatically make the connection between what they do and what you do! And once you've taught them that their behavior affects how the classroom is run, you must reinforce this understanding throughout the day by responding CONSISTENTLY to behavioral infractions.

Teaching students about the connection between their behavior and yours is a relatively simple matter of pointing it out. When students play around while lining up, say with a disappointed face, "Well, I guess you're not ready. Have a seat, please. When it's quiet, I'll line you back up again." When students look unhappy, say, "I know, it makes me unhappy, too. I don't want to be late for lunch, either. The people who were playing around are causing me to miss my lunch time, too! But this is what I have to do when students misbehave, because I want them to learn to make good choices." When students do line up correctly the next time, let them see how the right decisions also influenced the way things happen in the classroom by saying, "Wow! Almost every single person got right to their spot and didn't say a word! I'm so impressed! See how fast and easy that was?　We're actually going to have an extra minute for our lunchtime because we didn't have to wait around on anyone!"

Another conversation I have from time to time with my kids is about their behavior during projects and hands-on activities.　If they start off well, I reinforce their behavior by saying, "Teachers don't like using manipulatives when kids play around, talk to people, don't listen to directions, and don't clean things up the right way.　Those behaviors make teachers say, forget it!　But when I see you all following along with me, using the materials the right way, listening to what I'm saying...that makes me want to use manipulatives with you all of the time.　The more you behave like this when we do special projects, the more projects we'll do."

**Students need to see privileges for what they are, and work for them.
But they will only put forth effort if they believe it will impact the outcome.**

Conversations like the ones above have a tremendous effect on my students. When I say, "Today we're going to use fraction tiles," immediately five or six kids say, "Oh, thank you, Ms. Powell!"　The whole class sits up straight and folds their hands automatically.　They know from experience that I'll only give them a few chances before saying, "You all aren't showing me that this is something you want to do.　You're doing your own thing and you're not trying to learn.　Please put the materials back in their bag.　I'm going to give you a page in your workbook to do instead.　If you are responsible with that, then maybe we'll try again tomorrow with the manipulatives."

When students understand that their behavior impacts the way the classroom is run, they will be more motivated to cooperate with the routines and rules you've put in place.　They will demonstrate a more positive attitude toward you and a willingness to work together with their classmates toward a common goal.　They will show gratitude for the little things you allow them to do, and will think carefully about how to show you they are responsible and ready for additional privileges.

When You're Not Seeing Results

Never under-estimate the importance of teaching and reinforcing routines and procedures. In addition, you must set behavioral expectations and enforce them consistently throughout the year. It's critically important to model problem solving strategies and good character. If you're doing these things, you have a whole-class reward system in place, and you've developed individual plans for students who need extra support, you should notice a major change in your classroom since the first day of school. If you are not seeing results, the reason probably stems from one of two problems.

Unclear Expectations

The first possibility is that you think you've effectively taught students your expectations and are consistently enforcing them, but you're not. Your kids are still unclear about what to do and you need to spend more time teaching routines and procedures. This is usually the case when children are respectful towards the teacher, but need an unusual and excessive amount of support and guidance. Reread the section called "Precise Expectations" in Chapter 9, and make sure students understand how you want them to behave.

A Lack of Respect

The other possibility is that your students do not respect you. That's a very painful thing to consider, but if kids are ignoring your requests and disregarding the routines you've explicitly taught them, then you are dealing with a lack of respect. If your students are questioning you, arguing with you, and making up their own rules, then you haven't established that you're in charge. Your students may like you. But they don't respect you. Developing a good rapport is about mutual respect. You can bribe students to like you by giving them candy and rewards. You can never bribe someone to respect you.

Thousands of new teachers every year encounter this problem, especially in high-poverty neighborhoods (see Chapter 18). They follow the advice of every successful teacher and mentor in the school. Yet their students still run, yell, fight, talk over them, and generally create such a chaotic atmosphere that it is impossible for any real learning to take place. Clearly, this is a respect issue. And my theory is that the teachers who are not respected by their students are simply NOT BEING FIRM ENOUGH and NOT BEING CONSISTENT.

There are teachers who swing the opposite way, who are incredibly mean-spirited and uncaring. Their students pick up on the "I don't like you and I don't care about you" vibe, and respond accordingly. But most elementary teachers have the opposite problem. They care too much about making sure the kids are having a great time at school. They worry about being perceived as 'mean' and having their kids not like them.

I PROMISE YOU **that if you show elementary school students that you genuinely care about them by listening to and valuing their ideas, they WILL like you, no matter how often you have to take away privileges and correct them!!**

I remember my parents saying before they disciplined me, "This is going to hurt us more than it will hurt you." I never believed that until I became a teacher. There are times when I give myself a pep talk, like, *I really wish I didn't have to do this, but here goes*...and really lay into the kids. IT HAS TO BE DONE. It is not fun. Usually it doesn't feel good afterwards. But if your students are running your classroom, then you MUST reinforce ALL of your expectations, with no exceptions. Every. Single. Time. Never say to yourself, *Next year, I'm going to be much harder on my kids during the first month of school.* Don't wait—be strict with your students NOW! You cannot afford to waste a single day stressed out and exhausted while your students' education suffers.

Chapter 15: Teaching Children to Be Self-Reliant
Encouraging independence and self-sufficiency in the classroom

Do your students follow you around the room to ask questions? Are they constantly seeking your approval with comments such as "How does this look?" and "Did I do it right?" Are they unable to take out a textbook and turn to the right page without you guiding them through the process? Are your reading groups continually interrupted by students who can't work independently for longer than three minutes?

If so, then you need to address the neediness factor in your classroom. Children must be taught self-reliance, especially since some of them are babied at home by family members. They have to learn to problem solve for themselves in order to function in school and later in life.

The independence and self-confidence that many students lack is what drains so many teachers. They are exhausted from incessantly being the focus of everything that happens in the classroom. Many feel like traffic directors in a busy intersection, constantly on watch and telling everyone where to go and what to do. The whole system falls apart without them. But traffic directors are unnecessary when there's a working stoplight: things function in a fairly orderly way because there's an automatic and predictable system in place.

That system is what you need to create in your classroom—students need to rely on the procedures and routines they've learned, not you. They need to depend on their problem solving skills, and stop expecting you to make things right in every scenario throughout the day.

Setting Teacher-Student Boundaries

Getting the Teacher's Attention Appropriately

I use a lot of choral response during instruction and don't always have kids raise their hands to answer questions I pose while teaching. However, any unsolicited comments or questions must be preceded by hand raising. In kid language, that means students must always raise their hands when they have a question for me or something they need to tell me.

I never allow students to call out questions like "Can we use markers on this?" even if I am standing right next to the child. I'll smile and say, "Raise your hand first." I wait for the child to do so, then say, "Yes, honey" and listen to the question.

Students are also not allowed to come up to me while I'm sitting at my desk, teaching reading groups, assisting other students, etc. One of my pet peeves is having children follow me around the room to ask questions. I can't stand turning around and nearly stepping on a little person who's three inches away, waving a paper in my face and saying, "Is this right?" I'll say politely, "Have a seat and raise your hand."

Following the teacher around and getting out of one's seat to ask a question is a hard habit to break, especially since many teachers allow it. The mantra, "Have a seat and raise your hand" must be repeated many times for some children before it becomes automatic. You may feel silly making a child go all the way back to her desk and sit down, only for you to call on her so she can come back over to you, but it's necessary. If you say, "Next time, raise your hand," the child won't remember. The physical act of having to redo the whole process is what reinforces the procedure.

Your expectation for students to raise their hands before asking a question will need to be reinforced a lot throughout the year for certain children. Most kids will get it quickly if you don't make any exceptions and enforce the procedure consistently. If you do want students to be able to come up to you at certain points in the day, you can make that clear to them. During our writing block, for instance, students are allowed to bring me their journals so I can check whether they are ready to move on to the next step of the writing process. I put a sign on the board that says, 'Please come show me your work when you're done.' For the vast majority of the school day, students cannot just walk up to me for approval of something, so the sign signals that there's a special exception during this assignment. Also, I sit at the front of the classroom right by the sign during the writing block, and that change also signals to students that the procedure is different.

Using the 3 Before Me Rule

Another of my pet peeves is having students ask me questions that they should already know the answer to. I cringe when children ask, *Is it time for lunch yet? What chapter did you say? Are we supposed to write our names on this*?

A pro-active solution is to teach students the 3 Before Me rule. Explain to children that there are twenty kids in the class and one adult, so it's exhausting for the teacher to have to keep saying the same things over and over. Tell them that there are many issues which students should not need to consult with a teacher about because they can either figure the answer out on their own or ask a friend.

Introduce the 3 Before Me Rule: if you have a question, ask three people in the class, and if none of them can answer it, then you can ask a teacher**. *I like to teach my students that the first person they should ask is themselves*.** I explain that sometimes people feel lazy and want someone else to do the thinking for them. However, if they really thought about it they could usually figure out the answer on their own. We talk about how that's a very mature and responsible way to handle problems, and discuss the importance of drawing conclusions and making personal inferences, since these are terms that students will learn during reading instruction. For example, no should ask the teacher if it's snack time yet, because they can look around the room and draw their own conclusion. If they see nine other children eating, it must be okay to have snack.

I give an example of a 3 Before Me question, such as "What time is it?" and demonstrate how to ask myself the question first. "Hmm, what time is it? Can I figure that out myself? If I can, then I don't need to bother anybody. If I can't, then I should ask someone else. Let's see, I'm feeling confused about whether it's 10:30 or 11:30, so I will quietly whisper to the person next to me, being careful not to speak so loudly that everyone around me can hear. [In a whisper] Demi, can you read the clock for me? Demi knew the answer, so I could just go back to work.

Let's say she didn't know. What would I do next? Right, Stefan is on the other side of me, so I'll whisper to him, Stefan, do you know what time it is? Now if Stefan didn't know either, then I would have asked three people: myself, Demi, and Stefan. So now I can ask the teacher."

To help kids understand what questions they should use the 3 Before Me rule for, I have a few examples written on strips of paper and put in a bag. I call students up to draw a slip, read it, and call on someone to tell whether it's a 3 Before Me Question. I guide students to understand that something like, "Can I call my mom to tell her I forgot my lunch money?" is something only the teacher can answer, so the child should raise his or her hand right away. Something like, "What's the date?" is a 3 Before Me Question, because the child can probably figure it out by asking him or herself first, and checking with two other kids if needed. A grown-up is not the only one who could answer that question.

I also throw in some trick questions such as, "Can I get a drink of water?" and "Can I sharpen my pencil?" These are actually 3 Before Me questions because students should understand whether the teacher has given or withheld permission implicitly through instruction in routines and procedures. A child should not have to ask whether he can get a drink because he's already learned the appropriate times and can check the posted sign for reference. Similarly, a child would not need to ask me if she can sharpen her pencil, because every day, I only allow students to do that before 8:15.

If you use the 3 Before Me procedure with your students, you'll have to remember it when you hear kids whispering during quiet independent work. On more than one occasion, I've asked students to stop talking only to have them say truthfully, "I had a 3 Before Me question" (to which I respond, "Oh, okay. But make sure you're whispering because I can hear you over here"). It can be irritating to hear occasional chatter from students helping each other, but it's far better for them to problem solve with each other than to involve you in every trivial concern.

Responding to Attention-Seeking Behaviors

Praise vs. Encouragement

Sometimes students are too needy because they're used to hearing praise and compliments, and can't function without them. Psychologists sometimes call this approval addiction, and if children carry that into their adult relationships, they're in for a lot of heartache.

Children must to learn to rely on their own evaluations of themselves. Our verbal reinforcement should direct them to form independent opinions as often as possible. Even a positive judgment is in fact a judgment when it comes from another person.

Praise causes children to become dependent on us and our evaluations of how they're doing, whereas encouragement states what children have done so they can make their own evaluations. We need children to say, "I did it!" instead of, "How did I do?" Praise serves no real function—it is unnecessary when students feel safe in the classroom, and insufficient when they don't.

When a child says...	Replace this evaluative response...	With this one that fosters self-reliance...
"Does this look good?"	"Yes, it's beautiful!"	"What do YOU think?"
"Look what I did!"	"I'm proud of you!"	"You should be really proud of yourself!"
"Do you like it?"	"Yes, you did a great job!"	"You really worked hard! I bet you're really impressed with yourself!"
"Is this right?"	"Yes, very good!"	"The directions said to __. Is that what you did? Okay, so you've got it!"
"Do you think this is good?"	"I think it's great!"	"Is it your very best work? Then you should feel great about what you did!"

An important part of encouragement is providing non-evaluative feedback to students, commenting on what you see rather than judging it. Ask questions about what a child accomplished to draw his attention back to the work itself and motivate him to do more:

- I see you've written a lot for the middle of your story!
- I'm noticing a lot of hearts in your picture—you must like hearts a lot!

- You're finishing up your Morning Work! Now you'll get to pick a book to read. I wonder which one you'll get...
- You've solved every problem on this page!
- You finished reading that entire book in twenty minutes! I remember when it would take you several days to get through something that long. You're becoming more fluent all the time!

These types of questions and comments encourage children to take pride in their own accomplishments and stay focused on what they've done, rather than someone else's evaluation of it. They build students' self-confidence and self-reliance by encouraging the child to reflect on his own meaningful achievements.

Fostering Self-Control

Teacher Control vs. Self Control

When students follow the rules in order to get a reward that is meted out by the teacher, they are really behaving in order to please the teacher. It is the teacher's judgment that determines whether a child gets a prize, so the child's own reflection is irrelevant and self-reliance is not developed. And since it is also the teacher's evaluation that determines when a punishment is enforced, responsibility shifts to the teacher rather than the child for his own actions and he blames the teacher for the outcome.

If natural consequences are used and feedback is non-evaluative, the student learns to determine for herself whether a behavior was appropriate. Children learn what works and what doesn't based on results, rather than waiting for an adult to pronounce a behavior as acceptable or unacceptable. Understanding the effects of one's actions is what leads to having an internal locus of control and the ability to independently regulate one's own behavior.

Using Effective Questions to Redirect Behavior

It is absolutely infuriating when we as teachers have to repeat directions we've already given a million times. Students already know what they should be doing, so they tune us out, and we say it again. The cycle repeats endlessly. The teacher tells the student what to do and the child never learns self-control.

You can place the responsibility of solving the problem with the student. Ask questions that redirect behavior and require the child to determine a more appropriate action:

Commands in which the teacher tells the student what to do	Questions in which students must solve the problem on their own
Put that away right now!	Where should that paper be?
Get in line!	Where is your place in line?
Spit that gum out!	What is our rule about chewing gum?
Stop talking!	What should you be doing right now?

In response to the question, the child will typically pause, think, and then self-correct either through a verbal response or change in action. The teacher has not given a command for the child to rebel against, and the child has not had to 'give in' because she was never told what to do. The student determined the solution and chose her behavior. This then provides the teacher with an opportunity to reinforce appropriate decision-making by saying something encouraging:

- Exactly.
- Thank you for fixing that.
- Good choice.
- I knew you would figure out the right thing to do.
- You got it.
- Yes.

Of course, not all questions inspire self-reliance and problem solving. Many times we ask questions that we don't really want to hear students answer. Inquiries such as, "Why do I hear talking?" rarely have any productive response from students. They should be replaced with authentic questions that, when answered by the student, will provide a positive change in behavior.

Replace 'why' questions that students can't answer constructively...	With questions that prompt students to think of appropriate behaviors...
Why are you out of your seat again?	Where should you be right now?
Why do you have that on your desk?	What should be on your desk during math?
Why are you sitting there doing nothing?	What should you be working on?
Why are you pushing her?	Where should your hands be?
Why are you out of line?	How should you be standing?

Untangling Yourself from Petty Issues During Instruction

It's not necessary or appropriate to turn every minor dilemma into a major problem solving session. Sometimes you're beating a dead horse, sometimes the child isn't ready to accept the answer, and sometimes you're actually teaching academics and can't afford to bring the lesson to a screeching halt because someone stepped on a person's pencil and broke it.

Every primary-grade teacher needs a quick response to the repetitive complaints we hear daily. The goal is to reassure students that they are in a safe and orderly environment, encourage them to take personal responsibility for their actions, and teach them to problem solve independently... all while spending as little time as possible addressing the problem.

You cannot allow yourself to be sucked into arguments and circular reasoning with children, especially during instruction. The following are some of the lines I have used that seem to be the most effective in terms of satisfying the child and allowing me to resume teaching. These lines have worked with MY kids, as part of MY personal teaching style. Choose the ones that you think will be right for YOUR situation, and use them consistently. Soon your kids will already know what you're going to say before you open your mouth, and that consistency will work wonders in preventing further problems.

Student	Teacher
"Is it time for lunch/P.E./recess yet?"	(Looking at the clock pointedly) "Is it?" (Wait for the child to answer—the goal is for the child to figure it out for himself.)
"She said my pencil is ugly!"	(Very seriously) "Thank you for telling me." (No follow-up necessary.)
"What page are we on? What are we supposed to do?"	(Silence. Blinking. The child will figure out that she needs to look around the room, or ask another child, assuming you've taught the 3 Before Me rule or something similar.)
"I can't find my paper/book/eraser!"	(With a shrug and a sad smile) "Sorry, sweetie, I don't know where it is, either."
"I'm done!" "Look!"	(Nod solemnly. If repeated, say gently: "Okay, thanks. You don't need to show me any more.")
"My mom wants to know what time the field trip is on Friday."	(With 'teacher look') "Does this have anything to do with math? So when should you ask me? Thank you." [The correct answer for me is during morning warm up, recess, or bus call time].
"But he was talking, too!"	(Looking puzzled) "You're not in trouble because *he* was talking. You're in trouble because *you* were talking."
(When two children are both blaming each other) "I didn't do anything, she did!"	"You two are being very rude to each other and you're supposed to be working. Please control yourselves and be quiet. If you're still bothered by what happened, come tell me about it at recess."
"But she started it!"	"Then you need to finish it! How can you handle it next time when someone does that to you?"
"She said she's not my friend anymore!"	"It's okay for friends to get mad at each other and want some time apart. Let her cool off and try to talk to her tomorrow. I promise you that no second grader has ever stayed mad at a friend forever. Until she's ready, who else can you choose to work with?"

And of course, learn what lines DON'T work in your classroom. These are things I've actually heard teachers say (or have said myself in desperation) that should typically be avoided:

Teacher's Line	Why I Think It Can Be Ineffective
"Sit down!"	This is a direct command, which means it can cause a confrontation with some kids if barked like an order. I have found that a very firm, "Have a seat" works just as well and sounds much less like the teacher has lost control.
"Honey, don't you want to come over to the rug and have a seat?"	This line can cause a misunderstanding due to either the child's young age or a cultural gap between the child and the teacher. Many children regard these types of questions as a choice. *Why, no,* they think. *I wouldn't like to come over to the rug, I'd like to keep playing.* Who could blame them? A clearer but still kind direction is, "Come join us on the rug, Terrell." Remember, if it's not a choice, don't phrase it like one. Kids are literal thinkers.
Anything sarcastic	This is the hardest one for me personally because I have a dry sense of humor. However, sarcasm is lost on young children. It certainly feels good to say, but rarely gets your point across. Many times children think you are agreeing with them when you are being sarcastic, because after all, they say what they think. If you say, "Yes, the middle of a math test is the perfect time to go find your lunchbox on the playground, please, go right now!" the child is likely to do it! Little ones just can't grasp why anyone would say the opposite of how they really feel.
"If one more person talks out today, the field trip is cancelled!"	First of all, expecting the entire class to be quiet for a whole day is unrealistic. Someone will talk and you'll end up punishing the whole class for what one person did, which is unfair to the innocent and turns the class against the talker. But the worst part about this line is that you're bluffing. The bus is scheduled, volunteers are lined up, bag lunches are ordered—the class is going on the field trip no matter what, and an empty threat like this teaches children you don't mean what you say.

Teaching Kids to Solve Social Problems Independently

Considering Your Students' Developmental Level

The amount of explicit teaching you'll have to do in this area will depend on the age of your students. When I taught Pre-Kindergarten, I modeled and reinforced social problem solving constantly. In fact, it was one of my initial lessons on the first day of school. We talked about how to use our words when we were upset and to say, "I don't like that." It's almost impossible to argue with the statement, "I don't like that" because it expresses the person's own feelings with no judgment about the other person. I never forced the recipient of the comment to apologize because I wanted their words to be sincere. Instead, I taught to them 'to do something to make it right' or 'make it better'. This could be done by saying, "Okay" or "I'll stop" or "I'm sorry." If the child was hurt, the offender could ask, "Are you okay?" and sit quietly with the person until she was ready to go play again.

Older children have usually learned to problem solve and need a refresher course about what's expected at school after having been home all summer. They also need to understand your precise expectations for them and the level of intervention you're willing to provide in student conflicts.

With third graders, I typically explain on the first day of school that I expect them to work out their own problems because they are mature enough to handle them without my assistance. However, I will facilitate their conversations if they need me to. I define 'facilitate' as 'listen and guide'. That means I won't solve the problem for them, but I will listen as they talk to each other and guide them to make decisions together about what to do.

Discussing Physical Confrontations and the Self-Defense Argument

Students need to be taught about the consequences for fighting and being physically aggressive in school, and trained to respond to conflicts in other ways. I usually have an in-depth discussion about the concept of, "If someone hits me, my mom said I have to hit them back." This is an extremely common sentiment in some communities that cannot be easily deprogrammed in children. Many kids will be expected to fight back if something happens in their neighborhood, or even in their homes, and this expectation applies to school, as well. The families teach their children to defend themselves, as well as their close friends and relatives (i.e., if someone hits your cousin and you're standing there, you better stand up for your cousin).

The 'self-defense' concept is one that you must accept as reality for many children. You cannot control what happens outside of school. You can and should discuss the consequences of the street code, but you cannot change it. I try to be very practical with my kids when we talk about this during the first week of school. A sample conversation is written here. The tone should be non-judgmental, non-emotional, and very matter-of-fact, with a clear indication in your voice that you care about the children and you want them to make the best possible decisions for their lives. You are not just telling them what will happen if they are violent, you are trying to teach them to think about where violence leads.

I will caution that you are dealing with reality in the classroom and there's no room for sugarcoating (as you may have been taught to do with children). I can say from experience that kids understand and relate to conversations like the one that follows, and they learn to make good decisions when you speak to them from a relevant place.

A Sample Discussion About the Consequences of Fighting

"Let's talk about what to do when someone hits you or tries to hurt you in any way. What should you do in those situations? [Elicit responses, encouraging those who suggest the 'right thing'. Almost inevitably, someone will mention that they were told by their parents to hit back. If no one does, you can skip the next three paragraphs and talk directly about what happens when you hit someone in school].

"Okay, so let's take a look at what she said. Some people think you should do something back when someone pushes, hits, kicks, or tries to hurt you. That's called 'retaliate'. If you hit someone back or retaliate in your neighborhood, very bad things can happen even if the other person started it. Hitting someone is called 'assault' and it is a crime. You can go to jail for it. If the other person can convince a police officer that you hit them first, you could go to jail. Or, both of you go could go to jail for fighting.

"That's not all. Anytime you hit someone back, you're going to make them angrier, and they're going to hit you again. Then you will have to hit them again. That could go on for a very long time and hurt a lot. Also, you might retaliate against someone who is stronger than you or has more friends around who all gang up on you. You could get really hurt if no one is around to stop the fight. The person you hit back could also tell his friends and relatives and they could come and hurt you and your family later.

"I'm telling you all of this not to make you scared of people in your neighborhood, but to make you think twice before hitting anyone back. Fighting is extremely dangerous. You never know where it's going to end. It might not end until you're in the hospital or jail. So if someone tells you to do something back to people when they mess with you, you will have to decide whether that's the best decision. It is always your choice how to respond to people bullying you. But, there can be very serious consequences when you choose to fight back, and I really hope you think about that before you put your hands on anyone.

"So, I can't control what you do in your neighborhood, and I'm not going to mention those things again. I am in charge of what happens with you in school. Someone tell us about what happens if you hit someone in school, even if they hit you first... Exactly. Serious trouble. You will get an office referral, you could be suspended, which means you're not allowed to come to school, or even expelled, which means you'll never be allowed back in school. So you must learn how to talk out your problems in school. You will need to do that in other places away from your neighborhood, too: your after-school program, later on in college, and on your job... can you imagine if every time another teacher made me mad, I hit her?! I would lose my job! So to get an education and a job, you have to be able to solve problems using only words, even if someone tries to hurt you.

"What should you do if someone tries to hurt you in school? Right—if you tell a teacher, the OTHER kid will get in trouble. But if you hit the kid back, you BOTH get in trouble. You have to always tell me when someone tries to hurt you—don't ever hit back. Once you put your hands on somebody, I can't help you anymore, because you're in the wrong. But if you tell me that they tried to hurt you, and you used words and then told me, I can stand up for you and make sure that child is punished. So if you want my help, you have to do the right thing."

This is a very lengthy conversation (about fifteen to twenty minutes), especially since children will be waving their hands eagerly in the air to share their own experiences. I encourage a lot of discussion throughout the conversation because I want kids to make connections to their lives and ask questions that will help them make better decisions in the future.

Be prepared for a few off-the-wall statements. If someone comments, "My brother's cousin went to jail because someone brought a gun and said they was gonna shoot him but my cousin got a rock and..." gently stop the child by saying, "That sounds like some personal family information. We don't want to talk much about bad choices other people have made. We want to stay focused on how we can make the right decisions for ourselves." If a child asks a wacky question like, "What should we do if someone at school says they're going to beat us up after school and to meet them at the bike rack but we go the bike rack and they're not there, but they're waiting for us at our house..." interrupt the child and say encouragingly, "Let me stop you there, because it sounds like you're either making up something really outrageous that will probably never happen to any of us, like, what if a Martian lands on the school and shoots us? Or, you're asking me what to do in a specific situation that already happened to you or someone you know. If you're just saying something wacky, then let's forget about the idea for now and handle the situation if it ever comes up. We'll just apply our problem solving skills to any new issue and we'll get through it. If you're telling us about something real, then I'd like for you to speak to me about it at recess to talk about your personal situation."

I usually have the discussion again a few times during the year as situations arise. This reinforces what I've already taught the students and allows them to integrate new experiences with familiar information.

Handling Peer Conflicts As They Arise

Determining When and How to Intervene

When I hear students having problems with each other in the classroom, I rarely intervene and instead listen to see how the kids work things out by themselves. Many times they see me watching and start using appropriate problem solving strategies. If things end well, I compliment the children specifically on what I heard ("I heard you two arguing about who was supposed to be ahead at the water fountain. I thought that was very mature for Hallie to let Karen go ahead of her instead of continuing to debate back and forth. And I heard Karen say thank you when she stepped ahead. That was extremely polite. You all handled that exactly the right way"). If the conversation deteriorates and it's clear students will need help, I step in by saying, "Would you two like some help in solving your problem?" This is also my response when students tattle on each other. Many times children don't actually have a problem, they have a miscommunication, and just need help understanding one another.

An Example of Facilitation Using Active Listening

"Okay, take a deep breath. Let's relax. We're going to get a resolution and things are going to be fine in a moment. I'm going to have James tell me what happened, and Roberto is going to listen, without interrupting. Then Roberto's going to tell his side, and James is going to listen. Everyone will get to defend themselves. James, what's going on? Hold on, Roberto, it's James' turn, I promise you'll get a chance. Go ahead, James.... Okay, now let's hear Roberto.... James, do you have anything to say about that?... Roberto?"

I let the kids get everything out, responding back to each other until they run out of words, which is usually pretty quickly. I say as little as possible because I want the children to be able to repeat the same process when I'm not around. The only purpose I'm serving is as a facilitator—someone to listen and make sure things are done in an orderly manner. In this role, I use active listening techniques (repeating what the child has said and rephrasing things to make sure we understand each other, without interjecting any ideas of my own).

When they're done talking, I pick up on a common point or hint of resolution the kids were heading towards. "So James, you're upset because Roberto said you can't play football. And Roberto's saying yes, you can play, you just have to ask Antuan first, because it's his ball. Is that right? So we have a miscommunication here. What needs to happen now to solve this problem?... You have a plan. Roberto, you're going to go with James while he asks if he can play. If that doesn't work, you can let me know and I'll help you finish solving the problem, okay?"

If the kids are too emotional at that point, I steer the conversation toward a resolution by helping them understand each other's underlying feelings. "I'm hearing that you're both still angry and not quite ready to let this go. It sounds like James felt really upset because he was left out, and Roberto felt upset because James wasn't understanding what he needs to do. So the problem is, James wants to play, but the ball doesn't belong to Roberto. Do you think that Roberto, you could go over with James to Antuan and ask if he could play, too?"

There are a lot of different ways to help children problem solve—you can even teach them active listening techniques. For me, the most important thing is that I don't provide a solution unless the kids are totally stuck. I want my children to know that they can come to me if they need assistance with a dispute, but I don't want them to think that I will solve it for them. Over time, the kids realize that all I'm going to do is repeat what they've said to each other and ask questions. They recognize that they are responsible for coming up with a solution, and most of the time they feel good about trying to do this on their own.

Tattling

When children know how to effectively problem solve on their own, they won't become frustrated and resort to telling the teacher. Sometimes it seems as though children *could* handle a situation independently, but tell on each other for the enjoyment of getting a peer in trouble. ***However, students often tattle because they are unsure about which situations concern them and which don't***. One minute teachers say, "Don't just sit there, help her pick those crayons up!" and the next we say, "Do your work and let her take care of herself!" We say, "You *knew* he was writing those rude things on the cover of that book and you didn't do anything?!" and then an hour later snap, "Worry about yourself—that doesn't concern you!"

We must have clear expectations about how we want children to respond to rule and procedural infractions. I teach my kids to tell the person who's breaking the rule BEFORE they tell me. For example, if a student says, "Jason's on a game website instead of using the reading software," I reply, "Did you tell him that's against the rules?" If the child says no, I say, "Okay, go tell him. I'll watch." This almost always resolves the situation because the offending child is aware that I'm looking and responds appropriately. If the tattler says yes, she did tell the offender, then I say, "Okay, you've handled it the right way! Thank you!" and that's the end of it. Sometimes the tattler will insist that the offender didn't listen to her, so I say, "Go tell him again, and this time I'll watch." If that doesn't resolve the situation, I call the offender over myself and talk with him.

Teaching kids how to respond to one another's corrections is also important. Children have a tendency to say things like, "Leave me alone" or "Mind your own business" if the teacher has sent mixed messages about listening to peers. I decided several years ago that I would send a consistent message to my students that they are in fact responsible for one another, because that's the type of classroom community I want to create. "Worry about yourself" is a phrase that I try very hard not to use, and I expect the kids not to say those types of things, either. Instead, we talk about the difference between being bossy and being helpful:

> *"Being bossy is telling someone what YOU want them to do. Being helpful is telling them what the TEACHER needs them to do. Being bossy is saying, 'You have to play the math game my way.' Being helpful is saying, 'We have to take turns rolling the dice the way Ms. Powell showed us.'*

> *"When someone is trying to be helpful and remind you about a class rule, you need to say, 'Okay' or 'Thanks.' You should not get mad or argue with someone who tells you not to push in line, or that you shouldn't be playing with a toy in your desk. Your friend is being helpful, because everyone in our room is responsible for following the rules. Remember: when you make good decisions and follow the rules, people won't HAVE to tell you what to do, so if you want to be left alone, then do the right thing! If someone is trying to be bossy and tell you what THEY want you to do, then you need to say, 'That's not helpful'. The person should stop bothering you right away, and if they don't, you can let me know.*

> *"If you have a problem with someone not listening to you, you can tell me. I will watch you go back and talk to that person. If that doesn't work, I will facilitate your problem solving. But you need to talk to each other before you talk to me."*

Be very careful how you respond to kids 'telling on' each other. What teachers may view as a minor issue can be very significant to children, and if you disregard their feelings, you may have to answer to their parents later on. Children often complain to mom or dad, who then ask, "Did you tell your teacher? What did she say?" and the child replies honestly, "She told me to mind my own business" or "She said go play, don't worry about it." Therefore, your response must be appropriate and make a good 'sound bite', should the child repeat it. If I'm in the middle of a lesson or otherwise engaged and can't ask, "Did you talk about it with her?", I'll say in serious tone, "I will handle it" or "Thank you for telling me."

If you teach students how to help one another without being bossy, and how to respond appropriately when another child reminds them of a rule or tries to do social problem solving, you will encounter far less incidents of tattle-telling and see major breakthroughs in the level of self-sufficiency demonstrated in your classroom.

Chapter 16: Whole-Class Reinforcement Systems
Two simple plans for rewarding students' efforts toward self-discipline

It may surprise you to see a chapter on reward systems after reading so much information about intrinsic motivation and teaching children to self-regulate their behavior. However, there is a very definite place for whole-class rewards in the elementary classroom, should the teacher choose to use them.

Why Have Reward Systems?

Children have very high expectations placed on them in school. Most kids exert a tremendous amount of self-discipline for hours every day: sitting still, not talking, staying in line, listening when they're bored, struggling through challenging new material, having no control over their daily schedule, being told when to use the bathroom and when to eat, having to get along with immature and annoying classmates whom they're forced to sit inches away from all day long...think about how hard it really is to be a student!

There must be a balance between teaching students to behave for intrinsic reasons and having something meaningful to work towards. As teachers, we show up to work everyday on time because it's the right thing to do, not because we're expecting a reward...but we wouldn't show up at all if we weren't getting paid at the end of the week.

There has to be some significant motivation for people to put forth a great deal of sustained effort over time. Students should be taught to see the big picture and the value of their education in terms of future success, but they are *children*. They need to have a more immediate pay-off that's tied directly to the challenges they face every day.

One year, I decided not to have a whole-class reward system. I wanted my students to work hard because it was the right thing to do, and to respect me because I respected them. I stuck to my basic teaching philosophy as described in this book, and it worked. Students were self-controlled, followed procedures, and learned a lot. But they were tired. My district required me to use standardized test practice daily and the kids' minds were pushed to the limit without any end or relief in the foreseeable future. There was nothing in particular to look forward to in school. Summer vacation would come whether students were on-task and earned A's or drove me crazy and earned D's. What difference would it make in the quality of their daily lives if they tried their best?

When the same thing happened the following school year, I realized I had to go back to giving some sort of incentive for students to put forth the massive amount of effort required of them each day. There had to be a type of celebration or special time for those students who worked hard and genuinely tried to make good choices for themselves. That's when I began using the Bead System described in the second half of this chapter, and I've stuck to it ever since.

I *want* to give my kids rewards. I enjoy doing things that make them happy when I see their efforts and progress. **Also, I view whole-class reward systems as a type of 'positive consequence' for responsible behavior, rather than an incentive for it. If the rewards were an incentive, I would need to give more when children are unruly and less when they follow the rules. But the opposite is true.** With my most recent group of students, I actually increased the amount and type of rewards they could earn with beads because they were so consistently on-task. I *wanted* to give them more good things because they were so respectful, kind, and hard-working.

This chapter will explain in detail how to use two original whole-class behavior management plans, one using tokens and the other beads. Both are rewards-based, rather than consequence-based. The two systems are extremely flexible and can be adapted to fit the needs of any class. I hope that my ideas will inspire you to design a system that rewards students for their progress as they learn to be productive, responsible members of the classroom community.

The World's Easiest Token System

This was the first behavior management plan I designed for primary grade students, and the popularity of this system continues to astound me! I posted it on my website many years ago and had no idea just how well it would resonate with other educators. There are literally hundreds of teachers around the world who have used this plan, which I named 'The World's Easiest Token System' after researching complicated token economies that had me exhausted by the time I got through reading them.

The system described here was featured in the April 19, 2005 edition of Education World and was listed as a resource in a token economy article that was published in conjunction with that organization on the National Education Association's website shortly thereafter. While I love creating new plans and have since experimented with numerous other behavior management systems over the years, the World's Easiest Token System will always be special to me because of its powerful resonance with other teachers and its positive impact on so many classrooms.

Why This System Works

The token system is effective because it DOES NOT require:

- ➢ you to track each child's behavior in order to penalize or reward
- ➢ the entire class to 'behave' in order to be rewarded
- ➢ you to punish those who did behave due to actions of those who didn't
- ➢ the same behavioral standards for everyone
- ➢ students who are frequently in trouble to get all of the reinforcement
- ➢ any money to be spent on candy or prizes
- ➢ the staging of elaborate rewards
- ➢ a complicated class helper system (tokens assign many job privileges)
- ➢ class time that should be spent on academics
- ➢ a lot of maturity in students: even preschoolers can participate

Setting Up the Token System

Find some chips, tokens, cubes, or whatever items you can access—even small laminated slips of paper will work. 10-20 per child should be enough.

Assign personal identification numbers (PINs), and write them on your tokens. If your students don't have numbers for another purpose, assign them for this. (You could write children's names on the tokens, but then you will have to make a new set each school year and whenever new kids transfer to your class.) Keep each group of tokens sorted into separate sections in some kind of

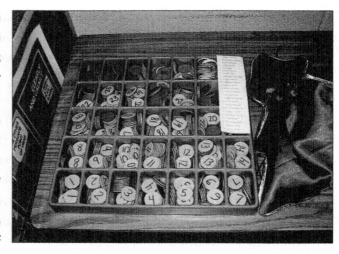

container, like a tackle box or craft supply organizer. Last, find or make a box or bag to put the tokens in when they are awarded. I use a sparkly purple and gold drawstring bag I found from a dollar store a few years ago. You only need one for the whole class.

Introducing the System to Students

Explain to your class that each teacher has a method for rewarding good behavior in students. Ask them to recall some of the ways other teachers have rewarded them, e.g., stickers, play money for a class store, or a paperclip chain to earn a pizza party. Be prepared to limit the discussion, as rewards will be a very popular topic!

Discuss with the kids how they might have earned those rewards in previous classes. Encourage specific responses. This is also a good way to set behavioral expectations for the year, and check prior knowledge. You may want to list their ideas, or write down just the ones that you will be reinforcing. Decide ahead of time whether you will also reward academics with the token system or if it will be purely social/behavioral.

Tell children that this year, in their new class, tokens will be awarded to the children who exhibit the behaviors you discussed and other appropriate actions. Stress that tokens will not be awarded every single time, but that you will surprise students and they never know when they will have a token added to the bag. This is an important point so that they do not wait to be rewarded each time they follow directions. You might also want to mention that if a child asks for a token, he will not be given one, no matter how good of a job he did. You are the only person who determines when tokens will be awarded.

Make a big production out of showing the token organizer and your special container, then demonstrate how you will award tokens. Tell a child that you liked the way she came in that morning and started working right away, so you will take a token with her number on it and put it in the bag. Tell another child you noticed he walked quietly in the hallway, and make a big show of putting in a token for him. Give specific reinforcement to each child in the class and add tokens to the bag. Tell the students that they will have opportunities to earn tokens every school day, all day long.

Demonstrate how you will pull tokens and give rewards. Emphasize that tokens will be pulled whenever you have a special job in the classroom, and how you might pull a token at any time throughout the day. If you will also pull tokens at a set time or on a specific day, explain that as well.

Begin using tokens for classroom privileges right away. If you go to music class right after the discussion, you could pull a token to determine who will line up first, or who will carry the chorus permission slips. Use the tokens frequently during the first few weeks of school so children can learn how the system works and make connections between their behavior and privileges.

How to Use and Maintain Your Token System

Put tokens in the bag whenever you see behaviors you would like to encourage. Pull tokens from the bag whenever you need to select a student for a privilege or special responsibility. Using tokens prevents you from having to recall who has 'behaved' recently and determine whether you are calling on students equitably. Since appropriate behavior is what causes tokens to be added to the bag, the higher the incidence of good behavior, the more likely a student will be to receive extra responsibilities and privileges.

Using tokens will simplify your helper system—you don't have to assign every conceivable job to a student, because you can pull tokens for occasional tasks. Use tokens when you need a student to:

> ➢ pass out art supplies
> ➢ take a message to another teacher's room
> ➢ work a problem on the board or overhead
> ➢ participate in a role play
> ➢ hold a book, poster, chart, or other prop while you teach
> ➢ call the other students to line up
> ➢ run irregular errands
> ➢ choose a read-aloud
> ➢ complete small tasks for other teachers
> ➢ monitor behavior when you are briefly out of the room
> ➢ help the Star of the Week
> ➢ bring you something from another part of the room/school
> ➢ carry things in the hall
> ➢ sit in a special seat
> ➢ read from texts to the class
> ➢ share journal entries
> ➢ serve as group leader for activities

You can pull a set of number of tokens on a certain day or time, such as every Friday at dismissal, to distribute additional rewards. If you give your students prizes, this would be a good way to do it, but this system does not require any tangible rewards or expense on your part.

Be sure that after you pull a token from the bag, you put it back into your organizer, rather than back in the bag. Empty out the bag every week, month, or quarter, depending on how many tokens you have and how often you want your class to have a fresh start. Students should be able to sort the tokens by number back into the organizer for you during indoor recess or dismissal.

More Ways to Use the Token System

☑ **Incorporate tokens with your classroom jobs.**

All routine jobs should be assigned to specific students. It would be very distracting to have to pull a token to determine who will turn the lights out each time you leave the room and who will collect papers, and having to do those tasks yourself is just as bad! You want instruction to be uninterrupted, so any regular classroom task which you want to be performed automatically without your supervision should be assigned. Use tokens only for privileges which do not have to be done automatically to maintain the flow of the classroom.

☑ **Have a 'Star of the Week' for times when you are unable to pull tokens**.

Sometimes at recess, in the hall, or at an assembly, a child needs to be chosen for a small task such as taking a note to another teacher or retrieving something from the classroom. Your Star of the Week, or VIP (whatever name you choose) can serve in this capacity. There may also be an unassigned task that pops up during a lesson, and rather than distract the class with tokens, you can ask the Star to do it. This seems fair to children and they do not question it. While you could have a Star Student for the day, I like assigning the Star job for an entire week so that I can remember who it is more easily. The Star can also share books and poems she likes, bring in a favorite item from home, eat lunch with you, or participate in any other activity that will make the child feel special.

☑ **Allow children to put tokens in the bag themselves for especially great accomplishments.**

This can become distracting if done during instructional time, so I would not recommend it as a regular routine. However, you can reinforce appropriate behaviors in a powerful way when you announce in front of the whole class, "Wow, Jasmine, you saw trash on the floor that did not belong to you, and you threw it away in order to be helpful. Thank you for being so responsible. Come put a token in the bag for yourself!"

☑ **Teach students to nominate each other for tokens**.

Choose a regular time of day, such your morning meeting or at dismissal, for two volunteers to tell about how someone in the class was a good friend or role model, and have that child put a token in the bag for his or her classmates. This encourages children to look for appropriate behavior in their friends and support one another in developing responsibility and good character.

☑ **Give tokens based on input from other teachers.**

If students know that a particularly good report from the P.E. teacher can earn them a token, they may be more likely to behave when they're not with you. I always told my students that if I heard another teacher or administrator compliment one of them, I would add a token when we got back to the classroom. My grade level team always knows my behavior modification plan and they make sure to comment when they see exceptional behavior at recess or in the hall.

☑ **Make tokens that say "Whole Class" to occasionally reward excellent group behavior.**

These tokens can be earned when all students have worked together and demonstrated excellence. Then whenever a 'whole class' token is pulled from the bag, a special reward can be given instead of the purpose you pulled the token for. If you pulled a token to see who would get to write on the overhead projector, for example, it would not be feasible for the whole class to complete the task. Announce the whole class reward, then pull another token to select who will use the overhead). The whole class token could mean:

- ➢ five minutes of free time at the end of the day
- ➢ extra recess or computer lab time
- ➢ extra singing or finger plays during the next morning meeting
- ➢ ten minutes of self-selected reading with friends of their choice
- ➢ time in class to begin homework
- ➢ any other reward that most students enjoy and that you are comfortable giving every time that you pull the 'whole class' token

The Bead System

A former co-worker of mine came up with the idea to use beads for behavior management, and when I tried out the idea for myself, I realized the possibilities for adaptation were almost limitless. I experimented with the format for awhile and tailored it to meet the needs of my class, and ended up with the system outlined here. The photo shows what might be the most ridiculous-looking behavior modification prop you've ever seen, but trust me, this system is simple, fun, and the kids LOVE it!

How the Bead System Works

Basic Principle

Students earn beads for demonstrating on-task, appropriate behaviors. A privilege is earned at the end of the week for children who have earned a pre-determined number of beads.

What You Need

> ➤ half a pipe cleaner for each child
> ➤ a small bag of identical beads (I use triangular ones that fit together)

How to Start the System With Your Class

1) **Explain the basic principle of the system to students.** Have them suggest positive classroom behaviors that could earn beads (following directions, not talking when the teacher's talking, etc.) and list them on a chart for the children's reference. (The brainstorming process was explained in more detail in 'The World's Easiest Token System' section of this chapter and can be used with any reinforcement method you use.)

2) **At the bottom of the chart, write the reward for earning the set number of beads each week and explain it to the class.** 10 is usually a good number if you want all your kids to be successful. Possible rewards could be participation in Fun Friday or free time. One year I let my kids participate in centers such as play-dough, watercolor paints, math manipulatives, and board games. This was the ONLY time they got to do those things in third grade so it was a HUGE privilege.

3) **Allow the children to ask questions.** Make sure you cover all of the FAQs listed here (adapting the responses to your own teaching situation).

4) **Show students how you have taped one end of a pipe cleaner to each child's desk or desk tag.** Tell the children that they are each responsible for their own pipe cleaner and beads. You can attach desk tags to the front of students' desks so that they don't play with them. Tape only the top of the nametag, so that students can flip it up while seated to add beads to the attached pipe cleaner.

5) **Give specific verbal reinforcement and a bead to each child in the class.** This allows children to see firsthand how the system works and buy into it right away.

What to Do at the End of the Week

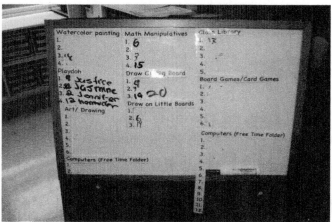

At 1:00 pm every Friday (or the last day of the school week), I ask students to turn in their beads, starting with the child who has the most. I'll ask if anyone has 20 beads, then 19, and so on. The children bring them up to me in their open palms for me to 'check' (you know which children's beads actually need to be counted) and then they put them back into my bead box. After a child has returned the beads, he can sign

up for a center on the wipe-off board chart. This way, the kids who earned the most beads get to pick first. (My kids can sign up using their name or their number, which is why you see names and numbers on the board.)

The children who did not earn the specified number of beads are to work silently and independently on an assignment of their choice.

Frequently-Asked Questions

▶ **What type of things should I give beads for?**

ANY behaviors you want to reinforce can earn beads. Besides the obvious good behaviors, I give beads from time to time for: wearing the school uniform, being on time for school, walking quietly in the hall, getting a compliment from another teacher, lining up quickly after recess, and cleaning up materials when first asked (those who keep working or play around quickly learn that when you say time's up, you mean it). I often give beads to kids for using time wisely, staying on-task, and completing a pre-determined amount of work in a set amount of time. For example, I'll tell the kids they have 15 minutes to do the front of a worksheet, and after that amount of time, I walk around and give out beads to those who have done so, making accommodations for individual kids as needed.

▶ **Do kids get beads individually or do you give them to the whole class?**

Both. Sometimes only a few kids earn them, and sometimes I'll compliment the whole class for a job well done and give them to everyone.

▶ **What do you say and do when you give beads out?**

Sometimes when kids are working, I'll walk around quietly and slip beads onto their desks and whisper encouragement. Other times, I make a huge deal and reward them in front of the class. Having the teacher smile at and compliment them is a greater reward than the bead itself for most kids. Often, I'll give beads to everyone when the class is doing a good job and give two beads to those who needed no reminders to stay on-task or did an exceptional job. Once in awhile when the majority of the class is talking too much and there's a handful of kids really working diligently, I'll say, "Wow, thanks, Joe and Dara. You two are determined to get this assignment done even when there's noise and distractions all around you. Come up and get a bead." The most important thing is to GIVE VERBAL REINFORCEMENTS along with the beads. The kids need to know exactly what they did right so that they'll do it again. There should be no mystery surrounding how beads are earned.

▶ Can children have beads taken away?

To keep them on their toes, I tell my class that I reserve the right to take away beads, but I've only done it two or three times and it was for really egregious offenses, e.g., lying to me, or forging a parent's signature on a report card.

▶ What if a child loses the beads or pipe cleaner?

I do not accept beads that are off a pipe cleaner. That's the only way to keep the beads from becoming a distracting jumble in the children's desks. I give new pipe cleaners every month because they do get raggedy after awhile. Anyone who loses the pipe cleaner must wait until I give out new ones (although I have made exceptions). Students who lose their beads are out of luck: I tell them from the start they are responsible for keeping them on the pipe cleaner until Friday.

▶ Can beads be saved from one week to the next? What if a child is absent for the reward?

Beads cannot be saved—students must be on their best behavior EVERY week. However, if a child is absent on the day of the reward, I allow her to be the first to choose centers the following week.

▶ What if a child is absent one or more days during the week and can't earn as many beads?

During dismissal, I have a student helper put two beads on the pipe cleaner of any kids who were absent that day. This makes up for the beads that children probably would have earned if their parents had brought them to school. I also give extra beads to students who miss a lot of my class because they are in special education pull-outs (provided I don't hear of any problems from the other teacher). For students who are in a special education or gifted program for several hours a day, I send a slip of paper with the child on Fridays and the ancillary teacher writes how many beads the child earned out of a possible total.

Please indicate how many beads the student has earned this week for following directions, staying on task, completing work accurately/on time, and for appropriate behavior. Feel free to write comments as needed. Thanks! ☺

Between 0 and 7 Beads

6	Feb. 4-8	Mar. 3-7
	Feb. 11-15	Mar. 10-14
6	Feb. 18-22	6 Mar. 17-20
6	Feb. 25-29	6 Mar. 24-27

► Can children request certain color beads/pick beads out themselves?

Every now and then I let the kids pick the beads themselves, but it has to be for something very special. I don't normally allow this because I want distribution to be quick. If getting beads distracts the kids from the on-task behavior I'm rewarding, it defeats the purpose. My motto is, you get what you get, and if you don't like it, I will be happy to take the bead back.

► Can children trade beads if they want to have specific colors?

I'll warn you, this is a disruptive practice, so in the beginning of the year, I would say no. However, the kids get really excited about making patterns, getting all the same colors, collecting their favorite shades, etc., and anything that increases their interest in beads is a good thing to me.

► Can children sell or barter with beads?

About three weeks after I first started the system, I heard someone say, "I'll give you three beads if you do these multiplication problems for me!" The very same day, I heard a rumor that a little girl had brought a bag of bouncy balls to school and was selling them for two beads each! I had a serious talk with the class about how this defeats the system ("The whole point of the beads is to reward people who make good choices, and if someone can be off-task but sell things and do other people's work for them in order to still get a reward, then the system doesn't work"). That's why I advise you to cover all these FAQs with your kids right from the start! After the talk, I didn't have any more problems with trading.

▶ Can children give beads away?

If a child has eleven beads and his best friend has nine, of course the child will want to share a bead so that his friend can participate in centers, too. But I tell my kids that this also works against the system because it allows children who make poor decisions to earn the same rewards as those who make good decisions.

▶ What if children steal beads or bring extra ones from home?

The children understand instinctively why this is unfair and have never tried it in my class. Having the pipe cleaners in plain sight provides a measure of

accountability: because they are always on display, the children keep meticulous counts over how many beads each person has. If several beads were to come up missing, everyone who sits around that child would vouch for how many he had, and would be quick to point out that suddenly, someone else has a few more. Also, I tell kids from the start that if they are ever caught stealing beads, they will not be able to earn ANY more for the rest of the year. (If that ever happened, I may actually talk with the class about lessening the 'sentence' after awhile so that the child who stole still has an incentive to behave: however, this threat seems so severe to them that stealing beads isn't worth chancing.) If some kids seem to have a miraculous number of beads on Friday, you can have a student helper do a mid-week 'Bead Check' and write down how many beads each person has next to their name on a class list.

▶ **What is the motivation to earn more beads once a child has met the minimum requirement?**

The kids with the most beads get to pick centers first. My most recent class was so on-task and responsible that I started giving prizes to the top three bead-earners each week. If there was a tie, I let multiple kids choose. Then I began giving stickers or pencil erasers to anyone who earned 15 or more beads, in order to reward those students whose behavior was really exceptional that week, even if other people had earned more beads. This is the ONLY time I EVER gave tangible rewards so it was a really big deal to my kids. I have a treasure chest with Happy Meal prizes and other trinkets that I collected for free. This really motivates the kids to stay on their best behavior all week and rewards those kids who consistently make good decisions.

▶ **What if children start expecting beads every time they do something good or argue about them?**

If a child is behaving because he wants a bead, he's behaving for the wrong reason. My rule is that if you ask for a bead, you won't get one. In life, sometimes you get rewarded for doing the right thing, and sometimes your good deeds go seemingly unnoticed, so you have to learn to be responsible regardless of the outcome. The bead system reflects that.

▶ **How does this system tie in with rewards for completing homework or class work?**

Completing one's work is an important part of being responsible and on-task, so you could stipulate that kids must earn ten beads AND turn in all assignments in order to have the reward. The problem you'll have to solve is that some kids behave all week but don't do their class work or homework, and others complete all their assignments but have trouble behaving. The beads become meaningless for these children.

One possible solution is to divide your center time/Fun Friday in half, so that anyone who either doesn't turn in all their work or doesn't earn ten beads misses the first half and participates in the second half. If someone doesn't do their work AND has less than 10 beads, they miss the entire time. This is simpler than it sounds and works beautifully.

▶ How can I use beads to target specific classroom behaviors?

Another extension of the bead idea is to have 'Bead Awards'. Write the criteria on the board, e.g., Best Job Following Along, Most Cooperative, or Most

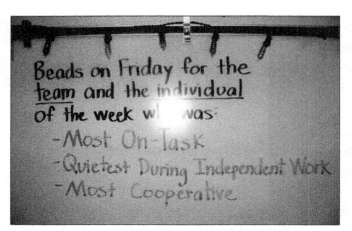

Improved. I like to use the same three or four categories for awhile and then reward students for a different set of positive behaviors I've noticed. Tell students that at the end of the week, you will select one team AND one individual who displayed the attributes shown. (The individuals selected may or may not be on the winning team.) Those individuals and

teams will each receive an extra bead. It is possible for one team or individual to earn all three categories, so the kids will be on their best behavior in hopes of racking up serious bead counts with this! Giving extra beads to those students who needed the fewest reminders to work hard during the week is a great reinforcement, because those children often get less attention than the ones who are always acting out.

▶ Are there any items other than beads that I could use for reward symbols?

The bead system is incredibly flexible and can be used in any number of ways to support the type of behaviors you want your students to exhibit. You could substitute dry beans, counters, tokens, or any other small item you'd like. The idea is to give students something to work for, and to reinforce their efforts on a regular basis.

Chapter 17: Meeting Individual Needs
Understanding and addressing the behavior of every child

Behavior modification encompasses several important components, such as developing a rapport with your kids, establishing procedures and routines, and setting up a positive behavior management or reward system for your whole class. However, there are children who need additional structure and support through special behavior modification systems. You will encounter students who appear to be uninterested in pleasing you or being successful in the classroom. Many of these children have disadvantaged home lives, disabilities and disorders, social difficulties, and other issues that have been working against them for a very long time. These deep-seated problems will cause the kids to struggle to meet your expectations, even though deep down they want to make good choices.

These challenging students are the kids who fail at whole class systems. They're the ones who are constantly losing their recess, being isolated from the group, not earning the sticker or treat, and so on. While one set of consequences should be set up for the entire class, it's unreasonable to expect all kids to act the same way, and therefore it's unfair to try to treat them all the same way. Rather than striving for equality, work for equity—treating students in a way that is appropriate and reasonable for their unique temperaments and personal situations. Equity involves encouraging students to develop and perform at their personal best. Every child brings a unique personality and set of experiences to the classroom, and therefore, not only will each child have different capabilities, each will need to be disciplined differently.

This chapter will show you how to examine children's motives and responses to discipline so that you can help them manage their own needs. It will also give you ideas for individual behavior plans, called Personal Improvement Plans, that will help troubled students become the best they can be.

Considerations When Disciplining: Needs and Response

Student Positions (Needs/Motives)

We all have reasons for acting the way we do. Our choices serve a function in our lives and provide reinforcement at some level. As teachers, it is our job to find out WHY a student is acting out and address those unmet needs. Ultimately, our goal is to teach the child to identify her own needs and problem solve ways to meet them independently.

I heard about student positions from a friend who studied them in graduate school. Read carefully, because this might be the only time I mention something I learned solely from a textbook! The positions approach to behavior modification contends that children act out for one (or more) of the following reasons:

> ➤ boredom
> ➤ excess energy
> ➤ need for power/control
> ➤ in search of attention
> ➤ to avoid failure
> ➤ because they are uninformed about expectations

If you can identify the reason why a child is misbehaving, you can determine the most effective response.

Makes sense, right? So why do many of us as teachers continue to have class systems which provide no solutions for students who are continually disruptive? For example, if you have a student who wants to assert power and control and starts talking back, being ordered to 'flip your card' will infuriate the child even more and does not address the root cause. If a child is playing around because he is bored, how is he going to feel more challenged and supported once the card is flipped?

Giving consequences for misbehavior is not synonymous with acknowledging the root of the problem. And since the root cause is different for each child, the consequences may need to be different, too.

For example, the day after I first learned about student positions, I had two second-graders who refused to walk in line and were trailing way behind the others. This was annoying me to no end so I decided to try to identify and respond to the kids' positions. I recognized that one of the stragglers was seeking attention, so ignoring it would have resulted in increasingly more disruptive behavior (I knew this well from experience with him). Quietly but very firmly I said to him, "Walter, I need you to be a part of our line. Off the wall and behind Rachel, please," and gave him the teacher look as he did it. I then paused and commented loud enough for the whole class to hear: "That's exactly the right way to walk, Walter. Now everyone is standing in line the right way. Thank you!" He received more attention for his good behavior than his misbehavior, and because I kept smiling at him as we walked, he was successful. (Of course, I did not FEEL like smiling at him, but it was either meet his needs or deal with a tantrum, and I knew which one was best for both of us!)

The other child who would not walk was hopping and jumping all over the place. His position was excess energy, of course. I gave him a reminder about hallway expectations, and when he started jumping again a few seconds later, I quietly asked him to go to the end of the line where he would not be disruptive and no one could see him. He happily marched (literally!) to the end and swung his arms around the whole way down the hall because he really needed to do so. When no one could see him or get hit by him accidentally, his behavior was no longer disruptive. (Had we seen someone important coming down the hall, I would have insisted on him keeping still for a few moments. The students know that when we are out of the room, we are representing our class and have to do it well.) The end of the line became his permanent place and I stopped fighting the battle of his excess energy.

Now, compare those results to that of 'card-flipping' or another punitive whole class system. Both boys would have gotten to red, undoubtedly, and neither of their needs would have been addressed. Both were lagging behind the rest of the line and could have been punished together for their similar offenses. But instead I tried to figure out why they were doing what they were doing and fix each individual's situation.

This is actually easier than it sounds once you know your kids. Anytime I saw Walter fidgeting after that, I knew why, and I tried to place him in a spot in the room where he wouldn't be disruptive. Students normally act from the same positions, or points of motivation, time and time again.

The idea is to accept the child's position, but not his or her behavior. In this way, you are working with, rather than against, the child. The positions are not the problem, because we have all experienced them at one time or another. In the classroom, we have to help students identify their positions and meet their needs in an acceptable way. Therefore, whenever responding to a student's behavioral issues, you should always ask yourself: what unmet need is the child acting in response to?

Student Response to Correction

In my experience, there are five basic responses to discipline that you will see children exhibit in the classroom. I would probably expect more kids of the first two types in affluent communities and more of the last two types in lower-income neighborhoods. This is due to cultural norms and the type of coping skills that are effective in each environment. The middle type, in which the student wants to be responsible but lacks self-discipline, seems to be a common characteristic of young children who are trying to learn how to grow up in any community. You will have a mixture of student temperaments and reactions to discipline in any classroom, and the information provided here is intended to help you meet each child's individual needs.

Student's Response to Discipline	How the Teacher Should Enforce Consequences
Tears up when disciplined; genuinely sorry or scared	-reprimand privately and quietly -give a reminder about consequences and enforce them only if the behavior is repeated
Appears sorry but quickly repeats wrong behaviors; 'talks a good game'	-reprimand privately and quietly, warning what will happen if another inappropriate behavior occurs -be extremely consistent about swiftly enforcing a MEANINGFUL consequence upon second and all later offenses -discipline without lecture: this student knows right from wrong and needs consequences to be quick and matter-of-fact

Wants to do the right thing but doesn't have the self-discipline necessary to follow through	-talk and reason kindly with the child: Why is it hard to do __? What can I do to help you make good choices? What can you do to help yourself? -encourage the child to problem solve by offering choices such as sitting alone or by someone else if a particular group of children is a negative influence or distraction -be patient with this type of child: she is learning how to self-regulate and you will see progress with an individual behavior plan
Subtly defiant or disrespectful (mutters, rolls eyes, sucks teeth)	-consider the trigger: some children are subtly defiant only when they have an 'audience' and will be respectful if you discipline them one-on-one; others are defiant only when they you show anger towards them and will remain submissive if you are calm and level-headed -don't do anything to turn the situation into a power struggle! You can try disciplining one time in front of the class (the child may back down and the behavior may not resurface once he realizes you insist on being in charge—this is more likely with younger students) but be prepared for this approach to backfire -use nonverbal redirection whenever possible or talk to this student privately, walking over to her rather than calling her over to you, because she may refuse to move -briefly state the inappropriate behavior and the consequence, enforcing it immediately without any emotion ("Hitting him was not okay. You need to sit by yourself over there.") -if the child protests, repeat yourself calmly and firmly ("You need to sit by yourself."). Do not provide any additional information for the child to argue with. -provide specific praise related to appropriate behavior when you see it: these kids are often attention seekers and have a poor self-concept
Openly defiant **(talks back, cusses, becomes violent, refuses to do anything you say)**	-follow the suggestions for the subtly defiant child -pick your battles: don't upset the child over something small such as humming in the hallway or not having his shirt tucked in -keep in constant contact with parents, especially when the child does something good, and be sure to document all conversations

-get an individual behavior management plan in place quickly so the child can learn to self-regulate and receive frequent positive reinforcement

-talk to the child's previous teacher(s), but keep in mind that kids behave differently for different people and are change and grow over time

-let the principal/behavioral specialist/guidance counselor know what's going on for documentation purposes and also for advice

-bring the child up at a child study meeting to look into special placement, services, and evaluations: most school systems have behavioral intervention steps that you need to follow

-find out what behaviors require office referrals and be sure to write them when the child has misbehaved severely (I used to avoid this, wanting to handle discipline problems in my own classroom, but once when a child needed to be suspended for a violent act, he couldn't be, because I had never written any previous referrals)

Being Consistent While Differentiating for Students' Needs

Showing Kids That You Decide What's Best for EACH Child

Sometimes teachers find it difficult to discipline equitably—that is, to treat all students in a way that is appropriate for their needs. They don't typically have a problem accommodating individual students, but they worry about being 'unfair' to the rest of the class or enforcing consequences inconsistently.

Your students must realize that your job is to make sure that every child gets what she or he needs to be successful. Every decision you make is based on what you believe will help them.

I say this to my class many times during the school year. When they ask why some kids go to pull-out classes, that's why. When they ask why Isabel is sitting at the back table when everyone else is at their desks, that's why. When they ask why Mateo's always at the front of the line, that's why. ***Because my job is to help decide what is best for every person in our classroom, and what's best is not the same for everybody, every time.***

If children are continually questioning how certain students are being disciplined or given privileges, then you haven't made this concept clear to them. Talk with the class about how being fair does not mean treating everyone the same. Give an example about bedtimes. "Would it make sense for your fifteen-year-old brother to go to bed at 8:00 when you do? What about for your baby sister to have to stay awake through the whole day until all the kids go to sleep at 8:00? Do certain family members always stay up later as a reward, or go to bed earlier as a punishment? Of course not. The parents set things up that way because it's what's best for each child."

Be very matter-of-fact when doling out consequences and explaining them. If a child questions why you didn't enforce the usual consequence for a child who didn't follow a procedure (for example, a child who pushed someone but didn't have to go to the end of the line), wink and smile: "I did the best possible thing for Darryn to help him make a better decision next time. Trust me. I know what I'm doing."

Low-Key Rule Enforcement

The discrepancy in treatment will be less obvious to students if your tone and word choice remain the same. ***Anytime you are calm when giving consequences, kids are less likely to question them.*** If you yell at and embarrass a child for running in the hallway, he is far more likely to get indignant when another child doesn't get punished for that same behavior. If you were respectful during the infraction and simply said, "Our rule is walking in the hallway. Please go back and show me you can do that. Thank you," the child is likely to not even notice when someone else runs and you don't make a huge deal of it, because you were so kind when he did it.

Handling Jealousy

I have found that children rarely question why other students don't have punishments or consequences enforced for misbehavior. They are far more likely to notice when other students get extra privileges. If a child asks, "Why does Chris get to stay on the computer when we have to get off?", you can repeat the mantra that you are doing what's best for each student. Or you can give a more specific response that's as honest as possible. "Chris stayed on the computer for an extra ten minutes because it was really hard for him to get his Morning Work done. You know how he usually plays around? Well, today he finished on time, so as a special treat, I'm letting him go on the computer. I'm hoping that will convince him to work as hard as you do. You're a great role model for him, because you do the right thing even without extra computer time. One day he won't need that kind of reward, because he'll automatically get everything done. You should be very proud of yourself for being such a responsible student."

Revealing Your Reasoning

I don't recommend telling children, "Because I said so" or "Don't question what I do." When students understand the reason for your actions, they are far more likely to be cooperative and support your classroom goals than if they are complying out of intimidation or blind trust. You can have a general discussion about how a lot of children have special issues they are dealing with. Talk about how 'some kids' get very angry and can't control themselves, so it's not always best for you to give a consequence right away. Those kids need time to cool off first. Discuss how some children have a hard time controlling themselves during instruction, and how they'd always be sitting alone if they got moved away from the group every time they forgot to raise their hands. Explain that you have to all be patient with those kids and help them learn to make better choices.

You can discuss specific situations in front of the entire class, as long as the tone is an accepting, affirmative one. If a child questions, "Why does Laura keep getting stickers for doing her work and we don't?" say, "Have you all noticed that Laura has a tough time staying in her seat sometimes? She does, and that's okay. We all have something that's hard for us to do. Right, Laura? See, that's something she's really working on. I'm proud of how hard she's trying. I want her to be able to do that automatically just like you all do. So I'm going to give her a sticker for each assignment she does without getting out of her seat. If you see me giving her stickers, that's why. The rest of you already know how to stay in your seats, so I give you stickers for other things, like getting A's and B's on your assignments. Soon Laura is going to be such an expert at staying in her seat, she'll just be getting stickers for doing her best work, too. So until then, if you guys see Laura getting stickers, know that it's because she's doing the right thing, and give her lots of compliments and encouragement. Will you help Laura and me with that?"

Explaining your reasons can prevent students from believing that you are inconsistent or unfair and builds their trust in your judgment. After awhile, they will stop asking about other children's accommodations and they may even start deducing things for themselves. I had a child say to me recently, "I know why Joshua gets that paper from you at the end of the day! You're trying to help him do better in class so you're writing things down for him to show his mom! And! It's working! Because I saw Joshua let somebody go in front of him at lunch!" Hearing that comment was so important to me because it demonstrated that students are internalizing the supportive, encouraging attitude of teamwork I've worked so hard to foster in the classroom. My response? "Hey, Lucas, that was really observant of you! I'm so pleased that you noticed the improvements Joshua is making. Did you compliment him when you saw him let the other kid in front? Ooh, you should! He'll be so excited to hear that you cared enough to say something! You're an awesome friend, Lucas!"

Violent, Defiant, and Emotionally Unstable Children

Children with extreme emotional issues are often placed in the regular classroom, sometimes with the benefit of special education labeling and support, and sometimes without. These children, more than any other, need to be handled on an individual basis: you will need to consider what motivates them to behave and what triggers them to misbehave. This process takes time and can be very frustrating in the beginning of the year. However, there are two major things you can do to help lessen the behavior issues while you learn how best to manage the child.

Strategy #1: Project a calm, unemotional demeanor, even if you have to pretend.

One of your most important jobs as a teacher is to stay level-headed and calm at all times. You have to be the stable, mature person when dealing with an out-of-control, emotionally unstable child. This can be extremely difficult, but these children often thrive (consciously or subconsciously) off of other people's reactions, so don't feed into any negativity or drama the child tries to create. Speak to the child in a low, matter-of-fact voice at all times and only show excitement when the child is behaving appropriately. You must be consistent with this. The child has to learn that if he wants to elicit a reaction from you or inspire excessive attention, he will have to do it with good behavior.

The added benefit of maintaining a calm demeanor is that it reassures the rest of the class, who may otherwise respond in kind to the chaos the disruptive child is trying to create. Your persona must always communicate that you are in control, nothing is throwing you off, and there's nothing a child can do to create an unbalanced reaction in you. This is much easier said than done, of course, but it becomes easier with practice.

Remember that a significant part of effective teaching is performing. You are an actor. You are acting like a calm, rational person even when you do not feel like one. This is a mask you must put on for the kids at all times. It's part of your unwritten job description. Later you can go 'behind the scenes' to talk to a colleague and let the real you come out, but as long as you're on the classroom stage, you have to act like a professional who cannot be fazed. Come up with a mantra of some sort to repeat to yourself when you feel like you're coming undone. Tell yourself something that puts the problem in perspective and helps you stay focused on the big picture. *I will not let a six-year-old control my behavior. I will act and not react. I am in charge. A little kid is not going to ruin my day. In a few hours, I will go home. This job is not my whole life.*

Your mindset must be totally independent of your circumstances. Make a conscious decision about how you will think and act in the classroom, and stick to it no matter what happens.

Strategy #2: Avoid power struggles and only command what you can enforce.

The second major thing you can do to decrease the control an emotionally unstable child has over your classroom is to avoid power struggles. Never give a directive that you can't enforce. When a child is being defiant, always give choices. Both choices must be acceptable so that you don't have to hold your breath wondering what the child will do next. Either choice must fit your ultimate purpose of maintaining authority over the classroom.

Replacing Repeated Demands With Expectation Reminders

Emotionally volatile and defiant children do not typically respond well to direct commands and confrontation, and will view constant nagging as a weakness. Instead of barking orders or repeating yourself, try to express a calm reminder that will reinforce appropriate behaviors without directly telling the child what to do.

Instead of nagging, pleading, begging, and demanding...	State a calm, firm reminder of the expected behavior...
Sit down!	Sitting.
Walk!	Walking.
Stop talking!	We need quiet.
Get in line!	We're in a line.
Come over here!	We're over here.

What to Do in a Stand-Off With a Defiant Child

1) Give choices to defuse the situation. There are occasions in which a child must be directly confronted about an unacceptable behavior that is interfering with instruction. If a student has been continually disrupting your lesson and has not responded to your attempts at redirection and intervention, you may need to remove him from the group. Say in a quiet, matter-of-fact tone, "I can't allow anymore interruptions when I'm teaching. Please have a seat at one of the back tables, away from the group." Then immediately resume your lesson if possible to prevent the situation from escalating.

If the child just stands there, say, "You can sit in a chair at the round table, or the rectangular one, you decide." This must be communicated calmly even when your heart is pounding with infuriation. Give the child about ten seconds of total silence to process his choices and make a move. If you look away from the child during that time, he may be more likely to do what you've asked because the situation seems less like a stand-off. You're dealing with a human being, not a wild animal, so it's okay to break eye contact! Also, your movement will cause the rest of the class to look at you in anticipation of what you'll do next, and disruptive children are usually more likely to cooperate when they don't have twenty pairs of eyes glued to them. During those ten seconds, act totally confident, as if you are so sure the child is going to go sit at the back table that you don't have to watch his every move. Briefly shuffle your papers, shift in your seat, put a paperclip over a textbook page—whatever. Then look back over at the child.

If he's complying, say, "Thank you. You made a good decision." Then pretend as though the situation never happened and continue with the lesson. You can address the child later on when instruction has been completed and the entire class is not watching. As long as the disruptive child is now quiet and in the place you asked her to go to, let the situation defuse. If the child is either not moving or else talking back, wait out the whole ten seconds before reacting. Sometimes children will backtalk briefly (*"Man! I didn't do nothing!"*) and then comply. Accept this action for now and address it later. Remember, your main objective is to continue your lesson, and that can't happen if you let your pride create a stand-off.

But if the student is showing no signs of cooperating, you need to make a decision quickly. Is the child's behavior so severe that staying with the group is impossible and he will have to be forcibly removed, or can you deal with the child later? The second option is ALWAYS preferable, because you will still be able to reassert control and 'save face'.

Let's look at the second option first, in which you continue instruction and address the defiance afterwards. Say nonchalantly, "You know what? I'm not going to waste any more time dealing with your attitude. That's not fair to the other nineteen students in this room who are making good choices right now and need my attention. I will deal with you *later*." Totally ignore the student and let him cool off until you can discuss the situation privately.

This scenario works, because even if the child is at his desk and not in the place you asked him to go, you are still making it clear to everyone in the room that this is your classroom, and you make the rules. Your word choice and tone clearly imply that the reason the child gets to stay at his desk is not because he wants to and you can't do anything about it. It's because *you* decided that the behavior wasn't worth your energy and you wanted to pay attention to the kids who were doing the right thing instead. *You* decided that the situation was so unworthy of any further time or attention that you'd deal with it later on, when you feel like it. And when you do handle the situation, the insinuation is, it won't be pretty.

This response will alleviate problems with almost any student for the duration of the lesson. The child may mutter under his breath or play around with something in his desk, but as long as you can teach without interruption, don't say a word until later on when you talk with the child. Once you've said you're going to ignore the child's situation, you must keep your word. If he continues to be disruptive, call for administration to remove the student from your room WITHOUT addressing him yourself any further. Just pick up the phone or get on the intercom and say in a calm voice that you need administration to escort a child to the office. (Many schools have a special code, such as code gray, in which all you have to say is the name of the code and someone comes immediately to the room.)

2) Remove the child from the classroom if the behavior escalates. If a child has disrespected you or become violent to the point where you cannot allow him or her to stay in the classroom, saying that you will deal with the child later is not a viable solution and the previous three paragraphs do not apply. Instead, you can give one final set of choices, both of which involve the child leaving the classroom. To do this, you must be confident that your principal, school security, guidance counselor, or other staff will be ready to come to your classroom immediately and assist you. If you're not sure how this works at your school, talk to the other teachers on your grade level and find out what type of support you can expect. Immediate intervention assistance is a very reasonable expectation and it is your right as a teacher to provide an environment that is safe for you and your students.

Say to the child in the same calm, assertive tone, "You didn't make a choice about which table to sit at. Your choices now are, walk down to the principal's office with Margerat and Jose [responsible students in the classroom] or have me call for Principal Jones to come up here and escort you down there himself." It's important to give the child a way to comply without making him admit outright that you've won the battle of wills, so say something along the lines of, "If you would like the first choice, please walk over towards the door." If the child begins shuffling over, say, "Thank you, you've made a good decision. Margerat and Jose, please walk him to the office. I'm going to call down there now so they'll be expecting you all. The rest of you, please finish your work. We don't want to make anyone uncomfortable by staring when they're doing the right thing now."

If the child does not choose to walk down to the office willingly, then say only one thing: "Okay, you've made your decision." Call the office and ask to have the child removed from the classroom. Until assistance arrives, totally ignore whatever the child is doing and try to resume normal classroom activities. You could also have students sit on the carpet so they are up close to you and you can read a light-hearted story, or have them work on something with the person next to them so there's other noise in the room besides the disruptive child's ranting. If a behavior is so extreme that you cannot possibly keep teaching, say, "You can either stop kicking the wall, or I can add 'kicking' to your referral. You decide."

If the child kicks harder and acts even more outrageously, then you know any further attention is only going to feed into the behavior so the child must be completely ignored. What you need to do is communicate to the rest of the class that the child's behavior is not acceptable, he will not get away with it, you are still in control, and everything is going to be fine. Shrug and say to the other kids, "Well, I guess he made his choice. He's going to have a very upset principal and parent today. I bet you all are glad that you're doing the right thing. Whew!" If you laugh a little bit at this part and let your normal personality come through, you will see visible relief on the faces of your students. This can be done even while the child is still making a scene, because you're communicating to students that the incident is over and you're moving on.

3) Reassure the other children and resume instruction. After the child is removed and things get settled following a major incident, I usually can't help letting out a big sigh and rolling my eyes up to the ceiling—it just happens! I say, "Oh, boy. That was pretty ridiculous. Whew. I am so glad we have such an awesome class and I don't normally have to deal with that kind of behavior from you all. I would much rather be teaching you about... what were we doing, anyway? [Smiling, so the kids know I'm pretending not to remember because I want them to recall the lesson] Oh, that's right, thank you... let's try to go back to where we were with force and motion. Ready to pick up where we left off? Okay, great. You all are fantastic."

Calming down the rest of the class is important. The other children may want to talk about what happened after the child leaves the room and will start murmuring to each other and breathing sighs of relief. If this happens, stay nonplussed and matter-of-fact. "I know it was kind of scary for you when he was throwing desks and yelling, but you are safe here. I am always in control and I won't let anything bad happen to you when someone behaves like that. Sometimes kids have a very hard time dealing with their feelings, and that's what happened to Thomas today. He's going to have to learn how to follow our class rules and deal with his angry feelings in an appropriate way. What kinds of things do you think we could do to help him? How should we treat him when he comes back in the room?"

You don't want to turn the class against the disruptive child and create an us vs. them mentality, because that will only lead to further isolation and frustration for the troubled child. Show the other kids how to relate to what happened by identifying the underlying emotions (*Have you ever been that mad? What did you do? How did that work out? Would you respond that way again?*) and elicit the children's suggestions for making the situation better.

Modifying Your Whole Class System for Individual Needs

Individual behavior plans do constitute additional work for teacher, no matter how simple they are. Therefore it is advisable to first try adapting the whole class system(s) already in place. Here are a few ideas:

- **Use your whole-class rewards (beads, tokens, etc.) to reinforce your troubled students' efforts toward behaving.** "Wow, he bumped into you and you chose not to push him back!" or "You took your paper out and put your name on it right away, without any reminders. Thank you!" After the first few months of school, these accomplishments might be too minor for the rest of the class to earn beads for doing. However, you can always whisper to an individual child and reward her privately if that's what she needs in order to be as successful as the other children.

- **Structure your routines and procedures so that there are more immediate and concrete rewards and consequences for the child ("Three Strikes").** For example, my students know if they are continually disruptive, they will have to move their desks and sit alone. But there are some kids that aren't able to monitor their behavior well enough to understand when this consequence will apply. Rather than developing an entire behavior plan for the child, I just say, "You're going to get three warnings a day about that behavior. If I have to say something to you about that more than three times, you will need to move your desk away from the group for the rest of the day. It's just like in baseball, except I'm giving you one extra chance—three strikes and THEN you're out!" When that fourth correction comes (and it normally won't using a consequence this immediate and clear-cut), I simply say in a firm and disappointed (not angry) tone, "I've had to stop teaching four times today because of that behavior. Your three strikes are up and you're out. Please move your desk back from the group. Thank you. I hope you will do better now that you are sitting alone."

♦ **Never underestimate the impact of a private word with an encouraging teacher.** Talking individually with the child usually has a powerful influence on behavior. Taking a few minutes at various points in the day to comment on good decisions and the reasons for bad decisions may be all a child needs for success the majority of the time. Call the child over to your desk first thing in the morning and say, "You've got a fresh start today! I know you're going to do the right thing. How are you feeling? Are you ready to do your best work? Go for it!" Whisper to the child in the hallway on the way back from specials, saying, "I loved how on-task you were during reading groups today! Keep up the great work when we do math this afternoon!" At the end of the day, stand in the doorway and pat the child on the back. "Hey, what happened today during science? You seemed really spaced out and you were playing in your desk a lot. [Help the child reflect on what she did and why]. Everybody gets distracted sometimes. I know you'll be more focused tomorrow. Have a great afternoon, honey!" The purpose is to let the child know you pay attention and care about everything she does. This is the personal touch that makes a world of difference to most kids. Taking a few minutes to talk everyday can eliminate the need for a more formal behavior plan—which is easier on you in the long run.

Creating Effective Plans for Individual Students

When is the Whole Class System Insufficient?

There are several ways to tell if your whole class positive reinforcement system isn't meeting the needs of a particular child. Here are a few possible signs:

- The student is rarely successful in meeting your whole class goal (earning the required number of beads, getting tokens, staying on 'green').

- The child's parent has asked to be notified daily about the child's behavior—or you think the parent should be, so the student is accountable and the parent can hopefully reinforce expectations at home.

- The child is getting into serious trouble at school, resulting in administrative referrals.

- The child is so needy that you're having to give almost constant reinforcement, encouragement, and redirection as a motivation to behave.

Designing Personal Improvement Plans

I prefer the term 'Personal Improvement Plan' to the more traditional 'Individual Behavior Plan', despite its unfortunate acronym, PIP. That's because my purpose is more focused on helping the child become a better person than on modifying his behavior. The PIP is designed to help the child reflect on her actions and connect them to logical consequences (and motivating rewards if needed). It is typically a contract or evaluation that is created in conjunction with the child and parent. Here are guidelines to help you design a plan that meets individual student needs, followed by examples of plans that I have successfully used with children:

☑ **Choose ONE specific area you want the student to improve upon**.

Some kids are just a mess all the way around, and there's no way you can address everything at one time. Choose one behavior that most interferes with learning, e.g., calling out, playing around in the desk instead of listening to the teacher, talking back, or arguing and fighting with peers. As you see improvements, you can add other criteria. The idea is to break down the task of being a responsible student into small, manageable steps so the child can experience success and build self-confidence.

☑ Explain the need for a plan to the child.

Form an idea about what you want to do, and then speak to the child about it. You could say, "I know how hard it is for you to control yourself when you get angry. I want to help you. I'm thinking of a plan that would have us talk about your choices at the end of every day. I have a paper that looks like this, and what will happen is, I'll give it to you each day during dismissal. We'll discuss your decisions and then I'll send the paper home for you to look at with mom. Do you think it would be helpful for you to talk about your behavior with me? Do you think that showing mom will help you? I'd like to bring her in so we can decide on this together. We'll meet with her tomorrow morning, and then start the plan right away. Does that sound like it will work? I'm proud of you for wanting to do the right thing, and I feel good about our plan. If we need to change anything later on, we'll talk about it, but let's give this a shot. I believe in you."

☑ Involve the child and parent in setting up the plan.

When you meet with the parent, leave things open-ended for his feedback, and emphasize that the plan's purpose is to provide the support the child needs to be successful. Present the information in a nonchalant way that clearly communicates you don't think the child is 'bad' and needs 'punishment'. Show enthusiasm and optimism about the entire process, and let both the parent and child know you are confident that the three of you will be able to work together and find a way to help the child be the best she can be.

☑ Make sure the rewards and consequences are effective for the particular student.

Not all PIPs have built-in rewards or consequences, because sometimes the child just needs verbal accountability and attention. If you feel that the plan will work better with incentives, by all means discuss those with the child and parent. To achieve the optimal results, you should not determine the reinforcements on your own. Some kids will work hard for privileges in the classroom (extra computer time) or to avoid consequences (having to sit alone). If you have a very supportive parent whom you know will follow through consistently at home, you can add rewards/consequences for there as well (extra video game time, or loss of it). If the parent wants to reinforce the plan at home but you have reason to believe that this will not be enough for the child, or the parent won't follow through effectively, provide classroom reinforcements as well.

Examples of Personal Improvement Plans

"Andre": The devious smart-aleck who could care less about school

Andre was the most difficult non-disabled student I ever had. This six-year-old was bright and athletic, but bad to the bone. Mischievous and totally lacking in self-control, Andre was almost impossible to motivate. There wasn't anything I had that he wanted. Sitting alone? No problem, he'd just throw crayons at the other kids to get their attention and talk loudly to himself nonstop. Losing out on free time? Who cares? He never did any of the assignments, anyway—every minute of the day was free time for him. Try to have a heart-to-heart with him? Forget it. He'd talk back or else just stand there silently and refuse to give me any information. Write a referral? He'd yell all the way down the hall, with school security yanking him by the arm so he wouldn't run off.

Andre's Personal Improvement Plan

My teacher will set a timer for me. When it goes off, I will think about the choices I made.

Good Choices	Bad Choices
Staying in my seat	Walking around without permission
Working quietly	Calling out and being noisy
Doing all of my work	Playing around
Allowing other people to work	Disrupting the class

If I made good choices, I will get a token. If I made bad choices, I will not.
At the end of the day, I will count my tokens.

If I get 10 or more tokens >>>>>>> I get a reward at home, such as extra video game time, football practice, or a special snack.

If I get less than 10 tokens >>>>>> I will have a consequence at home, such as no video game time, no football practice, or no special snack.

My mom and I will decide together what reward or consequence I should have each day.

Andre needed constant reinforcement. He had the most stringent PIP I ever used, in which we evaluated his behavior together as often as every fifteen minutes. If he was on-task, he would earn a token. Since there was nothing to motivate him at school, we used rewards at home that Andre could get if he earned a set number of tokens that day. The rewards were set up to be very flexible, since his home life was not the most structured.

Even though Andre wasn't interested in pleasing me, talking to him throughout the day was somewhat helpful because I was able to encourage him and provide support regularly. I could say, "You only interrupted Davis one time so far during Morning Work and you got one problem done—that's an improvement. Good. Now we're going to finish Morning Work, and then look at your checklist again. To get your next token, you'll need to finish the other problems, and work without disturbing anyone. Understand?"

Directions: Ms. Powell will let you know when it's time for you to check your plan. Find the correct time and put a checkmark by each task that you were supposed to do. Ms. Powell will write whether you get a token.

Time	Did I stay in my seat?	Was I quiet?	Did I do my work?	Did I let other kids work?	Did I earn a token?
8:45					
9:45					
10:30					
10:45					
11:00					
11:45					
12:00					
12:15					
12:45					
1:00					
1:15					
1:30					
1:45					
2:00					
2:15					
2:30					
2:45					
ANDRE'S TOTAL TOKENS:					

Eventually we were able to look at Andre's checklist only a few times per day. His behavior was managed, but there was no miracle improvement. Some kids are really hard cases and there's nothing you can do in six hours a day to undo everything that happens in the other eighteen hours. It's exhausting and discouraging to work with these types of kids. Fortunately they are few and far between in most schools, and the majority of troubled students will make improvements for you during the school year. Sometimes the cases that seem the most hopeless make the biggest turn-around, and not necessarily right away, so don't count any child out until the end of the year.

"Claire"- The emotionally disturbed child who wants to succeed

Claire was probably my second most difficult student. She was diagnosed with a myriad of disorders, and showed noticeable signs of being both bipolar and emotionally disturbed. Her moods were incredibly unpredictable—one moment she would write a ten paragraph essay, at another she would collapse onto the floor and sob if you suggested she write her name on a paper. There was absolutely no way to predict her behavior and therefore nothing I could do that would consistently help her. Claire got along well enough with the other kids, but refused to do the majority of her work and became hysterical if I insisted she complete it. Sometimes she would have to be forcibly removed from the classroom multiple times in a single day for loud, violent outbursts.

I worked closely with Claire and her mom to develop a PIP with many frequent and varied rewards. Claire lost interest in things easily and the plan was changed about once a month. Fortunately, Claire had a one-on-one assistant who helped her fill out her plan throughout the day and regulated her rewards and consequences. On days when the aide was not there or was pulled to do other things in the school, I filled in. It was time-consuming and tiring, but I got the job done.

Claire made more significant improvements than anyone thought possible during the year. The structure and routines that were part of both the classroom and PIP were probably a considerable help. Claire did go downhill at the end of the year when some outside factors in her life changed, but overall, this behavior plan did in fact manage her behavior. Like Andre, a miracle cure never appeared, but Claire was able to function for the most part—and that meant the rest of the class was able to learn.

Claire's Personal Improvement Plan

Time	Behavior	Reward	Consequence
8:00-8:15	Unpack backpack correctly Copy homework correctly Put homework on table	Choose a sticker to put in your agenda book	No sticker
8:15-8:30	Copy correct heading for MW and complete it	5 minutes of choice time	No choice time; must complete MW
8:30-9:30	Follow along during lesson Complete your assignments	Centerjobs	No centerjobs: must complete assignments during centerjob time
9:30-10:15	Stay on-task without interrupting reading groups or other students	10 minutes of choice time	No choice time
Prepare for Snack/Recess	Clean up area and get snack out with a teacher's help within 3 minutes with no outbursts	Carry stuffed animals outside during snack and recess.	Leave stuffed animals in classroom during snack and recess.
10:20- 10:45 *Snack and Recess*			
10:45- 11:15 *Specials*			
11:15-12:00	Follow along during lesson Complete your assignments	10 minutes of choice time	No choice time: must complete assignments
Prepare for Lunch	Clean up area and get lunch out with a teacher's help within 3 minutes with no outbursts	Carry stuffed animals to lunch.	Leave stuffed animals in classroom during lunch.
Lunch			
1:00-1:15 Prepare for Mrs. Justine's/ Dismissal	Pack up everything with a teacher's help within 3 minutes with no outbursts. Be in Mrs. Justine's room by 1:15 and back in the classroom by 1:50.	Carry stuffed animals outside at dismissal	Leave stuffed animals in backpack during dismissal
1:15- 1:45 *Mrs. Justine's: Math*			
Dismissal			

"Elijah": The kid with a good heart who just doesn't get it

Thank God there are more kids like Elijah in the world than Andre or Claire. Elijah wanted to do well, and was capable of doing so, but just didn't have a clue about how behave to appropriately. He had the world's messiest desk and lost his materials constantly. He forgot where to stand in line and couldn't remember the procedures for pencil sharpening and bathroom breaks to save his life, even by spring time. His social skills were even more lacking: he would give kids noogies to show he liked them, or poke them in the stomach with a pencil to get their attention. He simply had no self-help skills and no strategies for being successful in the classroom. Part of this was probably bio-chemical, since his mother was on crack-cocaine while pregnant, and part of the problem was an unbelievably chaotic home life, since she remained an addict. Elijah was the type of kid that any sensitive teacher's heart would go out to. Unfortunately, some of the adults who worked with him in the past didn't take the time to see him for who he was, and instead shamed, punished, and isolated him, which contributed to his socially unacceptable behaviors. Elijah needed a fresh start.

Today's Date: _____ Mom's Initials _____		
Check plus= excellent, check= okay, check minus= problems		
	Elijah Says	**Ms. Powell's Comments**
Class work completed correctly with no or few reminders		
Appropriate behavior in the classroom		
Appropriate behavior in the hallway, at lunch, and at the drinking fountain		
Appropriate behavior on the playground		

I designed a much more laid-back PIP for Elijah than I did for Andre or Claire. I simply provided verbal reinforcement and beads (part of our class reward system) throughout the day, and at dismissal I gave Elijah a checklist summarizing his behavior. His mom did read the form sometimes, but I also sent Elijah to another teacher at the end of the day so she could talk with and encourage him even if mom didn't. Elijah was intelligent and mature enough to know that whatever happened during the day would be recorded on that paper, and looked forward to seeing the summary each afternoon. The most effective element of the plan was the accompanying pep talks. I helped Elijah create a new identity: the 'old Elijah' was always in trouble and didn't have any friends. I worked ceaselessly to convince him that I saw a 'new Elijah', a boy that people liked and that completed his work and was successful in school. In a rather short amount of time, Elijah began buying into this idea, and changed his self-concept.

I didn't think Elijah was capable of improving much, but he made amazing strides during the school year. I changed the form so there was a column for him to reflect on his own behavior before I evaluated it, and his comments were remarkable insightful. He continued to have days in which he totally zoned out and reverted back to his anti-social behaviors, either because of physical or psychological reasons. On those days, I talked to him about being the old Elijah. He understood that the new Elijah paid attention and got along with the other kids, and when the old Elijah resurfaced, we discussed how to get back on track. The PIP helped Elijah in astounding ways—he was a great kid who just needed additional structure and someone to care about him.

"Derick"- The kid with the hot temper and bad reputation

I heard about Derick before he even stepped foot in my class. Everyone in the school warned me about this kid: *He's a huge bully, he'll cuss you out, he's lazy and won't do any work*...it was endless. After the second person gave me a heads up, I started cutting everyone else off. "Yes, I've heard about Derick, but I don't want to know any more because I want to be able to give him a fresh start without any preconceptions." I listened to the guidance counselor and the previous year's teacher only—and that was enough to shake me up! I can only imagine how nervous I would have been if I had let everyone tell me their horror stories about this child.

In the beginning, Derick tried me at every turn. But, he was never disrespectful. I was patient with him, developing a rapport whenever I had a chance to talk to him alone. At recess Derick told me all about his video games and his cousin in Nicaragua, and gradually he began opening up more and more. He continued to have problems with other staff members, getting referrals whenever he was out of my sight, but Derick worked hard for me. I praised him often, and talked to him about his anger management issues. I tried not to ever raise my voice and reprimanded him privately every time it was necessary—and that was fairly often in the beginning. But Derick needed someone to believe in him. I told him repeatedly that no matter what someone accused him of, I would always give him a chance to tell his side of the story, and talk with him about how to make better choices when he messed up.

Derick never needed a written behavior plan. Our agreement was oral. Being ostracized and pegged as 'bad' was Derick's biggest frustration, so isolation from the class was extremely detrimental. However, Derick would frequently play around and distract the kids sitting near him, sometimes getting into conflicts that deteriorated quickly into name-calling and very hurtful words. I had a private conversation with him one morning in the same manner I always did with Derick, taking on a quiet, serious, and firm tone and displaying my most disappointed-looking face.

"Derick, you know I care about you. I believe in you, and I know you want to make good choices. And what I've noticed is, your behavior towards your team members is not helpful. I've seen a lot of arguing and fighting lately, and you've been playing around instead of working. Have you noticed that too? Is there anything you'd like to say about that? It sounds like you have been getting very frustrated when Orlando bumps into your desk all the time. Unfortunately, I can't keep talking to you every time you get upset, not if I'm teaching.

"I'm going to have to give you three chances to do the right thing. I'll show you one finger for your first warning, two fingers for your second warning, and so on. If I have to show you four fingers, you'll have to move your desk away from your team and sit alone. It's just not fair to your teammates when you talk to them while they're trying to learn. And it's not fair to me when I plan out a lesson to help you guys learn and then I can't teach it because I have to keep stopping for you. Does that make sense? I know you want me to be able to teach, and you want to be able to learn. So I'm going to need your help on this. How about you monitor your own behavior so I don't have to say anything, and if I do, you'll get three chances before you sit alone. Does that sound fair to you? Okay, let's try that out today and see how it works. I want you to tell me at the end of the day whether you think this is a good plan for you. You can do this, Derick. I know you can."

This PIP helped Derick take responsibility for his behavior and made him feel capable of managing it, because he knew I was counting on him to pull it together. There were still incidents and we had to have several in-depth class discussions about how to respond to Derick's name calling and rudeness to his classmates. I guided the other children to understand that when Derick was angry, they needed to walk away and give him time to cool off. Derick would then approach them when he was ready to apologize and talk calmly. I asked the other children to suggest ways to help Derick control his anger, and someone suggested a stress ball. After the discussion, Derick approached me shyly, and I'll never forget what he said: "Thanks for having the class suggest ways to help me handle my anger, Ms. Powell." The stress ball turned out to be the perfect thing for Derick, who already had nervous energy and was always fiddling with something! And once he and the class had agreed on the appropriate course of action for whenever Derick got angry, the situations were diffused much more quickly.

Although Derick's Personal Improvement Plan wasn't written down, he took pride in having a private contract, something special that only he and I knew about. His home life always contributed to 'relapses' and issues outside of the classroom, but as a whole, once I had established a rapport with him and created an accepting classroom environment, Derick was an awesome student when he was with me. "Our agreement" was something that made sense to him, and he handled it with a lot of maturity.

Chapter 18: The Challenges of High-Poverty Schools
Tools to help you succeed with disadvantaged children

Let me start off by being perfectly clear on one point: not all children who are economically disadvantaged have behavior problems or work below grade level. Many children in high-poverty or Title I schools are talented, bright students who were born into low-income families. Title I simply refers to a federal program that provides additional funding to schools in which a certain high percentage of students qualify for free or reduced lunch. These schools may also be referred to as having low socio-economic status (SES).

This does not mean a school or its students are 'bad'. It does mean that the school is likely to have a disproportionate number of children who do not come to school prepared to learn. New teachers are often 'stuck with' these schools while veteran teachers select the cushier jobs out in the suburbs, and by Labor Day each year, I'm getting swamped with emails from disillusioned inner-city teachers who are ready to quit.

Most of the advice that follows is applicable for all teachers, because working with affluent populations is no walk in the park, either, and there are tough kids in every school. But this chapter is written specifically for and dedicated to those teachers working in our most challenging schools with the neediest populations. You are amazing, and I want to encourage you along every step of the way.

The Realities of Teaching in High-Poverty Schools

What You Weren't Prepared for in College

Teacher preparation programs in American universities are getting better about addressing the classroom realities that their graduates are about to experience.

But chances are, your college textbooks did not prepare you for teaching children who witnessed violent crimes the night before or haven't had anything to eat for two days. I know mine didn't.

There's a reason for this. College courses typically focus on effective instruction, not classroom management, and teaching high-poverty children doesn't require anything special in the way of lesson plans. Your activities should be hands-on, student-centered, and carried out within the context of very structured routines and procedures, just like you would use to teach any group of children. Also, inner-city schools typically receive additional funding for lots of innovative programs, materials, and staff development. Therefore, there is little information for textbooks (or for me) to provide about effective instruction in Title I schools.

The difficulty lies in being able to actually teach those wonderful lessons you've developed when one kid finds a switchblade on the floor, another throws a chair because he got a "B" on his math test, and a third is crawling under her desk and sobbing uncontrollably for no discernable reason (which all happened concurrently in my classroom one time as I tried to begin a social studies lesson). Those are the situations that teachers need help handling, and any new educator who accepts employment in a high-poverty school will need additional support in classroom management.

My Own Background and Experiences

It is easy to feel isolated and believe you are the only one who is subjected to the daily traumas that occur in many urban classrooms. But I know what you're going through. With only one exception, every school I have ever taught in was low-income (70-90% free and reduced lunch), and the population in one inner-city school was so impoverished that 99% of students received a completely subsidized breakfast and lunch each day.

During my fifth year of teaching, I actually moved into the inner-city of Washington, D.C. with a friend who was from the neighborhood. The community was just starting the process of re-gentrification and I was the only white person I ever saw in our high-rise, a former housing project that had been among the most the dangerous in the nation. I was able to experience first-hand what it was like for my students to live in a place where it was unsafe to sit outside even for a few minutes, to step around homeless people slumped against the building, to have a pizza place refuse to deliver to the neighborhood, and to see teenagers standing on the corner in broad daylight selling drugs. I viewed the situation as a temporary environment that I had consciously brought myself into for the purpose of experiencing life from a different viewpoint. I lived there by choice, and that could never compare to the daily trials of someone who was born into that environment and had no choice economically but to stay there. But it was an amazing experience that opened my eyes to a lot of things, especially in relation to what makes inner-city kids tick.

What follows are words of advice from someone who has spent time living and working in the inner-city and has a special heart for the teachers and students in that environment. I sincerely hope that the information I provide makes you feel a little less alone and helps you to clarify the direction in which to take your teaching.

Lessons Learned from a Teacher Who Didn't Make It

Okay, I don't mean that literally—she did physically survive. But after four years of preparation in college, this teacher only lasted two months at our inner-city school. My heart still goes out to this enthusiastic, loving teacher who just couldn't control her kids. No one from the district was able to help her, and after many chances, the principal forced her to resign or be terminated. I share her story not to scare you—new teachers being let go for lack of classroom management is extremely rare in nearly every school system. Rather, I'm presenting this information to help you identify any commonalities between your practice and hers so that you can be successful in your own classroom.

I'll call the teacher Miss Green. When I tell her story, it may sound like I'm being harsh or judgmental towards her, but I'm speaking out of a tough love. Inner-city schools are no place for the weak-minded, thin-skinned, or faint of heart. My own analysis of her teaching practice is far less harsh than the summation she got from her students every time they disrespected and ignored her.

Lesson #1) You must have self-confidence and inner strength that outmatches the toughest kids.

Here's what I observed with Miss Green. The children did not listen to ANYTHING she told them. Whenever another adult was around, the kids listened (more or less, of course). I went in one day to help with dismissal and it wasn't hard to get the kids in order, but as soon as I turned my back to leave, and I mean IMMEDIATELY, they got out of line, started talking—one even sat down at Miss Green's desk! It was like a light switch: when I walked in the room, the kids listened. When I walked out, the kids seemed to think there was no one in charge and weren't even aware that Miss Green was in the room. It worked that way with the entire staff—half a dozen of us showed her what to do and successfully managed her kids—but she just couldn't follow through herself when we weren't around.

She said what we said, and did exactly what we did. But there was some reason why it didn't work for her: an intangible something, the X factor, that Miss Green did not have. My theory? She didn't project confidence and calm assertiveness. She was missing a firm, loud, strong voice with a source of authority that comes only from a belief in one's self and one's abilities. Her tough demeanor was false, and the kids knew it—they did not believe in her because she did not believe in herself. She was inconsistent with rules, routines, and procedures because she did not have the confidence and presence of mind to enforce them with a well-founded assumption of mutual respect.

Many kids in the inner-city learn instinctively to be tough. They have strong personalities and know how to get noticed and get things done even in the face of overwhelming obstacles. These are qualities that young people have developed in order to survive in their environment. When you accept a teaching position in the inner-city, you are now a part of that environment, and you must adapt the same attitude of self-preservation. You must have an equally strong presence in the classroom. You must be a fighter, a person who can handle stress and pressure without crumbling. This is what the kids know, this is who they are, and it's who they relate to. Not all of them are truly strong, but the ones who earn respect in their community can fake it. Even when they are trembling inside, they maintain a tough exterior that says, "Don't mess with me." That's the mentality of a survivor. To be a real force for change in these kids' lives, you have to take on their best qualities and personality traits. *You* have to be a survivor.

Lesson #2) It's not just what you say, it's how you say it.

Miss Green gave directions but had no techniques for making sure they were followed except for repeatedly begging and giving stickers every fifteen minutes (literally) to the kids who did behave. She was not able to raise her voice above their voices when needed. When she gave directions, it was soft and phrased positively ALL THE TIME. She talked TOO much and the kids tuned her out. They responded much better to a serious "Pick it up, please," than her pleading, "Johnny, would you please help take care of our classroom by picking up the paper you just dropped? Great job, Johnny. Thank you for being a good part of our class." That kind of talk can NOT be used for every single direction given, especially not with that group of kids.

Miss Green needed to get an attitude in her voice at times, some sassiness: "Ex*cuse* me, if *I* am talking, YOU are listening," followed by a three- or four-second silent stare. She would attempt to say these things at times, but her tone sounded like she was pleading, that she was hoping that they would listen. It did not convey a confidence that when she told them to do something, they WOULD do it. Her tone needed to convey that she would figure out whatever it would take to get them to behave and not settle for anything less—some kids need firm reminders, some need to be called last to line up or miss out on an activity, some need to have security escort them to the principal's office. Her tone did not convey that she had a bag of tricks up her sleeve and was prepared to follow through all the way with each child.

I do not smile when my students misbehave. My face gets very, very serious, my eyes stone cold. I can be smiling as I teach my lesson and then narrow my eyes and lower my voice in an ominous tone to address a child who is playing around, then a split second later smile at the class again and finish my sentence. At first I felt like a schizophrenic, but I saw myself on videotape once and it doesn't look that way at all. It's more like, here's a teacher who's happy and enthusiastic because kids are learning, and now here's a teacher who turned tough with the one kid disrupting that process, without taking it out on the whole class. The other children get the same smile and positive tone they received before the reprimand because they had nothing to do with the problem.

In addition to lacking an authoritative attitude, Miss Green was also visibly afraid to get in her kids' faces when reprimanding them. In high-poverty schools, it's typical to have a handful of kids who tune you out if you don't bend over to their eye level and say what you have to say. Calling across the room or from three feet above when you stand next to them doesn't cut it. By being the only adult in the school who did not speak to her class in close proximity, Miss Green was communicating a weakness of sorts, as if she was afraid of what they would do if she were too close.

You must refuse to fear a child. Keep perspective of the situation and tell yourself, *I will live through whatever this child does next, and I will win in the end.* If students are used to yelling, don't be afraid to raise your voice at times until they can respond to the methods of communication that you feel are more respectful. I don't mean screaming at your kids—I mean using a commanding, authoritative voice. A lot of teachers don't want to speak loudly and firmly because it's not fun to do and they don't like speaking that way. However, there are a lot of things in teaching we don't want to do but have to in order to reach students with a diversity of needs.

Disciplining itself is not fun. IT IS EXHAUSTING having to stay on students for every single behavior for every second of the day. In one inner-city school, I rarely went more than two minutes without having to get somebody back on-task—*no talking, keep working, you can do it, I love how you're taking care of our books, no way, stay in your seat, great job walking, what's the rule about pencils?* There was no alternative. I could either get lazy or I could enforce my rules and enjoy the continuing payoffs. DON'T GIVE UP!

Lesson #3) Never reward behavior before related procedures are firmly in place.

Many new teachers know the importance of procedures and think they are teaching and reinforcing them, but in reality, they aren't. If your students don't complete classroom tasks exactly how you want them done the majority of the time, you're not done teaching routines. You must explain, model, practice, and reinforce appropriate behaviors before attempting to give incentives. For example, students can't have free time in the classroom until they've proven they can work independently. They can't have extra time on the playground until they've shown they can follow rules for using the equipment.

> **If students don't respect your routines and expectations for appropriate behavior, then any rewards you try to give them will result in chaos.**

One of the saddest things I saw happen with Miss Green occurred in the media center one day. She was picking up her kids from specials and wanted to distribute treats that she bought with her own money. She was hoping to reward them for walking quietly back to the classroom. This was not a terrible idea, given how far her students were from self-regulation and intrinsic motivation. She was trying to meet them at the level they were at and provide an incentive for behaving appropriately.

The kids saw the candy and began pushing and shoving each other, yelling, "I want that one! I want that one!" This didn't surprise me, because if kids are not taught how to respond appropriately to rewards, they will do things like that. Miss Green had no procedures in place that she could rely on to control the environment. This happened over a month into the school year, and her kids should have known never to approach her all at once. In fact, they should have been extra quiet to try to earn the reward, in which case they would have heard her announce that she wanted them to walk back to the classroom first. They should have then waited to be called by teams or individually to get their candy. But they didn't think to do that, because she never taught them how to wait.

So far the incident was pretty predictable. But the part that I couldn't believe was that Miss Green *still gave her kids the treats* after they nearly mobbed her! She allowed them to swarm around her and became completely flustered trying to distribute the treats without having the kids kill each other. I didn't hear a single thank you. The children argued with each other, stole pieces out of each other's hands, and ripped the bag open to grab every last candy. Miss Green had wanted to give out treats slowly and make the bag last for at least a week. The children had devoured the entire thing without her permission in under a minute. She looked completely defeated and totally worn-out. And now all of her candy was gone and her kids were bouncing around the media center on a sugar high without ever having accomplished the task of walking back to the classroom.

Watching this, I was simultaneously heart-broken for Miss Green and infuriated at her students. Those kids, in my opinion, deserved NOTHING. I would have raised my voice so they could hear me over the chaos and said loudly (not screaming), "No. Everyone have a seat. Sit down. Goodbye," and put the treats behind my back or up on a shelf as a symbolic gesture. I would have waited until everyone sat down and then laid into them in a normal tone of voice (kids do get quiet when they sense they are in trouble or something interesting is about to happen!). "I bought you treats with my own money because I was so proud of the way you behaved in media. But then I saw so many disrespectful behaviors. What did I see that was not okay?" I would have then called on the kids to tell me what they did wrong, because they did know better, they just realized that they could get away with atrocious behavior around Miss Green. They would be able to list every single unconscionable action, and I would fill in the blanks for anything they missed. "So you KNOW what you did was rude and you chose to do it anyway. I can't give anyone a treat after that sort of behavior. I'll be watching to see how things go during math. If I see people listening when I am talking, using the materials the right way, and cleaning up quietly, I will think about giving you the treats then. Now, I'm going to call you by teams to form a silent line back to the classroom."

I guarantee that if Miss Green had asserted control over the situation that way, her students would have thought twice the next time she tried to reward them. They still would have needed reminders and guidance, including reinforcement narration when she was ready to pass the treats out ("I'm going to call the quietest table to come up first for their treat. Watch as table one WALKS up to me, waits quietly in line, and walks back to their seat without saying a word except thank you—great job, table one"), but chaos of that magnitude would be in the past with a little more firmness.

It's great to reward students for good behavior, but only give them rewards they can handle. Miss Green's class couldn't receive candy during the fifth week of school because they still hadn't learned to sit and wait for her to give directions. (You can only imagine the impact of this problem on instruction.) Students don't have to be faultless in order to receive positive reinforcement, but until they're ready to begin self-regulation, they need to grasp that YOU are in charge of all tangible rewards and classroom privileges: who gets what, when it happens, how it happens. If students try to take over that process, they don't deserve anything other than a discussion on how to receive things properly the next time.

Lesson #4) When you correct misbehavior, be FIRM and don't worry about whether kids will like you or think you're mean.

A significant part of earning children's respect is by showing that you genuinely care about them as individuals—greeting them each morning by name, returning their hugs (if appropriate), listening and smiling when they talk, and so on. But most teachers whose kids walk all over them have the niceness thing down. They know how to show kids they care.   They just can't get kids to stop taking advantage of that fact.

What many teachers consider mean is typically not so in the mind of a young child, especially in high-poverty environments.   In fact, children may view our attempts at building their self-esteem as being too nice.   At home, many disadvantaged students do not receive praise for doing things halfway or for doing things they are expected to do.   If Marshaun was supposed to take his baby sister's things to her room and instead leaves them on the stairs, mom will probably not say sweetly, "Marshaun, thank you for trying to carry everything! Would you please take the bag all the way up the stairs?   There you go!   Great job, Marshaun!"   She would probably respond with something similar to, "Marshaun!   I said put that bag in your sister's room!"   When he finally does it, she would likely say nothing, because it was a simple task that Marshaun was fully capable of, and he was lazy about it until she repeated herself.   That type of conduct is not likely to inspire compliments from a mother who has worked two jobs that day and is taking care of four children by herself.

Now imagine that Marshaun comes into your classroom the following day and you ask him to put his pencil away.   He sticks it behind his ear instead.   Try to picture what's going through his mind when you then smile and say, "Oh, Marshaun, you're so silly!   Where does the pencil go?   That's right!   Good job! No, no, Marshaun!   Put it in your desk, please!   Alright, way to go!"   You think you're being encouraging and positive, and a child with a background similar to yours might see it that way, too.   But Marshuan's initial impression is that you have low expectations and are willing to baby him.   He doesn't have to be responsible, because when he plays around, he gets rewarded with attention, praise, and encouragement.   You smiled at his misbehavior, which must mean it amuses you and he should do it again next time.   *This* is how it's possible to be too nice, especially when working with inner-city populations.

Don't worry about a child disliking you for being strict and having high expectations. There is a special elementary school phenomenon that is absolutely astounding to all the teachers I know.   It applies in every classroom in which the teacher has shown students she cares about them.   ***Here's what happens: no matter how many times you have to discipline the class…they still love you.*** Young children have an innate loyalty towards their teachers that would rival that of a Labrador retriever towards its master.

There are days when I feel like the meanest person in the world and the kids line up to give me hugs on the way out the door at dismissal! I can ream a child out for misbehavior on the way to lunch, and then when I wave goodbye to the class at the cafeteria door, he'll shout, "'Bye, Ms. Powell! Have a great lunch!" I even remember a time in which I sent a child to the office for cheating on a test, and when she came back into the classroom with tears streaming down her cheeks, she came immediately over to my desk and said, "I'm sorry, Ms. Powell! I love you!"

Children need structure and thrive off of discipline. Sometimes the amount of love a child demonstrates towards the teacher is directly proportional to the amount of correction the teacher gives. Your most challenging students are often the ones who care about you the most.

This phenomenon is something that Miss Green never caught onto. She thought she had to earn the kids' affection by being permissive and understanding with their behavior. She didn't realize that her kids already loved her, because they knew she loved them. They had already seen the genuine smile on her face and sparkle in her eye when they walked in the room each morning.

Lesson #5)   Remove disruptive children from your lessons and focus on students who want to learn.

In high-poverty schools, there's almost always a small core of students who just do not follow the rules no matter what—they're always talking, out of their seats, pushing, making gross noises and burping on purpose, taking things from other kids, interrupting, and so on. I used to let those kids get to me—I would stop my lesson to address them, and feel my blood pressure rising! But ignoring them would only cause worse behavior.

One day as I started to get extremely frustrated during a lesson, I realized that 21 out of 23 kids were fully engaged and participating (typical kid stuff like playing with pencils not withstanding). I just decided (out loud) that I was not going to let those two kids put me in a bad mood because I was really enjoying the lesson and I could tell that the rest of the class was, too. The most disruptive child was put by the door where no one would be paying him any attention, and the less disruptive one was sent back to his desk from the carpet. And the lesson went beautifully from then on! In the past, I had allowed the misbehaving kids to stay on the rug because I was following what I knew from behavior modification textbooks about not excluding or embarrassing students, and I didn't want them to miss out on instruction (as if they were paying attention). But keeping disruptive kids with the group was not working. I learned to stop worrying about these trouble-makers' self-esteem when they were preventing the rest of the class from learning.

If students are noisy even after being removed from the group, I ignore them at first, then if I see that the other kids are distracted, I give a mean stare and get back to teaching. If it happens a third time, I let them know they will be removed from the classroom if they disrupt my lesson again. Removal from the classroom is part of my behavior plan so parents and administration are aware that I do this and support me. If the student does anything else, I make a big serious production out of having to stop my lesson, apologizing profusely to the class for the child's misbehavior, and ask, "Would you mind waiting quietly for two minutes while I take Carlo to Ms. Diaz's room?" They all nod solemnly and I walk the kid to another teacher, usually someone really tough. For documentation purposes, I fill out a form similar to the one below (available for free download at TheCornerstoneForTeachers.com) and send it with the child. I try to provide work for the student but getting that together takes even more time away from the lesson, so sometimes I let the child just sit there with his head down, or complete whatever work the kids in the other class are doing.

REMOVAL FROM CLASSROOM: DIRECTIONS & DOCUMENTATION

Date _____   Time Sent _____

Student's Name _____   Sent to _____

From ___*Ms. Powell (room 12)*___   Reason _____

Directions: complete the assignment below   put head down   do what the teacher's class is doing

Return to classroom: when assignment is completed   when the teacher needs you to leave   at dismissal

Comments from other teacher (if needed):

Note to student: Please stand inside the teacher's doorway until he or she asks you to come in. Ask if you can stay, and show this note only when the teacher asks to see it. Do NOT interrupt the class in any other way! DO NOT LOSE THIS PAPER! You will file it when you return to our classroom.

The majority of kids in some high-poverty communities are working below grade level, and a big part of the reason why is because there are so many behavior problems in the classroom. Teachers can't teach those who want to learn, and their hands are tied when it comes to discipline. Getting disruptive kids away from the ones who are trying to learn is critical in any classroom. Equally important is keeping the teacher's focus on instruction. Do not let yourself become discouraged or bogged down by the obstacles that your challenging students throw your way. Keep your mind focused on the children who ARE cooperating, who DO care, who WILL try their best. Go in to work every day and give everything you've got for those kids.

Part Five:
Planning Purposeful Instruction and Assessment

Chapter 19: Purposeful Planning
Gathering and organizing resources for effective instruction

All of us can think of a time in which we didn't understand what we were supposed to be teaching or how, and the impact our unpreparedness had on the flow and effectiveness of the lesson. There are no routines or procedures that can make up for a lack of clearly defined activities that achieve a common purpose. Why plan procedure practice if there is no ultimate goal for student learning? How can we meticulously plan our routines and daily schedule yet neglect to have a vision for what students will learn and achieve throughout the year?

Lesson planning is a very individual process that will vary according to your needs and preferences, the structure of your class, and mandates by your administration. I have taught in schools that left me completely on my own and gave almost total freedom as to which skills I taught and when. Other schools provided a pacing guide that told me exactly what to teach at every moment of the day with such precision that I could have told you in August what I would be doing at 9:45 a.m. on April 19th. Your situation could be at either extreme or someplace in the middle, which makes it difficult for me to give general advice about lesson planning. Instead, I'll try to provide guidelines to help you streamline the system you're supposed to use and reflect on your practice in a way that isn't overwhelming.

If you want to create a more unified, thematic approach to your curriculum that makes learning more meaningful for students, read on for ways to set goals, collect and organize resources, and create long- and short-term lesson plans that not only align with what your school district requires, but with what YOU know is best practice for your students.

The Freedom to Teach

Who Determines What You're Teaching?

It may surprise you to learn that I am in favor of stronger district mandates on the WHAT (but not the HOW) of curriculum implementation. I believe that each school district (in conjunction with nearby counties whenever possible) should provide long-range planning and pacing guides (or curriculum maps) that are based on state standards. These should be provided not as a restriction on teachers, but as a service for them. No new teacher should be left struggling to figure out how to cover everything in all the textbooks. We don't teach textbooks, we teach state standards, and those standards should be made clearly evident to every teacher. If you're assigned to a classroom, you should be familiarized with what the state expects for your grade level (and to some extent, the grade below and above you, as well). In my opinion, it is the school district's responsibility to provide its teachers with a pacing guide that outlines which skills should be taught with a suggested order of instruction that is logical and based on student needs.

When teachers are given an effective plan for implementing all of the state standards, the struggle to 'fit everything in' becomes far less overwhelming. Teachers are less isolated in their classrooms and can work together as a grade level team to share the responsibility of planning lessons, selecting photocopies to be made, and gathering relevant materials. Instruction is improved when it is tightly aligned with the state standards, and teachers are free to focus their attention on effective implementation strategies for their students.

Your Responsibility for Addressing Deficiencies in the System

You may not be provided with a district-designed or school-based pacing guide, or you may be given one that is insufficient or ineffective. The burden of designing an appropriate long-range plan then falls on you. I encourage you to do whatever helps you form a clear focus for your instruction and ensure that you are teaching ALL of your state standards without speeding through curriculum or lingering too long on one area. This might mean sketching things out in a rough plan, or creating a more effective pacing guide and submitting it for district use.

I once taught in a school that did not have its own pacing guide and relied on an outdated, fragmented plan from the district, so I pieced the various segments together and specified which skills I would cover each week. The plan was far more comprehensive than what was given by the county, and when I showed it to my team leader, the whole grade level adopted it. What began as a simple framework for effective instruction in my own classroom became a school-wide model. The staff worked together to create similar guides for each grade level, resulting in more unified instruction for the entire school. Not every teacher will want to take on this challenge, but if you see a deficiency in the way your school implements curriculum and you feel inspired to make a difference, I encourage you to contribute to improvement in any way you can. Create a vision for your instruction and share it with anyone who might benefit.

Lacking a clear focus for the school year is the opposite problem for some teachers. Unfortunately, some educators are forced to use a guide that tells them not just WHAT but HOW to teach (the strategies they must use and sometimes the exact words to speak). I've known teachers who could hear each other through the walls while each was saying the same sentence at the same time. This type of control disregards teaching as an art as well as a science, making the false assumptions that a) teachers have no professional discernment or innovative ideas to contribute, and b) that students will all achieve the same results if given the exact same instruction. Typically, scripted lessons are 'only' used during the reading block, but teachers within these institutions cannot plan effective instruction in any area when the learning environment is not based on what's best for students. These teachers must either work within their schools for change or seek employment opportunities elsewhere.

Planning Basics for All Teachers

Regardless of the amount of control you have over what and how you teach, in order to design and implement effective lessons, every teacher should have a:

- ➢ system for writing daily lesson plans that's easily managed
- ➢ long-range plan and focused vision you're working towards
- ➢ method for obtaining and organizing new teaching ideas
- ➢ plan for reflection on your teaching strategies and making improvements

Daily Lesson Plans

Using a Daily Plan Book

When I first started teaching, I used standard lesson plan books with one square for each subject. I wrote out every detail of what I planned to do to make sure I didn't forget anything. Over time, I felt like I was rewriting the same things too often, so I developed my own weekly lesson plan format in a word processing document (which can be downloaded on my website). Now I print it out and photocopy the pages back to back.

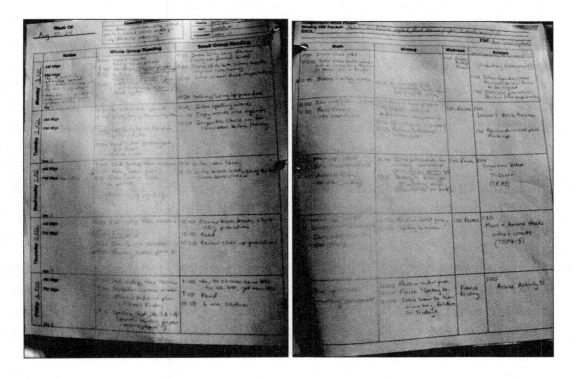

When I sit down to plan for the upcoming months, I copy the skill from my pacing guides into each lesson plan block and underline it as a title for the lesson, such as "Equivalent Fractions" or "The Inner Planets." When all the skills are written in for the time period I'm planning for, I go back and write activities related to the skills, one subject area at a time. Seeing the order in which skills will be taught for each day of the month helps me keep the big picture in mind as I plan specific lessons. I use my lesson resources to help me fill in the activities, pulling out the related drawer or magazine file boxes to see what materials and worksheets I have and setting up a pile of things to get photocopied.

Advice for Daily/Weekly Lesson Planning

♦ **Check your district requirements.** Some districts and administrators want teachers to write lesson objectives, homework assignments, how instruction will be differentiated, etc., in their plan books. Find out what is being asked of you and if it seems excessive, check with your union representative to determine your contractual obligations. I once worked for a principal that asked teachers to document far more information than would ever fit in our planning pages; in another county, I heard of principals who were requiring typed lesson plans to be posted online. In both situations, our contracts specified that we could not legally be required to do those things.

♦ **Consider typing your reading group plans if you follow a similar format each day.** I did this for language arts in one school because our 120-minute block was very regimented. I enjoyed the consistency of the schedule and found that printing out an outline of the block and then handwriting the specifics for the week saved me a lot of time and helped me feel more prepared.

♦ **Underline the materials needed for each lesson.** At the beginning of the day (or the afternoon before), you can quickly glance over the day's lessons and see what things you need to gather or prepare.

♦ **Design a rough outline of your plans for an entire month or unit, then fill in the details as you go.** There is something to be said for student-centered curriculum and basing future instruction on how well children are mastering the current skills. However, planning day-by-day or week-by-week does not enable you to focus on the big picture of what you want your kids to ultimately learn, unless you are following a pacing guide. You may not want to plan all of the activities for next month quite yet, but write down the skills or concepts you want to cover for each day, leaving yourself several days for review and catch-up activities. The week before you teach, you can choose the exact lessons and materials to use and fill them in your plan book.

♦ **Have a regular, uninterrupted time for lesson planning.** When I switched from third to second grade, I used to take all my manuals home every other weekend. (Of course, you may now be able to access most of your teaching guides online so it won't be necessary to drag everything around!) I would spend about two hours on Sunday afternoons planning. To me, it was worth the time investment because I felt so much more prepared at school. In other teaching situations, I knew the curriculum so well that I really didn't have to plan at home, although I did occasionally. The newer you are to the teaching profession/your grade level/your curriculum, the more important it will be to set apart time to really concentrate and create plans you are excited to teach. The longer you've been teaching, the easier it will be for you to work more spontaneously. I often write the skill or objective I want to teach and that's it: then, the morning of the lesson, I'll come up with a way to teach it that suits my mood, the kids' moods, and the day's schedule.

♦ **Use sticky notes to reflect on what did and didn't work for next year's reference.** I have one sticky for the week that I place on the bottom right hand corner of the page and write notes to myself for next year ("Measuring took longer than I thought—allow about 20 minutes" or "Kids loved main idea posters—give them time to explain with partners"). If your school collects lesson plans at the end of the year, you may want to write your notes on a separate sheet of paper, and then photocopy the notes and the lesson plan pages in June.

Long-Range Planning

Backwards Planning

Sometimes teachers plan activities and then give a test that has no correlation—maybe the lessons prepared the kids, maybe they didn't. Many times, there isn't proper alignment between instruction and assessment, unless your administration or district have spent extensive time on creating pacing guides and resources to address the problem. However, with the Backwards Planning method, you design the 'big idea' and essential questions first, then choose ways to assess whether kids have mastered those key concepts, and THEN activities to prepare the kids for assessment.

It takes awhile to move towards this type of instruction; I used to just follow the curriculum guide and hope the kids did well on the test. Eventually I started looking at the test first and then designing the lessons, and now I bring everything back to the key concepts daily and really keep things tightly connected. It's probably too much for a first-year teacher to do—I know I wasn't ready back then—but I encourage more experienced teachers to experiment with this type of thinking. It will revolutionize the way you teach and how your kids learn. For example, instead of just learning to locate places on a map and study random cultures in social studies, my kids are exploring the essential question: How do geography and history affect destiny? (Meaning, how do place and time affect the way people live their lives?) All of my assessments were based on the state standards and were designed FIRST, so I know my lessons are tightly aligned and preparing students to demonstrate mastery in essential skills.

Using Pacing Guides to Teach the Standards, Not the Textbook

Pacing guides or curriculum maps are outlines of what objectives/ themes/concepts will be taught and when, and help you keep your lessons focused on state standards. Aligning your instruction and assessment with state standards is NOT the same thing as 'teaching to the test'. Your standards are the grade level expectations—things that all children should know before moving on to the next grade level. Therefore, those are the things you should be teaching. They may be more in-depth than what is outlined in your teaching manuals, or your manuals may include additional skills that students in your state are not required to master until later on. For example, my state standards require third graders to learn about Roman numerals, but the concept is not included in our math text; conversely, students are not required to learn about light and optics, yet the science textbook includes these topics. Publishers do their best to align teaching materials with standards, but there are always gaps. Teach your state standards, not your textbook. This is most easily done when all of the standards are mapped out in a pacing guide.

Developing a Repertoire of Teaching Strategies

Too Many Ideas, Too Little Time

Even with the aid of a curriculum map or pacing guide, many teachers over plan and get frustrated because they can't squeeze it all in. There are so many things we want our little ones to learn and it's just not possible to do everything!

Like most teachers, I collect ideas, lessons, and worksheets throughout the year. Anything related to a specific theme, skill, or concept is filed in a clearly labeled file folder, which I don't go through until it's time to teach the particular unit. However, the behavior management strategies, vocabulary builders, routines, character-building activities, and morning meeting ideas I collect get lost in the shuffle, because they don't go with any particular concept or unit. At the end of the year, I always feel disappointed that I never got to try a certain game with the class, sing a special song, read a specific book, or address a particular world event or problem.

Have a Specific Timeline for Implementation

I created a Year-Long Planner to help me implement all the great ideas I'm just dying to use but never make time to squeeze in. It's organized by month and category, so that each month I'm using new ideas. This system provides enough time for kids to get comfortable and familiar with activities without things becoming tedious. And of course, I go back and use some of the previous month's ideas from time to time,

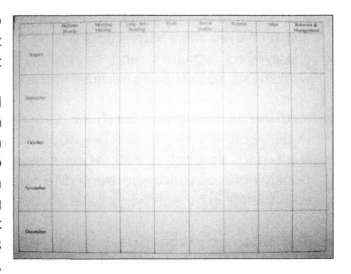

especially when the kids request it. You do have to accept the fact that you can't use every idea every year. Pick the ones you like best and concentrate on those.

Inexpensive Ways to Get New Teaching Resources and Ideas

- **Buy and resell on online auction sites:** These websites have lots of great stuff, some new, some used, and all are serious bargains! Be careful, though—it's addictive! I usually buy, read, photocopy and take notes, then resell. The items are considered used, but that really doesn't take much off the value. After all, the next buyer doesn't care if you were the sole owner or the fifth one, as long as the materials are in good condition.

- **Local library:** You would be surprised at what your local library might have! There are usually a variety of workbooks for parents to help their kids succeed in school. I have also seen books of reading games, early childhood learning-readiness activities, and craft books. Photocopy what you need at school for free. Also, do an inventory search on the library's website. There aren't many copies of each title—usually one per system—but you can place a hold on any book you see online in the library catalog and they will send it to your local branch at no charge.

- **Other teachers:** Of course photocopying an entire resource book breaks copyright laws, so I can't advocate that... but do recognize that other teachers in your building have likely spent hundreds of dollars on books, most of which they don't use. Borrow those resources and write down any ideas you like! I am known for sending out emails to an entire grade level (not necessarily my own!) or even the entire school asking for a specific resource—math games, cause/effect activities, and so on. I have an incredible assortment of worksheets and activities because of the generosity of co-workers!

- **Retiring and resigning teachers:** One retiring teacher I know set up a 'store' in her room on the last teacher workday of the year. Everything was free for the taking, although donations were requested. There were tons of resource books, none of which she wanted to lug home to store in her garage! Ask your friends in other schools to let you know when their colleagues retire.

- **The Internet:** Who says teacher resources have to be in book form? Nowadays, just about any printables or lesson ideas you need can be found for free online!

Organizing Your Ideas

Keeping Track of Activities from Magazines and Books

It's so hard to remember (not to mention organize) all of the great ideas you come across. Here are ways you can keep track of the tips and techniques you collect:

- **When you read an idea you like in a magazine you own:** I suggest ripping it out and filing by subject (such as for a lesson on money) or by month (such as a winter activity). I don't ever go through old magazines to find lesson ideas, but I do look in my files and review the things I ripped out. It's hard to tear up a beautiful resource, but if that's the only way it will get utilized, then it's worth it. Although it's more work, you could also photocopy the articles.

- **When you read an idea in a book you own:** Mark it up so it's useful to you! I put a checkmark by the idea if I think it's worth remembering, two checks if it's something I'd like to try, and a star if it's something I absolutely must do. I keep several sticky notes inside the front cover, labeled with 'To Make,' 'To Photocopy and File,' and so on. As I read ideas I like, I write the page numbers down on the appropriate sticky. I differentiate between materials I need to gather and create, and things the kids can color/cut/get together for me, since the things they can do usually get accomplished right away. I'll often prioritize different ideas on the sticky notes by starring anything I want to make or get together right away. If I'm feeling lazy, I'll just write 'equivalent fractions— see Mailbox Oct. 2008' on a sticky and  put it in my fractions file folder. Then when it comes time to teach fractions, I have to go through the trouble of pulling the resource to see what was in it, but at least I knew it was there. Nothing's worse than finishing a unit and realizing you forgot you had the perfect activity!

- **When you read an idea in a book or magazine you *don't* own:** Use sticky notes to mark the pages you want to photocopy. If the idea is very brief, you could write it on a sticky note instead and then put it in your files. For example, the sticky in the lower left hand corner of the photo shows how I list all the pages in a magazine that I want to photocopy. The one above it lists the things I want to make (with page numbers or just little drawings or notes). The others on the right side are stickies that will be filed according to the skill or concept written on each.

◆ **When you read an idea for a game:** You could just put all game ideas in a binder or folder. I like to photocopy each game idea I see, then cut it out and glue it to an index card. The front of the card has the directions,

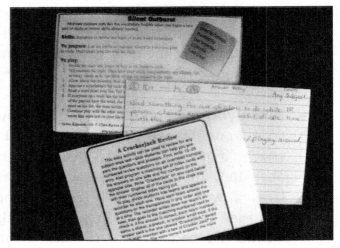

and the back has the category the game goes under (e.g., math or spelling), along with my adaptations and reflections. I also like to add symbols indicating how much prep time is needed, whether it's an active or quiet game, and if it's for teams or individuals, but you don't have to go that in-depth. After lamination, the cards are filed in an index card box. I do a review game before almost every test I give, and if the rules are written inside some random teacher resource book or buried deep in my file cabinet, I'll never remember or utilize them. This way, tons of review ideas are literally at my finger tips and require very little planning.

◆ **When you read something online:** Print and file, or, if it's a large collection of ideas, cut and paste into a Word document, then print and file. I always make sure I have the website or title somewhere on the page (usually this is done automatically by the printer—check the bottom of your pages) so I can refer back to the site, and also in case I share the idea and need to give proper credit.

◆ **When you see or hear about something another teacher does:** I have a camera phone and try to take a picture to help me visualize the idea later. I'll print the photo on regular paper and jot notes on the side. If it's just something a teacher mentioned to me, I try to write it down on my infamous sticky notes and place it in the appropriate file folder.

◆ **When you discover an ongoing routine or strategy you want to use:** I record the ideas using one of the strategies above, then add it to my year-long idea planner so I can be sure it gets fit in.

Building a Personal Reference for Topics That Interest You

One summer, I decided I wanted to learn to use a word wall—not just have it up on the wall, but actually teach with it. Although word walls were encouraged by the district, they weren't part of our curriculum, and I had very few resources. So, I typed 'word wall' into an Internet search engine and clicked on 'Search IMAGES' (not websites). I copied and pasted into a Word document the photos that looked interesting to me and then printed them.

Next, I typed 'word wall activities' in and did a regular Internet search. I printed everything relevant and helpful. I also bought a word wall book, photocopied the pages I wanted, and resold the book online to get most of my money back. Last, I hole-punched the pages and put them in a binder.

You can see the bottom of the page where I wrote notes about tips I picked up from the photos—how word walls were hung up, word organization, colors that

were used, etc. I then went through and marked the pages up to my heart's content! I used the following system:

- Headings/New Topics: orange highlighter
- Subtopics: yellow highlighter
- References/web addresses: green highlighter
- My notes: red pen

I made little notes in the margins about possible ways to tailor the ideas for my own classroom and things I wanted to research more. Whenever I found new ideas about word walls, I added them to the binder.

Organizing Internet Resources

How many sites are saved on your 'Favorites' list? If you're like me, probably a million. You can't tell what half of them are, the links don't work when you click on them...you know the drill. But what's even more frustrating is the dilemma of being on a really great website with links to other really great websites—should you leave the first site? Or bookmark the second site and come back to the first one? Or just bounce from site to site until you're out of browser windows and your computer freezes up?

My plan isn't perfect by any means. But if you're lacking a system altogether, these tips should be helpful:

- **Use your 'Add to Favorites' function!** There's no way to track everything without becoming familiar with this tool. (They're called 'Bookmarks' on Macintosh computers.)

- **Enable the 'Links' toolbar.** If you add websites to this folder in your Favorites, it will put all links from the folder at the top of your browser window. This is perfect for links you use on a daily basis. If you put a folder in the Links folder, it will make that whole folder appear at the top of your browser.

- **Set up folders that make sense for you**. Delete the standard ones. Your folders should encompass every type of site you could possibly bookmark, but you shouldn't have more than a dozen or so to keep things simple. Here's my current list of education-related folders:

  - **To Peruse**: Sorry for the pretentious-sounding name, but 'peruse' is the most concise word I could think of for a title! This is the most important folder I have for keeping teacher sites organized. Anytime I'm at a site that links to another, I click on the link, take a thirty second glance to see if I think it would interest me, and add it to my 'To Peruse' folder if I'd like to spend more time there. Then I go back to the original site and finish what I started. Anytime I have a few minutes, I click open my 'To Peruse' folder and pick a site! I usually have twenty or more sites at any time in this folder. After I look at them, I either delete or add to...

  - **Teaching Stuff**: Resources I use all the time.

  - **Projects:** Any big projects for which I'm collecting resources go in here, and if I'm doing multiple projects, I create additional folders inside the Projects folder.

- **To Print:** I stick links in here and print all at once when I have a chance. I have a folder inside this one called 'Print At Work' for extensive classroom-related printing to save on my own ink and paper.

- **To Make**: I often see forms I want to use in the classroom but that need to be altered before I can print them. I stick the links in this file, and when I have time, I edit them and then print.

♦ **Always add new links to a folder.** Don't let sites accumulate in a huge list. The more random links you have, the less likely you are to remember what they're for and utilize them. If nothing else, they can go in your 'To Peruse' folder for when you have time to explore them more fully.

Reflecting and Planning New Strategies for Next Year

There are a few questions I ask myself in preparation for each new school year. Reflection is an ongoing process, but the summer is a natural time to really think things out and get everything in order. Here are the questions, along with my honest responses from a few years ago:

1) What aspects of teaching did I stop enjoying this year?

I kept falling behind on my grading; therefore I needed to re-evaluate the type and quantity of assignments I gave and when and how I graded them. My math warm-ups got really dull, so I needed to find a book or Internet resource to give me some fresh ideas. And science was such a pain—I needed to figure out a way to make it more hands-on and get my materials together in advance so I wouldn't be scrambling around at the last minute.

2) What concepts or skills did the students have a lot of difficulty mastering?

Converting measurements, telling time, adding details to sentences, and using proper punctuation were concepts my kids struggled with all year. I also had a hard time getting children to slow down and check over their work. Additionally, I had a big problem with stealing in the classroom, and name-calling persisted among a small group of children no matter what I did. The methods I used to address these issues, both academic and social, were obviously not as effective as they could have been, so I needed to read, visit chat boards, search the Internet, and collaborate with my teammates to develop better strategies.

3) What type of students do I want to produce? What's the main thing I want all my students to remember from spending a year with me?

My goal was for children to want to learn, and recognize that learning takes place everywhere all the time, not just in school. I wanted them to begin questioning what they're taught and critically analyze what their friends say, what they read and see on TV, and the subliminal societal messages that are reinforced daily through stereotyping. Therefore, I needed to point out inconsistencies and mistakes in texts, teach strategies for analysis in reading, use current events in social studies, and show students how to be active and not passive learners. I needed to plan for specific strategies to reinforce these priorities on a regular basis and not get caught up on whether students could round to the nearest hundred or identify a noun without relating those lessons to a meaningful context.

Reflecting on your teaching helps sharpen your focus and generate enthusiasm for the following year. It is so important for teachers to BE the life-long learners we talk about with our students. When you create new goals for yourself and consciously look for ways to improve your teaching, you will enjoy your profession for many more years to come.

Chapter 20: Managing Small Group Instruction
Strategies for facilitating guided reading groups and transitions

The structure and components of literacy instruction vary widely around the nation and even within school systems. Many schools get new literacy programs or mandates every single year, with little continuity between the changes. As a general rule, most elementary teachers are required to teach reading for 90-120 minutes per day, with some parts of the reading block conducted whole class and some parts in small groups. The whole class part is pretty straightforward. It's the small group component that stresses teachers out. They're not sure how to provide literacy instruction on the appropriate level for every single student, and they worry out about keeping everyone on-task for the entire hour.

Your school system will most likely mandate or recommend a structure for your reading block. What they probably won't explain is how to manage it without inducing daily migraines. That's where this chapter of the book comes in.

There are a lot of different things you can have the rest of the class doing while you teach reading groups: centers, centerjobs, partner reading, partner work, making words, independent work, silent reading, computer games, and so on. In the past, I have called the whole thing our Literacy Workshop, since it consisted of a variety of elements. Look at what your school system requires and then fine-tune the plan until it works for you.

For the purposes of this book, I'll assume that your small group reading block will contain some combination of the following elements:

- **Independent work:** This is a set of assignments that students complete on their own, generally in silence. Independent work is usually comprised of pencil and paper tasks such as worksheets, but could be hands-on activities such as making words.

- **Small group instruction:** For 10-30 minutes per day, students meet with the teacher to work on skills and concepts that are developmentally appropriate for each individual. Typically the groups are homogenous (below, on, and above grade level, known as BGL, OGL, and AGL). However, groups can be flexible, in which children who need to work on a particular skill are temporarily grouped for instruction on that skill. Groups could also be formed heterogeneously so students can learn from and help each other.

- **Silent, Self-Selected Reading:** This can be a highly unstructured time in which students read whichever books interest them, or it can be structured to include a reading log and conferences with the teacher.

- **Computers:** If there are multiple working computers in the classroom, students may take turns completing activities online through web quests or use computer software programs provided by the district or teacher.

- **Centers:** This is a broad term that typically refers to activities that are supposed to be hands-on, differentiated for varying ability levels, and open-ended.

This chapter will clearly explain the process of structuring each reading block component: how to choose materials, how to introduce routines, and how to assess learning. The chapter will conclude with tips for smooth transitions in between each rotation and ideas for keeping the whole class on-task throughout the reading block.

As you read, I'd like for you to keep in mind three important things:

1) **It's okay to feel overwhelmed by this part of your schedule.** Reading is my least favorite subject to teach because the concepts are so abstract, and because I have to teach it for 150 minutes per day. The good news is that 'hard to teach' and 'tedious' do not equal 'impossible'! While I rarely look forward to teaching reading, I don't hate it, because I have routines and systems in place that make it relatively painless for me and meaningful for the kids. So if the idea of teaching reading exhausts you, don't worry—your feelings are normal and things will improve!

2) **You don't have to make any decisions at the beginning of the school year.** Small group reading instruction doesn't typically begin until at least the third week of school, sometimes later. Get to know your class. Familiarize yourself with your materials and the expectations of your administration and school district. Focus on implementing the procedures and routines for the rest of the school day to prepare students for reading group rotations.

3) **Don't be afraid to change things mid-year or more than once throughout the year!** I typically switch up reading block components and routines five or six times a year. The changes aren't necessarily drastic, but I like to experiment with new things, and the adjustments keep children interested, too. The key is to explain clearly why you are making changes so the kids understand that they will benefit from them, and to be precise about your new expectations so that kids can adjust quickly. Children are intrigued by fresh materials and systems, and will embrace them willingly if they understand exactly what to do. So as you read this section, know that you CAN and SHOULD change things later on in the year if they're not working as effectively as you hoped. You are not locked into one way of doing things for the entire school year. Think about what's best for your kids right now, then act upon your professional judgment.

Making Decisions About Your Reading Block

Here are the decisions you will need to make before you start your small group reading block. Remember, you have a few weeks after school starts to get this together! I've put the choices in a logical sequence, but you don't necessarily need to complete the steps in this order.

- **Begin organizing your area and materials.**

- **Decide how many reading groups you will have.**

- **Determine which small group block components you will have, and how long each will last.**

- **Choose the order of your rotations.**

- **Select the materials children will use for each component of your small group reading block.**

- **Determine how you will assess students' work and progress for each component.**

- **Decide how to introduce routines and procedures for the block to your students.**

- **Choose how you will facilitate transitions and keep the class on-task.**

The information you're about to read will help you make these decisions in an informed way. There's a lot to digest, but take it slow, and be open to adapting and changing your ideas. The great thing about the small group reading block is that you can be creative and experiment with lots of different strategies, materials, and procedures.

Organizing Your Area and Materials

Your organizational system will probably be revised many, many times throughout the planning process. My suggestion is to read over the ideas below, consider what you think will work well for your situation, and then modify and adapt those ideas as the rest of the small group format is decided.

Guidelines for the placement of your reading group area in the classroom were outlined in the first chapter of this book. Ideally, you should have the materials that you might want to use during a reading group (e.g., workbooks, little readers, wipe-off boards, pens, and word tiles) in one location near your small group table. Then have a separate and nearby location for the materials you access daily or on a routine basis. Here are two examples of how I have accomplished this:

❖ **Possible Set-Up: Teacher Passes Out and Collects Materials**

Several years ago, I kept all of my guided reading materials on the large shelf you see in the left photo on the next page. I used the small rolling cart (shown in the right-hand photo) only for reading group supplies that I accessed daily. I just

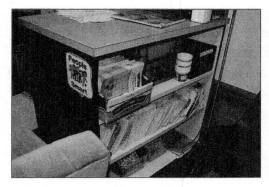

wheeled the cart over to wherever I needed it (the table, the rug area, or student desks if I went to a small group of students instead

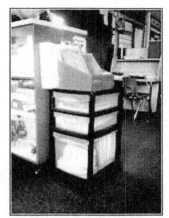

of having them move to me). The materials on top were things I needed for all three groups: my binder with test scores, running records, small group notes, etc., along with pens, pencils, and dry erase markers. Each of the three cart drawers held materials for a different reading group. So, when it was time to teach a particular group, I just opened the drawer and had the appropriate readers, teacher's edition, and props right at my fingertips.

❖ **Possible Set Up: Kids Access and Return Materials Themselves**

This is the shelf behind the reading group table in my current classroom. I store anything that might be utilized during a small group in the cabinets underneath the shelf. On top of the shelf, I keep all the materials that are used on a regular basis. The three crates in the middle hold supplies for each of my three reading groups: red, yellow, and blue. The whiteboard on top tells the children how to prepare for group that day. The top of the board says, 'Please Bring to Small Group' and tells the children which materials to bring over to the table. Underneath, it says 'Be Ready To Begin' and explains what students should do once they are at the table. Typically I have students use the pencils, pens, and highlighters from the blue container on top of the crates. Having students use my writing utensils ensures that everyone has the needed supplies and no one wastes time digging through their desks.

Each group's materials are stored altogether in the colored crates. (If you like the idea of having a separate container for each group but are short on space, remember that crates can be stacked vertically). When I call, for example, the red group over to meet with me, the six children in that group go to the red crate to get their workbooks. The board tells students whether they should open the workbooks to a certain page or begin a particular assignment.

There is also a color-coded plastic bin inside each crate. These hold quick reads appropriate for each group's reading level. If students need to complete an assignment independently during the small group time, I put the box of books on the table so they can read while they wait for others to finish. The books are short but I do have bookmarks with the students' names on them so kids can pick up where they left off last time if needed. The bins of books are also handy when I know a group will not be able to start on time because I'm finishing up another task. I then write on the board (where it says 'Be Ready to Begin'): *Read a book from the book box*. I know that students will sit down and read quietly, fully engaged, until I'm ready to start instruction.

Determining Small Group Reading Block Components and Group Rotations

Deciding on the Number of Groups and the Materials for Each

The choice of small group reading materials may be mandated by your district. In all likelihood, you will be provided with resources or guidelines for what each group should be taught during small group instruction. You might modify your decisions about materials and number of groups once you get to know your class, but talk to your team leader and figure out what's typical and expected in your school and base your plans on that.

If you're doing homogenous grouping, three is the traditional number of groups: below, on, and above grade level. Once students have become fluent readers (intermediate elementary), the tasks completed in groups will become more similar and ability grouping is less crucial (as opposed to first grade, for example, when some kids don't know letter sounds and others are reading chapter books). However, most school districts require teachers to pull groups based on like ability.

When your groups are too large, or the range of abilities is too broad, you may need to have four groups. I did this one year because my OGL group was difficult to teach—I had some kids who were barely out of the BGL group and some who were almost ready for the AGL group but not quite. You may also have a situation like I did one year in third grade, in which the BGL group had to be split up. Most of the group was only a year or less behind, but I had three kids who were on a first grade level and had already been retained: they needed extra help that the rest of the group was too advanced for.

What to Do With Kids Who Don't Fit in Any Group

You may have an outlier child: one who is so far ahead or behind that there is no appropriate reading group. Check with your reading specialist and team leader to see how your administration wants you to handle this situation. Some schools have resources and programs in place and have set ideas about how these children should be taught. If your school doesn't, it's going to be up to you to meet the child's needs.

If the student is advanced, you may be able to work with an upper grade level teacher to obtain supplementary materials for the child to work on independently, with occasional conferences with you. Or, the other teacher may be able to take that child into his reading groups. If the child is significantly behind the rest of the class (such as a new English Language Learner, or ELL), it can be helpful for the low child to sit in with the OGL group to see appropriate peer-modeling. However, you will need to provide instruction at her ability level, perhaps with materials from the lower grades. I typically pair non-English speakers with a high-achieving child for about 10-15 minutes during the reading block. The two children work together to help the ELL complete below grade level materials and practice reading little books and sight word cards. Computer programs can also provide the individualized instruction that you cannot.

Another Approach: Flexible Reading Groups

I prefer flexible grouping with my third graders because it prevents them from feeling 'labeled' or limited, and they can practice just the skills they need. I give mini-benchmark tests for specific skills on a regular basis: kids read a short passage and answer 5 multiple choice questions. I grade the papers quickly, and then pull the kids who need to review it for a small group. In this way, flexible grouping allows the teacher to take advantage of teachable moments and individualize instruction.

To use flexible grouping, simply set up a rotation schedule that doesn't include time spent with you in guided reading: only include centers, computers, silent reading, and/or independent work. Call the children you want to see when you are ready to teach them, and when you're done, they can return to the regular rotation.

You can even have regular homogenous groups and still pull groups flexibly from time to time. Set up a rotation that doesn't include guided reading, and then pull either your homogeneous groups or your flexible, skilled-based groups, depending on what you need to accomplish for the day. This is not confusing for students if you explain what they will be doing: let them know whether you will be pulling 'regular groups' or 'flexible groups'.

Selecting Your Small Group Block Components

You will need to look at your school district's mandates and principal's expectations to determine which specific tasks students will be doing, e.g., silent reading, computers, centers, and/or independent work. If you are a new teacher and you don't have to use centers, I would advise you to skip them your first year. The next chapter will explain how, when, and why centers should be used, but anyone trying to simplify their teaching should feel free to leave centers out of their reading block schedule.

Making a Schedule

Your grade level team leader will let you know what criteria your school uses to determine which reading group each student should be placed in, and how many groups to have. You will probably have three groups and an hour to see them all, so that's twenty minutes each. You'll need to plan for transition times, because it will take 1-4 minutes to get everyone settled. Here's one way you can set up your rotations:

	1st Rotation	2nd Rotation	3rd Rotation
BGL	Centers/Computers	Small Group	Independent Work
OGL	Small Group	Independent Work	Centers/Computers
AGL	Independent Work	Centers/Computers	Small Group

Here's an example of a rotation if you have four reading groups (which is harder to arrange than if you have three). There are four rotations, each lasting fifteen minutes:

	1st Rotation	2nd Rotation	3rd Rotation	4th Rotation
BGL	Small Group	Independent Work	Centers/Computers	Silent Reading
Low OGL	Independent Work	Centers/Computers	Silent Reading	Small Group
High OGL	Centers/Computers	Silent Reading	Small Group	Independent Work
AGL	Silent Reading	Small Group	Independent Work	Centers/Computers

If you have four groups and you're short on time one day, you can just do three rotations: combine two of the groups for the day and have them go through the rotation on the same schedule.

It can be frustrating for some teachers to stick to such a tight schedule. I dislike having to stop a lesson after fifteen minutes when the kids are on a roll. One year I saw each group for thirty minutes and only met with two groups a day. BGL kids were taught every day in the first time slot, and OGL was in the second slot on Mondays, Wednesday, and Fridays. The AGL kids took the second slot on Tuesdays and Thursdays, and on the other days, they worked with one another on projects.

Choosing the Order of Your Rotations

The order of rotations shouldn't be random: you can base it on your students' needs. For example, one year my BGL kids often had a hard time sitting still and concentrating for long periods of time, so right after whole-class instruction, I would send them directly to the computers. Another year, with a particularly challenging class, I tried to schedule my struggling readers in the first and second rotation when I still had energy and I knew we wouldn't run out of time (my last group often got shortchanged, time-wise). It can also work well when you teach your OGL group last. My AGL group one year was very creative and self-motivated, and meeting with them between my BGL and OGL groups gave me a break of sorts—the kids didn't need as much structure and I could facilitate rather than teach.

Whichever order you decide, I encourage you to keep the same schedule every day. This routine will make things flow more quickly because students know where to go without you telling them. Explain and practice the rotation extensively at the beginning of the year and have the schedule posted where everyone can see it.

Independent Work During the Reading Block

The Purpose of Independent Work

Creating appropriate independent work assignments is really the key to behavior management during guided reading: if kids are engaged in developmentally-appropriate tasks, you will have far less worries about anyone acting up or playing around.

The purpose of independent work is not only to keep kids quiet while you teach small groups, it's to show you what kids can do completely on their own. The work completed during independent reading is a true measure of students' abilities.

Choosing Materials

Independent work assignments will be influenced by your school and district requirements, but any worksheets, workbook pages, tests, or practice activities that students can do by themselves could be used. To be effective, the materials you choose must be:

> ➤ challenging but not so hard that students have to ask for help
> ➤ open-ended so that students cannot claim to be 'done'

➢ lengthy enough to last the FASTEST child the entire work period
➢ self-explanatory so children can work independently
➢ quiet so you can teach your groups

Independent Work Management Tip: Reading Folders

An excellent way to structure independent work is through Reading Folders. I was introduced to this concept through the administration at one of my schools—it was a mandate, and it turned out to be a highly effective one! Whenever my students are to work independently during our small group time, they know to take out their reading folders. I give them a checklist of everything inside and the order it must be completed in, and collect the whole thing on Fridays.

The reading folder assignments are differentiated to some extent for ability but mostly for pace of work completion. The faster kids have more assignments (the last few things on the list are fun, so the children aren't being saddled with extra work) and the slower kids have fewer requirements. The requirements are called 'Must-Do's' because they must be done by Friday in order for students to participate in Fun Friday activities. There are other activities on the checklist called 'When Done Choices'. These are high-interest activities which students should complete after their Must Do's are finished. This way, every child has something to work on at all times during independent work. If the 'When Done' choices are completed early, students can read materials from their book boxes.

On Fridays, I call each student up to my desk to ensure that the work was completed in its entirety and that all papers have names on them. Students then turn in the papers, sorting them into like stacks so that they are ready for me to grade. New reading folder contents and checklists are passed out on Mondays.

Assessing Independent Work

The way you assess the work students complete on their own during the reading block depends on how well you understand the work's purpose. Independent work shows what students can complete without any assistance, so in general, it provides an excellent opportunity for assessment. I grade the majority of work my students do during this time. The only papers I don't grade are the ones that were just for practice (such as those that duplicate another assessment) or ones that are too time-consuming to grade. Each week, when I look through students' independent work, I can get a pretty clear picture about each child's progress.

Independent Reading During the Reading Block

Is Self-Selected Reading a Waste of Time?

There is a substantial amount of research showing that students who read for at least thirty minutes in class every day score better on standardized tests and have higher reading comprehension levels. However, that research also points out that reading time must be regular, uninterrupted, and structured. It's the STRUCTURE that most of us leave out. Teachers must monitor what students are reading and teach children to choose books that are appropriate for their reading level and interests, and students should be logging what they read and reflecting on it either formally or informally. So the question is not about whether kids *should* be doing voluntary free-choice reading in school, it's about how we can make the time meaningful for them.

There are several programs in which students read books of their own choosing, e.g., Self-Selected (or Sustained Silent) Reading, both abbreviated as SSR, and Drop Everything and Read (DEAR). The difference between these programs is the level of structure and amount of teacher monitoring required. To avoid any associations with or preconceptions about other programs, I'll refer to the system described in this chapter as Independent Reading Time, which is inspired primarily on research by Regie Routman.

What Students Do During Independent Reading Time

Remember that children, like adults, are more motivated to read when the subject matter is interesting to them, so if we want kids to read, we need to give them opportunities to figure out what they like and spend time with those materials. After all, if you love mysteries and fashion magazines, you're not going to pick up a science fiction book or fishing and hunting magazine, and that's okay. Students can develop the habits of good readers using whatever materials they select. Independent reading time may be the only time of the day in which they are not told exactly what to read.

You will probably want your students to keep a record of their independent reading (a reading log) of some sort if they are in second grade or above, and you may want them to keep a simpler form in the younger grades. I encourage you to allow students to respond to the texts they select in ways that are natural for them. Some kids will just want to read, which is great (and to be expected in the younger grades). Others will want to keep detailed summaries in their reading logs, or write down quotes and passages they like. They may want to write down other books they want to read about a topic, or make notes for themselves to follow up on an idea. Whatever you have modeled for students, they will want to do! These are habits of good readers and we as teachers need to encourage them.

When I read nonfiction books, I frequently write down ideas I want to use; when I read novels, I sometimes am reminded of a movie I want to see or food I want to try, and I jot those down somewhere, too. I would be very frustrated if I was told that I couldn't do anything except read for twenty or thirty minutes, at which point all the connections to my own life would be lost, so I don't push that 'reading-only' rule on my students. The vast majority of students' independent reading time will be spent reading, but don't be afraid to let them interact with their reading materials just because it's unconventional.

I also think it's important to allow students to be comfortable during their independent reading time. All of my kids choose a special spot they can go to read if they would rather not be at their desks. I reserve the right to ask a child to choose a new spot any time they become disruptive or distracted by the people who are near them. If a particular group of kids one year are very mature, I allow them to choose new spots whenever they want—most ask me every few weeks, "Can I move my spot to __?" and I almost always approve. Other classes need far more structure with this process.

Holding Conferences During Independent Reading Time

Students' independent reading needs to be closely monitored to make sure kids are achieving the goals you've set together. To do this, you'll need to conference with students individually. Doing this during independent reading time allows you the rare opportunity to get to know the children's personalities, interests, strengths, and weaknesses individually while all other students are meaningfully and quietly engaged. Just a few purposes for these individual conferences are to ensure that students are:

> ➢ selecting books on their reading level
> ➢ understanding what they read
> ➢ progressing in their fluency
> ➢ reading a variety of texts
> ➢ using reading strategies you've taught them

Set up a schedule for conferencing that meets your kids' needs and fits into your specific teaching context. You may want to use your reading group time one day per week to talk with the kids in each group about their reading. If students are completing Independent Reading outside of your small group reading block and are all reading at the same time, you can meet with 1-3 kids per day so that each child has a conference monthly. Primary level students will need more frequent conferences than those who are basically fluent readers, and you may want to check in with struggling readers more often.

What to Do During Conferences

Have the student bring the book she is currently reading and her reading log to the conference. In your conferences, you can have the child read excerpts aloud to you, give an oral retelling, reflect on her book choices and progress, set goals, and so on.

You can take anecdotal records, use a checklist, take notes on index cards, organize a binder with a section for each child, or utilize any other system that allows you to keep meaningful notes about children's independent reading. In general, most researchers emphasize that students should not be graded on independent reading, so you don't have to include anything about it in your grade book. Students are reading for the sake of reading itself, so we as teachers can enjoy this time without making it more complicated than it needs to be.

Teaching Procedures for Independent Reading

Lots of modeling with distributed practice is key here, just like with every other classroom routine. Decide on guidelines for your students, such as:

> ➤ choose reading materials that you like and understand
> ➤ continue reading for the entire time
> ➤ stay in your special spot
> ➤ record all books in your reading log

Start with a short amount of time, such as ten minutes, and walk around to make sure kids are able to follow the guidelines. Gradually increase the amount of time students are expected to read independently, and when you are confident the class can stay on-task, begin holding conferences and/or small groups. Remember that conferences don't have to be held back-to-back, so you can interact with and redirect children as needed between conferences. You will probably want to teach your students not to interrupt conferences except for emergencies, just like you do for reading groups.

Individual Book Boxes

It's easier for students to remain meaningfully engaged in reading when they have a variety of self-selected texts available. While some teachers allow their students to go to the classroom library as needed to choose new books, this can be distracting, especially with younger students who read shorter books and may need to make multiple trips to the library (at the same time as their friends, coincidentally) during every independent reading block.

Many teachers, myself included, have individual book boxes or baskets for their students. The book box system and check-out methods are explained in Chapter 7, Maintaining a Classroom Library.

Keeping Authentic and Meaningful Reading Logs

I provide students with a two pocket folder like the one shown on the next page. However, I let my kids keep their reading logs in any format they want: a composition book, a beautiful journal, a trendy little notebook or binder, etc. I know I prefer writing in something that brings me pleasure to look at, and students do, too.

You have to model, model, model how kids should keep a reading log, but do allow them to modify the basic format to fit their needs. Some children will want

to draw a picture for each book they read; others will write summaries and include quotes from the books, and still others will want to write the title and author and that's it. If your procedures and expectations are clear, students will be able to take on the responsibility of determining what works best for them.

More Information About Independent Reading and Conferences

If you are interested in creating a meaningful self-selected reading time in your classroom, I encourage you to visit TheCornerstoneForTeachers.com. There is a lot of information there that is beyond the scope of this book, including links to some incredible resources and printable forms of all kinds: reading log forms, conference sheets, posters, and much more.

Facilitating Small Group Reading Instruction

Introducing Small Group Routines and Procedures

Students should practice completing independent work for several days before you introduce small groups. Teach them what to do if they have questions about their assignments (my rule is, try your best and ask me about it when the reading groups transition).

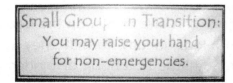
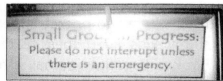

If you have a small group sign like the one pictured, explain how it works to students, then sit at the table by the sign while students work independently. If someone raises their hand with a question, point to the sign.

If you have computers, self-selected reading, or other components built into your rotation system, you can add those in after a few days of independent work. Students should practice switching from one component to another quietly and staying focused on the task at hand. If you will be holding Independent Reading Conferences, you can begin those at this time, as well.

When you are sure the majority of the class is capable of doing sustained work without disrupting others and are demonstrating this consistently, you can introduce your reading group board, if you have one. The board explains what students should bring to small group and how to prepare each day. Tell them you will be calling the groups over one by one to practice the system. You will not be teaching the groups yet because you want to make sure everyone can complete independent work. Reinforce your small group procedures for each group of children and have them read silently or complete a worksheet. You should sit with them the majority of the time, but may still need to walk around the room to assist or correct those students who are having trouble with independent work.

It will probably take about a week of this sort of practice before you begin teaching the groups. On the day small group instruction actually begins, make a big deal out if it. Tell the children how proud you are that they've proved their ability to work by themselves, and how they can finally learn to read in small groups. Make the initial activity a very fun one so students have a positive first impression. Don't plan anything that requires a lot of supervision or facilitation from you the first week, as you will still have interruptions. If students fall short of your expectations, don't let anything slide. Address problems right away and practice your procedures until students get them right.

Keeping the Class On-Task

During small group instruction, position yourself so you can see the entire classroom and survey the room with your eyes often. I always glance up from the group once or twice a minute to make sure everyone in the room is on-task. This only takes about two seconds each time and I do it when my group is not looking at me (while another child is speaking, or when they're reading and writing). The process is very similar to glancing in your rear-view mirroring while driving. The more experienced you become at teaching, the more natural glancing around will become until you do it automatically.

If someone in centers or independent work is off-task, attempt to make eye contact first. A stern look should get them back on track, and often misbehaving children are looking at the teacher, anyway, because they know they're doing something wrong. If you can't get eye contact, focus on the small group again for another thirty seconds or a minute. If you look back up and the child is still misbehaving and won't look at you, you have a choice. You could choose not to say anything and then after the group ends, give a consequence that is consistent with your behavior management system. Or you could give your group a brief task ("Tell your partner about...") and get up to whisper to the child. Your final choice is to call across the room to the misbehaving student. This last method is quite disruptive to the whole class, but can be very effective especially in the beginning of the year because it reinforces your expectations and lets the kids know you ARE watching them.

If a handful of students cannot work independently, sit them either away from everyone else or near your small group table. Some children will be on their best behavior if they're seated near you, but others have such limited self-control that their actions would only interrupt your small group. Disruptive students must be seated in a place where they cannot distract others, and if certain children continually pose a problem, explain your reasons for having them sit alone. Consistent appropriate behavior should result in them being allowed to sit with the class again on a trial basis. You can also tell off-task students that if they don't do their independent work, they can't go to centers or on the computer—it's a package deal.

Transitioning Between Groups

Have children do guided reading, independent work, and centers (or whichever rotations you include) in the same order daily. This routine will make things flow more quickly because students know where to go without you telling them.

Allow 1-4 minutes in between groups to answer questions VERY quickly and get students settled in their new places. Be strict—if one group ends at 10:25, you should be teaching the next by 10:30. And yes, this IS possible!! Using a timer is highly effective: I announce that the next group will begin in two minutes, and when the timer goes off, I start teaching. Give rewards and verbal reinforcement, and establish consequences for stragglers—do whatever you have to do so that reading instruction is not compromised.

You could also have a warm-up on the board for your upcoming small group, such as rereading the story with a partner or writing two sentences to explain what they think will happen next in the story. This way students get their full twenty minutes of differentiated practice even though you may only be teaching for fifteen.

Assessing Student Progress in Groups

Some school systems don't require reading group work to be assessed at all. I support this philosophy because it assumes that teachers are capable of informally assessing students' progress over time using their own judgment. **The purpose of small group instruction is for students to have direct and guided practice in skills, so any assessment that takes place should focus on tracking progress and guiding future instruction.**

If you must keep records for your reading groups, I encourage you to use simple forms that stick to the focus of tracking progress and not assigning formal grades. If your district doesn't mandate a complex system, just write the skill at the top of a checklist and use a basic scale to indicate if kids are mastering what you teach (such as S for secure, P for progressing, and E for emerging). I've done this in the past when it wasn't required just as documentation of learning during reading groups and to help me plan upcoming lessons.

Chapter 21: Rethinking Centers
Creating a simplified system for independent hands-on learning

For years, I had a page on my website called, "Hundreds of ideas for inexpensive, easy to make, fun centers...and how to run them." However, I've since asked myself, do teachers really needs hundreds of new materials to create, or do they need an effective system for managing reading instruction? The more I learn about the teaching profession, the more I'm convinced it's the latter, and in 2006 I changed the entire arrangement of the centers/literacy pages to reflect that perspective. If you leave the website feeling as though you have MORE WORK on your plate, I've done something wrong. I want the site—and this book—to make your teaching easier and more efficient.

Rethinking Centers in the Classroom

Centers have become an obsession with many teachers. Maybe it's the creative side of us, wanting an opportunity to make cute games and activities, or maybe it's bewilderment about what students should be doing while we're teaching reading groups. Either way, it's a cause for concern, because centers have routinely turned into something time-consuming, expensive, and difficult to manage, and children aren't transferring the skills they are practicing during centers into other tasks later on. In many classrooms, centers have become an elaborate system that wastes the time of both children and teachers.

Teachers DO NOT have to spend hours creating centers to teach reading effectively. If centers are serving a meaningful purpose in your classroom, that's wonderful.   My goal is not to discourage you from using centers, but to encourage you to:

1) **Question whether centers are the most effective use of time for both you and your students:** Ask yourself, what purpose do centers serve in

my classroom, and is there a more efficient method that could accomplish the same things?

2) **Strive to create a reading group rotation system that makes teaching EASIER for you and more meaningful for students:** This system may or may not include centers.

Potential Benefits and Drawbacks of Centers

Centers can be a time for students to practice the skills that were taught in class through activities that encompass a variety of learning styles. Centers can also be an opportunity to reinforce concepts for children who do not always learn best through traditional teaching methods or who need hands-on experiences.

Unfortunately, centers frequently consume hours of the teacher's prep time and result in an expensive, chaotic management nightmare. Many times, they ultimately consist of free play or busy work in which children practice skills in isolation and never transfer them to authentic tasks.

What Else Are Kids Supposed to Do?

I encourage you to read the book, "Reading Strategies" by Regie Routman. It will revolutionize the way you structure your reading time and will leave you feeling energized and ready to simplify all of your instruction. The book is based on the philosophy that students should spend the majority of their time in school *reading*, not doing activities about reading. If you are in support of this theory, may want to have students do one or more of the following during your small group reading block in place of centers:

- **Independent reading:** Each student chooses a book on his reading level.

- **Reading group follow-up activities:** Children can finish reading or reread the book(s) you began during reading groups, or explore a related or extension text.

- **Meaningful projects**: These are generally related to shared reading experiences.

All of these methods have engaged my students as much as or more than centers. Having a child read a book on a topic he's interested in and that's on his reading level is ALWAYS a good use of time. It's also a very quiet activity, which is helpful when you're teaching reading groups. Book-related projects can be incredibly engaging if properly designed because they are authentic and purposeful. Best of all, both reading and projects require far less prep work and management than centers do.

Centers don't have to be used only for reading group time!

If you really think centers are useful for your kids, you can still have children complete authentic reading tasks during your group rotations—simply schedule centers for another time during the day. Here are some opportune center times for your daily schedule:

-Morning Work: I love the idea of having children unpack, sharpen pencils, and delve right into center activities—what a motivation for kids to be on time for school and to get started working! You would never have to worry about kids being off-task due to boredom, and you could lengthen or shorten the time each day to suit the number of tasks you need to complete (attendance, checking homework, etc.).

-Indoor Recess/Fun Friday/Free Time: Use centers as a reward for your students. Give them an hour every Friday afternoon as part of your regular schedule, or as part of your behavior management system in which children have to earn free time for centers. Alternatively, some teachers allow their students to earn up to 10 or 15 free minutes at the end of every day (subtracting/adding minutes according to pre-determined behavioral standards). The class could work for time to use centers at the end of the day instead of free time—that's extremely motivating for them and more beneficial.

-As Part of Your Instructional Time: I frequently use my whole-group time to introduce activities that will become centers or at-home games. The entire class plays games at once, so I can go around to ask probing questions and challenge students' thinking. This strategy is very effective and I use it almost daily in my math block.

Traditional Centers: Making It Work

If you do choose to use centers during reading group time, they can be a fabulous hands-on learning experience when properly designed and managed. Remember that their primary purpose is to provide differentiated and hands-on instruction. I urge you not to go through the trouble of creating and maintaining centers just so your kids have something to do while you teach reading groups. I especially advise first-year teachers to forget about centers until they can confidently run their small group time with simpler components.

I have used a variety of center systems in my classroom over the years,. The next section of this chapter will explain the choices you will need to make as you create your center system. At the end of the chapter, you'll read about a variation of traditional centers called centerjobs.

You have a number of decisions to make when designing your center system. The possibilities are unlimited, so have fun and be creative!

Decision 1) Will your centers be used in different areas throughout the room, or will students take the centers back to their desks?

Many teachers have students sit at their desks to do centers because it's more orderly or because the classroom has limited space, but some of my centers have distracting materials so I usually had students sit at designated points in the room. This also allows kids to move around the room and sit in a different place. I've managed this in several different ways. In one classroom, I had signs identifying each of the multiple intelligences, which I hung around the room so students knew where to sit (by the sink, on the rug, etc.). Centers which had activities requiring more room were in open areas or in quiet corners.

If you don't have room for separate center areas, don't despair—very few teachers do! At one school, I was in a classroom about half the size of my current one, so I had students sit in groups of six, and one group of six at a time used centers. The kids all took center materials back to their seats unless the activity required them to be someplace else. Centers can work just as well at students' desks—all you need is a well-organized, compact method of storing them.

Decision 2) What type of centers will you have?

I encourage you to have AS FEW CENTERS AS POSSIBLE for management purposes. It is not necessary to have an overhead center, a making words center, etc. Instead, try having 3-5 work stations or center areas, and have a small variety of materials in each.

One year, I designed centers to incorporate the multiple intelligences. Another year, I had centers for each subject area. There are innumerable ways to create centers and no shortage of ideas online. If you need ideas, check out my website or do an Internet search for "easy reading center ideas."

Decision 3) How will you organize your center materials?

One way is to have a drawer or container for each subject area or type of center. Put a pocket (similar to those in the back of library books) on the front of each drawer. Each child is assigned a number and given an index card with that number on it. When a child takes materials from a drawer to his desk, the child puts his index card in the drawer's pocket. (Sometimes children can be allowed to take the whole drawer, if that's easier than removing the materials.) With this method, you'll only need to switch out the materials inside each drawer about once a quarter because there are a variety of activities inside them.

If you're a new teacher, someone who has not really used centers in the past, or an experienced teacher who is tired of trying to keep up with complicated and time-consuming center set ups, I have good news. You can create work stations, or 'stations' for short. Here are the advantages of this system:

- You can rotate new items through periodically without having to add a lot at once.

- Instruction is differentiated by skill level, so kids can work independently on tasks that are challenging for them but not over their heads.

- Students are more motivated to complete the work because there is an element of choice.

- Kids can't be 'done' with the station because there are other materials to choose from.

- You can include meaningful activities that take multiple days, since a child can continue working anytime she goes to work stations.

Getting started with stations is quite simple. You will only need 4-5 of them. Stations can be spread out in labeled areas around the room, or kept in one central location for students to bring back to their desks,. The idea behind stations is that each one encompasses many different activities. There's certainly nothing wrong with having lots of different center areas—but you'll have to make more materials and keep a tighter rein on your management as students try to figure out where to go and how to use the materials. Limiting the amount of stations or centers you have enables children to work more independently, freeing you to teach. You only need one work station for each skill or related set of skills students will be practicing: Word Work, Reading Comprehension, Spelling, Writing, etc.

Within each station, provide differentiated choices using labeled containers. Keep all the materials for a station in one rolling cart, with a drawer for each reading group or ability level. (Alternatively, if you're using shelf space, have all materials on a shelf, with different bins on the shelf for each group.) Students can choose any materials you have in the drawer or bin for their level. You can change or vary the materials as you teach new skills (rather than having to change all of the materials at one time), and there will always be plenty for kids to work on. Children can do the same thing more than once if they choose to for additional reinforcement.

__Another Approach: Mixed-Ability Center Groups__

If you like having a student-centered classroom with lots of center time, you can try something else innovative: having center groups. Choose your groups, taking into consideration student personality, and have children in each center group rotate through the various work stations or activities together. Be sure to use mixed-ability grouping: if all of your below grade level readers are in centers at the same time, they'll have no one to help them.

If you use center groups, you can do either flexible reading groups (in which you pull the students who need to work on a specific skill, so groups are always different) or traditional homogenous grouping. Either way, you simply have the whole class working on centers for the entire reading block, with no set rotations. Then call each reading group to you when you are ready. Students will leave their centers and then return when you're ready for them to go back. This arrangement gives you much more freedom to meet each child's needs through the type and amount of instruction you give. It also allows you to send kids back to centers if they have finished the reading group task early or have demonstrated mastery, freeing you to continue working with those who need additional support.

Decision 4)   How will you determine which students go to which centers?

Here are a few of many possible options:

- **Tracking forms:** Give each child a list of all the centers. Students check off each center as they rotate through in order.

- **Spinner/Posted Schedule:** The spinner pictured has numbers on it, each representing a student. I turned the spinner one center to the right each day. So for example, if your number was 4, on the day shown in the photo, you would go to Nature Smart, number 19 would go to Picture Smart, etc. These were Multiple Intelligence centers and some had a lot of activities in them, so the students would often be assigned to the same center two days in a row. This worked well because absent students had a chance to go to the center they missed, and allowed kids to complete more in-depth tasks.

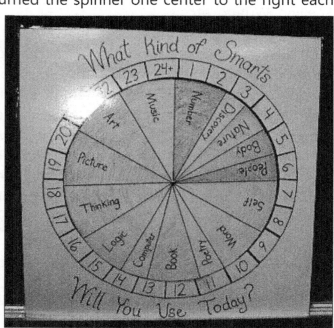

- **Student Choice**: Typically teachers who use this method do still require every child to complete each center eventually, but if you have a lot of center activities, students can do them in any order (choosing whichever center is available to them on a given day). Students can mark off which ones have been completed on a center checklist. If you have choices within each center, a child can occasionally do the same center twice and still be able to practice new skills.

Decision 5) How will you assess center work and keep kids accountable?

The idea of having to grade open-ended, differentiated, subjective center work sends a chill through my bones...as if centers weren't time-consuming enough! Typically when teachers feel obligated to grade center work, it's not because they want to know what students have learned—that's what independent work time is for. Teachers grade centers because they want to ensure that learning is taking place and they feel the need to give students some kind of accountability. There are many simpler ways to accomplish these goals than grading every single center activity:

- **Teacher observation and student self-reflection:** My students used to complete center work in their journals so there were no papers to photocopy or grade. Occasionally I would check journals, walk around and observe students in centers, or have kids reflect in their journals afterwards about what they learned or practiced. If I could tell from their practice that students were using center time to their full advantage, that was evidence enough for me.

- **Regular monitoring of each child's work:** I once used a system with second graders in which they placed their papers in a large pocket chart (one pocket for each child). An accordion file folder with a section for each child would have also worked fine. I flipped through the papers about once a week to make sure students were on the right track, and after about a month, when the whole class had completed all centers, I took out the papers. Sometimes I graded the ones I thought were the most indicative of students' progress and abilities, then stapled the rest together and used a 'Read But Not Corrected' stamp. Other times I sent all the papers home ungraded. This system kept students accountable because they were responsible for turning in their work daily. They never knew when I would check it and they understood that all work would be reviewed and sent home.

- **Grading work for each center:** The simplest way I've found to take grades on center work is to have a large manila envelope (basket, folder, etc). in each center or in one designated place in the room. As students complete the work for a center, they check off their name or number on the checklist attached to the envelope, and slip their work inside. At the end of the week or month, anyone who has not completed a center can be given an opportunity to do so (maybe on a Friday afternoon). When the checklist shows everyone is done, collect the envelope and grade the papers inside. This can be more effective than having kids keep all their own work in a folder or journal because it's so much more efficient to grade a whole stack of like papers at the same time.

- **Grading specific tasks or centers:** If children choose which centers to go to and you grade certain ones, you don't have to specify which you'll be grading so kids will work equally hard on all tasks. Conversely, you may want to tell students which centers will be graded so they can prioritize their time: if a graded center is not being used by another child, they should choose that one first. Graded centers can be changed monthly, and non-graded centers approximately every other month.

- **Student-developed center rubrics and point systems:** Discuss as a class what the expectations are and determine point values for each expectation. The trainer at a literacy workshop I took said she told her fourth graders they could get 100 free points towards their reading grade every week just for doing the right thing in centers. They kept all their center work in individual folders, which the teacher looked through on a regular basis (Monday- BGL group, Tuesday- OGL group, etc.). If they had completed the work, they got 100 points. She had a big disclaimer for her kids that the quality of center work would affect the points earned—if the child had clearly rushed or made up answers, points were taken off. Also, she would start subtracting points if children were playing around in centers. This seems like a very reasonable system that could be easily implemented and that children would really buy into.

- **Keep center work in a binder that's graded quarterly:** I know a fourth grade teacher who had her students keep all of their center work in a binder, with one section for each type of center. The binders were collected quarterly with a grade given based on effort and completeness. The teacher used the math center work for one math grade, reading center work for one reading grade, and so on. This was a generally a boost for most kids' averages. The work was then stapled and sent home. I love this method because it's so low-maintenance for the teacher and provides great accountability for students.

Decision 6) How will you introduce center routines and procedures?

The beginning of the year is always the hardest but it will get easier if your students are well-trained on how to use and clean up the materials. Many new teachers believe they should have centers up and running within the first week of school. I don't even THINK about centers until the class knows how to work independently while I teach reading groups. Centers don't appear in my classroom until at least a month into the school year, and even then, I introduce each center very slowly, one at a time, modeling EVERYTHING. Center usage is taught like all other procedures and routines. The kids role-play how to use the materials, solve problems, get help, and put the materials away. Without this foundation, centers (and consequently, reading groups) will be a time of chaos in which little learning takes place. You will need to go very slowly with this process and do LOTS of modeling to show what you expect. Here are some guidelines for easing children into the center routines you've created at a manageable pace:

♦ **Introduce centers after children can complete independent work without your assistance.** See Chapter 20, Managing Small Group Instruction, for tips.

♦ **Once they've got that down, show kids EXPLICITLY how to care for centers.** Explain how centers are stored, used, and cleaned up. Be extremely detailed and assume students have no knowledge of the materials. For example, if you have a sandwich bag with pieces in it for one of your centers, model putting the bag back and ask if you forgot anything. Someone will notice you did not close the bag, and you can explain to the class why it is so important to always keep the bag sealed shut. If you skip this step of explicit modeling, you will pay for it later. I have taken the lazy way out before and been very upset when materials were not used properly. However, I had no one to blame but myself because I never took the time to teach my kids how to care for the centers.

♦ **Introduce each center individually.** This takes forever but will save you from having to answer the same questions repeatedly, and it will leave the kids dying to try the centers out! In Head Start, we called this the Guided Discovery process. Think about it as guiding students through the proper way to discover and explore the materials.

- **When students have been familiarized with each center, tell them it is finally time to try them out with your monitoring.** Explain that when the kids use centers, you will not be able to help them because you'll be teaching small groups. Tell the class that because they are still learning, for the rest of the week, you will be walking around to answer questions while they practice centers, but once small groups start, they'll be on their own. Allow the entire class to go to centers simultaneously so that you can give your full attention to monitoring. Look to see if the materials are being used correctly, and if children are on-task. Use reinforcement narration periodically and performance feedback afterwards as you normally would.

- **After a few days (once the class has demonstrated their ability to use centers), discuss procedures for when they have questions at centers but you are teaching a small group.** As a class one year, we decided that our rules would be to 1) reread the directions to yourself, 2) ask your partner or someone near you in a whisper voice, and 3) just do the best you can. The third rule became our center mantra. I repeatedly emphasized that it was okay if children were not using a center exactly as the directions specified (our centers were very open-ended) as long as students were on-task and practicing literacy skills.

- **Next, have half the class practice centers and the other half practice independent work, with NO QUESTIONS or help from you.** After twenty minutes, give performance feedback and reiterate your expectations. Have the class switch tasks without assistance, debrief once more, and thank them for working independently. Tell the class you think they are ready for reading groups and you believe you can trust them to stay on-task, work quietly, and respect your small group instruction.

- **Emphasize to students how precious your reading group time is—you absolutely cannot afford to discipline the class when you are teaching reading.** You wouldn't tolerate disturbances during whole-class instruction, so don't allow it during small groups, either. One year when I had a difficult group of 27 children, I created a very structured system for responding to misbehavior during center time. Every time I had to interrupt my small group to speak to someone, I noted the infraction on a class list I kept on my clipboard, and after three chances, that person could not go to centers for a week.

Sample Centerjob Form

Subject	Centerjob	Day Started	Day Completed
Reading	Read an Amelia Bedelia book. Write at least 5 examples of multiple-meaning words or figurative language. Explain what Amelia Bedelia thought each word or phrase meant, then write the meaning that was intended.	M T W Th F	M T W Th F
Language Arts	Choose a book from the reading area. Write the name of the book and the author. Then read the book. Write down the page numbers and examples of at least 10 action verbs WITH helping verbs. You may want to use a t-chart to help you organize your information.	M T W Th F	M T W Th F
Writing	Design a postcard showing what your community looked like a long time ago. Explain at least three ways the landscape has changed. Use ideas from our fieldtrip to the Old Davie Schoolhouse. Follow the postcard format in the writing area.	M T W Th F	M T W Th F
Math	Create a building or design using 5 solid figures. Make a drawing of your creation. Then label the number of faces and vertices each figure has.	M T W Th F	M T W Th F
Social Studies	Choose a state from one of the atlases. Trace an outline of the state. Color it using different colors to represent the state's topography. Be sure to provide a key explaining what each color represents.	M T W Th F	M T W Th F
Science	Complete the activity on Science Flip Chart pg. 123. Use the plants in the science center for your observation.	M T W Th F	M T W Th F

Centerjobs: An Individualized, Self-Paced Alternative Center System

You might consider using centerjobs if you've ever thought to yourself:

"Are my kids really learning anything in centers?"
"I can't grade everything they do in centers—what am I supposed to do with all their work?!"
"I need something for kids to do when they first come in each day."
"I feel like I'm always giving busywork to kids who finish early."

Centerjobs (or workjobs) are a set of individualized tasks that students complete using hands-on materials. They can be completed within any center or work station system you have set up, and/or can be used when students finish early or have extra time. You can also provide time for centerjobs as a part of your daily schedule, e.g., during the last half hour of the day or for Morning Work.

The purpose of centerjobs is to:

1. Individualize instruction
2. Allow each student to work at his own pace
3. Give meaningful work for when others are in reading groups
4. Provide authentic tasks for early finishers
5. Allow for hands-on experiences when materials and resources are limited
6. Encourage independent work and time management skills
7. Permit students to leave their desks and move around the classroom in an orderly way
8. Ensure that students are working on specific objectives and not 'playing in centers'
9. Motivate students who are distracted or disengaged during whole-group instruction

AND BEST OF ALL

10. Allow teachers to focus on instruction, because centerjobs take very little time to prepare and assess!

Centerjob FAQs

How long does it take to prepare centerjobs?

Once you get the hang of it, about 15 minutes per week, and you can reuse them from year to year. I keep blank centerjob assignment sheets as well, so I can handwrite tasks in for the weeks when I'm not able to plan ahead like I like to. If your centerjobs are monthly, it will take longer to prepare, but you won't have to make them as often. I go through the reading curriculum guide and pull a lot of the suggested cross-curricular activities that we rarely have time to do. I also choose activities that I don't have class sets of materials for, such as tasks that involve special books, a globe, computers, etc. For example, when we read a story in our reading series about space, students used their centerjob time to read for information (finding a drawing of the solar system in one of four books I provided) and draw a diagram that illustrates the planets' relative size. I didn't have enough books for the whole class to do this at once, but with centerjobs, it didn't matter.

How do you keep the centerjob plans organized?

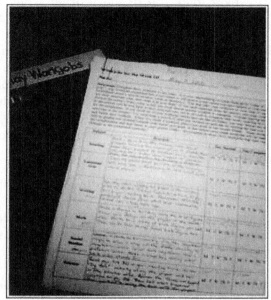

I keep a little black folder like the one pictured for each month, with copies of the centerjob sheets inside. On one copy, I highlight the materials needed and note in red ink any problems or suggestions for the next time I use them. I try to type the centerjobs so I can edit them each year, but I had gotten a little lazy by May when this picture was taken! I paperclip examples of student work and any written directions to the forms for next year's kids. The materials for the centerjobs are kept in magazine file boxes (available at office supply stores for a very small cost) labeled by month.

How do you explain the centerjobs to students each week?

I plan a shortened reading lesson each Monday so I can provide about 20 minutes to go over the centerjob instructions. Students will have already read over the assignment sheet for Morning Work to familiarize themselves with the tasks. Then we read each task together. I show the kids where the materials are kept and give any special instructions about caring for them and cleaning the areas when they are done. If needed, I also demonstrate how to complete the assignments and point out any work samples. Students generally have few questions during the week about centerjobs because I try to base the work on concepts the class is already familiar with, and I make the tasks pretty straight-forward.

When do students do centerjobs?

I originally designed centerjobs for students to complete while others were in reading groups. However, I also allowed my students to complete centerjobs if they finished other assignments early (I kept a 'When Finished' sign on the board which indicated if they should do centerjobs, read a book, or do another assignment). When centerjobs were due weekly, I always provided time on Friday afternoons for students to finish.

Do students ever use traditional centers?

When all centerjobs are completed, the child may select freely from other materials in the center areas.

How long does it take for students to complete centerjobs?

However long you as the teacher want them to take, because you design the tasks! I like to plan for about thirty minutes a day for the average worker (while the others are in reading groups), so 2.5 hours per week. With six subject areas, that's about twenty minutes per task. If one task will take longer, I try to design a quicker one in another subject area. If you want your early finishers to do centerjobs, you can make extra tasks for them as a group (design a standard centerjob assignment sheet for the rest of the class, then add a few extension activities and print copies for the kids who need more tasks). Once you learn the system and your kids' needs, you can differentiate centerjobs so that your higher-level kids and fast finishers have lengthier or more difficult tasks.

How many students are allowed to do the same centerjob at a time?

It depends on how many kids can comfortably fit in each center area—usually about four. Students can always take materials back to their desks and work there if the area is full.

When are centerjobs assigned and collected?

I used to collect them on a weekly basis: the assignment sheets were passed out and reviewed on Mondays and all work was due on Fridays at dismissal. Later, I designed the tasks to last several weeks or even a month. Instead of having students circle the day they started and completed the centerjobs, I left the sections blank for them to write in the exact dates.

How do students keep their papers together and track their work?

The children each have a plain file folder for their work. If a child loses his folder, he has to start all over or get a zero for the assignments. There is a section on the assignment sheet for students to circle the days they start and complete each task. This tells me not only how long it takes for the child to complete the work, but how long specific tasks are taking so I can modify as needed in the future. It also holds the child accountable for his or her time ("You didn't circle any centerjobs on Tuesday—what were you doing that day?").

What if students don't finish them?

If a lot of students have not finished their centerjobs by Friday afternoon, I glance over their assignment sheets and write 'OK' on the unfinished tasks I will excuse (the ones I don't plan to grade) and write 'Finish Monday' on the ones I will grade. Then for Morning Work on Monday, I give students about twenty minutes to complete whatever they have left. If you assign bi-weekly or monthly centerjobs, it will be easier for all students to have time to finish.

What happens if students play around or continually don't do their centerjobs?

Your kids will be very motivated to do centerjobs, so it's not like trying to get them to do worksheets or stay focused during lectures! However, some children just aren't ready for the required level of self-direction. They are unable to track what they've done, clean up after themselves, and organize their work. For these kids I try first to modify their assignments and provide greater structure. For example, I may have them do centerjobs in the order they are listed on the assignment sheet, or give fewer centerjobs. I might also require the child to show me his work each day so I can help him manage his time ("You have two days left to finish four centerjobs. How much time do you think would be reasonable to spend on coloring this science task? If you spend more than ten minutes on it tomorrow, you probably won't get to finish Social Studies. So tomorrow we'll look at the clock when you start and set a timer for ten minutes."). If certain children continue to play around, disrupt others, or be irresponsible with time despite the increased structure and assistance, I don't allow them to complete centerjobs the following week. I give them alternative assignments (workbook pages or something not as fun) so they can earn grades for the two or three centerjob assignments I plan to correct. When they finish the alternative assignments for the week, they read a book during centerjob time.

Are centerjobs graded?

Only the assignments I want to be assessed are graded, usually 2 out of the 6. It depends on the subjects I need a grade for that week, as well as which assignments are in an easily-graded format. I generally won't grade a centerjob that requires line-by-line reading in order to save time—I just check those off and students get credit for completing them.

How long does it take to correct centerjobs?

I generally spend about a minute on each student, so around twenty minutes for a week's worth of work. On Fridays, students staple their papers to the assignment sheet in the order they are listed. I can already tell if something has not been completed by looking at the assignment sheet, so I don't have to dig through the pile of papers to make sure everything's there. I glance through the assignments I don't plan to grade and put a checkmark beside them on the assignment sheet. Then I look over the ones I do want to assess and write the grades for those on the assignment sheet as well. After I've gone through the stack, I transfer the grades from the assignment sheets to my grade book and then send the packets home. When centerjobs last several weeks, it takes me longer to grade them because the assignments are more in-depth, but I have to do it less often, so it's a trade-off.

Chapter 22: Standardized Testing
Preparing, surviving, and even having fun!

Managing a classroom full of students who are stressed out about standardized testing requires special considerations. I know of children who have gone on anti-anxiety medications, vomited the day of the test, started shaking and crying uncontrollably, and refused to go to school because they were so worried about how they would do.

Preparation for state testing can be extremely stressful for teachers and students. In some schools, children are constantly drilled, while in others, the emphasis is on authentic instruction as much as possible. Regardless of the expectations in your school, students do need to learn the skills that are assessed on state tests, and you'll need to address the issues that come with having high stakes testing. This chapter will help you explain the testing situation to your students and build their self-confidence so that the process is as painless as possible. I'll also explain ways that I prepare children academically for state testing without sacrificing meaningful and developmentally appropriate instruction.

Preparing Psychologically: "Why are we doing this?"

☑ **Have a class meeting about WHY students have to take so many tests.**

Ask what is a test, anyway, and why do teachers give so many of them? Take the children's ideas first, and guide students to understand that teachers use test results to guide future instruction. In the case of standardized tests, the community and government want to make sure that kids are learning and that teachers are all doing what they need to do to help. Explain that when people notice areas in which kids don't do well, the teachers will realize there is a problem and help children make improvements.

☑ **Set a purpose for test-taking.**

Students should understand why they are learning things in school and how the information will be useful to them in the future. This is especially true for standardized testing, because it's difficult for students to see the relevance to their everyday lives. Try to help students make real-world connections as often as possible.

☑ **Explain test-related vocabulary and scoring criteria.**

I discuss with my class why the tests are called 'standardized' (it's similar to standardized measurement units—everyone uses the same tools so it's easy to make fair comparisons). It's important to make clear any other test-related vocabulary the kids don't understand. Many of the words are too large for them to really grasp, but since kids are the ones who have to take the tests, I think they should be taught to understand our conversations about them. I also explain the scoring criteria so that the children know what they will be working towards.

☑ **Put the test into perspective using the context of other assignments.**

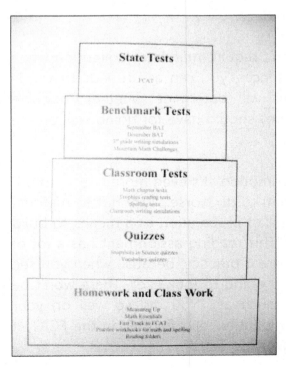

Students don't always understand the weight that high stakes tests hold. I explain that these are the assessments seen by parents, principals, superintendents, the governor, sometimes even the president. These are the most important assignments and it is crucial to give them your greatest effort. I explain to my kids that the test scores will be published on the Internet, in the local newspapers, and so on. I stress that we want the community to know how hard we have worked and to be proud of us.

I do try to discuss this in the context of how it is important to do our best work on every task that is given to us in life for the satisfaction of a job well done. More often than not, a student will bring this point up, making a much bigger impact than if I had mentioned it myself.

We also talk about standardized tests in relation to other work. We discuss the purpose of homework and class work (to practice skills); quizzes (to check what students know prior to testing them); classroom tests (to prove what students know and can do independently); benchmark tests (for the school district to check and track progress), and standardized tests (to find out how well students are doing in relation to other children in the school, county, and state, and to make sure they are ready to go to the next grade level). I give examples of each type of assignment to make the concepts more concrete.

☑ **Don't be afraid to express your own feelings about the test**.

It's often reassuring for kids to see that even grown-ups have to deal with testing pressure! You can be an excellent role model for handling stress. I tell my kids that most teachers don't like giving the FCAT (our state standardized test in Florida), and most kids don't like taking it, but the test is something that we have to do, so we should stick together and do the best we can.

☑ **Make a conscious effort to reduce test anxiety.**

This is much easier to do in states that don't require mandatory retention when children fail standardized tests. In those places, you can assure kids that only their attendance and report card grades will determine whether they are promoted, and discuss other motivations they should have for doing well on the test.

In states that do tie test performance to promotion, it's even more critical to put kids at ease, because anxiety can cause them to do worse. I try not to mention the test very often, other than in the context of preparation as a means to build student confidence. For example, I'll say, "This reading assignment has a lot of FCAT-style questions. This is going to be great practice, because when you see the actual test, you'll already know what it's going to look like! There won't be any surprises!" I'll also make comments such as, "You did so well on your geometry assignment! When you have to identify solid figures on the FCAT, it will be no problem for you! You are really working hard!"

Preparing Academically: "Will this be on the test?"

☑ **Regulate the amount of materials you use that are formatted to look like standardized tests.**

Much of test-prep work just makes kids want to scream every time they see a multiple choice question or paper with bubbles to fill in, and causes them to feel too burned out to try their best when it's time for the real deal. It's great to have kids become familiar with the testing format, but there are so many other ways for children to demonstrate their knowledge than through multiple choice questions. This is especially true in science and social studies (or whichever subjects are not tested at your grade level)—you can use more authentic and interesting assignments for those areas. Unfortunately, the trend in many school districts is to add test-prep materials for those subjects so that students are doing test practice all day long. I try to avoid that scenario as much as possible for the sake of my students' sanity and my own.

☑ **When you do give test-prep work, approach the whole thing nonchalantly and build up students' confidence.**

Tell the class that you are going to show them a paper that looks a little bit like the state test they'll be taking. This means that when they do take the state test, they will already know what it looks like and won't have any reason to be nervous.

☑ **Practice assessing anonymous work samples as a class.**

Most students love an opportunity to be the teacher! In one school system, I put short answer essay responses from previous classes on the overhead and had the kids score them according to the same rubric that was used by the official scorers. We talked about which responses would earn a "3" (the top score) and discussed what was missing from the lower-scoring essays. The kids showed on their fingers what score they would give, 0-3, and talked with partners about why they gave the score they did. This really helped my students become mindful of what they were being assessed on. After some practice, when a child turned in a poorly-written response to a question, all I had to say was, "What score would YOU give this?"

☑ **Teach test-taking skills and provide timed practice.**

The focus of instruction should always be on producing good readers, not good test-takers, and the relevance of skills to real-life tasks should be emphasized as much as possible. However, students need to have strategies in place to use on the test: circling key words, proving their answers, answering questions out of order if needed, and so on. These strategies must be explicitly modeled and practiced often enough for students to do them automatically. Children should also be taught: what to do if there are unanswered questions and only two minutes left for the test, how to make a decision when they don't understand the question, and HOW they are supposed to check their work when they're done. Provide sufficient practice so that students get comfortable with being timed and using their strategies.

☑ **Give as much feedback as possible on practice tests.**

Grade practice tests right away and go over the results so kids know how they're doing. Explain to each individual which skills are their strong points and which are weaker areas, and suggest ways to improve. Typically, teachers have a lot of data about student progress, but they keep the information to themselves. I encourage you to be honest and direct with your students about where they stand so there are no surprises. Anytime you see gains, be sure to point them out so the child can see her progress and build self-confidence.

☑ **Stop doing practice activities a week before the test.**

A struggling child is not going to magically learn to accurately answer comprehension questions five days prior to a high stakes test. Gear things down a bit to de-stress the kids and have them practice their skills in more authentic ways. I give kids a break from homework during the week of the test, explaining that their assignment is to get lots of rest and play outside as much as possible so that they don't feel stressed and are ready to concentrate in school.

During the Test: "Can we take a break now?"

☑ **The importance of pep talks (especially individual ones) cannot be overestimated!**

Certain children need to have some pressure put on them, or else they'll be lazy during the test. Others are already anxious and need someone to bolster their confidence and relax them. I like to call each student over to my desk on the first day of testing and provide words of encouragement and tips that I know will benefit them. Hearing, "I know YOU can do this!" makes a world of difference for most of them!

☑ **Have kids make test affirmation posters and read them aloud regularly.**

The week before testing begins, I have students brainstorm all the reasons they feel confident about taking the test while I write them on the board. Usually we can list between ten and fifteen reasons, ranging from the practice activities we've done to the focused work in small groups to the independent reading students did at home. We even list things such as, "I'm getting a good night's sleep before the test" and "I'm eating a healthy breakfast" and discuss how important those actions are. Students create little affirmation posters for themselves, writing down the reasons that are relevant to them and adding creative decorations. I laminate the posters and children stand up on their chairs each morning before testing and shout their affirmations. I reiterate the importance of BELIEVING the words as they're speaking them, and the pivotal role of self-confidence. Being nervous makes things worse, so I encourage my kids to speak positively about the test experience ("I felt a little nervous this morning, but now I'm confident because I keep thinking about how hard I've worked this year").

☑ **Take all the test breaks that are allowed, and find quiet activities for children to do during them.**

If you have multiple test sessions in one day, you may have breaks in between them. With short breaks (5-10 minutes), it can be hard to get students calmed down again before the next test section. Use fun, quiet activities to help the kids de-stress and gear up for the next test session.

De-Stressing Activities for Test Breaks

Silent math ball: Using a store-bought inflatable math ball (or beach ball with numbers written all over it in permanent marker), have the students stand in a circle and toss the ball to one another. Whoever catches the ball looks at the number under his right thumb. He then says a number sentence that goes with it (e.g., for 12, he might say 3x4=12 or 13-1=12), then tosses the ball again. You can have each child toss the ball back to you and you can toss it out to a new person if you want to make sure the game is fair and there are no wild throws. Anyone talking during the game is out. As a variation, you can have kids say a real-life math fact about the number her thumb is over. For 12, you might say there are 12 months in a year, or for 4 you might say there are 4 legs on a chair. You can also pass the ball around the circle instead of tossing, or sit on the floor and roll it. With a mature group of kids, this can be done with several balls simultaneously, either in small groups or as a whole class. Silent math ball is best used during the breaks for reading tests, so students aren't overwhelmed with math activities.

Chalkboard drawing: This can be free-time, or you can give specific directions, such as to draw a large triangle and then turn it into any object students want to create, e.g., a piece of pizza, rooftop, or diamond. It should be a time that requires little thought and allows students to stand and use large- rather than fine-motor skills.

Simon Says: Take turns being Simon and creating actions for the rest of the class to mimic. You may not want to have people sit out if they make a mistake because kids who are out don't get the chance to move around, and children may incite some arguing about whether someone did something correctly, which takes away from the quiet of the game. You can also play Simon Says silently, more as a mime activity, to keep kids calm.

Clapping games: Have students sit on top of their desks or stand, just for a break from their chairs. Clap out a pattern and have students clap it back. Invite volunteers to think of the patterns. Remember to consider the noise level if nearby classes are testing.

Play make-believe games: Pretend you're an airplane taking off. Pretend you're a dinosaur. Pretend you're an astronaut walking without gravity so you keep flying away. Be creative! The kids will love this and may have ideas of their own to contribute. You can also have the class sit in a circle and pretend that they're passing an object. It can be an object that's very heavy, very light, oddly shaped, sticky, etc. It's even better when you have students pretend to throw or roll it to someone else in the circle...especially if you create a rule that they can't talk. It's a lot of fun to pantomime. Another great make-believe game is when you pretend you need to take a shower, but only one drop of water comes out of the tap. The idea is to make that drop of water clean your whole body without letting it go down the drain. When you are leading this activity, you should move slowly and try to get the students to stretch as much as possible.

Do a mirroring activity: Start a motion and have the kids mirror it. Raise a hand, raise a leg, jump, and so on. Once they have the hang of it, let the kids take turns being the one that the class mirrors.

After the Test: "Is it over now?"

☑ **Have a celebration!**

Let the kids decide what they want to do. You can hold a discussion earlier in the week so that students can anticipate their reward throughout the testing period. Everyone can contribute $1 towards pizza delivery, or you could watch a favorite movie and play games. Extra recess time is also fun if the weather allows!

☑ **Don't try to teach any new material the rest of testing week.**

Most administrations will allow testing week to be a 'down time' in which students can complete art projects, watch educational videos, and do hands-on projects. Remember that testing is extremely stressful for the kids, and it is a relief for them to just relax a little bit. Putting any extra demands on children right after testing isn't fair to you or them.

☑ **Take time for yourself to relax and de-stress.**

You deserve a treat—take a hot bubble bath, get a manicure or pedicure, go to 'Happy Hour' with your co-workers, buy yourself something special, or even take a day off! In many ways, it feels like testing week is the culmination of all the hard work you've put in for months. Don't forget to reward yourself!

Making Test Week the Highlight of the Year

Believe it or not, it is possible for students to look forward to test week! Let them know at the beginning of the year when you first start talking about the test that you have lots of fun things planned for them. Refer to those activities often to keep the momentum going.

Just what ARE those activities? A few years ago, I put a request on the Internet for teachers to share ways they make testing week fun. The ideas that I got back were fantastic! Here is a sampling of the ones I liked best:

■ "We make test-taking survival kits I found on a website a few years ago. The kids really love them. They get stickers, gum, and new pencils which they especially love, plus other stuff to help them 'survive'."

■ "You'd be surprised how one stick of gum leaves an impression! As we talk about getting ready for our test, that's the first thing my kids ask—are we going to get to chew gum? They look forward to testing week! We started this practice when all the high stakes testing took effect. We were looking for ways to help the kids relax, and gum seemed like a cheap, easy thing to try."

■ "We have breakfast every morning before we test. I have made pancakes, eggs, and waffles, and brought in things like donuts, muffins, and cereal." *Note: I tried this idea a few years ago and loved it so much that it's become a testing tradition! I send home a note asking parents to provide bagels, muffins, fruit, granola bars, etc., and set up a buffet for the kids. Eating breakfast together really helps calm the class down and creates a bond that reassures them that we're all in this together.*

■ "I only test in the morning, so I have to fill many afternoons. Some years I had theme afternoons. We did a carnival one year and the kids loved it! We had games related to probability and just general carnival games. It was a lot of fun."

■ "I talk to the P.E. teacher and she sometimes allows us to use the gym. I either give the kids free time or we cruise around on scooters or play a game together."

■ "We had a board game afternoon. The kids brought in games from home and they played all afternoon."

■ "We always make a big art project. The past three years, we made tissue paper butterflies. These are very involved, so this is a perfect time for us to take time out of our schedule to do them."

■ "I let the kids vote on free time inside or outside for the last half hour of the day."

■ "I let them have snacks before and after the test sessions. Since we do our nutrition unit during testing week, we try to have snacks from the different food groups."

■ "We do large art portfolio books, one page each afternoon during test week."

■ "At the end of the test on Friday, when all has been turned in, we walk to the far edge of the playground and on the count of three, we scream as loud as we can, 'It's over!' Then we run around like we are chickens with our heads cut off. I buy poppers (plastic bags you blow in then squeeze to pop so paper confetti comes out). We shoot them off to celebrate the end of the test."

■ "We go outside and fly styro-foam airplanes, have races with little jumping frog toys, and take walks while blowing bubbles."

■ "On the last day of testing, we celebrate with an ice cream party."

A Final Note: Choose Your School and District Carefully

In many instances, the only thing high stakes tests measure fairly accurately is the socio-economic status of the student body. Therefore, I refuse to work for any administration which puts undue pressure on teachers to perform miracles.

I once taught in a school district that was emphatically geared up about the tests, especially since we had the second-lowest scores in the state (and also the second-highest rate of students living in poverty). However, my principal was reasonably laid back and let us know that he had confidence in our teaching abilities. He was not into excessive meetings and constant test practice and checking lesson plans—his theory was that we should strive for a sound educational program all year long, and the test was just one piece of the big picture. That year, we made Adequate Yearly Progress (AYP) in every area for the No Child Left Behind Act, and that was certainly evidence that our school's focus was where it should have been.

Another school where I taught had an opposite but equally successful approach to testing. The administration felt that the students needed a lot of structure and explicit instruction in how to succeed with the standardized test format. Our daily schedule was closely monitored and the vast majority of our materials were considered test-prep. This scenario has the potential for disaster, but because of the principal's attitude, the set-up worked. We as teachers felt supported because the administration was closely involved and knew exactly what was going on, offering specific guidance as needed. We had all of the materials we needed and then some, and every resource was put into place to help struggling students so that one person was not left holding the ball when children were unsuccessful.

The common factor in those two schools was a supportive administration who made decisions based on what was best for the students. Principals who operate out of fear and create tyrannical working environments will have great difficulty retaining good teachers and keeping kids happy and motivated. In such schools, teachers are often afraid to leave because they've been duped into thinking that the next school could be worse, and that all teachers everywhere feel constantly under the gun to raise test scores. I assure you, there *are* schools with healthy learning and teaching environments. If high stakes testing has made you and your students miserable, I would strongly recommend considering a transfer to place where you are respected as a professional.

Chapter 23: Eliminating Homework Hassles
Choosing an effective and manageable program for <u>your</u> class

There are a number of reasons why teachers assign homework: because the school district requires it, to provide skill reinforcement at home, to show parents what kids are practicing in school and enable them to support learning, to review previously-taught concepts, to prepare students for upcoming tests, and to teach skills that there wasn't time to cover in class. This last reason is the only one that isn't particularly appropriate: homework should be a time for reinforcement of skills already learned and students should be able to complete assignments independently. Sending work home that students cannot do will result in frustration and reinforces incorrect practice and misconceptions.

The reason(s) you give homework will influence how much you give, what type, whether or not you grade it, etc., so it is critical that you answer this question before planning any further: Why are YOU assigning homework?

Choices to Make About Your Homework System

There are endless ways to manage an effective homework program, and I can't begin to describe them all here. What I'll do instead is pose several questions you'll need to ask yourself when designing your homework program. I'll list the questions altogether first, and then go through them one-by-one to give you some ideas and suggestions for determining what's best for your class.

There are NO RIGHT OR WRONG answers to these questions: it's about what's developmentally appropriate for the age group you teach, and what fits the needs of your particular students. My homework system changes each year to reflect the age, personality, socio-economic status and home environment of my students so that the assignments are relevant to kids and manageable for their families.

1) How often will you assign and collect homework?
2) How long should it take your students to complete their homework?
3) What type of assignments will you give?
4) How will you communicate assignments to students?
5) How will homework be collected?
6) How will you check and/or grade homework?
7) What will be your policy on late, incomplete, and make-up work?
8) What consequences/rewards will you tie into your homework program?

1) How often will you assign and collect homework?

Most elementary teachers give homework daily, but there's no hard and fast rule about this unless your district requires something specific. A preferable option, in my opinion, is to use weekly homework packets. I dislike this concept in theory because I believe homework should consist of DAILY reinforcement, not a four-hour marathon the night before homework is due. However, on a practical level, weekly homework seems to be the best solution for most families. It works well for students from upper-class backgrounds who may be run ragged with soccer and piano and ballet practice every night, as well as for students from lower-class families who may have a lot of responsibilities at home while their parents work.

I used weekly packets for several years, emphasizing to the parents and kids that homework should be done over the course of the week, and then leaving the schedule up to them. I assigned new homework packets and collected the old ones on Fridays. This meant students had an entire week to do their homework (Friday to Friday) and could get a head start on it over the weekend, or wait until the following week to begin.

To create the packets, I had my kids gather all the worksheet or workbook pages for the week, as well as blank paper for spelling, and put the papers in the order they were listed on the homework assignment board. When I checked the previous week's homework to see if it was done, I also checked the new packet to make sure the assignment was copied word-for-word, everything was spelled correctly, and the papers were in the right order. Once the child had everything ready, I stapled it and initialed the corner so the parent would know that the child had copied the assignments correctly. The stapling procedure is what really held the kids accountable—they couldn't have a real packet, only a pile of loose papers, until they had correctly written the assignments.

The packets were wonderful when I checked homework because everything was already in order, making it easy to tell if something was missing. Also, not having to collect homework during the rest of the week saved me a tremendous amount of time.

In addition to regular homework, I also give Home Learning Projects (HLPs). Depending on the particular class I have, I assign HLPs every month, bi-monthly, or quarterly. The HLPs are projects that allow for much more creativity than typical homework assignments. They also prepare students for the research projects and long-term assignments that are frequently given beginning in fourth grade and provide practice in time management. Students are given a choice of two to three topics to research and present to the class in a format of their choosing. Posters, dioramas, crafts, songs, poems, and booklets are very popular. Oral language, speaking, and listening skills are practiced and assessed during the presentations. HLPs are designed so that students can be successful with minimal parental involvement, but most families enjoy getting involved and often attend the student presentations. You can find more information about Home Learning Projects at TheCornerstoneForTeachers.com.

2) How long should it take your students to complete their homework?

This is different from asking how much homework to give: 'how long' refers to your determination about what is a developmentally appropriate amount of time for your students. You may need to modify assignments for some children to make them more or less challenging, but overall, should your kids spend twenty minutes on homework? Thirty minutes? An hour? Your district will most likely have a policy on this. Generally, child development experts recommend ten minutes for each grade level, i.e., 1st grade=10 minutes, 2nd grade=20 minutes, and so on. Many teachers require a time of self-selected independent reading in addition to the regular homework. When I gave daily assignments, my kids spent thirty minutes a night on written work and thirty minutes reading, for a total of an hour.

A word of warning: no matter how much homework I give, I ALWAYS have at least one parent who complains that it's too much, and at least one parent who complains that it's not enough. Usually there are more of the former than the latter, but this happens almost every year. You can't please them all. The best way to handle this, in my experience, is to determine with your grade level team how much homework to give and be relatively consistent with one another. Parents and kids do talk to one another in their neighborhoods and it's not uncommon for a parent to approach a teacher and say, "How come you give two pages of math and Mrs. _ only gives one page? Why does Mrs. _ give special projects and you don't?" It's not necessary for the whole team to give the same assignments, but it works in your favor if there is not a huge discrepancy between what your students do and what other students in the grade level do for homework.

If particular parents want extra homework for their children, I tell them I would be happy to suggest supplementary activities. I emphasize that the best thing parents can do is read with their children and provide time on the computer to utilize specific sites I recommend. The kids do enough paper and pencil tasks in class and as part of regular homework—bombarding them with worksheets doesn't tend to improve the situation.

I also send home parent surveys a month after school starts to find out how long it's taking the children to do their homework and whether the parents think their children are getting too much, not enough, or the right amount. If a parent indicates there is a problem, I call them and we discuss ways to make the work more or less challenging. In one situation, I allowed the parents to read to the child before bedtime in place of self-selected, independent reading. The child recorded the information the same way on the reading calendar and no one knew the difference, but it made that family's busy schedule a little less hectic. In another situation, a child really struggled with math and took three times as long to complete the work as the rest of the kids. I began circling selected problems for the child to complete, or assigning just the odd problems, and the child did the rest if there was time.

Some teachers disagree with this practice, saying if you give parents an inch, they'll take a mile, and you should be firm and consistent with your policies. However, very few parents or students require these kinds of accommodations, and it's been my experience that the more flexible you are with parents in areas that matter to them, the more flexible they will be in the areas that matter to you. My goal is equity, not equality, and that means trying to give each child what she needs.

3) What type of assignments will you give?

Decide if you will assign the same homework each night or vary it. Perhaps every Monday you'll give the same assignments, every Tuesday a different set of assignments, etc. Maybe kids will have choices about the type of assignments they do (such as for spelling), or you'll alternate between tasks for different subject areas. Perhaps you don't want a set format so you can assign whatever the kids need that day. You might even differentiate homework based on students' needs.

4) How will you communicate assignments to students?

There are several ways you can present homework tasks:

- **Provide students with a copy of the assignments**: This saves time and ensures that everyone has the correct information. I recommend this method for grades K-2, when copying assignments is very difficult developmentally.

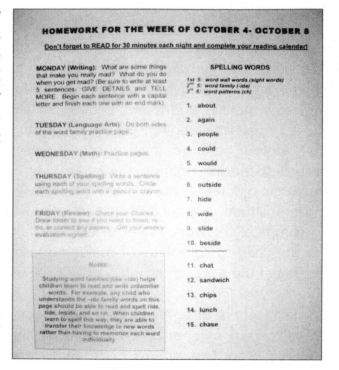

- **Have a homework assignment form for students to fill out**: Write the assignments on a transparency copy of the form, place it on the overhead projector, and have students copy it onto their own blank forms. This system allows you to change or add to homework assignments as needed throughout the week, and doesn't take up any space on your board. When students are absent, it's easy for them to see what they missed when they look at the transparency. The two photos on the next page show assignment sheets I've used in the past.

- **Write assignments on a designated spot on your board for kids to copy**: This works well because unlike with transparencies, the homework is always visible throughout the day. The photo below shows a homework board where I listed assignments that students were to copy in the mornings. I required the class to turn in their assignments in the order in which they were listed on the board so when I checked their folders, the spelling work would be in front, with reading right behind it, then math, and so on. Any missing work forms were placed in the very front, along with notes or forms from parents. This kept me from having to dig around to find papers and helped the children determine whether they had forgotten to do an assignment. I was introduced to this system when I co-taught with a former first grade teacher: she said if six-year-olds were able to use it successfully, then our third graders should be able to, also. She was right!

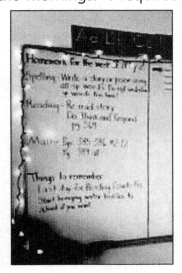

  Teaching kids to keep their assignments in a specific order takes a tremendous amount of patience and modeling for the first several weeks, but the payoff is SO worth it.

- **Use a laminated poster or wipe-off board to display assignments for students to copy**. I like this method because the poster is easily visible at all times, but I can take it down if I need space on my whiteboard.

- **Use the Internet:** It's also a good idea to post homework on a class website in case students lose their assignments, are absent, or go out of town.

Unless you choose the first method or teach the upper elementary grades, you will need to make sure students have copied homework assignments correctly. Even at the end of the year, my third graders still make careless errors when copying, so I've just accepted that I will always have to check behind them! Sometimes I have a Homework Helper who does this job for me.

One trick that has really worked for me no matter how I display homework assignments is to have kids copy the assignments in the morning instead of before dismissal. I prefer it this way because a) checking to ensure kids have copied assignments correctly at the same time that I collect homework prevents me from having to deal with homework twice everyday; b) dismissal can be hectic and we often run out of time; and c) kids leave for illnesses or other early dismissals throughout the day. You may not explain the homework until after your lesson is taught, but your kids will have already copied it. If you need to change the assignment, have students erase and write in the corrections.

5) How will students keep their homework organized?

If you don't design a system for helping kids keep up with their assignments, most of them won't HAVE a system. Children are prone to lost homework, and even with solid procedures in place, you'll still find papers crumpled in the bottom of backpacks and old assignments shoved in random folders. It's critical for teachers to establish a simple system that kids can organize themselves to minimize lost homework. The photos show a student's BEE (Bring Everything Everyday) Binder. Homework packets and notes to/from home are kept in the front pocket. Papers that should be taken out at home are left in the back pocket. This system could also work with a two-pocket folder instead of a binder.

6) How will you collect homework?

Collection may seem like a minor part of your homework program, but it's an important routine that needs to be considered. Will kids turn in their work as soon as they enter the classroom, after copying the next day's assignments, or at the end of the day? Will you have the class pass their work in, or will you have a special file tray in which students will individually place their assignments? You may even want to go around to each student's desk to check homework.

I've tried all these methods and found each effective, depending on the classroom situation. Some years, students handled the collection process independently. Each child stapled together his work for the week and placed it in the in-box for my review at a convenient time. Other years, my method was to call each child up to my desk one-by-one so I could personally check homework. This was time-consuming, but it was an extremely effective way to hold kids accountable for their work, and wasn't a big strain on me because I only checked homework on Fridays.

With some groups of children, I've found it helpful to have students fill out a missing work form when they don't complete a homework assignment, then turn the form in with everyone else's homework. That way, every child turns in something and I don't have to wonder if I missed a child's paper. After I marked the missing work down in my grade book, I stuck the form in the back of the index card box (as pictured) and had a student file for me at the end of the week. (Each child wrote her number on the form so the filer just placed each form behind the corresponding number in the box.) Missing work forms were shown during conferences and sent home quarterly for parent signatures.

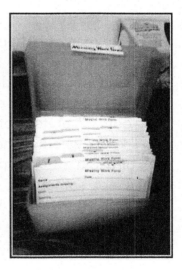

7) How will you check and/or grade homework?

You can assign letter grades and percentages or just mark the work as complete, incomplete, or missing. A separate homework grade can be given if that's part of your district report cards, and/or you can average homework assignments for each subject into children's subject area grades.

Missing Work Form   Name _____   Date _____   #_____

_____ Reading log   Reason: _____

_____ Math practice pages   Reason: _____

_____ Writing   Reason: _____

_____ Bi-Weekly Folder   Reason: _____

_____ Current Events   Reason: _____

_____ Other:_____   Reason: _____

Usually I glance over the work to make sure it was done completely and correctly: if the child didn't understand a concept, I reteach it briefly one-on-one and send the child back to his seat to redo it. I do assign letter grades for Home Learning Projects. The basis for points is outlined on each project checklist so everyone is graded as objectively as possible.

There are many teachers who claim that if children take the time to do the work, we as teachers should take the time to grade it. Some teachers also add that their students would do sloppy work if they thought it wouldn't be checked. You'll have to use your professional discretion and determine what's best for your classroom. I prefer not to grade homework because it's practice work only. I don't know whether the child actually did the work, or had someone do it for him, or had a lot of help. It's not a good indicator of what the child really knows, so it's not something for which I want to record a grade. The purpose of homework in my classroom is to reinforce skills, so grading it is unnecessary: the work is either complete or incomplete.

7) What will be your policy on late, incomplete, and make-up work?

I require parents and students to sign a contract to indicate they are in agreement with my policies. When I taught in an affluent area, I had a lengthy class handbook that spelled out my expectations very clearly. Here is an excerpt from the handbook's 'Homework Policies' section:

"Please note: Late homework for reasons other than an excused absence cannot be accepted, even with a parent note! When a student is missing an assignment, he simply fills out a Missing Work Form which documents exactly which assignments were not turned in and why, and staples the form to his homework packet. When I check to see if homework is completed, I circle any missing or incomplete assignments and keep the Missing Work Form for parental review during conferences. Most parents choose to have their children complete late assignments simply so the child gains the academic benefits from the work. When they do so, I mark the assignment 'Late' so that parents are aware that no credit was awarded but that I have noted the child's effort towards the skill practice. Students who are missing assignments use their Fun Friday time to complete make-up work, as well.

"Occasionally true emergencies come up. Please know that two or three missed assignments each quarter will not hurt a child's grade. I appreciate your cooperation with regard to my late work policy, and I assure you that the entire class benefits from the way it decreases the time devoted to checking homework and increases time for learning.

"If you notify the office of an excused absence, please let me know that you did so with a quick note in the agenda so I can send home make-up work. Many of the activities we do in class are hands-on, involve class discussion or teamwork, or are otherwise unable to be duplicated at home. For these assignments, I simply mark the student in my grade book as having had an excused absence so they are neither penalized nor credited for it. No make-up work is provided for unexcused absences, as permitted by school board policy. Make-up work for excused absences is due two days after the student returns to school (i.e., for a Monday absence, the student returns to school and gets the make-up work on Tuesday and must turn it in by Thursday in order to receive credit).

"Homework is marked in my grade book as 'Complete', 'Incomplete', or 'Missing'. If homework is done with an excessive amount of errors, I generally give it back for students to redo during Fun Friday. (No credit is taken off as long as the work was done; however, students quickly learn to do things right the first time or else they end up with double the amount of work.) I go over the assignment briefly with the child to determine whether she did not understand the work or simply chose to rush through it. If the student needs extra help, I reteach her one-on-one before having the child complete it during Fun Friday.

"Turning in accurate, timely work is an important life skill that I try to teach students early on. I put a tremendous amount of effort into designing effective lessons and assignments and I expect students to work equally hard to complete them, as it is for their own benefit. I appreciate your support in this area as we work together to instill a solid work ethic in the children.

"Parent signatures are REQUIRED on agendas each night! I use the agendas to communicate about missing work and behavior issues each day and it is crucial for families to maintain two-way communication. Signing the agenda lets me know you are aware of your child's work habits and social growth and have reviewed the homework for completeness and accuracy. I encourage you to look at your child's homework, rather than ask if it was done, and make sure the work your child shows you matches up with the assignments written on the homework packet, as many times a key element has been left out."

8) What consequences/rewards will you tie into your homework program?

When I first began teaching, students who did not turn in their homework missed recess—that was just standard procedure for almost every teacher I knew. Now, many teachers believe this practice is developmentally inappropriate, because children need to move around and release energy—often the kids who don't turn in homework are the ones who need to run around the most!

My current school district does not allow teachers to take away recess for missing homework because of the obesity epidemic in our country. While I understood that reasoning, I wondered at first what leverage I could possibly have for getting kids to turn in their work. For an entire year, I had no consequences or rewards tied to homework, and I have to admit, I saw absolutely no correlation between recess privileges and the regularity of homework being turned in. In every class, there are always a handful of children who just don't turn in their work. For this reason, I am convinced that taking away recess is not an effective way to get kids to do homework.

Most years, I do give a reward for those who turn in their homework all week. One year I did Power Hour, which is a 30-60 minute block of time scheduled at the end of the week for kids to play educational games, have free time in centers, or enjoy some other fun activity in the classroom. If other teachers were doing Power Hour at the same time, we often opened our classrooms to one another, so that students who wanted to do an art project went to one classroom, those who wanted to play board games went to another, and so on. Students who didn't turn in all their work had to complete it during Power Hour, and if they finished early, they either found other work to do or I assigned them work. This is an effective motivator for most children, especially in the older grades when they are mature enough to wait for a delayed reward. It works especially well for weekly homework packets, because I collected the work on Friday mornings and then immediately gave the reward to those who earned it.

Another reward for students who do their homework is to have a picnic outside during lunch or watch a movie in the classroom while they eat. This is an awesome motivator because it doesn't detract from instructional time, and provides the added incentive of getting to eat with the teacher. I only do this when 90% of the class has turned in their homework so that peer pressure will work in my favor. Although I don't announce who didn't do their homework, the children always ask each other, "Did you do it? Did you do it?" No one wants to be the person who forgot their homework and caused the class to miss out on the movie. This system creates a very high percentage of homework being turned in.

Chapter 24: Quick and Easy Assessment
Minimizing paperwork to focus on student learning

If you're taking papers home with you on the weekends to grade, or spending hours before and after school trying to update your grade book, I have great news for you—assessment doesn't have to be so time-consuming! By rethinking the way you teach students and evaluate their learning, you can take the hassle out of grading. In this chapter, you'll learn how to manage the grading process and determine whether kids are really 'getting it' in simple, easy ways.

Rethinking Paper and Pencil Work

Alternative Activities

Almost every teacher could afford to rely less on worksheets and utilize other types of student responses more often. Using manipulatives, oral discussions, partner work, games, and group activities can also give a clear picture of what kids are learning. Yes, you need written documentation of how kids are doing, but not for every skill, and certainly not for every practice activity. Non-written assessment methods are just as valid as those that produce a finished product. You can grade kids on participation (an easy 'A' for most children) or just let them enjoy the learning process without recording any grades.

Using Page Protector Sheets

You can put dittos in page protectors and have kids use vis-à-vis markers to write on them. This is a great way to save paper when giving timed math fact quizzes, handwriting practice, and so on. A quick squirt from a water bottle and a paper towel are all it takes to erase.

Using Individual Dry Erase Boards

Use wipe-off boards for instant individualized assessment during lessons. Purchase a piece of shower board from a home improvement store and have it cut into 12x12 squares. This will provide you with thirty individual dry erase boards for around ten dollars. If the school can't give you dry erase markers, ask parents for donations, and use tube socks or felt squares for erasers.

Dry erase boards can be used in place of almost any paper assignment, and are far more motivating for kids. To use them, have your class helpers pass out the materials. Give students thirty seconds to 'test their markers'. During this time, they can draw or write whatever they want, and let you know if the marker has dried out so that you won't hear any complaints during the lesson. If a marker seems to be losing ink during instruction, tell the child to finish working with it that day and then throw it away after the lesson, rather than putting it back with the others when markers are collected.

Model dry erase board procedures like you would any other, and train students to only write what you write and erase when you erase. This will take a lot of practice initially, but the logical consequence for students who don't follow along or who race ahead of you is to use pencil and paper instead of the board, so students will be eager to follow your directions. When you give a problem, have students hold up their boards for you to confirm their answers. When you nod, they can put their boards back down on their desks and wait quietly for the next instruction.

There are endless possibilities for dry erase boards. Students can even put manipulatives on top of the boards and write labels next to them. The boards can be used to create graphs, charts, thinking maps, and more. You can even take questions directly from an end-of-chapter test or related worksheet by writing the problems on your overhead projector and having students solve on their boards. The idea is to have students practice the needed skills and problem format using a method that is motivating for them and easier for you to assess. By the end of the lesson, you will have a clear idea of who is demonstrating mastery because you will have seen every answer each child gave, as well as how long it took each child to determine the answer, and the strategies used to find it.

Informal Assessments (No Grading Required)

Using 'Benchmark' Students

Choose three students as your 'benchmark': either three on grade level kids, or one above, one on, and one below grade level child. When those three children start to tune out or show significant difficulties, change your instruction and reteach in a follow-up lesson. When those three kids demonstrate mastery, it's probably time to move on to the next skill.

The same thing can be done with written student work. Look over 3-6 papers from each assignment you are not grading to see if students are getting it. You can choose papers randomly or view selected students' work (I choose low- to average-performing students. I know certain children almost always master what I teach, and certain others very rarely get it the first time, so I pick students that typically fall in the middle range.) Check just those 3-6 papers for common mistakes or excessive errors to see if you need to reteach.

Quick Checks for the End of a Lesson or Day

- **Informal reflection questions**: After you've taught your lesson, have students answer a reflection question with a partner or group. You can walk around to hear individual student responses and then call on a select few kids to share their answers with the class. Ideas for questions include, *When will you use this strategy again to help you as you read? If we had a new student in our class, what would you tell him about community helpers? When will you use estimating again when you're not in school?*

- **3 Things Poster/Calendar**: At the end of the day, have kids work in teams to brainstorm the three most important things they learned that day. Teams can then write their ideas on sticky notes to attach to a poster (or write directly on the poster). You can also use a large desktop-style calendar. This is a good way to help children differentiate between 'important' and 'interesting', which is a mistake they often make when identifying main ideas and supporting details. Encourage children to focus on the things that they will probably need to know later on. At the end of the month, talk about what you've learned. Bind the posters together to make a class book. You can also choose the three most important things for the week and/or month and circle them.

- **Learning Timeline**: You can record important classroom events on adding machine paper that is taped in a long strip across the wall. Each day, have the class discuss the most important things you've done or learned that day, and have a student volunteer write the date and activity on the tape, drawing an illustration to go along with it. You could already have the date written out for uniformity. The assessment value is in the class discussion, but the timeline itself will provide a record of student learning and help children see how they are acquiring new skills.

- **Exit Tickets:** Also called 'Your Ticket Out the Door', these are small scraps of paper that students use to write what they've learned after a lesson. Children hand them to you when leaving for lunch, specials, or dismissal. You can change the exit ticket topics to fit the purpose of your lesson. Examples of prompts include: *How will you use addition to check your work from now on?; Name the planets in order from the sun; How can you tell the difference between a square and a cube?; Give one fact and one opinion about dogs;* and *Name two things you will do differently in writing tomorrow after learning about capitalization.*

A Simple Way to Tell and Track: Do They Really Understand?

One of the hardest things to gauge as a teacher is whether the kids are actually 'getting it'. Sometimes I teach a lesson and think I have everybody with me, and then give an assignment and realize it was the five brightest kids in the class who knew it all and the rest of the group just followed their lead.

I especially need to know if my kids are grasping math concepts, because I teach new skills in that subject more often than in other subjects, and so much of the content knowledge is cumulative. I can't move on to three-digit subtraction if kids still don't understand two-digit subtraction, but I can't do two-digit if they don't understand regrouping, and I can't do regrouping if they don't understand place value...and on and on.

I designed the form shown as a simple and fast way to tell what kids can really do on their own and to formulate a plan for reteaching when necessary:

1) After teaching a lesson, I give students an independent assignment and tell them to show me when they finish. The assignment is usually a workbook page that is closely aligned with the format I just taught. The assignment is typically short, maybe 10-20 problems—just enough so I can see what kids know. I fill out the top of the form shown (concept, assignment, and date) for my records while I wait for the kids to complete their work.

2) When a student brings me his assignment, I circle the problems he missed and go over the correct answers. Usually this is a quick process in which I just clarify one or two problems that were wrong. I put a checkmark or sticker at the top of the paper and congratulate the student on completing the assignment. (If the child has missed several basic problems, I either reteach right there on the spot, or give him a bit of guidance and send him back to his seat to try again, if I think he's capable of correcting the work independently. When the child comes back and shows me he understands how to get the answers, I put a checkmark on his paper.)

3) After viewing the child's work, I write his name in the appropriate column on my form. I base the placement on what the student did independently, and not on whether he understood the concept once I went over the assignment with him and retaught.

Math Concept: _____		Assignment: _____	Date: __/__/__

Mastered	Progressing	Emerging	
		Needs Concept Instruction	*Needs Basic Skills Practice*
1			
2			
3			
4			
5			
6			
7			
8			
9			
10			
Enrichment:	*Follow Up:*	*Follow Up:*	

Whole-class Follow Up: _____

Absent:_____

4) Once I've checked the assignment, the student works on a fun math practice paper while waiting for the others to finish. I place these at the front of the room in a consistent spot, and the child is allowed to take one back to his seat after I've checked his work on the initial assignment. Sometimes I staple multiple papers together to create a packet that students keep in their desks and take out as directed.

5) Later that day or the following, I work with kids who just aren't getting it or need extensive reteaching. There are usually a handful of children who miss so many problems that explaining it to them individually would take five or ten minutes each, so I provide basic concept instruction at a more convenient time for all of the children who need it.

I use the assessment form to look for patterns in the class' progress as a whole and to track individual student growth. I also use the form to plan future instruction. When the majority of the class' names are in the left two columns, I know I can move on to the next concept or skill.

Ways to Involve Students in the Assessment Process

❖ **Have students correct their own papers.**

I don't advocate having children grade each other's papers, and some courts have disallowed this practice. If I were a child who got a bad grade, I wouldn't want my peers to know. But, having children correct their own work can be a great experience.

Ask students to put their pencils away and take out a crayon or pen to self-correct. My students always use blue so parents know that any corrections marked in that color were written by the child. Let the class know that anyone caught with a pencil out will have their paper taken away and graded by you, and if they are caught changing any answers, they get an automatic zero with the paper photocopied and sent home with a note for parental signature. (I had a very sneaky class of 28 kids one year, so I assigned a 'Grading Monitor' to walk around the room as an extra pair of eyes while we graded—she was a student who typically got A's and I would grade her paper myself later on.)

Having students grade their own work saves time and provides immediate feedback as to what type of errors they are making. When children self-correct the same type of assignment repeatedly, they can also see improvements or stagnation in their progress over time. Sometimes I like to have students reflect in the top margin or back of the paper before they grade it ("How well do you think you understand this skill?") and afterwards reflect on what they learned by grading it, using one or more of the following prompts: *Did you understand the material as well as you thought you did? What parts of the assignment were easiest for you? Hardest? Is there anything you need your teacher to help you understand better? On a scale of 1-10, how well do you think you understand what we learned?*

❖ **Grade papers while students are working on them.**

I know of a teacher who assigns two papers, the most important one (to be graded) first, and a lesser or reinforcement paper to be completed second. Students work independently and the teacher either circulates around the room to check their work or calls them to her desk. The teacher grades the paper with the student watching, asking him to make corrections as needed. She records the grade right then and there, and the student works on the second paper (which just gets a checkmark). This method saves the teacher time, provides individual assistance and feedback to kids, and ensures that grades are recorded right away without a stack of papers piling up.

❖ **Give students the answer key.**

Here's an example of how answer keys can be a great tool. In the back of our math textbook, there were five short practice tests that my kids needed to do right before state testing. I gave the children an answer sheet that provided space for responses to all the questions and had them do one test each day for a week. Whenever they finished, they came over to a table where I had a few photocopies of the answer key. The children used pens to correct their work, then came over to my desk to show me how they did. I went over any problems they missed and sent them back to their seats to work on a high-interest activity. At the end of the week, I collected their answer sheets and recorded all five grades in my grade book. The students loved this! They're always excited to do even the most mundane assignment when they know they'll get to see the answer key.

What Not to Grade

I'm personally giving you permission not to grade every assignment! To determine whether or not to grade something, ask yourself:

> ♦ **Is this a true assessment of what kids have learned?** Group activities, partner work, and teacher-led assignments usually are not good indicators.

> ♦ **Is this the only assessment of a particular concept or skill I have given?** If you are giving two papers on proper nouns, you don't need to grade them both—one can just be for practice.

> ♦ **Does this assignment measure a skill or concept I need to know if students are mastering right now?** Some assignments are just given for review, and others will be assessed after a few more lessons.

There are two types of assignments that you don't ever need to grade, in my opinion. The first is homework assignments. If you give two assignments per night, say spelling and math, and you have 25 kids, that's 50 papers to grade every night, or 250 a week! Shave hours off of your grading time by collecting homework and recording whether or not it was completed. If it was, students get a 100; if it wasn't, they get a 0. You could also give a 50 if the work was begun but incomplete. Simple as that.

Remember, some kids have a lot of parental support at home, some have none, and still others have 'helpers' who do the entire assignment for them. Homework is NOT a true measure of what a child knows and from my perspective, is not worth the time it takes to grade. If you don't believe this, compare the class work and homework grades of the kids in your class. You will probably find that some get A's on things completed at home but mysteriously 'forget' the skills on class work and on tests. Grade only the work you see being done right in front of you, in class.

The second type of assignment I recommend not grading is work done with a substitute teacher. The fact is, if you aren't there, you don't know if a child copied the work, was allowed to work with a partner, received excessive help from the sub, or was given no clarification at all even though you would have helped if you had been there. Students do not turn in work of the same quality when you are not present, just like with homework. Chalk it up as practice work, use your 'Read But Not Corrected' stamp, and send it home.

What to Do With Work You Don't Grade

Rather than placing a checkmark at the top of ungraded papers, try using a special stamp. This is an especially important consideration when a paper has errors on it—giving it a checkmark can send the message to students and parents that you are not looking over work or that you are being careless. Stamps like the ones explained below (purchased at a craft or teacher supply

store/catalog) prevent that misunderstanding. Some of the stamps can also be used for work that IS graded to provide additional information to the parent about how the grade was earned:

- **Read But Not Corrected:** This stamp is perfect for those papers you choose not to grade or mark on at all. Parents will expect the papers to have mistakes that you did not point out.
- **Completed Together In Class:** Place this stamp on papers that students did while following along with you. This lets parents know that their children did not get all of the answers correct by themselves!
- **Completed Independently**: Stamp this phrase on papers that students did on their own. You may choose to mark mistakes, or not.
- **Completed With Help:** This tells the parent you had to give a lot of assistance to the child: if the assignment was graded, it lets the parent know that the grade doesn't reflect what the child can do independently.
- **Partner Work/Teamwork:** Use this stamp for papers that students did with other students. Teamwork assignments are rarely graded by most teachers because they are not fair assessments of what students have learned, so this stamp is a very useful one.

You can even have student helpers stamp papers for you. The child will not see anyone's grades so there are no confidentiality violations. It's an easy, fun job that saves a lot of time for you.

And by the way, you can occasionally throw papers in the trash. Most teachers feel guilty doing this, but it's okay! Sometimes rather than stamp practice assignments that don't provide assessment information for me and will probably be unclear to parents, I just toss them out. I also throw away papers that almost the whole class bombed—if I'm not recording the grade, there's no sense in sending home F's for all the kids and causing their parents to freak out for no reason. I just toss the papers, reteach, and reassess.

Meaningful Assignments That Are Easy to Grade

When you need to assign a formal grade, give assignments with easily-graded formats. Multiple choice, fill in the blank, and matching are obvious examples, but there are ways to make even those formats simpler. For example, you can have students write their answers on a separate sheet of paper so you don't have to flip through the packet and find the answers that students circled or bubbled. You could also photocopy blank bubble sheets and have kids mark their answers that way. With these methods, you can reuse the same tests year after year and save on photocopies.

Another great format that can be used as an occasional treat is color-by-answer assignments. Print out simple coloring sheets from the Internet or use coloring book pages. Write problems in different areas of the picture and make a key. For example, you could write a math equation in each section (if the answer is less than 10, color it blue; 10-20, color it red), or write special terms or vocabulary words, e.g., color nouns yellow and verbs green, or color words with two syllables purple and three syllables blue. The possibilities are endless. Kids LOVE these, and you can grade each paper within seconds simply by looking to see if the colored page looks like a correct student sample.

Using Simple and Consistent Markings

Choose your color for grading and use it exclusively. I use red because it stands out well and makes it clear to parents and kids what I have written vs. what they have written (my kids often correct their own papers using blue pens). Red is the traditional teacher color, and I think that some of us as adults are kind of 'scarred' from seeing red marks on our papers as kids. However, a young child hasn't had those types of experiences and therefore there are no negative connotations for them. I also use red ink for all of my stamps, so the kids associate red with positive messages, too.

I think seeing numerous corrections can be intimidating in any color, so it's more important to focus on what types of marks you are making on the paper. Be sure to use simple, quick markings, and be consistent with them. For example, I don't make big Xs by or circle wrong answers, I just draw a slash through the problem numbers.

Try not to make more work for yourself. I once knew a teacher who wrote the correct answers next to wrong ones on EVERY student paper. That's great for the kid and parent (assuming they actually read each paper) but it took her a half an hour just to grade a set of spelling tests! Another teacher I know circles the correct answers and leaves the incorrect ones alone. This helps build student confidence and makes marks from the teacher a good thing (the more, the better!) rather than a bad thing. I love this concept, but again, I wouldn't do it for the whole class because it is too time-consuming.

Staying Organized and Current With Grading

Keeping Papers from Piling Up

Try not to let students' ungraded work sit out on your desk: until you're ready to grade, leave it in the file trays where kids turned it in. Messy piles accumulate so quickly! If you have a good filing system, it should take less than ten seconds to find any stack of ungraded student work in your filing trays. Use the ideas in Chapter 4, Avoiding the Paper Trap, so there will be no more confusion about what's already been entered into the computer grade book, what's has been graded and what hasn't, etc.

Don't let papers go ungraded for more than a week, tops. This is easier said than done! However, more than once I have been in the middle of grading a tedious math worksheet when I realized I had already tested the kids on the material. What's the point of grading the practice class work at that point? It was too late for me to assess whether or not the kids were getting it, and because I never provided them feedback on how they did, it's possible that a number of them had used the assignment to practice incorrect strategies. It was a waste of time for me and them.

Finding Time to Grade

In the past, I've set aside certain times of the day to grade papers, such as during students' Morning Work, while the kids used math centers, or right after dismissal. Every day during the predetermined time, I tackled whatever papers the kids had created since the day before. This was a very effective way to make sure that papers never piled up. I now typically grade all papers for the week at one time (during Fun Friday). This is manageable because my students complete most of their written work in workbooks and journals which are not graded. I know other teachers who stay after school one day per week to catch up on their grading.

Taking Papers Home to Grade

Although I've never regularly taken papers home, I do have an organized file folder system for transporting and keeping track of papers that I prefer to grade at my house. Sometimes I've used three folders for each subject (class work, homework, and tests); other years I just had one folder for each subject. Additional folders can also be useful:

- **Already Graded—To Be Entered in Computer:** I kept my grades electronically and put papers in this folder until the grades were entered.
- **Already in Computer—To Be Filed:** I would empty this folder into the basket of papers for students to take home.
- **To Review/Redo With Class:** When there were a lot of errors I wanted to go over, I placed the papers in this folder.
- **Incomplete:** These would be stapled to weekly evaluations on Friday as weekend homework.
- **Make-Up Work:** I normally graded make-up work every two weeks and kept it in this folder until I was ready to correct them.
- **No Names:** I filled this file if I was going to try to find the papers' owners later—most of the time, those papers got zeros and were put in the trash.

Tips for Quickly Assigning Formal Grades

☑ **Use a slide chart grading aid (easy grader).**

This little device allows you to have any number of problems or questions in an assignment and calculates the grade. The easy grader prevents you from having to choose a basic number of questions for an assignment, such as 20, in order to make each question worth 5 points each. With a grading aid, having 27 or 34 questions is no problem. You can buy these for about $5 at teacher supply stores, or do an online search and download one for free.

☑ **Grade an assignment on criteria for multiple subject areas.**

If you assign a reading passage with questions about living organisms, you can take reading AND science grades from the same assignment. A population graph activity may provide you with social studies AND math grades. At the top of students' papers, write the subject area and grade for each, e.g., 'Rdng- B, Sci- A'.

☑ **Collect grades from several workbook pages at a time.**

This is a useful strategy for grading assignments in workbooks when children aren't supposed to rip the pages out. It works best when you need the grades for documentation purposes and don't need them for information on student progress. Collect the workbooks and record grades all at once for several assignments by flipping to the page numbers that students completed. You can even have students fold down the page corners to help you find them more easily. This process is much more efficient than collecting workbooks or journals after every single assignment. If for some reason you must do it that way, have students stack their workbooks while they're still open to the right page so you don't have to flip through them.

☑ **When grading multi-page assignments, grade the first page for each student, the second page for each student, and so on, rather than grading the entire test for one student at a time.**

This is an invaluable tip that I learned years back, and it has saved me countless hours. When grading one page at a time, you tend to memorize the answers, making it easier to spot errors. If there are a lot of problems on each page, write the number the student got wrong at the bottom of the page, such as –0 or –3, and then after you have graded the whole stack, go back through and count up how many each student got wrong by looking at the minus-however-many that you wrote at the bottom of the pages.

☑ **Use accurate student papers instead of making answer keys.**

After the first quarter of the school year, you'll have a pretty good idea about which students will have the right answers on their papers. If you don't have an answer key for an assignment, check two or three of those students' papers against each other first, and find one that is basically correct. Mark corrections for any mistakes on the paper, then use it to check all other students' work against. This is much quicker than making an answer key, and if you photocopy the child's paper, you can save it and use it for the key again the following year.

☑ **Make an answer key transparency.**

For lengthy assignments or those you plan to use for several years, make photocopies of bubble sheets (like those used on standardized tests—check the back of your teacher's guides) and have your students fill in the bubbles instead of writing answers on the test or blank paper. Make an answer key on a blank transparency using a permanent marker. When you are ready to grade, place the transparency over a student's paper and count how many bubbles don't match up between the student's sheet and the answer transparency. I grade my students' Scholastic Reading Inventory tests this way and can get through an entire class set (45 questions each) in less than 10 minutes.

Tips for Keeping a Grade Book and Averaging Grades

☑ **Give letter grades instead of percentages.**

Not every school district allows this, and not all teachers like the idea, but this will save you so much time! Essentially, instead of having to calculate the exact percentage a child earned, such as 84%, you just write "B" in your grade book.

This makes it much easier to glance over your grades and see how a child is doing and also how well the class as a whole scored on a particular assignment. At the end of the marking period, average the letters out mentally, or if the grade isn't immediately clear, assign each letter a point and average it that way (A=4, B=3, C=2, D=1). If your report cards don't allow for plusses and minuses to be given, this makes even more sense. Grading isn't rocket science in elementary school—don't make your job unnecessarily difficult.

☑ Only use weighted grades if your district mandates that you do so.

Have every assignment count equally, instead of weighting tests to be equal to 50% of students' overall grades, homework as 25%, and so on. This will save you massive amounts of time at the end of the quarter.

☑ Simplify the way you calculate homework grades.

At the end of the quarter, I simply go through and count up how many assignments were missing. If there were 42 homework assignments given in a marking period and a child did not turn in 3, she gets a 39/42 and the computer automatically translates that into a letter grade and percentage out of 100. If your district requires you to assess homework separately for report cards, then that's your grade. If your district expects homework to be included in each subject area's average, you may be able to use the same homework grade for every subject, rather than differentiate with a reading homework grade, math homework grade, etc. After all, children are either doing homework or they're not, and that choice will usually impact their grades in all subjects equally. Also, if you rarely give social studies, science, or health homework, combining all the homework assignments ensures you will have a homework grade in every subject.

☑ Use a computer grade book.

I was hesitant to start this method because I thought it would be a pain to have to record grades and then enter them in the computer, but if you back up your files, you don't have to keep a paper grade book at all! A computerized grade book allows you to pull up a child's average at any point (such as when a parent calls), and at the end of the quarter, all you have to do is print out the grades.

Part Six:
Implementing Instruction Effectively

Chapter 25: Teaching Techniques That Minimize Off-Task Behavior
Fifteen tips for keeping all kids actively engaged

In college, I was always taught that elementary-aged children can't stay focused for very long, and how it's best to break up their learning with movement, music, and play. What I never understood was, with all those interruptions, how was I ever supposed to teach? If the kids have to be ready for standardized tests in just a few weeks, and I've got them all focused with a great momentum going...am I supposed to stop and let them sing a wiggles song?!

Then, when I got my first classroom, I figured out what the real key is to keeping kids on-task: variety, variety, variety. When kids need to move around during the middle of a math lesson, it doesn't have to be with a trip to the playground or a stretching exercise that totally detracts from learning—the movement and learning can be connected! You can be as creative as you want in designing lessons that have kids standing up, switching seats, and doing related movements. Kids will listen more closely to your instruction when they know that at any moment, they could be asked to do something fun and out of the ordinary.

Another tip I picked up during my first year was from an early-childhood workshop I attended. The speaker adhered to what is a basically a fifteen minute guideline: never do any activity longer than 15 minutes with preschoolers. And you know what? It works with children of all ages! Just when they start getting antsy, it's on to something else.

Several years later when I moved up from preschool to third grade, I noticed that my students could work on certain projects for an hour or more and complain when it was time to stop. Then, when I gave other tasks, they would start playing around after five minutes! I knew that holidays, the time of day, and deviations from the daily schedule such as fire drills and assemblies can all influence student behavior and throw off even the best-planned lesson. But I started picking up on a general pattern: if the task was well designed, meaningful to students, and required their constant and active participation, they could stick to it for far longer than 15 minutes and really get into higher-level thinking processes.

I developed something I call the FMAP guideline to follow when designing and implementing lessons: Fifteen Minutes, Active Participation. This is based on my discovery that when I switched tasks at least every 15 minutes, my kids were more involved in the lesson and displayed fewer behavior problems. They also retained more because the information was broken into smaller chunks and I was more likely to engage them in their preferred learning style or modality.

FMAP in Lesson Design

Creating Effective Lessons With FMAP

The FMAP guideline is primarily followed during instruction in a spontaneous or intuitive way. However, it should be incorporated into your lesson planning ahead of time whenever possible.

It's much easier to use the lessons you were given by your school district. But we all know the difference in our students' behavior when we have an interesting, well-designed lesson and when we use a textbook-based one that we never bothered to tailor for own classroom. The feeling of satisfaction that comes from teaching without constant interruption and knowing that students were successful in learning makes the time spent planning well worth it. And the best part is, it takes less planning to teach this way after the first year you've tried it. Not only can you reuse ideas and materials, you know the outcomes that are expected and getting your students to master them becomes intuitive.

Reinterpreting Basic Lessons Using the FMAP Guideline

You can take a general lesson plan from your curriculum guide and reinterpret it using the FMAP guideline:

An example of a 60-minute traditional math lesson typically provided in curriculum guides

5 min.   **Warm up** (independent written task, usually 3-5 problems in the text)
5 min.   **Review warm up** (teacher-led with student volunteers providing answers)
30 min. **Teacher Modeling, Guided Practice** (teacher explains, writes on board, asks questions, students answer; might involve some manipulative usage)
15 min. **Independent Practice** (worksheet or textbook problems)
5 min.   **Review/Assessment** (teacher asks questions, volunteers answer)

Yawn. I almost fell asleep typing that. The poor kids sit at their desks for the entire hour. There's no way to tell whether every student really mastered the concept taught, or to ensure that the class is even paying attention while the teacher blabs on and on, interacting with the five kids who always want to be called on. And which part do you think the teacher usually loses the kids on? The meat of the lesson—modeling and guided practice. It doesn't fully involve the students, and it goes on too long.

Let's see how the FMAP (Fifteen Minute, Active Participation) guideline might reinterpret that schedule—remember, activities can be shorter than 15 minutes, but not longer unless they involve every student's active participation, and that means more than simply listening to a lecture or discussion:

Example of the same 60-minute math lesson using the FMAP guideline

10 min. Warm Up/Review
This could be a different partner game every week to practice basic skills. It could also be a textbook or workbook assignment, a fun activity sheet, writing a fact family, a higher-level thinking story problem, or a math sing-along with a CD. A review of the warm up can be done whole-class, or with a partner/group.

5 min. Introductory activity
Kids sit on the floor at the teacher's feet as he leads them in an anticipatory set that grabs their interest, e.g., a short role play, a real-life problem to be solved, or a song/chant.

---

10 min. Teacher Modeling
The teacher conveys the concept to be taught in concise, simple language, using lots of props, examples, the board or overhead projector, and student input as much as possible.

15 min. Guided Practice
While still sitting on the floor, students use manipulatives, wipe-off boards, or other props if possible to practice the concepts taught under the teacher's guidance.

15 min. Independent Practice/Partner Work
Students go back to their desks and complete a task by themselves to demonstrate mastery, or work with a partner if the lesson is a multi-day one. The tasks vary: further manipulative work, worksheets, math games, writing about what they learned, and applied problem solving. The teacher walks around the room to see who needs additional assistance and keeps kids on-task.

5 Min. Closure/Review/Assessment
Students respond to the teacher's questioning with as much movement and creativity as possible—standing up or sitting to show whether they agree/disagree; writing an answer on an index card with markers and holding it up; or even just sitting *on* their desks instead of *at* them while reviewing a skill in unison e.g., skip counting or chanting a multiplication table. The closure could involve revisiting the introductory activity or another real-world application.

The basic components of the lesson are still present in the FMAP version. The teacher still teaches concepts from the state standards. But students are actively participating, and are not given the opportunity to daydream during lengthy modeling and discussion sessions. The teacher keeps the kids close to her during the most important part of the lesson to ensure they are on-task before releasing them to the distractions of their desks. Children get to move around in ways that add to—rather than detract from—the lesson, and a broader range of learning styles are addressed. By following the FMAP guideline, you can help ensure that students are learning and on-task the majority of the time.

Using the FMAP guideline will also encourage your students to follow the rule about not interrupting the teacher ('When I'm talking, you're listening'). Children will be more attentive to your words when they know they will be constantly called on to participate in fun and interesting ways. They will follow along with you because they can't wait to see what will happen next!

FMAP in Lesson Implementation

Creative Implementation Doesn't Take a Lot of Planning!

You might be saying, "Sure, that sounds great, but when am I going to find time to design creative hands-on activities? It takes me hours each evening to plan for the lessons already in my curriculum guide!"

Designing innovative lessons takes time, but creative implementation can be very spontaneous. It's about involving students in instruction and saying and doing things in different ways to keep their interest. Once you acquire a repertoire of teaching techniques that minimize off-task behavior, you can apply them to any lesson you present.

The following tips are designed to help you implement your lessons in a way that involves lots of variety and motivates students to stay engaged in the learning process. You should incorporate these ideas into your instruction in a natural way that makes sense for you and fits your teaching style.

Tip #1) Make your whole-class, teacher directed instruction as quick as possible.

Direct instruction doesn't typically allow children to construct their own knowledge, which is the main way they retain information. What's the point of teaching if the kids won't pay attention or remember what you've said? The more hands-on activities, partner/group work, centers, games, field trips, walks, songs, and technology-rich lessons you use, the more kids will learn. Present the concepts you need to introduce as briefly and simply as possible. Then give kids a variety of tasks to practice with your support.

Learning can be facilitated most effectively through small group instruction and individual conferences. Students are much more on-task when working in a group of six than in a group of twenty-six. We as teachers know this already from our reading instruction: we teach a whole-class mini lesson, then let the kids practice in centers and other independent activities while the teacher provides small group assessment and skill reinforcement. Now we need to learn how to simplify that process and repeat it for other subjects, especially math.

Tip #2) Ask students to do little tasks during direct instruction to keep them involved.

Many teachers are used to being solely in charge of leading instruction and making decisions during the course of a lesson.

Traditional Method of Teaching Students to Solve a Math Problem

"62+18. First I add the eight and the two. What do I get, Maurice? Good, ten. I put the zero here and carry the one. Then I add the 6+1, plus the one we regrouped, and I get what class? Very good, 8. The answer is 80."

In this example, the kids interacted three times. The teacher did all the thinking and explaining.

The FMAP Method for Solving a Math Problem

"I need a two-digit number—Shane? OK, 34. Now I need another two-digit number. Make it less than 50. Keri? She says 17. The problem we created is what? [Class: 34 plus 17]

"Who can tell us the first step? Jonathan says to add 4 plus 7 to get 11. So, I'll just put 11 down here at the bottom, and we're all done! Thanks, Jonathan! [Kids start laughing and protesting] Wait, I can't just put 11 at the bottom? But Jonathan said 4 plus 7 is 11. Jonathan, you gave the wrong answer! [Kids laugh harder and insist Jonathan was right and the teacher was wrong] Oh, I see, Sara says I need to put the one at the bottom and regroup the one from the ten's place over to the ten's column.

"So what's next? Maria? Put your finger on your nose if you agree with Maria's answer. Griffin, you agree—tell us why you think that answer is correct. So I add 3+1 and then add the 1 that I regrouped and get 5. Class, the answer is? [51] Excellent.

"[Notices Josh is picking at his shoe and Wanda is looking out the window] Josh, we'll write the answer in a different color so we don't get confused. Which color do you want? Okay, green, and let's have Wanda come up and write the next problem for us. Wanda, choose someone to tell us a two-digit number..."

With the FMAP example, the kids interacted twelve times, including several whole-class responses. One time, the teacher asked students to show their responses by putting a finger on their nose if they agree, enabling her to see who understands and who doesn't and allowing the kids to move and participate. Even the kids who were completely disengaged were drawn back in with a question they could answer despite not following along. The kids created the problem and explained how to solve it. The teacher was silly and joked around with the kids, which made learning more fun and held their attention. She gave them ownership over the smallest decisions, such as the marker color, and even had a child write the next problem, freeing her to facilitate from the back of the room and ensure participation from everyone. Obviously this process takes longer, but children will get more out of three math problems completed with their full attention and involvement than ten problems with them halfway zoned out.

Tip #3) Whenever someone writes on board (including you), have the rest of the class also write at their seats.

This doesn't work for all lessons, but it's a good principle in general. If you want a few kids to put the correct answers on the board, for example, have everyone complete problems at their desks with pencil and paper (or better yet, individual dry erase boards). You can then circulate and ask students who have done the work correctly to put the answers on the board. This way the entire class is working and not just waiting for the child to write the answer.

Tip #4) Ask students to write on the board whenever possible so you can focus on your instructional techniques.

One day, for example, my class was reading a map to find out which states have deserts. As the children mentioned each one, I started writing them on the board so the kids would be able to spell them correctly during the activity. After the second state, I realized my attention was being taken away from the class because I was writing, so I had a high-achieving student finish the task for me. I was then able to walk around and make sure everyone was participating and comprehending.

Tip #5) Have children SHOW their answers on their hands.

Our class recently had a dispute over which digit in a particular number was in the thousands place, the 3 or the 1. The kids showed on their fingers which digit they thought was correct. This required everyone to participate without having to speak in front of the class, which is scary for some kids, and allowed me to see who needed more practice with place value.

Tip #6) Have kids make specific hand gestures to represent different needs or responses.

This can be done simply: "Put your hand on your head if you think the answer is the Atlantic Ocean; put your hand on your ear if you think it's the Pacific." Or, you can create a more complex system to use all year long, i.e., have kids show one finger to ask a question, two fingers to make a comment, three fingers to clarify the assignment, four fingers to ask permission for the bathroom, and five fingers to answer a general question or participate in class discussions.

Another way to use hand signals is to designate specific gestures for a particular lesson. When analyzing our writing, I put a diagram of a hand on the overhead with a specific criterion written on each finger: index finger means not enough detail; pointer and middle fingers touched together (so as not to make a rude gesture, of course) means off-topic; ring finger means the writing needs text support; and so on. I put anonymous copies of former students' writing on the overhead and the kids showed on their fingers what the problem was in each piece of writing.

Tip #7) Use songs to teach and get students' attention.

I've used songs for our morning meeting, particular lessons and topics, lining up, cleaning up, and just to focus the kids before a lesson. Nothing quiets a group of wiggling youngsters like a familiar song—they'll stop talking because they want to sing! Teach them to always fall silent when any song ends and wait for directions.

Tip #8) Periodically have students stand up as part of your lesson, not as a break from it.

This technique is easier to incorporate than you may think. When we compared numbers recently, I had two kids stand in opposite corners of the room with small whiteboards. Each child wrote a number and, on my signal, flipped over his whiteboard for the class to see. Students stood next to their desks and used their hands to make the greater than/less than sign to indicate the smaller number. The whole activity only took about five minutes—and that was five minutes that the class got to stand up instead of doing paper and pencil work.

Tip #9) Try using Think-Pair-Share (TPS).

This is a method of ensuring that everyone gets to participate, even those students who take longer to process information. With TPS, you pose a question and have the kids think in silence about the answer, then pair up with the person next to them, and finally, share what they thought. I use hand signals to represent each part, then clap out a pattern and have the kids clap it back to me to signal that the whole class is coming back together. Some students get tired of TPS after awhile because it's slow and they're used to a fast pace, but if not overused, it's a great teaching technique.

Tip #10) Be silly, use dramatics, and borrow some techniques from the gospel preachers!

If you have ever been to a charismatic Christian church, you may have noticed that the congregation does not sit quietly and passively by. The preacher will often have the congregation repeat things back and say things to their neighbors. The ministers use these techniques to drive home their most important points.

I use similar methods when my kids need to 'wake up' or when I'm saying something very crucial. In a very dramatic and maybe even silly tone, I'll say, "You can only change one variable at a time in a science investigation—how many variables? *One!* That's right, tell me again, how many variables can you change at once? *One!* Turn to somebody next to you and tell them, 'You can only change one variable at a time!' [Have the kids do it] How many variables? *One!*"

The kids really get a kick out of this technique, and many of them feel quite comfortable with it (even if you don't!).

Kids usually love anything unexpected, so whatever we as teachers do to liven things up is appreciated. I know of a second grade teacher who will give spelling tests lying down on her desk and stand on a chair to make an important point. She's a natural actress, and that style isn't for everyone (especially if behavior management is an issue), but I can't imagine any child dozing off in HER class!

Tip #11) Move students' seats often.

Many teachers don't feel this is necessary, but I have found that the longer I leave kids near each other, the more comfortable and chatty they become. That's great for partner work, but children tend to become increasingly talkative and playful during inappropriate times. Think about it: the first time you sit next to a stranger at an ongoing workshop or class, you are probably fairly quiet, but after a few days of being next to that person, you know her life story! One of the many advantages of moving desks frequently is that you'll keep kids from getting too comfortable with each other and distracted during instruction. If your classroom routines are firmly in place, you can even move students in the middle of a lesson for variety: set a timer and give everyone ten seconds to sit in a different chair, or move one person from each team to a new place. You could even move the whole class over to the rug. Do whatever needs to be done to wake kids up and get them interested in what you're about to do.

Tip #12) Develop a repertoire of very short, kind things to say to refocus kids without sacrificing the momentum of the lesson.

Did you ever notice that when you reprimand a student in a normal or even soft tone of voice, the entire class stops what they are doing to eavesdrop? The whole class' concentration is broken because a single child was doing something that probably only distracted one or two people (or maybe just the teacher!). And if you're trying to teach and you interrupt yourself with a drawn-out speech on the importance of paying attention, forget it. The whole class loses their train of thought. I still have to give myself frequent reminders about this one—*The middle of a lesson is not the time for a lecture: say only what's necessary to get kids back on track.*

Situation	Not Listening?	Still Not Listening?	*Still* Not Listening?
You've called on a child but the rest of the class is chattering.	"Okay, let's hear what Tony has to say."	[Step closer to the talkers] "Let's listen, Tony might be asking a question that you want to know the answer to."	[Loud and firmly] "Tony, you can ask your question as soon as you think the class is ready to listen with respect."
You made an important point that the class didn't respond to.	"I'll say that part again. Listen closely…" (pause for effect)	"Janice, can you repeat what I just said for anyone who didn't hear?"	"Abdulia, why do you think it's important to remember that?"
You gave a direction but kids are muttering to each, "What did she say?"	"Class, which page are we on? [The ones who did hear respond loudly and in unison] Thank you."	"Wonderful, I see an entire team that has found page 67."	Begin the lesson with a reference to the instruction: "You should now be on page 67. Take a look at the caption next to the photo and raise your hand when you know which habitat is pictured."
You're ready to begin the lesson but kids are still rummaging through desks and talking.	"Show me you're ready to begin by having your crayons and scissors out, and your hands on top of your desk."	"Justin, you're the first one to be ready with your materials out and hands in your lap. Thanks for your cooperation."	"Your crayons and scissors need to be on your desk before I get to zero." (If someone does not make the cut-off time, ask him to put his head down while you give instructions. After everyone begins working, quietly ask the child to get his materials ready. Don't walk away until he's got everything in place).

Tip #13) Use proximity control and teach around the room.

The most effective teachers I know rarely, if ever, sit down. They are constantly walking around the room. They stand next to students who are off-task, wordlessly bringing them back to attention simply by hovering near them or quietly laying a hand on the child's back or desk, all while continuing the lesson. There is something about walking around that makes students think, "I better be doing my work, because someone is watching." Sitting down, even if it's near students, just doesn't have the same effect. If you think back to workshops you've attended, I think you'll agree that people talk less to one another and stay more focused when the presenter is always on the move.

Standing up constantly is not a realistic expectation, because it's exhausting to be on your feet seven hours a day. I don't often sit during the first quarter of the school year, but I do like to rest later on, after the kids have proven they are able to meet my expectations without me constantly standing over them. When the kids do independent work, I'll pull my chair and a rolling cart to the middle of the room so that I'm close to all the students. I still get up and walk around frequently to send the message that kids have to stay on-task. During instruction, I walk around constantly, even though it's tiring, because the results are worth it. If you can learn how to teach from the back, sides, and middle of the room, you will see a significant improvement in how well your students pay attention.

Tip #14) Know when to abandon a lesson.

If you're trying to teach and the majority of the class is completely off-task no matter how many times you redirect them, consider the timing. Early release days, the last period of the day, the hour before a field trip, etc., are going to be very difficult times to teach. If the timing is good, consider your lesson. You *know* when a lesson is boring or poorly-designed, and you can abandon it immediately and try another activity. Get out manipulatives, assign a partner activity, or move on to another subject and catch up later.

If you have an engaging lesson that you are giving your all for and the kids are just being rude, tell them so and end the instruction. Several times a year, I may have to say to my kids, "You know what? You're showing me that you really don't want to listen to me today. You're talking, playing around, and not answering my questions. I put a lot of time into figuring out the best way to help you understand this, and to make it fun for you, and it's not fair for you to ignore me. I'm not going to teach when you don't want to learn. I apologize to those of you who were doing the right thing, but your classmates have ruined it for you and me. I'm going to grade your spelling tests, and you may do page 323. All of it. I don't want to hear anyone say that they don't know how to do it, because I tried to teach you and you ignored me."

This honesty really gets through to my kids! They struggle through the assignment so quietly you could hear a pin drop while I gather my patience and do something worthwhile with my time. After about five minutes, I ask, "How many of you are ready for me to try teaching the lesson again?"   The overwhelming majority, if not all, of the kids will raise their hands, and I begin where I left off with a slightly shortened version of the lesson. The kids are much better listeners at that point because they have seen how difficult the material is without a teacher's instruction and have learned not to take my help for granted. Teachers have feelings, too, and it's important for kids to learn that.

Tip #15) Give kids a break when THEIR minds are full (not yours).

If you've ever sat in a teacher in-service for an entire day, think of how you felt after six hours of even the most interesting presentations. Once during a particularly intense workshop about a topic I was really passionate about, I found myself completely unable to take in any more information. Even though I hated to miss anything, I stepped outside to get some fresh air and a drink because I knew I just couldn't process anything further until I took a break. For the first time it occurred to me that off-task kids might actually WANT to pay attention but their brains might be too full to learn anything else. Because most kids don't have the introspective skills or vocabulary to verbalize this, it's up to us as teachers to recognize when kids are into a lesson but just need a break, and make sure we provide them with one.

Chapter 26: Making the Most of Every Moment
Maximizing time on-task and encouraging participation

Researchers have found that elementary students spend an extraordinary amount of school time not engaged in learning tasks, e.g., getting drinks, standing in line, waiting for other students, and so on. In addition to wasting academic opportunities, transition times also tend to lead to behavioral problems because students have nothing to do but wait (and as we all know, young children are notoriously bad at waiting).

To make the most of every moment with students, you will need to give precise directions and clearly enforce your expectation that students will follow them the first time they're given. You'll need to call on children equitably to make sure each student is on-task and grasping the lesson content. Finally, you'll need to facilitate smooth transitions between lessons and lesson components to maintain the momentum you've built and keep students focused. The ideas that follow will help you consider each of these areas and maximize the amount of time your students spend on-task.

Giving Clear Directions

1) Get your kids' FULL attention.

You can do a 'hand check', in which you say those exact words and kids raise one or both hands in the air, waiting for your directions. Don't say a word until you see EVERYONE'S hands! You can say "Hands up [kids do it], Make them friends [clasp hands together in the air], In your lap/on your desk [lower clasped hands and listen]." Or you can say "1,2,3, eyes on me" and have the kids say back, "1, 2, eyes on you." Another alternative is, *If you can hear me, clap once; if you can hear me, clap twice* or clap out patterns and have kids echo them back. You can sing a special song or recite a poem—it doesn't have to be about transitioning, just something the kids know and can participate in. A variety of techniques can be used—but make sure you are not talking before they are listening.

2) Keep the directions as brief as possible.

The younger your students, the less they will be able to remember. Multi-step directions can be nearly impossible for English Language Learners and children with ADD/ADHD to follow, so be mindful of their needs, as well. ***Sometimes the problem is not that children aren't listening or paying attention; they just can't process everything that we've said.***

3) Teach students not to start any task before you give the magic signal.

If you ask kids to take out a book and turn to a certain page, most will immediately start banging around in their desks for the book and won't even hear the page number. Instead, say, "When I give the signal, please take out your crayons and math workbook." Your signal could be a hand gesture, bell, clicker, code word, or just saying "go." Beware that most kids associate the word 'go' with a race, so if you don't want them rushing, choose another word. One teacher I know calls her signal word the 'magic word' and often chooses something silly, such as 'pepperoni', as in, "When I say the magic word *pepperoni*, you will clear your desks. [Pause] Pepperoni." Remember that using signals is a procedure that students will need to practice many times.

4) Ask students to echo page numbers back to you.

When you give directions, say, "We're going to be on page 180 in our blue math workbooks. Which page?" and have the whole class echo the page number. If you've given a multi-step direction, you may want to write the page number on the board and point to it as you and the children repeat it. You can also hold up the book so the class can see which one you're referring to—you would be surprised how many kids get their books confused.

5) Have students repeat multi-step directions to you or a partner.

If you want children to put away a journal and pencil and take out a library book, say so and then ask, "What two things do you need to put away? Right. And who can tell us what you need to take out?" or say to a child at the furthest end of the room, "Robert, could you repeat the directions for anyone who didn't hear them?" Having the directions repeated by a peer is helpful because the child will likely paraphrase, giving students the opportunity to hear things in a different way, and students not sitting near you may be able to hear better if a neighbor is speaking instead. If you do this often, students will pay especially close attention to your directions, in hopes of being called on to repeat them. You could also say, "Tell someone sitting next to you what four things you need now," and have the entire class do so. Make sure students know to wait for the signal before taking action.

Getting Students Actively Involved

Equitable Participation

For students to fully participate in instruction, they need to understand your expectations. What should they do when they know the answer? What should they do when they have a question of their own? They also need to feel comfortable speaking in front of their peers, knowing that you will never intentionally degrade or embarrass them. In addition, you need to ensure equitable participation. Calling on children with equity refers to something far deeper than 'fairness'—it means that you make decisions based on what is right for each individual child. This is an important part of instruction, because it gets all kids actively involved in learning and allows you to assess their progress.

Two Methods of Student Response

There are two ways you can have students participate in class: through individual answers (in which you call on a student to respond) or through choral response (in which the whole class recites the answer together). Both strategies are useful when implemented correctly. You will need to explicitly teach your students when to call out and when to raise their hands, and teach procedures for each expectation. For example, you could use hand-raising as your general policy and have a signal, such as your hand cupped to your ear, to indicate when you want the class to just say their answers. Use the term 'choral response' to differentiate for kids between saying their answers together as a class (which is appropriate), and simply calling out (which is not appropriate).

The following guidelines will help you determine when to use individual responses and when to use choral response, and how to implement both effectively.

Using Choral Response

Choral response is effective whenever stopping to call on specific students would slow down the lesson's momentum. For example, when solving four digit addition problems, I call out each step of the problem and have all students give the answer, as in "7 + 3? [10!] Plus 2 more from where we regrouped? [12!]" I use choral response during lessons whenever the answer is one or two words and I'm looking for a precise response.

Type of Question	Why Choral Response is Effective
We said yesterday that the three states of matter are SLG... [solid, liquid, gas]	Students will all give the same response. You can tell by the kids' volume and the certainty in their voices whether most of the class knows the concept well, or is still catching on.
So the girl in the story stopped playing basketball because her dog... [died]	You're giving the entire class the chance to practice and demonstrate cause/effect understanding, and with this quick check, you can be sure the kids didn't miss a subtle connection before finishing the story.
Let's use the world map to find out where this article takes place. We read that the orangutans are in which country? [Kenya] And we know that Kenya is in which continent? [Africa] So let's find Africa on our map.	The kids are drawn into the lesson and kept on-task by the opportunity to provide information. This is more engaging than having students listen while you lecture about the continents, and prompts students to recall information for themselves.

The primary benefits of using choral response are that it engages the entire class and makes it easy to determine how many students are following along and have the right answers. You don't have to waste energy trying to keep excited students from calling out and you can channel their enthusiasm to get the other kids interested. It's very hard for children to daydream when others on both sides of them are saying loudly, "4! 12! 17!"

Choral response can be difficult to manage if you don't understand when to use it. It's only effective when everyone is saying the same thing. If students are all shouting something different, that's just calling out. Choral response is unified. There may be a short delay or echo with responses, but that doesn't detract from the goal or format of the lesson. If students do give different responses, you can guide them to a consensus. Children can do this by themselves if there are only one or two dissenters ("No, it's 8! 8! Because it's 2 x 4!" and everyone will start saying 8), or if there's a wide disparity, you can facilitate ("Okay, hang on a second. Let's figure this out. Some people are multiplying 2x4 and getting 8, and others are adding 2+4 and getting 6. Raise your hand if you think we need to multiply. Raise your hand if you think we're supposed to add. Okay, let me find someone to tell us why they think it's multiply...").

Type of Question	Why Choral Response is NOT Effective
What are some things the ancient Egyptians invented?	There are too many possible responses and it will be hard to hear children's individual answers.
How can you tell which stage of development a butterfly is in?	The answer is too long, and children won't all use the same words. It will sound like they are all talking over each other.
Why do you think most people in our community don't recycle their canned goods?	This is an open-ended, subjective question and student responses will vary. The teacher will want to address each child's statement and ask probing questions to encourage higher-level thinking.

It's important for students to understand how to differentiate between questions they should raise their hands to answer and those that they can answer using choral response. The 'default' mode in my class is choral response, so to signal that children should raise their hands, I restructure the way I ask questions. I'll say, "Raise your hand if you can tell us the main idea of this paragraph" or "Let's see who can explain how to read this graph..." After a few weeks, most students can tell instinctively what to do, and they start using choral response for quick answers and raising their hands when they want to share a personal idea, interpretation, or explanation.

Maintaining Control During Class Discussions and Instruction

Because they're allowed to 'call out' so frequently, I rarely get upset when I ask kids to raise their hands and they forget. If a child is calling out, it's usually because she's interested in what we're talking about and excited to participate, which is exactly what I want. When I've clearly said, "Raise your hand if you know..." and a child still calls out, I usually ignore it because she'll either self-correct or the other children will whisper, "No! Raise your hand!" and the child will do so. Sometimes I'll address the behavior either with a gesture or verbal reminder, and always with a smile ("Raise your hand please," or "Hang on, I want to hear what you have to say, but I need one person to talk at a time."). If the child apologizes, I nod encouragingly and say, "It's okay. You have something important to say and you got excited. No problem."

You may be wondering if my lessons descend into total chaos sometimes. They don't because my students have been taught that I am the discussion facilitator. I can usually silence every student simply by speaking (see Chapter 13, Teaching Work Habits). Any time students hear me talking, they know they need to stop whatever they're doing. That includes when working in centers or independently, in the hallway, and during dismissal, but especially applies when I'm teaching. Therefore, if students accidently call out or contradict each other during choral response, I am always in total control, because whenever I talk, the kids get quiet. This is a basic show of respect for me and my authority in the classroom. You can hold the same expectation in your own classroom, even with very young children, and I encourage you to do so. Once this procedural expectation has been modeled, practiced, and reinforced for students, you will have a great deal of flexibility in your instruction.

Note: Allowing students to call out (use choral response) during instruction is a teaching strategy that's used when *the teacher* poses a question. It is a completely different scenario than tolerating calling out when *students* pose the question.

Students should not be shouting things like, "What page are we on?" and "I don't get this!" and "Can I color this when I'm done?" at any point during the day. Anytime my kids need me to answer a specific question or give them permission for something, they know to raise their hands. I do not allow students to approach my desk or follow me around the room to ask me things. If someone has a question for me during instruction or wants to make a comment to the class, she must raise her hand and wait for acknowledgement. Whenever students call out to share information or ask their own questions, I correct them by saying, "If you have something you want to tell us, please raise your hand." I may also make comments such as, "I didn't ask you any questions, so you shouldn't be talking," or "Raise your hand if you need me for something."

Tips for Eliciting Individual Student Responses

☑ **Ask the question first, wait 3-5 seconds, THEN call on a student.**

If you say a name first, only that child will listen to the question, because the others already know they won't be asked to respond. Using wait time will allow all students to participate, since slower thinkers will realize they'll have a chance to answer and will put forth more sustained effort.

☑ **Use equity sticks to make sure you call on students fairly.**

Have each child's name written on an index card or popsicle stick. Flip the cards or pull a stick to determine who to call on. Students love the element of surprise with this—there's something about the use of props that makes this technique seem like a game!

☑ **Know when to call on students that you know have the right answer.**

If you are reading about floods and want someone to recall whether rivers have fresh water or salt water, pick someone who can quickly say "fresh" and move on. When you need a fast answer, waiting for the 'low' kids or someone who wasn't paying attention detracts from the lesson and slows down the class. Another great time to call on the higher-achieving kids is when you want to know HOW they know something or the reasoning behind an answer. Most kids have a lot of difficulty explaining things, and after an average performer gives a correct response, a 'higher' child can sometimes help "add to what he said" by explaining how the answer was derived.

☑ Know when to call on lower-achieving students.

When you are checking for understanding, call on your 'average' and 'low' students first—assuming your highest kids already know the answer. Call on the lowest kids to answer your simplest questions so that they feel capable and successful, and talk them through the harder questions. Try not to brush off wrong answers and go on to a higher child: give hints and ask follow up questions at least some of the time so the child ends the dialogue on a positive note and was accountable for his answer. And of course, when you ask critical thinking questions to challenge your highest achievers, you can call on other kids to respond, too: since you posed the question to the whole class, all of the children will be engaged and thinking.

☑ Deal with students who always know the answers on an individual basis.

Some children understand that they can't be called on every time and don't pout or cry. Others need more ego stroking. If you have a needy child, place her in the front of the room and occasionally ask her to mouth, whisper, or show the answer to you before you call on someone—a quick nod in that child's direction is sometimes all she needs. You can use Think-Pair-Share techniques so the child can talk often, sharing with a partner instead of the whole class. Occasionally I'll also say with a broad smile and a wink, "I know YOU know. I want to see who ELSE knows." That way the child feels acknowledged and sees that I recognize her expertise.

☑ Tell students why you can't call on every hand, every time.

If you have lots of sighing and disappointed faces when students don't get called on, explain your logic. Give students a choice: you'll call on every single hand every single time you ask a question and everyone can stay at school until 6:00 p.m., or they can let you use your judgment and call on a few people only. I throw this one out there when someone moans because I moved on without getting his input. The children laugh and make a decision very easily! After all, time constraints are the real reason we can't call on every student: we have to keep the lesson moving, and kids might not realize that this isn't a personal rejection of them or their ideas. One warning: you may have some kids who would love to stay all night, so be wary about this one backfiring. If a child says he wants to stay, smile and tell him you'll give tenth grade worksheets to do all night long. Once you've established your reasoning, don't allow students to complain when they don't get called on: say, "You know I can't call on you every time. I need you to be grown-up about this."

☑ **If a child never raises his hand, rely on other ways to check for understanding.**

Some people are by nature more introverted and don't enjoy speaking in front of a large group of their peers, especially when they're out of their element. I don't 'force' them to very often. To tell if shy children understand the lesson, ask one-on-one during independent work times, or check the pencil and paper work they complete during instruction. Using individual dry erase boards is a great way to check student understanding without anyone having to talk. Students don't need to tell you in front of the whole class for you to know if they're getting it, and participation can be as simple as staying on-task, listening carefully, and looking at the speaker.

Supporting Students' Answers

Sometimes kids say something totally off because they weren't paying attention or they just don't get it, and that can be frustrating to a teacher. However, it's important to respond as positively as you can to each answer if you want to create a safe learning environment in which students feel comfortable taking risks. If a child is totally off base, I may just say, "Keep thinking—I'm coming back to you." This encourages the child to stay on-task because she knows I will ask another question soon. Other ways to support each answer, especially when the child is close to the right idea, is to use comments such as:

> ➤ *Very close!*
> ➤ *She said ___. Who can add to that?*
> ➤ *Hmmm... (while nodding and smiling approvingly)*

> ➤ *You're on the right track!*
> ➤ *You're getting there!*
> ➤ *Would you like to choose someone to help you?*
> ➤ *Okay, I see where you're going with that...*
> ➤ *You're doing some good thinking!*

You should also support non-answers and the kids who say "I forgot" or "Never mind" when you call on them. If a student is totally unable to respond, the following question will almost always elicit a comment you can probe further: *I know you don't have the answer, but if you were going to say something, what would you say?* You can also give the child a choice: *Would you like to call on someone to help you, or do you want me to help you get it?*

It's extremely important to teach children not to laugh at others' answers and how to respond supportively. Generally, my kids will say things like 'good try' and wait patiently for me to talk through questions with the slower kids. But my class one year started off behaving very cruelly at times. They would openly sigh, roll their eyes, and groan if someone took too long or gave a wrong answer. I really had to work hard to teach them to sit silently and wait for their peers to think through things.

We did a role-play in which I gave everyone a really tough math sheet and then asked some of my worst culprits to answer the questions orally, rapid-fire. During the first minute of the questioning, I asked the class to be intentionally rude and impatient, laughing at the kids who didn't know the answers. We discussed how that made them feel. For the second minute, the class was asked to be silent and wait, then praise their classmates for eventually getting the correct responses. This experience was followed by another debriefing. To drive the point home, the children worked in groups to create posters listing what to do and what not to do when others are answering questions.

Children will pick up on your cues, so be extremely careful about how you respond to incorrect answers. If a student asks something you've just answered, say in an upbeat voice, "I just answered that question." If you show irritation at any time, children will emulate that. It's extremely painful to hear yourself through the mouths of your students when you haven't been a good role model.

Transitioning In Between Lessons and Lesson Components

Many teachers lose a lot of time transitioning from one subject area to another, or from one part of a lesson to a part that involves different structure or materials. It's important to convey to kids that you expect them to stay on-task even though the lesson is shifting. Here are some transition tips to help you keep your lesson momentum going:

☑ **Use timers, bells, and music to signal the beginning and end of activities.**

You can play a specific song when it's time to clean up, or ring a bell when a project needs to be finished. Decide whether you want your students to freeze when they hear a particular sound and wait for directions or immediately respond to what they heard, and teach them accordingly.

☑ **When transitioning from one subject area to another, get the kids immediately focused on what's coming next.**

"You all did a fabulous job with staying on-task during our rounding numbers practice today. Now you will be learning a new vocabulary word in science. When I give the signal, and not a second before, you're going to put away your math books and look for the new word in your science books on page 64. You will raise your hand as soon as you find it. [Pause to let the directions sink in] When I give the signal [pause], please put away your math books and take out your science texts. Okay." Write 'New vocab word pg. 64' on the board to help visual learners and those who will not be able to remember what to do after putting away their math books. This is a lot of information to give, but when you use this strategy frequently, it will become easier for students to follow. Kids will be so busy trying to discover the new word before anyone else that they won't stop to play in their desks or talk, and they'll be in the right mindset for the instruction that follows.

☑ **When you're ready to start teaching, start a backwards countdown.**

This is AFTER you've given directions and the majority of the class is ready: a countdown rushes the stragglers and gets the entire class focused. The countdown should be quick most of the time, not drawn out, or the kids will lose interest. I have found backwards counting to be most effective because the ending number is always clear. (Sometimes kids forget if you said you were counting to five or ten...or was it twenty?) There doesn't necessarily have to be a consequence for students who aren't ready after the countdown. Kids will hurry anyway, because they think they're in a contest. When you get to zero, just start your lesson. "5,4,3,2,1,0... Okay. Someone tell your partner what you learned yesterday about the three types of angles." There will usually be 1-3 kids who are still not ready, no matter what you do—at that point, move on without them, giving gentle reminders to individuals as needed. If you have a simple reinforcement system (such as beads), you could also give a reward every now and then to those who are ready on time.

☑ **Limit the materials your kids will need during instruction to shorten transition times and minimize distractions.**

In a typical math lesson, my kids may need journals, math books, manipulatives, and crayons. Because their work spaces are small, most students don't like to have a lot of clutter they're not using and will often sneak things back into their desks when I need them to keep everything out. However, if I stop the lesson for kids to get materials out or put them away, the class may start talking and become distracted. The best solution is to limit the number of materials needed for a lesson. If we'll be using dry erase boards, I don't require the class to reference their math textbooks—instead, I will copy the problems onto the board or overhead. If children will be doing a worksheet later in the lesson for independent practice, I have the kids do their practice work during instruction on the back of the worksheet instead of on a separate paper. This not only reduces the amount of times they go into their desks, but saves paper, as well.

☑ **Decide if you want kids at their desks or on the carpet, and move them only once.**

Start on the floor and then go to desks or vice versa. If it takes two minutes to get them to the next place, and another minute or two to get them re-focused on the lesson, plus two more minutes to return the original spot and two to get focused again, that's eight minutes wasted. Multiply that times the number of subjects you teach and you've lost 15-30 minutes every day.

Create Structured Time-Outs for Students' Minds

Sometimes students need a break between lessons. Fortunately, there are ways that they can clear their minds that are quick and structured enough not to deteriorate into chaos. A few ideas are:

- **Brain Breaks:** This concept is based on recent research proving what teachers have always known: young students have attention spans of only a few minutes and need to have frequent breaks for physical stimulation and exercise. The research is often associated with Howard Gardner's Multiple Intelligence theory and brain-based learning studies, which are having an increasingly profound impact on what we know about how kids learn best. You can do an Internet search on 'brain breaks' to find out what type of activities you can do with your children.

- **Yoga:** There are excellent books and free online videos to help you incorporate yoga into your classroom. Even one minute of yoga stretching and breathing exercises can help calm and focus your students. To find resources, visit <u>TheCornerstoneForTeachers.com</u>, or type 'kids yoga in the classroom' into a search engine.

- **Music:** Songs are a great way to bridge lessons in a structured way and allow students to use their brains and bodies creatively. Chants and raps are equally effective, and perfect for teachers (and kids) who don't like their singing voices. There are links to many resources for using music in the classroom on my website, including sites that have free downloads for children's music, great transition songs with lyrics and sheet music, and more.

Chapter 27: Hands-On and Cooperative Learning
Using manipulatives, concrete materials, and group work effectively

In many classrooms, students love using hands-on materials and cooperative learning strategies almost as much as their teachers dislike using them! Teachers appreciate the concepts theoretically, but management presents a special set of challenges that may or may not be worth taking on. Students must be taught how to work with others and use materials during instruction without losing focus of the teacher, and that is a daunting task. However, once this is accomplished—and it can be, in a matter of weeks—the possibilities for instruction are expanded almost infinitely.

Of course, that's assuming that you have time for these teaching strategies. It does take longer for students to work in groups, and manipulatives drag out lessons for considerably more time. Before doing these things with your class, you will need to completely buy into the idea that students will understand and retain information more fully when they experience it for themselves. In general, they will get more out of a two-day lesson with manipulatives than a one-day lesson with paper and pencil tasks: even though more time is expended initially, the end result is less reteaching later on. Children also grasp some concepts better when their peers explain, and through the process of teaching and discussing with one another, they deepen their own understanding.

The good news is that once your students understand their responsibilities, both hands-on and cooperative learning experiences will run much more smoothly and quickly. Well-defined routines and procedures will expedite the transitions, keep kids on-task, and maximize the amount of time spent learning.

Using Hands-On Learning Effectively

Inexpensive Ways to Get Materials

- **Other teachers:** Don't be shy—see what everyone else has and isn't using. The longer someone has been in the classroom, the more he's accumulated and just can't part with. Put the stuff to good use!

- **'Super Center' Marts:** These types of stores sell plastic teddy bears, coins, mini clock matching games, and more for very reasonable prices. Also check the sale shelves to see if there are any materials you can repurpose for use in the classroom.

- **Dollar Stores:** These are a fantastic resource for manipulatives and hands-on learning materials. Dice, cards, tiny erasers in different shapes, stickers... there's always something new, and it's all within your budget.

- **Make them:** I found a book of patterns (snowmen, dinosaurs, hearts, etc.) at the library, photocopied what I needed, and had the kids color them. After laminating, the kids cut them out. I program the pieces (shown in the photo) using permanent marker according to the skill we're doing, then spray them with hairspray to remove the words and reprogram. I also made manipulatives once when teaching division—I noticed my kids had a hard time keeping their groups of counters separate. I used the die-cutter to make little dogs (the school mascot) on bright construction paper and laminated them. I put ten in each 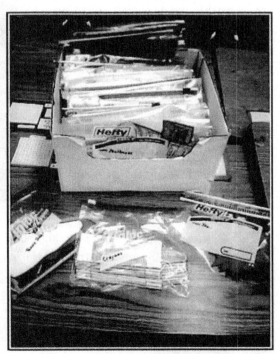 baggie so the kids had a visual separation for their counters (we called the counters 'bones' for the activity—as in, "Take 10 bones and divide them among 5 dogs. How many bones does each dog get?").

Organizing Materials

You will probably want to have your manipulatives and hands-on materials already counted out and in baggies. This is a lot of prep work but only needs to be done once. The Math Helpers have an easy job and you can be sure everyone has the same materials. In most cases it does not take longer than two minutes to get an entire set of manipulatives distributed to the class when you already have them counted out. Even if you have individual student math kits from your school district, you may want to take out the most-commonly used materials and keep all like manipulatives together so that students don't have the distraction of an entire kit.

Here's one way I've stored frequently-used manipulatives. I bought this organizer from a discount store for about $20. My Math Helpers grab the appropriate bin and pass the materials out, then slide the bin back on the rack. Materials we use less often (e.g., place value blocks and coins) are in the student's individual math kits.

I've also used a large black rolling cart with one drawer for each math unit. I opened a drawer, gave the materials inside to the Math Helper to distribute, and returned them to the drawer at the end of the lesson.

Distributing and Collecting Materials

☑ **Try to give each child his own set of manipulatives, rather than have kids share.**

Borrow from co-workers, scrounge around in supply closets, make them yourself—whatever you need to do. When kids share manipulatives, they HAVE to talk. It's already difficult to get them to focus during hands-on learning, so when you add talking to the equation, your lesson has gone down the drain. However, this doesn't mean that kids have to work by themselves all the time. For example, if you are comparing numbers, have the kids pair up and each silently show a different amount with base ten blocks. On your signal, each child shows her number to her partner and compares. This type of cooperative learning is far less distracting when students don't have to argue over pieces from a shared bag.

☑ **Have specific students in charge of distributing your manipulatives, and teach them a set procedure for moving around the room.**

Teach your Math Helpers how to pass out materials to students around the room to ensure all students get what they need. If there is no set pattern for distribution, your helpers will probably backtrack, stop to look around, give someone two of something, forget about an entire cluster of desks, etc.

☑ **If you have individual math kits, teach your procedures for handling and using them.**

I have each kit labeled with a number, to correspond with the number assigned to each student. My Math Helpers pass out the kits (or call out the numbers and kids walk over to get the kits themselves). The kits must stay unopened until everyone has theirs and is sitting silently. I then tell the class which manipulatives to take out, demonstrating how to do so (carefully taking off the lid, lifting out and showing the correct materials, gently snapping the lid back on, and placing the kit under a student's chair), then I give the signal for the class to do the same. After all students have placed their kits under their chairs and have their hands folded, I demonstrate what to do next and the lesson begins. When it's time to clean up, the kids have until a three-minute timer goes off to have all pieces back in their kits correctly. They love the idea of a race!

☑ **Have a set place for stray manipulative pieces that kids find.**

Somehow, my kids are always discovering fraction tiles and place value blocks on the floor and in random places around the room. I keep a colorful candy dish near the manipulatives so that any time a child finds a lone manipulative piece, he can put it in the dish. The next time we use manipulatives and are putting things away, the Math Helpers empty the dish and return stray pieces to their proper place. This technique works well with puzzle pieces, small building blocks, and other hands-on materials your students may use. Even Pre-Kindergarten students are capable of using 'the dish', although with young children, it may be more practical for you to restock the pieces yourself.

Keeping Students On-Task With Manipulatives

Introducing Manipulative Routines

I don't recommend using hands-on learning until students are successful at meeting your expectations for following along (see Chapter 13, Teaching Work Habits) because you will need to insist on the kids' FULL attention when you are teaching with manipulatives. Don't be tempted to let students get away with playing around just because they're using manipulatives.

I have two basic guidelines regarding manipulative use: #1: Don't touch the manipulatives until the teacher gives the initial signal, and #2: When you hear the clicker signal, you must take your hands off the materials immediately. These expectations are explicitly taught, modeled, practiced, and reinforced for some time before students consistently follow them. Our first few math lessons with manipulatives are very simple so that students can focus on practicing the procedures. Any child who can't follow either rule has their manipulatives taken away. This is a logical consequence that should be enforced consistently.

When distributing the materials, you can review your expectations for both manipulative usage and 'following along'. If a student does not meet those expectations, you can give a single verbal warning: "Your counters should look just like mine. If you are playing around, you will lose the privilege of using manipulatives." If the child violates that warning, say in a calm and matter-of-fact tone, "You have chosen not to follow along with us. You need to put your manipulatives back in the bag and see if you can follow along better when you don't have the counters to distract you." If the child does in fact pay attention and participate as much as possible after the manipulatives are cleaned up, I will sometimes allow him to try again with the materials later on. However, the general expectation is that once your manipulatives are put away, you don't get to take them out again until the next lesson.

Using vs. Playing With Materials

The difference between using and playing with materials needs to be taught as part of your procedure practice, as well. Model various ways of moving the manipulatives and have kids discuss whether you are using them or playing with them. For example, when learning about place value, my kids always want to make pretty designs or stack up the amount of base ten blocks they are supposed to be showing. So, I do those things in front of the class and talk about why they're not part of the expectations for following along (i.e., students are focused on their own activity and not watching and listening to the teacher; they are also falling behind because playing with manipulatives takes longer).

I explain to kids that their job is to show the amount as quickly as possible with their manipulatives and then either raise their hands or wait quietly (depending on the lesson). Constantly rearranging manipulatives counts as playing with them when the student is obviously not paying attention, and that is grounds for losing access to the materials.

When I first start using manipulatives with the kids, I model the practice on the overhead (or board, using magnetized pieces) and insist that students' materials look EXACTLY like mine. If mine aren't in a cute design, or lined up exactly even, then the kids' materials shouldn't be, either. Later in the year when procedures are firmly in place, I allow more freedom for students to arrange things in a way that makes sense for them visually.

At the beginning of the year when the materials are new to the class, I let students play with their manipulatives before using them in our lessons. Later in the year when we have time, I try to let those students who worked hard and used their materials the right way have a few minutes to play with them after the lesson.

Making Abstract Concepts Concrete Across the Curriculum

Math is the easiest subject to teach using hands-on strategies because of the obvious provision of manipulatives. Science instruction isn't difficult to make hands-on when you have organized materials and your procedures for distribution and cooperative work are firmly in place. Social studies can be almost completely hands-on if you allow students to actively discover history and the world they live in (I have a tremendous amount of resources for this at TheCornerstoneForTeachers.com because social studies is my favorite subject to teach.)

It is far more difficult to do hands-on learning with reading, but it can—and should—be done as often as possible. Think about the type of activities you would typically place in centers and see if you can incorporate them into either whole-class or small group reading instruction. You can also have students make their own manipulatives. For example, instead of having children do yet another worksheet about prefixes, show them how to write words in large print and cut them apart to separate the base from prefixes and suffixes. These can then be mixed up and placed back together to form new words.

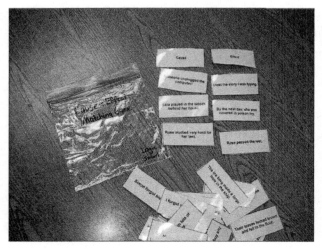

Another example is to cut apart a list of related causes and effects and give each student one slip. On your signal, each class member then finds the person with the corresponding cause or effect, and when everyone's paired up, they discuss their reasoning as a class. Later for an extension or assessment, give each student a copy of the cause/effect list to cut apart and match up independently. Kids can glue them on construction paper in two columns, one for causes and one for the matching effects. They could even make four columns *(This/ Caused This/ Which Caused This/ Which Caused This)* and put the two slips in the middle columns. Students could then write an initial cause and additional effect in the extra columns. For example, a child could match up *overslept* and *late for school*, and then in the first column put *stayed up too late the night before,* and in another column all the way to the right, put *didn't get to do my Morning Work* for a further effect. If students complete this activity collaboratively, you will probably hear a great deal of quality discussion and debate.

There are many ways to make learning more hands-on. It will require some creativity and innovation on your part, and that's what makes teaching so much fun. You don't have to do this for every lesson or even every skill, but work on a few things each month. If you come up with two hands-on activities every month, next year you'll have twenty fabulous lessons right off the bat. Many of your ideas can be adapted for other skills, so the more you try, the more strategies you'll have.

Using Cooperative Learning Effectively

When to Use Cooperative Groups

You can use the following three guidelines to help you choose whether to plan a cooperative group activity:

- Are negotiation, debating, collaborative problem solving, or team work skills being taught, practiced, and/or assessed?

- Will children be able to learn the material more effectively with peer support than without it?

- Do students need a break from independent work and teacher-directed activities?

Generally, I do not plan cooperative activities unless the lesson meets at least two of these guidelines.

Partner Work vs. Group Work

I use partner work far more often than group work because it's so much easier for students to get along with one other person and the accountability level is

higher. Having assigned partners makes the transition process quicker, so use student input to create suitable partner lists for each routine part of your day, encouraging children to select people that they work well with but are not necessarily their friends. When you begin partner work, ask children to raise their hands if their assigned partners are absent, and allow anyone without a partner to choose a pair of kids to join. Change the partner assignment every few weeks as students' needs change. If needed, partner one can be in charge of getting materials and partner two can return them.

Determining Group Placement

Use your objectives to determine whether you want to choose the groups, have students choose groups, or have them arranged randomly. I choose groups when I want to have a balance of high, middle, and low achieving students in each group with few personality conflicts. For activities in which I don't mind a lot of talking and some playing around, I let the kids pick their groups. I choose groups randomly for activities that are just for practice, won't be graded, or don't require a lot of prior knowledge or skill.

Choosing Groups Based on Learning Styles and Intelligences

If students will be creating projects or presentations, it may be advantageous to have a variety of strengths represented within each group, i.e., someone with interpersonal intelligence to take charge of the group and solve disputes, a verbal-linguistic child to do the writing or oral presentations, and a visual-spatial child to illustrate. This will ensure that the group runs smoothly and each student is able to express what she has learned in ways that are comfortable for her.

Using Sticker Cards to Divide Students Into Random Groups

If you want four kids in each group, cut index cards into quarters. Place identical stickers on each of the four sections of an index card. Repeat with a different sticker for each card. These can be laminated for durability. When you are ready to use them, shuffle the cards and randomly pass them out upside down on students' desks. I have kids wait for my signal, then flip their cards and walk around to find their group members. When the group is together, they come up

to me so I can see who is in the group and take their sticker cards, and I let them choose where in the room they would like to work. If you have an odd number of students, then the child whose sticker card did not match a group can choose any group to join. You may want to warn your students about trading sticker cards to switch the groups around—my policy is that if I see a child trying to trade cards with someone else, she has to work alone during the activity.

<u>Managing Cooperative Learning</u>

♦ **Introduce and reinforce your expectations for cooperative learning as discussed in Chapter 13, Teaching Work Habits, and do so ONLY after students are able to work independently**. Group work skills must be taught, modeled, and practiced. They can be introduced once students have consistently shown the ability to 'follow along' and 'stay on-task'.

♦ **Set up a system for monitoring the noise level and have consequences when kids get too loud.** You could turn on soft music and tell students that if they can't hear the music, they are too noisy. You could have a visual on the board, such as a stoplight, to show when the noise level is getting too high. Remember that the concept of 'quiet' must be taught like any other procedure. If students do not meet your expectations, you can give specific warnings to individuals that they will lose their group work privileges if they cannot work quietly. Give three whole-class warnings about being too loud, and then students must either work silently for five to ten minutes or end the activity altogether. After this happens a few times, the kids begin to self-regulate, and they will say things to each other like, "Shh! If we're not quiet, she's gonna make us clean up!" That's much more effective than having YOU warn them!

♦ **If you are asked the same question by two groups, you may want to stop the whole class to clarify and take additional questions.** Sometimes things are unclear to students when they seem obvious to the teacher. Rather than going over and over the same questions, give a pre-arranged signal for everyone to stop and hear your clarification ("Listen carefully, this may be a question that you want to have answered, too.").

♦ **Be prepared to 'jump start' each group after 2-3 minutes to make sure they have begun working and resolved any initial differences in opinion.** Wait until the group is settled in one spot and has their materials out, and then check on them. You may want to summarize what the group is about to do to make sure they have a starting point: "So Michelle is going to read the first question, and then Ahmed is going to answer it? And you're taking turns with each section? Great, okay, go ahead, Michelle, first one."

♦ **Use a rubric or checklist for students to grade their group's collaboration.** Have students indicate whether the group stayed on-task, worked together, etc. You may also want them to grade their individual performance and/or their group members' performances to make sure that everyone was pulling their own weight. This evaluation is for accountability purposes only. I use a form that was included in the teacher resource guide for our social studies curriculum.

♦ **Use a timer or bell to get the class' attention and signal when time is up.** When students hear the bell, they should get quiet to hear your directions.

Group Jobs

Many teachers find it useful to assign a job to each person in a group. This way, the division of labor is more equitable and students don't have to come to a consensus about who will be doing each task. Examples of group jobs include:

Speaker (alerts the teacher if there is a problem and presents to the class if needed); Materials Manager (gathers and returns supplies); Peace Maker (helps all group members work respectfully and supportively); and Scribe (does the majority of writing for the group). Having group jobs is especially helpful when cooperative learning is used in conjunction with hands-on learning in science.

Group Leaders

For ongoing, regular group work, upper elementary students can be assigned group leaders. My third graders last year were supposed to use a special math workbook everyday for two months before our state testing. Because I was already doing direct instruction for the first hour of our ninety-minute math block, I decided to have kids do the special workbook for the last half hour together in groups.

I assigned each group a mathematically proficient leader who I knew liked to play teacher. Each morning, the class would do a page in the workbook for Morning Work. While the other kids finished their assignments, the group leaders would meet together to discuss their answers and then go over them with me. I would ensure that every leader understood how to get the answers and how to explain them to their group members. I also emphasized that their role was as a LEADER (who helps students follow the *teacher's* directions) and not as a BOSS (who tells the group to do whatever *they* want them to do—see page 192). During our math block, each group of children met and the leaders went over the answers. The group then completed a second page together under the leader's direction.

To help motivate students to do their best work, I selected a 'sticker person' in each group. This person was usually a child who needed a leadership opportunity but did not have strong enough skills in that area or in math to lead the group. His job was to award stickers at the end of the group time as an additional reinforcement (one sticker if a child was trying his best, two if he was also being respectful and supportive). Over time as the groups bonded, the leaders asked if they could provide additional rewards for their group members, bringing in certificates from the dollar store and their own stickers and treats.

I gave an extra sticker to one group each day for exceptional cooperative work. This was an easy way for me to reinforce appropriate behaviors. I might say, "The excellence award today goes to group two [the others would clap and cheer for them]. They had one group member who wasn't getting a concept, and I heard Natalia say, 'Let me see if I can explain it another way' and taught the person a different strategy from the one the leader used. When the person understood, Chelsea said, 'I knew you could do it!' and the leader said, 'Good job!'. That's exactly the type of support I should be seeing."

This process took quite a bit of modeling and reinforcement initially, but after daily practice for two weeks, the groups worked unbelievably well together most of the time. I reminded the group leaders that they could use any type of instructional format they saw me use (e.g., completing the page together, having students do the work on their own and then reviewing it as a group, doing a few problems independently and showing it to the leader to go over it one-on-one). The leaders emulated me in so many ways it was a bit unnerving, actually. I heard one of my girls say, "Okay, let's stop there a second. You know what I notice about this section? All of the problems say 'how many more'. Why do you think that is?" The group members politely raised their hands and shared their opinions, and then they highlighted what they believed were key words in the question. It made my day to see how well the kids had internalized my expectations for working respectfully and supportively with their friends. That's not to imply that things were orderly and peaceful all the time...but with ongoing practice and reinforcement, appropriate interactions became the norm rather than the exception.

Solving Social Problems During Group Work

Teaching Respect and Support

Most of the social problems that students have during cooperative learning stem from a lack of respectful and/or supportive behavior. As discussed in Chapter 13, demonstrating these two qualities is an important requirement for any children wanting to work together. By the time you're ready to use cooperative learning, students should have already

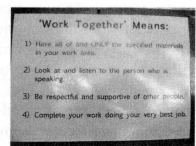

begun to develop an understanding of the concept of respect, because it was defined when you introduced your class rules and is reinforced on a regular basis through situations as they arise (see Chapter 2, Planning for the First Weeks of

School). Being supportive or helpful is a concept that will have to be taught primarily through ongoing reinforcement. Explain to students initially what the term means (supporting each other, helping out, encouraging others) and assist the kids in coming up with examples (clapping for people, saying 'good try') and non-examples (making fun of answers, laughing *at* people rather than *with* people, sighing impatiently).

Throughout the school year, you will need to help children develop the concept of being supportive. You will have to MODEL being caring and accommodating at all times so that the classroom environment is permeated with those qualities. Students will then begin to imitate you and you can comment on what you see, saying things such as, "You told her she did a good job. That was very supportive of you," and "You patted him on the back and told him it's okay when he messed up. Very supportive!" and "You all worked as team to care for her when she hurt her leg. I'm sure she appreciates your supportiveness." You can correct inappropriate behaviors by using the term, as well: "Laughing at his mistake is not being supportive." With time, being respectful and supportive will become your classroom standard, and students will intuitively determine whether comments and behaviors meet the criteria.

When Group Work Doesn't Work

If you don't like the way your students are interacting with each other after several weeks of cooperative learning practice, I recommend not using the strategy for awhile. Either your expectations for group work need to be retaught and modeled again, or students need more time to learn respect and supportiveness. Tell the kids exactly why you've suspended use of cooperative learning and what you expect to see from them in order to have the privilege reinstated. When you notice that children are following along during instruction and are on-task during independent work, you can begin reintroducing cooperative work procedures. Partner work is easier to handle for most kids and your class may need to practice that for awhile.

Some classes never get to the point where they can work well in groups. Or, individual students may not be able to handle it. Make sure you are being fair to your students before disallowing cooperative work. When you are positive that you have done your part to convey and reinforce expectations, you can temporarily remove the privileges when necessary.

Chapter 28: Time Management for Kids
Meeting the needs of slow workers and fast finishers

I can't begin to tell you how many emails I've received from teachers at their wits end about this dilemma. You know the one: the whole class is completing the same simple math test, but Mr. Brainiac is done in less than three minutes (*why didn't he qualify for the gifted program?* you wonder for the millionth time), while another child is still picking at his pencil eraser twenty minutes later (and his name isn't even on the paper yet).

And to complicate things further, there are always two other children who are done shortly after Mr. Brainiac, neither of whom have the slightest clue what they're doing—one could care less and basically wrote anything that came into his head, and the other who *thinks* she's the Brainiac and can't be convinced to check her answers because she's POSITIVE they're all correct. Then after the distraction of the pencil eraser has finally been resolved and you think everyone's done, you realize you've forgotten about your true slow worker, the one who was diligently plodding through the test the entire half hour it sat in front of him, but just processes things so slowly that he's still not even halfway through.

This situation frustrates teachers every single day, but imagine how irritating it must be for the kids! Many of them feel rushed through every assignment without a second to breathe, while others are bored to death while waiting for their peers to get through tasks that they were able to complete in seconds. Fortunately, there ARE solutions.

Tips for Teaching Kids to Manage Their Time Wisely

TIP 1) Try structuring your schedule so that everyone's not doing the same thing at the same time.

It's only logical that when children work in small group rotations, centers, and through individualized programs, they don't HAVE to keep pace with the rest of the class. Teachers who do very little whole-group instruction rarely complain about the fast/slow finisher problem. (I'm not one of them, but if you have this type of curricular flexibility, take advantage of it!)

TIP 2) Teach students to always READ when they're done with class work.

There are lots of cool systems teachers have set up for their early finishers: centers, centerjobs, customized worksheet/activity packets, games, etc., but they all require a lot more work on the part of the teacher than simple self-selected reading. The number one correlate between high standardized test scores as well as advanced reading ability is regular, consistent reading. Students HAVE to read in order to improve their skills. If you have a system for children to choose high-interest books and keep them handy, you'll never again hear the words, "I'm done—now what?"

TIP 3) Have a 'When Finished' sign perpetually posted.

I keep my sign on the board with little magnetic arrows that point to whatever the assignment is. Most of the time, kids are supposed to read when they're done. Sometimes I need them to finish their Morning Work or some other assignment, and I write that below the sign. I train my students to ALWAYS look at the sign when they finish their work so they know what to do without disturbing anyone. I have a plain arrow I use when there is only one task, and two arrows that say 'first' and 'then', respectively, when there are multiple instructions.

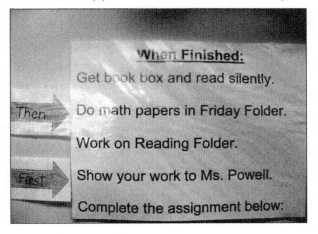

TIP 4) Give 10, 5, and 2 minute warnings before time for an assignment is up, and provide lots of opportunities for students to grasp those time concepts.

Unfortunately, announcing the minutes left for an assignment is not enough to train most primary level students how to manage their time: they still don't understand how to estimate how long things will take. They THINK they can do the last ten problems in two minutes and are shocked when you tell them they're out of time.

You will need to consciously help students develop the concept of time. Give frequent math drills so they can learn exactly how long a minute is. Read to them for ten minutes daily and reference how many pages you read in that time. Have kids mark where they're at on their papers at the 10-minute warning, 5-minute warning, and so on, and discuss with children (from time to time as a whole class and then individually as needed) how much work they're able to accomplish in each time period. Then when you give warnings, they should be able to estimate whether they'll need to speed up or not. I often walk around while students are doing guided practice or independent work and say either, "Good, keep going at that pace and you should be fine," or give hints such as, "You're going to need to draw your chart more quickly in order to finish on time—try using a straight-edge so you don't have to keep erasing your lines."

Regardless of whether students ever master these concepts—and most won't until they're older—you are still teaching them to use their time wisely, and you're preparing them for timed standardized testing. There are tasks for which you must have students stop working at a designated time, and giving warnings makes that demand a lot easier for children who are engrossed in their activities.

TIP 5) Set time limits for each part of a project so kids stay on-task.

We're on a tight schedule in my school so there's absolutely no leeway if kids want to spend an extra fifteen minutes on something. For example, science must be from 1:20-1:50 daily. One day, I had a project I wanted to do with the kids so I explained to them, "We have thirty minutes, and that's it, so I'm going to set the timer for each step and you must keep up." I modeled step one, which was cutting, and set the timer for three minutes for the kids to cut. Scissors were put away after three minutes, period, and if someone didn't have something cut out, they just wouldn't be able to use that piece. I modeled the next step, which was to color, then set the timer for four minutes, and when it went off, all crayons were put away.

When I keep things this regimented, I occasionally pass out beads [part of our class reward system] for kids who are done with a particular step on time. I plan the activity so that we have five minutes left at the end for kids to catch up on anything they weren't done with. I don't usually run things so robotically, but it's a necessity at times. I'm not going to be the only one to shoulder the responsibility of teaching a concept in a set amount of time, nagging the kids to hurry up while they play around without a care in the world. If we have limited time, I explain that to the children and teach them how to work with me as we manage our time together.

TIP 6) Use timers for EVERYTHING!!!

Kids respond to timers like magic because timing an event turns it into a contest. You can time kids on anything and they never seem to tire of it. You can also buy classroom timers with red, yellow, and green sections on them that sound verbal warnings as each color changes. These provide automatic reminders so you don't have to say anything.

TIP 7) Make a "Not Finished Folder" for each child.

If you give students a lot of worksheets and assignments on loose-leaf paper, it can be difficult to collect them all when many kids aren't yet finished. One year when I realized that many of my students were not turning in all of their work, I started a Not Finished (NF) folder system. Whenever time was up for an assignment, I instructed the class to pass completed papers in and put incomplete work in their NF folders.

Because I generally provided ample time for my students to complete their work *if* they stayed on-task, I only allowed kids to do their NF folders during Fun Friday. As soon as they finished the work, they could have their free time. Missing out on Fun Friday was a HUGE deal for them, so when I announced that anyone who wasn't done in a few minutes would have to put the work in their NF folder, the children became extremely motivated to finish. Alternatively, you can have kids access their folders anytime they have a few moments to spare, which

is a great option if you don't give your kids an opportunity to earn free time.

I kept the NF folders in the organizer shown here. I didn't let kids keep the folders in their desks because I didn't want papers to get lost, and I wanted to be able to see who had which papers still incomplete. Sometimes when there were lots of kids who had work to be turned in, I had them empty their NF folders by sorting the completed papers into piles on the back table. Any miscellaneous papers that they didn't see a pile for were put in the basket (pictured on the right in the photo below). After all NF folders had been turned in at the end of Fun Friday, the Paper Collector paper clipped each stack

together and put them in my file trays to be graded. I usually graded all of the classes' papers together, but sometimes I would have already graded the rest of the class' papers and would just quickly go through the ones from the NF folders and insert the grades in my grade book. Many of the assignments in the NF folders were not graded, just practice, so I put a stamp or checkmark and sent them home.

TIP 8) Help kids learn to manage their time when you give projects by telling them what you are grading on.

If you're not grading the illustration, tell students that, and talk about how they need to spend the bulk of their time on what will actually be assessed: their writing. When the illustration will be graded, be specific about what students should spend time working on. For example, if you want your kids to make a diagram of something and label it, write a checklist on the board of the criteria you are looking for. With repeated teacher guidance and practice, students will learn that they should spend their time creating and labeling the required parts of a diagram and only add details if they are finished early.

TIP 9) Teach kids to write first, THEN illustrate, THEN color.

As a general rule, have children do the writing part of an assignment first, then the drawing portion when they are finished, followed by coloring if they have time. I don't advocate illustrating or coloring as part of an assignment unless it's either a) for children just learning to write, or b) a truly valuable use of students' time and not just something for them to do while the others finish. If illustrating or coloring is integral to the assignment, include it, and teach children to complete it last. This prevents kids from spending twenty minutes trying to get one tiny aspect of a picture just right without ever completing the actual assignment.

Logical Consequences for Students Who Don't Get Work Done

If you want to give a reward for turning in all class work on time, you can use the privilege of sitting with a group or team. I make sure my kids understand that anyone who does not get their work done during the week has probably been playing around and talking too much, so that person will be able to get more work done if he sits alone. If a child has any work that is not turned in by Friday afternoon, he must sit and work alone for the entire following week (with his desk pushed back from the group). I do make individual accommodations as needed for kids who have special needs, work more slowly, were absent, etc., typically by shortening or excusing certain assignments.

The children who have to sit alone fall into one of two personality types. The first is the kid who normally gets everything done but was too distractible that week: five days of sitting alone is enough to ensure that won't happen again! The second personality type is the kid who really can't get anything done with peers around. This student must unfortunately sit alone most of the time, but the bottom line is that she will turn in her assignments with much greater consistency than if she had her friends nearby. Children are in school to learn and get their work done above all—that is a greater priority than socialization. Also, having these kids away from the rest of the group enables the others to get their work done without disruption, so everyone is more successful.

Planning for Fast Finishers and Slow Workers

Handling Students' Workload Needs on an Individual Basis

We'll never have a class in which all students work at the same pace. The goal is to keep everyone engaged in meaningful learning activities all the time. For some kids, that means they need to have extra projects and assignments to complete while they wait for their peers; for other kids, it means they need you to teach them how to manage their time and get things done on schedule. This is not as difficult as it sounds! Predictable classroom routines and lots of positive reinforcement will make a huge difference in how smoothly your classroom runs.

Understanding your students' needs can also contribute to classroom efficiency. There are a myriad of reasons why students finish their work more slowly or quickly than the rest of the class. In this section, I'll help you identify and determine how to best meet the needs of each child.

Note: These strategies address student work rates, not behavioral issues. If you have students who are not completing work because they are easily distracted, talking, playing around, or concerning themselves with everyone's work but their own, then you need to reteach and reinforce your procedures for staying on-task, as explained in Chapter 13, Teaching Work Habits. Provide related rewards and logical consequences as needed to address behavior problems.

The Brainiac: Finds every correct answer in less than three minutes

 ♦ **Have your 'When Finished' sign up and use it CONSISTENTLY.** The Brainiac is almost always going to finish early and needs to have something productive to do so that he does not need to interrupt you.

 ♦ **Have a long-term project or independent study for the Brainiac to work on.** Sometimes I have my Brainiacs create a presentation or report on a topic of interest to them, and I frequently have my above grade level reading group complete a novel study with corresponding projects that they can complete when they have spare time.

◆ **Try making an extensions menu in which early finishers can choose between various activities that extend their learning.** One format is a Tic Tac Toe in which kids pick three activities that form a horizontal, vertical, or diagonal line. This ensures that kids are completing a variety of assignments. You can design activities which incorporate the multiple intelligences or learning styles if you want to individualize or differentiate instruction.

The Christmas Tree Kid: Fills in answers without reading the questions ("Cool! I made a design like a Christmas tree!")

◆ **Teach the entire class structured ways to justify or prove their answers.** Strictly enforce adherence for the Christmas Tree Kid. For reading, you may have students underline where they found their answers in the passage. For math, students may circle the key words in the problem that told them what to do. Make it your regular classroom routine for students to show their thinking on their papers, and you'll see far fewer children making random guesses.

◆ **Provide timely and helpful feedback on student performance.** If kids know they won't find out how they did on a test for two weeks, they'll be less likely to care about the results. Similarly, if you give graded papers back without explaining how the assignment was scored and what children need to do to improve, kids will become discouraged and just write anything. It can be difficult to make time for this and to help young children understand assessment and progress, but make an extra effort for your Christmas Tree kids.

◆ **Be sure students understand the importance of the work they're doing**. Let them know that EVERYTHING they do counts for a grade (which is true—even if a particular paper is not graded, all of their work is taken into account when you write progress reports).

- ♦ **Also make sure students see the relevance of their work**. Explain how the assignment they are doing will help them later on ("This spelling practice is going to help you communicate your ideas more easily when you write" or "Learning to recognize genre will make it easier for you to understand how to read everything you come across in your life, from magazine articles to comic books to advertisements, because you'll know which strategies to use").

- ♦ **Give additional incentives for academic work from time to time**. Some kids are not motivated intrinsically, or by grades, or even by the threat of being retained. They need a tangible, immediate reward. I randomly give out stickers or beads for students who earned A's and B's on a particular assignment. If I am grading papers while the kids are in the room, I'll tell them, "While you finish your worksheet, I'm going to grade your math test. I'll let you know how you did in a few minutes. I'll also give a bead to those who earned an A or B or made a lot of improvement from their last math test." After grading, I'll call out the names of the kids who met the criteria and the class claps for them as they come up to get their reward. For some of my Christmas Tree kids, this is the only incentive to really work hard. Because I do it for all subject areas, every child has a chance to shine and the rewards are pretty evenly distributed among the class.

The Overly, Unfoundedly Confident: Won't check her answers because she's *positive* they're all correct

- ♦ **Talk to the class about individual strengths and weaknesses**. I share with my kids that when I was a student, I was incredible in reading, but horrible with math and science. That meant I had to try twice as hard in those subjects, and had to check my answers because many times they were incorrect. I then help the kids identify their strong and weak subject areas and set the expectation that EVERYONE is better at some things than others, so it's okay not to be great at everything.   As you teach different subjects throughout the day, try to encourage kids you know are weak ("Hey, you figured that out quickly! You must have been practicing! This is going to get easier for you because you keep working hard!").

- ♦ **Have kids grade their own papers as often as possible**. They can use pens to do this so you can ensure no one changes their answers. Talk with the kids who think they have everything right: *How do you think you did on this* *assignment? What was hardest for you? Which strategies could you use next time to make sure you do better?*

♦ **Give regular progress updates to support kids in taking an honest look at what they're accomplishing.** Again, it's great to do this for everybody, but make sure you do it for the Overly Confident Kid. ("On the last three reading tests, you had a D, a C, and another D. How do you feel about that? Do you think you need to improve? Do you want to? Let's look at the type of questions you're missing and try to come up with some ways to help you do better.") Remind the child as she takes the next test to slow down and use the strategies you discussed, and provide feedback on her progress as soon as possible.

♦ **Many times the Overly Confident Kid is actually a Christmas Tree Kid in disguise—the child doesn't REALLY think the answers are right, he's just too lazy to go back and check.** The strategies for the Christmas Tree Kid are often very effective with this type of child, too.

The Dawdler: Takes twenty minutes to put his name on the paper

♦ **The 'Time Management Tips for Kids' in this chapter are aimed primarily at the Dawdler.** This type of child just has no concept of time or time management, most likely because he is young. Use timers, reminders, etc., to help him develop the ability to monitor himself independently.

♦ **Stick to a set time for regular classroom routines.** Any daily activity can be used to teach time monitoring skills: Morning Work, buddy reading, warm-up games, etc. I give my kids eight minutes every day to play a math practice game: I set a timer and the kids adhere to it. Because the class plays the same game all week long, they learn to manage their time—I hear them saying things such as, "Come on, we gotta hurry up, because yesterday we only had seven cards done when time was up. We gotta try to get more today." They develop a sense of what they are able to accomplish in eight minutes and become very realistic about how they can and should use their time.

The Slow Processor: Needs an entire hour to answer ten questions

♦ **Consider modifying assignments**. If there's a section of the assignment that requires the child to write out an entire sentence, have this child just write the answer. If using scissors to cut something out takes forever and you're not concerned about the child having fine motor practice during the activity, ask one of your Brainiacs to do the cutting for your Slow Processor to allow more time for the actual work.   There are endless modifications you can use: anytime you don't think part of an assignment contains critical practice or assessment information, it can be eliminated for the Slow Processor.

♦ **Shorten assignments**. If you can tell whether the student understands the concept with five problems, there's no need to waste the whole morning having the child complete fifteen problems. You can circle select questions for the child to answer, or teach her to always do just the even or odd numbered problems.

♦ **If you use a Not Finished Folder, allow the Slow Processor to complete the work in it anytime he has a chance so that it doesn't pile up**. Many of these types of children are very diligent workers and will ask to catch up on their folders before the morning bell rings, at lunch, etc. This is fine as long as it's their choice.

♦ **Try not to send unfinished work home with Slow Processors.** Chances are, it takes them twice as long to complete homework, too, so adding incomplete class work to the pile will result in hours of torture each night.

The Perfectionist: Spends ten minutes writing and rewriting the date until the dot over each 'i' is a concentric circle

♦ **Check to see if the child is a Dawdler in disguise.** This child may not know how to manage time and may think she can make things look exactly how she wants and still be able to complete the assignment. Once the student realizes that there are deadlines that must be adhered to, your 'Perfectionist' may suddenly learn to accept crooked letters and smudges on her paper.

♦ **Bring perfectionist tendencies to the child's attention, because he is probably not aware of the immense pressure he's putting on himself.** You might say, "I noticed that you spent about ten minutes making this line straight with your ruler. Take a look at my line on the board. Is it exactly straight? Nope, I didn't even use a ruler! Do you know why? This isn't an art project and it doesn't matter if my line is straight. Everyone will be graded on the information they write IN the chart, not on how beautiful the lines ON the chart are. If I were grading how pretty your chart is, what do you think you would get? But what AM I grading on? And what grade do you think you would get if I took your paper right now? So let's concentrate on making a chart quickly so we can focus on the data we need to put inside it."

♦ **Let the child experience the consequences of being a Perfectionist.** When time is up, have a talk with the child while the others pass in their papers: "Were you able to finish? What weren't you able to do? Did you notice whether the kids around you finished? What is different about the way they completed their work and the way you did? Unfortunately, you're going to get a very low grade on this assignment because it's incomplete." Because the Perfectionist wants everything to be just right, realizing that poor grades come with being overly analytical can be a strong motivator to move things along.

♦ **Be sure to praise Perfectionists when they allow themselves to make acceptable faults.** For example: "Wow, Destiny, I know that you love for your paper to look neat, and you had to erase over there. But instead of crumpling up the paper and starting all over like you used to, I see that you chose to just erase, rewrite, and keep going! That's awesome, because now you're able to keep up with the class and you aren't falling behind. It's okay to have eraser marks. I can see you're doing your best work, and I'm proud of you!"

Part Seven:
Partnering with Parents, Colleagues, and Administration

Chapter 29: Creating a Support System
Collaborating with staff to maintain a positive work environment

One of the most difficult conundrums of teaching is the necessity of working as part of a unified system while having very little contact with others within that system. We spend 80% or more of our workday with no adult interaction whatsoever. We have a bit of small talk in the office before school, an exchange of greetings with the specials teacher as we drop our kids off, less than a half an hour to eat with the handful of colleagues who have our same lunch shift, and maybe a meeting at the end of the day. The other six hours are spent in the trenches, alone with students.

As if that weren't isolating enough, the time that we do spend with adults is very rarely expended on collaborative reflection and the sharing of classroom practices. Our meetings are about procedures and testing and problems with individual children, and we never quite make time to talk about improving our instruction as a team.

Creating a positive work environment can be very difficult when teachers have little influence on the school climate and few opportunities to create a true support system and bond with their colleagues. This chapter will explain how to identify negativity in the school and surround yourself with positive, forward-thinking people. It will outline ideas for gaining administrative support and working effectively with staff. Lastly, it will provide tips for utilizing your support systems to develop your own teaching style.

Working With Non-Instructional Staff

Non-instructional employees are the major players in keeping the school running smoothly, yet they rarely get the respect they deserve. For example, cafeteria staff have important and incredibly stressful jobs that are even lower-paying than ours! Can you imagine spending hours every day in a noisy cafeteria saying the same thing over and over to kids who forgot their lunch number, don't have any money, touched food that they weren't taking, threw a milk carton at the kid behind them, etc.? I don't know how they do it. I always try to have an extra smile and word of encouragement for cafeteria staff. In some schools, they are known to be very temperamental, being kind and giving extra portions to teachers they like, and being rude to the teachers who breeze in and expect perfect service. Be patient and polite with the cafeteria staff—after all, they are preparing your food!

The custodial staff is another unappreciated group of people. They are often criticized for their underperformance, as if three people could really give a deep cleaning to 35 classrooms, a cafeteria, and an office in one evening. Remember that these workers are not making extravagant salaries and they have a very, very dirty job. Do whatever they ask you to do: have kids stack chairs at the end of the day, leave the trash cans in one place, and so on. When you see your janitors, ask how they're doing and apologize for any messy glitter projects you've done that day. Let the custodians know that you recognize how much work they have and that you appreciate what they do. In my experience, custodians will go the extra mile for teachers that are kind and understanding with them.

Your school secretaries can make your life easy or a living hell, depending on the relationship you have with them. These people are the front contacts for angry parents, crying children, demanding administrators, and irritated teachers all day long. The annoyances that secretaries deal with will blow your mind if you ask about them. I had a secretary tell me once that she had a parent call every single day to ask what the breakfast and lunch menus were. The secretary told her that the information was available online and in a calendar sent home monthly. The parent replied, "I know, but it's easier if I just call *you*." If you think your job is stressful, try answering the phones and running the front office for a day. At least teachers can shut the door and run the classroom their way with their rules—secretaries are at the mercy of every wacky personality in the school and community. For that reason, it's important to be patient with your school secretaries. They're trying to handle the affairs of a thousand or more children sometimes, and it's normal for them to get confused and forget about things you've asked for. Have a ready smile for your secretaries, and go easy on them. I guarantee you will forget to give them your attendance or other paperwork at some point throughout the year, so show the grace you expect to receive.

Gaining Administrative Support

An administration that likes and believes in you is one of the best support systems you can possibly have. Here are some ideas to consider as you work towards a productive, positive relationship with your supervisors.

◆ **Find out what issues your administration is particular about and attend to them.** Is it being on time? Having a neat classroom? Following lesson plans precisely? Ask other teachers which things are particularly important to your principal and assistant principal, and make sure you accommodate them on those issues.

◆ **Be attentive when administration speaks at meetings.** I can be as bad as the kids when it comes to being quiet when someone else is talking! But when the administrators are addressing our staff, I try to listen attentively and take good notes to send the message that I respect what they have to say.

◆ **Smile and be friendly.** Even when you're stressed, try to look calm and in control. When your administration pictures you, they should have a mental image of you smiling and looking confident and outgoing.

◆ **Demonstrate good classroom management, especially in the hall.** Good management is a sign of good teaching, and although the two are not always related, being able to control your class sends the message to administration that you have a similarly strong presence during instruction. It's a signal to everyone you pass that you have reasonable expectations for your students and that they respect you enough to abide by your rules. Be encouraging with your kids when you take them to the cafeteria and special classes, speaking calmly and firmly as needed and praising their good behavior. Show that you have developed a rapport with your students.

◆ **Speak positively about your work.** There's no point in airing your dirty laundry, complaining about minor problems, or making comments that call your expertise into question. Teachers often complain about how 'low' their classes are and how they can't imagine how they'll ever get everyone working on grade level by June. This kind of 'negative publicity' serves no purpose. Have confidence in your kids and yourself when speaking about what's going on in your classroom.

◆ **Respect the hierarchy.** Don't ask your principal a question that a colleague could easily answer. Conversely, don't go over your administrator's head and ask a district supervisor about a situation that should have been handled in the school.

◆ **Don't expect administration to solve all of your discipline problems.** There are teachers who write referrals every single day for their students. In my opinion, this should be done only when absolutely necessary. Your administration is trusting you to handle student issues within your classroom unless there is a very extreme case. Overburdening administration with petty behavioral concerns is a quick way to lose your reputation as a self-sufficient and highly effective teacher.

◆ **Pick your battles.** If you are asked to do something that is too much for you, or goes against what you believe is appropriate for your class, decide whether you can go along with it anyway or if you must conference with administration. If you resist every mandate that is passed down, you will be viewed as difficult. Speak up only on the things that you MUST. I usually try see my principal no more than once or twice a year with concerns of any type in order to develop a reputation for being a cooperative team player. Then, if something is really bothering me, my principal will be more likely to take me seriously because she or he knows that I don't complain about much. If you decide not to speak up because the administration's mandate is reasonable or is something that must be done, then grin and bear it. If you have to follow the directive anyway, you might as well do it with a good attitude.

◆ **Recognize when mandates are out of your administrator's hands.** I cannot tell you how many times I've heard teachers complaining about something horrible their principals did when in fact, the principal was forced to act by a regional supervisor. Many of the ridiculous demands that are made on teachers come from someone in the superintendent's office, especially after the district was almost sued for something. I've had principals put a stop to birthday parties in class, footballs during recess, and comp time for staying late during Open House. I was initially perturbed until I asked colleagues for the reasoning or spoke to friends at other schools—I then discovered in each instance that the district had changed our rules and the principal had graciously taken the fall for it.

♦ **Thank them regularly for their support.** This is obviously easier when your administration actually supports you on a regular basis, but anytime your supervisors do something caring, be sure to point it out verbally or in a quick note or email. Be genuine in your gratitude and not obsequious— if you have a reputation for being positive, saying thank you to your administrators will not appear to be a vie for favoritism. Compliment your principal and assistant principal in the same way that you notice and comment on little things that your students do well. Administrators don't hear positive feedback very often and will appreciate your kind words.

Collaborating With Colleagues

Three Types of Teachers to Avoid

In every work environment, there will always be negative people. You'll be able to figure out who they are after a very short amount of time. Try to limit your involvement with these three types of teachers:

• **The Complainer:** This teacher can have three weeks off for Christmas and still come back to school whining that the vacation was too short and she can't wait to get away from the kids again. She always has too much paperwork, can't get through to parents, and claims she's never informed about school events and procedures. Nothing is ever good enough for the Complainer. Your response? Avoid her and her friends at all costs. The more time you spend with Complainers, the unhappier you'll become. There are certainly enough things in the teaching profession to be unhappy about, and talking about them incessantly will make the situation worse.

- **The Fear Monger:** This teacher enjoys exaggerating things and always looks for the worst possible scenario. He'll tell you, "Oh, you can't do THAT! You'll get fired if you do something differently! We've always done things *this* way." He is opposed to trying anything new or stepping outside the box. The best option: Don't tell the Fear Monger about anything you're doing in the classroom—you'll only get discouraged. Find someone who is realistic and knows what's going on to give you real advice.

- **The Bully:** Perhaps the saddest character in any school is the Bully. This is the teacher who constantly nags and yells at her students for every minor infraction and can't find anything good to say about them. The bully's controlling ways often extend to other teachers as she manipulates staff into seeing things her way and being on her side. Every year the Bully is stressed out by the incompetence of certain teachers or administrators and how 'bad' her class is. This is a person you want to totally disassociate yourself from. When you have to be around her, stay positive about your class and your workplace. Don't give the Bully the slightest encouragement to bash her students or anyone else.

Three Types of Teachers To Surround Yourself With

I like to have certain people on my side in any school. Sometimes I'm fortunate enough to know more than one of each of these teacher types, and when our personalities click, I spend as much time with them as possible:

- **The Practical, Down-To-Earth Old Timer:** This teacher has been at the school forever, and knows the administrators inside and out. She can predict how parents and the community will respond to new things you want to try. She knows what type of discipline will work. She knows what will get you in trouble and what won't. The Old Timer is an expert at keeping documentation and always has herself covered. If you want to know what you can and can't get away with, ask her, because she's great at clarifying procedures. The Old Timer won't intimidate you—in fact, you'll always feel relieved after talking to her because you'll understand exactly what's expected and the best course of action to take.

- **The Enthusiastic Friend:** This teacher is usually new to the profession: he's excited about teaching and loves trying new things. He's fun to be around, makes you laugh, and helps you when you're stressed. This is the person to eat lunch with and sit near during meetings. The Enthusiastic Friend is a great person to share ideas with about what's working and what's not because you'll always have more energy after the conversation than you did before it started.

- **The Expert Role Model:** This teacher may not be as fun to hang around as the Enthusiast, and she might not be as knowledgeable about how to work the system as the Old Timer. But the Expert is one of the most incredible teachers around: she understands children and best practice and her lessons are amazing. The Expert stays late to help other teachers and is actively involved in school events. This is the person to go to when you need strategies for improving your lessons or dealing with students' socio-emotional issues.

While it's great to associate with all these types of teachers and many other positive, forward-thinking faculty members, it may be advantageous to pick one confidante as your mentor and tell only that person your problems. The whole school does not need to know about your argument with a parent or a students' atrocious behavior in your classroom. ***People you don't know well should see and hear mostly good things about what's going on in your classroom, because very few people will ever get to see you in action—you will be judged as a good teacher or a bad one based on your reputation.***

Finding a Mentor vs. Finding Your Own Teaching Style

I have to mention one important caveat here: You must develop your own personal teaching style. You may eventually emerge as one of the three teacher types above, but don't do so consciously. Let yourself discover your own classroom identity, and never try to emulate any one person completely.

When I first started teaching at the elementary level, I wanted to be like the teacher in the room next to me who had been in the classroom since the late 1960's. "Mrs. Jackson" was voted Teacher of the Year, had amassed tremendous resources for every topic and skill, and her class was the best behaved in the school. My only experience in teaching had been with preschool and severely autistic students, so I had no clue what to expect from my new class of eight-year-olds. Since Mrs. Jackson had it all together and was so well-respected, I figured that she would be the perfect mentor. In my naivety, I didn't realize that she was incredibly strict with her students and very demanding of their families.

I modeled my practice after hers and started raising my voice when students misbehaved, and enforced swift punishments on anyone who dared to defy me. I took away recess for any minor infraction and expected my students to work nonstop for every minute of the school day. I also refused to budge an inch with parents. Once a mother showed up for a 2:30 conference at 3:05, after our contractual hours were over. The parents were immigrants each working multiple jobs and the mother had taken time off to meet with me. I asked Mrs. Jackson if I should hold the conference or not. "It's after hours," she replied flatly. "If you do it this time, you'll have to do it every time."

There was some truth to Mrs. Jackson's advice, certainly, but I still regret turning that mother away, especially since I never did get to meet with her or her husband. There were a lot of things I began to wish I had done differently. I couldn't understand why I didn't enjoy the interactions with students anymore. I didn't realize that Mrs. Jackson's methodology just didn't fit my personality.

I may not have ever learned that lesson if something hadn't shaken me out of complacency. One day, Mrs. Jackson told me that she had a former student come back to visit her. I thought that was awesome and couldn't wait to hear about the conversation. But apparently, the young woman had said to her, "You made me feel like I was stupid and would never amount to anything. So I just had to come back and let you know, I'm the CEO of a major corporation now, and I would NEVER treat my employees or my children the way you treated me." I was horrified, but Mrs. Jackson shrugged and said to me, "Please. That girl ain't no CEO. She never had the brains for that. She was a liar in my class and she's a liar now." That's when I realized that just because someone's experienced, knows content, produces high test scores, and can control students' behavior does NOT mean they are someone I want to imitate!

Obviously this principle applies to less extreme situations, as well. I know teachers who are silly and act crazy with their kids. Others have a very high tolerance for noise and chaos and have a million things going on in their classrooms all the time. Still others are very serious and 'by the book'. I'm not like any of those teachers. Yet ALL of us are extremely effective: we love our jobs, we have an excellent rapport with our students and their parents, and our kids make tremendous learning gains each year.

You can't take someone's teaching style any more than you can take someone's personality. You had to learn how to be yourself and accept yourself when you were growing up, and the same is true now in the classroom. Part of teaching is a science and you can follow best practice that's been proved by research, but the other part of teaching is an art. You can't copy art. It has to be original. And it won't feel right if it comes from a place other than inside of YOU.

If I had known all of this when I first met Mrs. Jackson, I would have had an entirely different relationship with her. I still wouldn't have classified her as one of the three personalities to avoid, because she didn't complain constantly, spread fear and conformity, or hate her kids. She was actually the Practical, Down-to-Earth Old Timer. But she wasn't someone I needed to keep close to me because her teaching style simply didn't match mine. She was a good sounding board and had lots of great advice, which I should have taken with a grain of salt and weighed against what I knew to be true for my own perspective on life and teaching.

What works for other people won't necessarily work for you. I caution you against modeling yourself too much after any particular teacher, myself included. I get many emails from new teachers saying that they want to be just like me. I find those statements to be misguided, because you can never be someone other than yourself. If you try to be me or any other teacher, the best outcome you can hope for is to become a second-rate replica. You have to be an original, a unique compilation of all the knowledge and experience that's been a part of your life. Amazing teachers are amazing people. Take everything that makes you who you are and pour it into your classroom practice. THAT'S what will make you the best teacher ever.

The presence of a good mentor will help you explore different techniques and methodologies and find what works for you. Learn from my mistake and never copy someone else's style blindly, or say and do things that don't sit right with you. Trust your instincts, and remember that who you are OUTSIDE of the classroom is very similar to who you are INSIDE the classroom. Let your real personality come through, and stay focused on your vision of the kind of teacher YOU want to become.

Chapter 30: Creative Family Outreach
Building a rapport and empowering parents to support learning

Involving parents in their children's education is an undeniably important role for the classroom teacher. However, supporting parents can sometimes feel like just one more thing to add to your already lengthy list of things to do. This chapter will help you develop a positive outlook on your relationship with parents, and provide simple ways to keep the doors of communication open. You'll also learn some creative and innovative methods to get reluctant parents involved and build the enthusiasm of those parents who are already anxious to be participate.

A Healthy Mindset About Working With Parents

Make Parents Your Partners

Teachers have to make a *conscious* decision to partner with students' families and accept them just as they are. You and your students' parents all have one thing in common: you want what's best for the children. Even when you don't agree on what IS best, remember that parents are doing everything than can with the resources they have.

It's easy to blame parents for the things that are wrong with our students, but even when you know that a parent is fostering a child's negative behavior, be careful not to come across as accusatory or blaming. If parents think you are attacking their child, they will naturally side against you, causing more tension in the classroom. Do everything in your power to create an alliance with the parent for the benefit of the child, approaching the situation with an attitude of, *Here's what I notice at school, tell me what you have observed at home, what can we do together to help your child?*

Know Your Community

Get to know the area you teach in, and tailor both your outreach and expectations accordingly. Go online and find out about your school's demographics, preferably before you even go on the job interview for your position. Consider the language(s) that students' families speak and the countries they're from. Look at children's registration cards and find out about the career fields of your kids' parents. Get to know what your families have to offer and utilize them!

It's also important to understand what your community's expectations are for education. Many families in affluent areas like to be deeply involved with education. They appreciate your efforts to provide unique opportunities for them to come into the classroom and like to send in supplies regularly. They expect you to allow them to participate fully in their children's learning, and you will find it difficult to maintain a positive rapport if they feel pushed out of the educational process. Conversely, many families living in poverty will not have the time or resources needed to become actively involved in the school community. You will become frustrated if you expect them to supply materials and commit time they don't have. These parents will likely appreciate translators for conferences and progress reports, and value simple, caring communication about their children's progress. No matter where you teach, you will find some parents at each of these two extremes and many in between, so above all, be prepared to meet the needs of individuals. Your efforts towards meeting each family where they are at will work wonders in building a rapport and helping children be successful in the classroom.

Accept That Not Every Parent is Going to Like You

This is a fact that's hard for many teachers to come to terms with and I have to admit, it's still hard for me. But the truth is, there will be times when you bend over backwards for families and it will not be appreciated. In some communities, it's not uncommon for teachers to be cussed out and physically threatened. I say this not to create panic but to prepare you—I wish someone had told me before I started teaching that just because *I* know I'm doing a good job doesn't mean all of my families will agree!

Some people take their personal problems out on everyone around them, and just like there are positive people and negative people in general, there are positive and negative parents. The key is to develop a thick skin and not take conflict personally. If you've made a mistake, admit it and make amends. If you know in your heart that you've done the best job you can do, relax and let it go without rehashing the situation a million times with every person you see.

Make Parents Feel as Valued as Their Children

When you talk to parents, be sure to thank them for whatever efforts they make in helping their children. It's easier to show appreciation to certain families more than others, but a single mom working ten hour days to support three kids will probably be grateful for any kind of positive commentary you give. I've thanked parents for getting their (horribly behaved) child to school on time each day, and complimented them on always packing a nutritious snack (for a child who forgets his homework and basic school supplies every day). Find and acknowledge the positive wherever you can find it. There are very few people who compliment parents on a job well done, and I've had MANY moms and dads tear up when I tell them what a good heart their child has, and to keep doing what they're doing at home.

Making parents feel acknowledged and valued is also easy to do in written communication, because you can type one basic note or form and use it for many situations. If a parent writes me a letter and I don't have time to respond the same day, I send home a 'received your note' form to let them know I got their message and intend to respond as soon as possible. If they send in tissues or dry erase markers, I assure them the supplies made it safely with a 'thank you for supplies' form. When they place Scholastic book orders, I send home a book order thank you, as well. Once I have printed and photocopied these forms, they take only a minute to gather and distribute to students. The forms keep me from having to follow up on matters later and they support timely and consistent communication with parents. (You can download all of them on my website.)

Be Flexible and Accommodating

I encourage you to be reasonable and supportive when working with students' families. They are often dealing with personal issues that we as teachers have no idea about, from financial troubles to divorce to difficulties with their children. If you think YOU'RE stressed out from dealing with a hyperactive and immature student, imagine if you were responsible for PARENTING that child! There are reasons why parents behave as they do. Believe the best about people until they prove otherwise. When a child is late everyday, it could be because the parent has no form of transportation, or has been in the hospital, or is taking care of an elderly parent.

If a family is going out of town and requests make-up work, provide something basic for the child to complete. If a parent shows up on the wrong date for a conference, adjust your schedule if possible and meet with her, anyway. If a family has had an 'emergency' and requests an extra day to complete homework, allow it one time. It's not necessary to treat grown adults like they are children who must have all rules strictly enforced every single time. Aren't we as teachers late to work sometimes? Don't we occasionally lose things? Don't we need reminders about meetings and forgiveness when we forget to turn in paperwork? Give families the benefit of the doubt when you know they are not trying to take advantage of you.

Tips for Fostering Ongoing, Two-Way Communication

☑ **Notify parents of positive behavior, too, especially when kids are having problems.**

I have a set of "Good News From School!" postcards that I address for each family at the beginning of the year. Periodically, when I notice a streak of particularly cooperative behavior or academic gains, I fill out a short message and mail them off (my school provides the postage). I can tell who hasn't gotten a note home yet by looking at the pre-addressed cards left in the stack. I also try to write specific, personal comments on progress reports and weekly evaluations to let parents know I recognize their children as individuals ("Jacob has really enjoyed learning about habitats—his ocean mural was so creative!" or "Shauna showed me the book you bought her! She has a knack for history, and I'm glad you were able to help her learn more about a topic that really interests her. Let me know if you need suggestions for more resources—there's a great exhibit coming to the museum next month"). A simple phone call can have the greatest impact of all— most parents have never been called by a teacher unless their child was in serious trouble, and having you call to report good news will leave a lasting impact.

☑ **Have a method for regularly updating parents on changes in student behavior and work habits.**

Parents hate finding out about problems that have been going on for weeks or months. If you sense that a child has become disinterested in school, has been getting in conflicts more often on the playground, or has been out of his seat more than usual, jot these observations down on a weekly contact form that parents sign and return. This not only lets parents know what's going on, but also keeps children accountable for their behavior and provides written proof that you have informed families about your concerns.

☑ **Teach kids to keep communication and documentation organized.**

Have a designated folder or binder for children to safely transport all notes to and from home. I call ours the Home-School Folder. Whenever you pass out papers for families to see, have children take out their folders and place the papers inside. Explain to students that when they arrive home, they should show the folder to a parent, and if there is anything for the parent to send back, the child should place the paper(s) in the Home-School folder. When arriving in the classroom each morning, students should check their folders to see if there's anything they need to give to the teacher. Provide a designated place (your in-box) for students to place all correspondence from home.

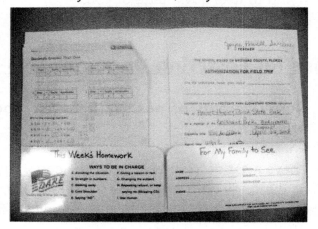

☑ **Provide a class handbook.**

When I taught in an affluent area with highly-involved parents, I expanded my parent letter into a handbook that students kept in their binders so parents could reference it as needed. I included my policies on everything from class parties to behavior modification strategies to standardized test preparation. I also made this information available for reference on our class website.

☑ **Send home surveys twice a year to elicit parent and student feedback.**

If you're like me, you sometimes wonder if parents feel informed about what's going on in the classroom and if they understand your expectations. Type up a few of these questions and allow parents to share their thoughts, even anonymously if they choose. Remember that not everyone will like everything you're doing in the classroom, so stay focused on the big picture that forms when you view the survey results as a whole. I have learned a lot about my strengths and weaknesses through these surveys, and keep them as documentation as well. Even if parents do not return the forms, at least I know their input has been requested and welcomed.

Parent Interim Feedback

I recently sent home an interim report letting you know how your child is doing in school. I would like for you as the parent/care-giver to have an opportunity to share how your child is doing, from your perspective.

Please circle your answers below for each topic. If you indicate that there are any problems, please write me a short note on the reverse side. Then send this paper back to school with your child. Thank you for your input!

Amount of homework	Not enough	Just right	Too much
Difficulty of homework	Too easy	Just right	Too hard
Bi-Weekly Work Samples	Not helpful	Helpful	Very helpful
Quality of my child's work	Not satisfied	Generally satisfied	Very satisfied
Child's attitude towards school	Does not like it	Okay	Enjoys school
Child's attitude towards teacher	Often negative	Okay	Usually positive

Please add any comments, questions, or suggestions to the back if you would like.

_____   _____
Parent's Name   Child's Name

☑ **Send home weekly, bi-weekly, or monthly newsletters.**

One year I used class newsletters called the 'Ask Me About...' to help parents find out what their kids had been learning. Too often when parents ask what a child did in school that day, the answer is "nothing" or something vague, and the 'Ask Me About...' provided specific questions parents could use to get specific answers. There was also a Guest Columnist section, in which students took turns writing about what they learned that week. Parents loved that feature and often saved the newsletter that their child helped write.

☑ **Incorporate technology to foster communication.**

There are lots of fun ways to do this! Here just a few, in order from easiest to the most time-consuming:

- **Email:** Create an email list and periodically send parents updates about classroom events. Many parents like this because they can keep a paperless record.

- **Digital Cameras:** Once you have parental permission on file for taking photos, go crazy with the digital camera! You can email pictures to parents, put them on the class website (again, with permission), and print them out to send home to parents. Some of the awesome things kids do, especially in the primary grades, aren't written assignments, and photos are the perfect way to share their accomplishments.

- **Class website:** Utilize a class website to post homework, spelling words, upcoming events, and more. There are several sites that offer free hosting for teachers and you can have your webpage up and running in a few hours. Most of the formats are so user-friendly that you don't need any prior experience with web design. Run an Internet search using the terms "free classroom web hosting" and see what's available.

Creative Opportunities for Parents to Get Involved

If the families in your community are anxious to be a part of your classroom, there are many easily-managed ways to facilitate their efforts. Some of the following ideas might also be useful for inspiring parents to get involved when you've had difficulty gaining their support. Regardless of where you teach, providing innovative resources and programs for families to participate in their children's education is always worth the effort. Try something new each year— you can maintain the activities you like and modify or replace the others with something different.

◆ **Allow parents to journal with their children.** Create Family Journals using composition books or sheets of notebook paper stapled together with a construction paper cover. The Family Journals can stay in students' binders or Home-School folders. Every two weeks (or more often as the individual child has time and interest), students can write a message to a family member, and take the journal home for the person to reply. The teacher doesn't need to mark the journal at all; it's just another way to help parents support learning and provide students with an authentic purpose for writing.

◆ **Use Family Literacy backpacks or something similar with fun activities parents can do at home.** I call mine "Kids Into Thinking" (KITs), and I send home one each week to help kids learn math facts. It takes awhile to create these, but you can download many of the forms and materials you'll need at TheCornerstoneForTeachers.com. You'll find the benefits are worth the time you spend making the activities, especially since you can use the same ones year after year. Also, many curriculums include games, drawings of manipulatives, and parent letters that can be reproduced for home usage, and there are lots of activities on the Internet that you can give parents so they can support learning.

◆ **Provide academic resources that families may not have at home.** Parents often have a hard time helping with math homework because they don't have concrete materials. Send home photocopies of manipulatives (such as fraction tiles and place value blocks) for students to cut apart and use. You may even want to have kids make the materials in class and store them in sandwich bags so that the materials are ready to go home.

◆ **Start a Family Fitness Program.** I tried this one year to support a statewide push to fight childhood obesity and experienced great success! Encourage students to exercise for at least 20 minutes three times per week at home. There is no penalty for not participating in the program; however, there can be incentives and prizes for those who do participate. The term 'exercise' is used loosely to indicate any sort of physical activity, e.g., soccer practice, basketball games, bike riding, jump roping, playing tag, or walking the dog. All students need to do is record their activity on the calendar in their planners (or on a photocopy of a monthly calendar page) and turn it in at the end of the month. While the entire family is not obligated to participate, many families begin taking walks together, playing ball, swimming, and so on. The Family Fitness Program is a motivator for everyone to get more active—including the teacher!

♦ **Hold parent workshops to teach families HOW to support student learning and make them feel welcome in the classroom.** I present these monthly or bi-monthly. Workshops can be done before or after school and are an awesome way to provide a window into the classroom for parents. The following page shows the list of 'Family Festivities' I provided one year when I taught in an affluent community and had a group of very involved parents.

♦ **Invite parents into the classroom as Mystery Readers.** Once a week, have a special guest come into the classroom and read a favorite book to students. Parents can sign up using a sheet in the classroom or through a written note or email. This is a great way to get kids excited about reading and allow parents to interact with the class in an appropriate and educational way.

♦ **Create a Star Family of the Week.** This can be done instead of a Star Student of the Week or as part of it! Have kids bring in photos of the whole family and share traditions and family memories.

♦ **Provide opportunities for families to volunteer...at home.** Many parents want to volunteer but work during the day: send a survey asking for ways they would like to help at home whenever they have time (coloring and cutting out materials, assembling resources for centers, etc.).

♦ **Suggest books for families to read together.** Send home a recommended reading list for your grade level. You could even form a Family Book Club that meets right before school once a month or quarterly. Families could talk about the books they've read and make new recommendations.

♦ **Send home monthly or bi-monthly Home Learning Projects for families to do together**. Have students present their projects to the class and invite parents to come and watch. You can find out more about Home Learning Projects (HLPs) and download sample projects at TheCornerstoneForTeachers.com.

Sample List of Parent Workshops

Month	Event	Description of Outreach
September	Open House	The most important event of the school year—you will get to see our classroom and what we do each day, as well as receive essential information about school and class policies, the FCAT, upcoming events, and much more. PLEASE plan to attend this!
October	Get-To-Know-You Breakfast and Scavenger Hunt	Start your week off with a good breakfast and great company. Come meet the other children in your child's class and put faces with all those names you've been hearing! Your child will take you on a scavenger hunt around our classroom to show what we've been doing and how our day is organized. You'll also get a chance to talk with other parents in a relaxed setting.
November	Thanksgiving Celebration	The children will have pumpkin bread and other fall treats awaiting you as they share their social studies projects. They will also present the charities and community outreach opportunities they have chosen to get involved with and you'll see examples of the many ways we are reaching out to those who are less fortunate than ourselves.
December	Holiday Traditions Tribute	The Home Learning Project for December will involve students sharing their family traditions at the holidays. Projects will be on display and each child will take 2-3 minutes to describe how his or her family makes the holidays special. This will be a very unique time of food, songs, art, and much more.
January	FCAT Jeopardy	What skills does the FCAT test, anyway? You'll know for sure after this! The children will design FCAT-style questions for families to try to answer (this is more challenging than you would think!) and quiz the parents in a game-show style format. There will be a prize for the family who earns the most points!
February	Valentine's Math Blast	Come join us for a time to celebrate being with the people you care most about, and learn how to help your child be successful in math. Families and students will work together through a rotation of hands-on math activities with a Valentine's theme.
March	Writer's Workshop	At this festivity, students will share their writing portfolios and participate in a demonstration writing lesson to show you how writing is taught in third grade. You will see what the state expectations are in preparation for the writing portion of the FCAT introduced in 4th grade. A fourth grade teacher will also stop by to answer any questions you might have.
April	Pizza Picnic	April tends to be a fabulous month in South Florida, and we're going to get outside and enjoy it! Come be a part of a whole-class family pizza picnic out on the lawn. Science Fair projects will also be on display for parent viewing.
May	Parent's Day Breakfast/ End-Of-Year Celebration	We'll have a potluck brunch to celebrate both Mother's Day and Father's Day. This final event for the year will be full of surprises for mom, dad, and the other adults that are special to each child.

Chapter 31: Keeping Parents Informed
Choosing a system to update parents on behavior and academics

Sending home daily or weekly evaluations to keep parents updated on behavior and work habits is generally not a requirement for teachers but is certainly worth considering. Reports may be sent home for the entire class, or only for particular students. If you have a very involved group of parents who would appreciate having regular feedback, I would suggest have a routine system for every child in the class. It may also be helpful to do reports for every child if you have a very challenging class that would benefit from extra accountability. It's okay to wait and see how things go with your particular group and then introduce a reporting system to individuals or the whole class a few weeks into the school year.

This chapter will help you determine a workable method for updating all of your parents or just the ones whose children need to be held accountable. It will also help you decide whether to update parents daily or weekly about behavior and explain ways to do each successfully. Additionally, this chapter will help you consider the most effective way to update your students' families on academic progress. This may be accomplished through sending home graded work in a folder for parents to sign, creating an individualized newsletter, or by utilizing a bi-weekly report form. I will present each of these options here and suggest ways you can adapt them to fit your classroom needs. At the end of the chapter, I'll explain a low-stress way to hold parent conferences using a student-led format.

As always, the forms featured in this chapter and many more are available as free, modifiable Word documents at TheCornerstoneForTeachers.com.

Behavior Reports

Choosing Daily or Weekly Communication

There are advantages and disadvantages to both daily and weekly reports. Consider the following information to determine what will work best for you and your group of children:

Communication Style	Pros	Cons
Daily Reports: Each day in students' planners, you use simple codes to indicate whether homework and/or class work were completed and note any behavioral issues.	-permits daily two-way communication -more immediate reinforcement for good and bad choices -the teacher doesn't have to record behavior for a week and then transfer the info to a form	-requires the teacher to record information daily -requires parents to sign off daily
Weekly Evaluations: Once a week, you total up missing work and behavioral issues and write them on a form for parent review.	-gives parents a quick summary of work habits/social skills -requires less of the parent: good for communities where family involvement is hard to get -can be easier for the teacher because reports are only done once a week	-does not provide immediate feedback for kids -notifies parents of a problem a few days after the fact, unless the teacher also writes a note the day of the incident

Daily Behavior Reports

A daily evaluation of children's behavior can be done for individual students as needed, or for the entire class. To manage daily reports for all students, I've used agenda books or planners ordered by the school. Each day at dismissal, I had students pack up and bring their agendas over to where I was sitting in a rocking chair. After I signed off on a child's agenda, he sat down on the rug to wait for his bus to be called. If there were any problems during the day, I explained them using the key shown here. Parents signed off in just one place each night, because the daily evaluation was right next to the homework assignment. The following key was pasted prominently in the front of each student's agenda. For the first few weeks of school, I also had students glue a copy onto each week's agenda page for easier reference until parents and students learned the code.

Sample Code Key:

Category	Abbreviation	Meaning
Homework	Circled assignment	Not turned in
	Circled with INC written above it	Incomplete homework
	MK-UP MISS.	Make-up work not turned in
Class work	MISS. CW	Missing class work
	INC. CW	Incomplete class work
Work Habits/ Social Growth	P	Playing around
	T	Talking out of turn
	D	Disrespectful
	H	Hallway behavior problems
	NF	Not following directions
Comments	1	Thank you for doing such a good job today!
	2	I'm proud of you for turning in all your work!
	3	Your behavior was excellent—make sure you turn in all your work tomorrow.
	4	Let's have a better day tomorrow.
	5	Please see comment in note section.

Sample Agenda Page Using Codes:

	[Student copies assignments here]	**[My codes and parent signature here]**
Monday 8/8	Math worksheet	1 ☺ *R K.*
Tuesday 8/9	Math pg. 8 Map worksheet	1 ☺ *R K*
Wednesday 8/10	Write a poem using spelling words.	4 (P, T) *I spoke to him about this— Thursday he will be More focused in class. R K.*
Thursday 8/11	Math pg. 11 Read pgs. 2-6 in Science.	3 *Not sure why this HW assignment wasn't turned in— he did it last night. R K.*
Friday 8/12	No homework Have a great weekend!	*He found the HW in his backpack!* *Great! R K.*

Other Ways to Do Daily Reports

◆ **Stamp children's hands, agenda books, or homework with special stamps.** Smiley face stamps are good to use (don't give a stamp if there were problems and write a note in the child's agenda to explain). Or you could use a set of stamps, with one particular stamp indicating the child had a great day, one for an okay day, and another for a day that had a lot of problems.

◆ **Use washable markers to make an X, star, or other symbol on children's hands or agendas in a color that symbolizes the behavior.** This method is often used by early childhood teachers because of its simplicity. For example, green=good day, yellow=okay, red=problems (with the specific issue explained in the agenda). I do caution you to be careful about putting a red mark directly on a student's hand, because it physically labels the child as 'bad' for everyone to see. If you have students who frequently earn a 'red', you may want to use a different, more private system for them.

◆ **Have children fill in a simple form or calendar at the end of the day**. The kids color that day's square green if they had a good day, yellow for an okay day, etc. The teacher announces that it's time for everyone to color their square green and calls over the 'non-green children' to discuss and mark individually. The teacher can then initial's each child's form to show parents that their children used the correct color, and can add notes as needed.

When a Parent is Unwilling or Unable to Check Daily Reports

If the parent is not a disciplinarian, you have the option of sending the daily note home anyway, and having the child show it to another teacher at the end of the school day for additional reinforcement. I once had a student whose father was deceased and whose mother had substance abuse problems. I sent home the daily note as documentation of the child's behavior, and sent the child to a colleague that I knew the student liked and respected. She talked to him for a minute at the end of each day, praising the child for improvements and encouraging him through mistakes. The child really looked forward to that attention and I saw a marked improvement in his behavior quite quickly.

Weekly Behavioral Evaluations

The Purpose

Weekly evaluations are a report on social skills (behavior) and study skills (work habits). Most school systems require teachers to grade primary level students in these areas using either a letter grade or numerical system (i.e., 1's, 2's, and 3's). Weekly evaluations are a quick and easy way to:

> ➢ have a highly structured yet simple system for recording behavior
> ➢ update parents on children's work habits and social skills
> ➢ notify parents when class work/homework isn't being turned in
> ➢ hold children accountable for their choices
> ➢ provide rewards/consequences for work habits and social skills
> ➢ keep documentation that you've notified parents about issues

Evaluating Behavior

Weekly evaluation grades are based on a check system used for recording students' behavior using the tracking form shown here. When students have behavioral issues, make a checkmark. Next to each check, write an abbreviation for the infraction (T for talking, F for fighting, etc.). At the end of the week, total up how many checks each student has and assign a Social Skills grade using the key shown on the weekly evaluation form. To save space, you could write just the infraction and not make actual checkmarks, as shown below.

Example of Tracking Form

Name	Work Habits: Homework					Work Habits: Class Work					Work Habits Grade	Social Skills Grade	Social Skills				
	M	T	W	R	F	M	T	W	R	F			M	T	W	R	F
1 Joshua											A	C	T T P	T D			P
2 Cara											A	A			O		
3 Carlos		Sci									B	B	T NF				O P
4 Dylan											A	A					
5 Maria		Sp Read				Math					D	B	T	P P			

One Version of a Weekly Evaluation

Week	Teacher's Comments	Parent Signature
Date: _____ Social Skills: _____ Work Habits: _____ Missing HW: M T W TH F		
Date: _____ Social Skills: _____ Work Habits: _____ Missing HW: M T W TH F		
Date: _____ Social Skills: _____ Work Habits: _____ Missing HW: M T W TH F		
Date: _____ Social Skills: _____ Work Habits: _____ Missing HW: M T W TH F		
Date: _____ Social Skills: _____ Work Habits: _____ Missing HW: M T W TH F		
Date: _____ Social Skills: _____ Work Habits: _____ Missing HW: M T W TH F		
Date: _____ Social Skills: _____ Work Habits: _____ Missing HW: M T W TH F		

Note: These are NOT your child's academic grades for the subject areas (math, reading, etc.). These grades reflect behavior and whether homework and class work are being completed and turned in on time, NOT whether your child has mastered the information taught. Please look for work sample forms, mid-term progress reports, and report cards for updates on your child's academic progress.

T=Talking   P=Playing Around   O=Out of Seat   D=Disrespectful   F=Fighting
NF=Not Following Directions   A= Another teacher had a problem

Social Skills Key:

A= 0-2 checks
B= 3-5 checks
C= 6-8 checks
D= 9-11 checks
F= 12 or more

Work Habits Key:

1 letter grade is subtracted for each missing or incomplete homework (HW) or class work (CW) assignment, and each time the child is not prepared for class with appropriate materials:
A=0, B=1, C=2, D=3, F=4 or more

Evaluating Work Habits

You can use the same tracking sheet to record whether students have any missing or incomplete homework and class work assignments. At the end of the week, give a work habits grade to each child (see the key on the bottom of the weekly evaluation form). If your school district uses a numerical scale for work habits, just convert the letter grades to whatever system your district uses. For example, if the scale is 1-3, then use this key: 1=Outstanding (0-1 checks), 2=Satisfactory (2-3 checks), and 3=Improvement Needed (4+ checks).

<u>Weekly Evaluation FAQs</u>

► How long do weekly evaluations take to fill out?

It takes about 10-30 minutes to complete forms for the entire class, depending on how much you want to write. I usually put more information at the beginning of the year, and by the third quarter, I've pretty much made all the complaints and given all the compliments I'm going to make for a child and pare it down more. If I see a student accomplish something remarkable during the week, such as writing an insightful journal entry or mastering a math concept he's been struggling with, I'll write a comment on the evaluation right away before I forget. Adding information to the forms throughout the week as things happen saves time on Fridays, and provides the parent with more specific feedback.

► Are there any rewards or consequences tied to the evaluations?

Only if you want there to be! You can set up a behavior modification system in which a student who gets three checks in one day has a consequence enforced. (Some offenses, such as fighting, lying, and stealing, can automatically get 3 checks and result in a more serious consequence.)

If you prefer to keep things rewards-based, you could try something I did one year on Friday afternoons called A/B reward. Any child who had gotten all A's and B's on her weekly evaluation could participate and the others completed practice work at their seats. A/B reward was usually a thirty-minute educational movie, but sometimes I would give the class free time or do an art project.

If you don't want (or aren't allowed) to give students free time, you can reward A and B students with a certificate. All the kids who get the award stand up and come to the front of the room, and the others clap, cheer, and congratulate them. Then the ones who didn't earn the award stand up and the ones who did get it clap for them and say, "Keep trying!"

You will also notice that many parents give or take away privileges for their children based on weekly evaluation results. My students regularly celebrated being able to go ice skating or to the movies over the weekend because they had earned A/B Reward.

▶ **Can weekly evaluations work with individual behavior modification plans? What if a kid gets 20 checks every single week?**

One year, I had a child whose behavior was so inconsistent that he was driving his family and I both crazy—he'd get an A in social skills for three weeks, then an F, for no obvious reason. I'll call him David. I met with David's parents and we signed a Personal Improvement Plan (behavior contract). It basically said that David was responsible for bringing home what he came to term his 'check book'—a leftover agenda book the school used with the upper grade students. I would record how many checks he had each day and what they were for, and he would bring the agenda home for his parents to sign. This daily reinforcement provided the structure David needed as a supplement for the weekly evaluation.

We also created a different set of expectations for David. If he had 2 or fewer checks for the day, he was allowed to have his normal TV and video game privileges. If he had more than 2 checks, he was not allowed to watch TV or play video games for the entire evening. Because he was allowed to get up to 2 checks a day (which would be 10, a D, by the end of the week), he would only have his privileges revoked over the weekend if he had more than 10 checks. Any D and F letter grades would be kept on my grading records because social skills grades were recorded on report cards, but they were not to affect his A/B reward or privileges at home.

The accommodations increased communication between home and school, provided more immediate consequences and rewards for David (since waiting until Friday was ineffective), and supplied solid documentation of his behavior for my own records and those of his doctor and the special education coordinator. It was also very little work for me, since David was responsible for giving me the 'check book' each day—if he forgot, he automatically lost privileges at home. He did an excellent job of remembering and really thought hard about his actions each day because of the high level of accountability. By the end of the year, David was only allowed to have 1 check per day and was put back on the regular grading system with the rest of the class.

▶ What if a student loses his or her weekly evaluation?

Since I used a tracking form to record students' behavior and work habits, it didn't matter if kids lost their weekly evaluations in terms of my own records. I did have consequences for students, however, so they would learn responsibility. If they didn't bring back the form by Friday, I gave them a check for being unprepared and wrote the child's work habits and social skills grades on a sticky note for the parent to sign. Although the forms were occasionally lost, no child ever had to get a replacement more than once in a school year, and the vast majority of students were very good about holding onto them. Insisting that the form be carried to and from school in a two-pocket folder or binder is a helpful strategy.

▶ What if the parent isn't responsible enough to sign the evaluation?

This is less of a problem than you might think, especially if you are clear with children that you will not accept excuses such as "I told my mom and she said she'd do it later" or "My dad forgot." It's the *child's* behavior and work habit report, so it's the *child's* responsibility to deliver the paper and make sure it's reviewed by a responsible adult. In very unstable households, I have allowed grandparents, aunts, uncles, and adult cousins to sign.

▶ How do you collect the evaluations and make sure they're signed?

I had student helpers collect the forms and write on a sticky note whose was missing. Each day, the helpers consulted the note, which stayed by the file box that weekly evaluations were kept in, until all the children had returned the form and the helpers had crossed off every name. You can also use a 'Have You Turned In Your...' board as shown in Chapter 11.

Reports on Academic Progress

Don't Wait for Report Cards!

Most daily or weekly evaluations address work habits and social growth but don't give a clear picture of how students are doing academically. We all have conscientious and well-behaved students who are working far below grade level, and conversely, kids who are always in trouble but still manage to get good grades. The typical weekly evaluation form can leave parents and children feeling very surprised when report card time rolls around if the teacher isn't clear about the form's limitations!

Experienced educators should definitely consider having a regular method for updating parents on children's academic growth. If your school system has already overloaded you with paper trails, this may not be needed. But if you'd like documentation of how you routinely provide student progress information to parents, I have several methods you can try. I've listed them in order from the simplest to most complex. Each one can be adapted to include social skills and work habit information, as well, so that you don't have to do a separate behavior report.

Option A) Send home graded work in a folder for parents to sign
Option B) Combine a newsletter with academic and behavioral reports
Option C) Use biweekly work sample reflection forms

Option A) Sending Home Graded Work in a Folder

This can be done weekly or bi-weekly. If you want to be sure that parents have seen the folder contents, have a page glued or stapled to the inside for them to sign. One of the simplest ways is to type up the dates for the entire quarter and have a blank spot for parents to sign each week.

Another way to send graded work home is to staple all of the work together for each child. The parent then signs the top page and returns the ENTIRE packet for you keep in student portfolios for documentation. This also prevents sneaky children from throwing out poor grades and only showing the 'good papers' to mom and dad. You could also have a paper on the front for the parent to sign instead of the work itself. This paper could be a class newsletter, behavioral report, or reflection on student work.

Option B) Combining a Class Newsletter With Academic/ Behavioral Reports

One year, I stopped sending home regular newsletters and combined them with student progress reports. I completed these bi-weekly but you could do them weekly if you prefer. I kept a basic template on my computer's hard drive and typed in updates based on the graded work that would be sent home with each child. I relayed information about what we had been studying and what the upcoming skills would be.

I then printed out a copy for each child and hand-wrote individualized comments, sometimes in great detail and sometimes with checkmarks or smiley faces in each section unless there had been a problem. If a student had done poorly or exceptionally well with a particular skill, I made sure to note that. It took me about an hour to complete the newsletter/individual report for every child in the class every other week.

The forms were sent home with the students' graded work. Parents kept the work and returned the signed form for my records.

Sample Class Newsletter With Academic/Behavioral Report

_____Justin_____'s Newsletter and Report For April 13-27

Homework Completion			Class Work Completion			Work Habits/ Effort		
1	(2)	3	(1)	2	3	(1)	2	3
Week ending April 20- ☺ Week ending April 27- *Missing spelling*			*Justin has been so responsible!* ☺			☺		

Language Arts/ Reading	The fact/opinion activity you see in the folder was quite difficult—however, there should be an improvement by the end-of-chapter test. *Nice work so far, Justin.* Your child has now learned how to write all cursive letters! See the upper-case letters packet in the folder. We will continue practicing cursive writing daily. FCAT Practice Test- *Check out how well Justin did on the author's purpose questions! I'm going to work with him on main idea in small groups next week.*
Math	Two digit division- *Great!* ☺ We will begin division with remainders next week- please see the attached game you can play to help your child with this concept.
Social Studies/ Science	Our world history unit is going well! Thank you Mr. Yahua for doing the presentation on ancient Egypt! *Justin loved the sequencing activity for mummies!* In science, we are learning about animals and food chains. Ask your child about the predators/prey activity we did outside.

Parent Signature/Comments: (PLEASE SIGN & RETURN THIS PAPER BY FRI. MAY 4th)

Key: 1: Outstanding   2: Satisfactory   3: Improvement Needed

REMINDER: Field trip forms and money are due on Friday 5/14!

Option C) Bi-Weekly Work Samples

Here's the method I used several years ago when I had a group of very involved parents who wanted frequent, detailed updates on academic progress. Because this particular class was so well-behaved as a whole, I had individual behavior plans for the kids who needed them and just left a small space for work habits/behavior on the bi-weekly work sample form (although you could easily expand it for your own class).

I sent home graded work in a bi-weekly folder with a form that detailed the student's academic progress. What distinguishes this format from that of most reports is the student reflection component. I taught children how to look through their folders and notice overall patterns of weakness, strength, and growth, and conferenced with kids individually to discuss their observations. This page and the next show an example of what a completed form might look like. The information all fits on one page when the margins are set at .5 inches all around.

BI-WEEKLY WORK SAMPLE FOLDER FOR
Rasheed   :   Mon. Oct. 8th– Mon. Oct. 22nd

Area of Development	Teacher Comments	Parent Comments (Optional)
Reading/ Language Arts	Difficulty distinguishing between main idea and details. Expository writing has been more detailed!	Yes, his writing is better! How is he doing on the narratives?
Social Studies/ Science	Please work on state capitals	We'll practice this weekend.
Math	WOW! You've really mastered four digit addition!	
Work Habits/ Behavior	Thanks for helping our new student this week. You've been very responsible!	Great!
Other	The Spanish teacher says you need to practice color names.	

Student Reflection

I am most proud of _____ my math test _____

because __I practiced on the computer every night and it paid off!_____ .

I chose to put the following in my portfolio: _____ my energy and motion poem _____

because _____ I used similes and metaphors and that used to be hard for me.

Last time I wanted to improve _____ map skills _____ .

When I think about how I've done in this area in the last two weeks, I think __ that I need study some

_____ more because I still don't get the compass rose and I didn't memorize the state capitals.

I would like to improve _____ on state capitals and cause and effect _____

To do this, I plan to __ play the state capitals game during centers and use FCAT Explorer on the

computer. _____ .

Teacher comments on reflection:
Glad you noticed the state capitals problem- you'll do better next week! ☺

Parent comments on reflection:
Can't wait to see your science poem at the conference! Good job on the math test!

Conferences Held	Please Sign	
_X_ Student-Teacher	Student Initials	__D.L.__
____ Student-Parent	Teacher Initials:	__AP__
____ Student-Teacher/Parent	Parent Initials:	__RL__

**PLEASE KEEP ALL WORK SAMPLES AT HOME AND RETURN THIS SIGNED FORM
TO SCHOOL BY FRIDAY, OCTOBER 26th**

Benefits of the Bi-Weekly Work Sample System

It usually took me 45 minutes to complete the forms and 45 minutes to conference every two weeks. That's only 90 minutes twice a month to:

> ➢ gain a comprehensive view of whole class/individual progress in all areas
> ➢ discuss growth and set goals with students individually
> ➢ provide detailed feedback to parents and students on academic progress
> ➢ maintain student work portfolios with meaningful student reflection
> ➢ document communication with parents on all areas of development

How the System Works

Here's an outline of the basic process:

1) Print one form for each child every two weeks.
2) Save all graded student work during the two-week period.
3) Briefly review each student's work and write comments as appropriate.
4) Let students view their work and select pieces to pull out for their portfolios to be shared at parent conferences.
5) Have students read your comments and fill out the student reflection box.
6) Hold 2-5 minute student conferences to discuss the child's work and reflection. (You can do half the class every two weeks so each child has a monthly conference.)
7) Check off whether a conference was held, then comment on reflections, and sign.
8) Send the form home along with student work for parent signature.
9) Keep signed forms in student portfolios for review at conferences.

If you want to save time, try typing directly into the form so you can reuse certain comments or announcements for multiple children. I would often look through a folder of student work, type the child's name and comments into the form, then print it. I then moved on to the next folder and repeated the process, not saving any of the changes, just printing from the same basic form each time. I could usually get through the whole class in half an hour this way and the forms looked very professional. The kids did their reflections afterwards, instead of beforehand, which worked equally well.

The Purpose of Sending Home Papers Bi-Weekly

The emphasis here is on noting patterns of progress while identifying problems in time to reteach and provide additional support. This is harder to accomplish if you send work home every day or even every week. For example, let's say you're teaching geometry. If you return graded papers each day, they'll probably get tossed in the trash or abandoned in the bottom of backpacks—parents never see them because most don't have time to look over a child's work every single day. When papers are sent home weekly, parents are more likely to look at them; however, the problem arises when they see something a child isn't doing well on and start freaking out.

Including two week's worth of assignments allows the parent and teacher to see progress. You might note in the math section, "Aisha's project clearly shows that she understands plane figures. She had trouble identifying angles at first, but doing the test corrections helped. You can see how much better she's doing with them on this week's quiz." Or, you might *not* notice progress and can comment on that, too, as well as some changes you want to make to your instruction ("Aisha has struggled with all the plot/conflict activities we did—I'm going to pull her for extra small group work this week"). Making such notes will solidify in the teacher's mind just how well each child is mastering concepts, which is difficult when grading stacks of papers. The bi-weeklies are a great time of reflection not only for students and families, but for me. The forms help me gather my thoughts before parent conferences and report cards, and serve as great documentation.

Setting Up the Routines and Procedures

Remember, you have every other week "off" since these are bi-weekly folders. I liked sending home folders every other Friday. On the Thursday prior, I had student helpers put graded work into individual folders with the work sample evaluation forms. Whenever I had time that day, I began reviewing student work and writing comments on the forms. I then had students review their work and reflect on it for Morning Work on Friday so no time was taken from instruction. I conferenced with students during Fun Friday or recess, which they enjoyed. Finally, I sent the folders home at dismissal with a due date of the following Friday.

Successful Parent Conferences

The Case for Student-Led Conferencing

Many teachers feel hesitant or nervous about telling parents that a child's been behaving badly in the classroom. Those feelings are misplaced. It is not YOU who should be worried—it's the CHILD! Let HIM explain what's been happening! If he hasn't been doing any work, let HIM break the news. And similarly, you should help HIM identify what needs to change and develop a plan for improvement. Even when the issues are academic, it benefits the child when his input about the problem is sought and he feels like a valued member of a parent-teacher-child team that works together to create solutions.

Conferences are about the student, so why should the teacher and parent do all the talking? In student-led conferences, the child is not only present, but is put in charge of explaining her progress, reflecting on accomplishments, and setting short and long-term goals. The benefits and purposes are:

> ➢ to show parents and students that their opinions and experiences are valued by the teacher
> ➢ to empower the child to take responsibility for his learning
> ➢ to give the parent and teacher a chance to hear the student reflect on her progress in her own words
> ➢ to reassure students that the parents and teacher are there for support
> ➢ to hold students accountable for their academic and behavioral choices
> ➢ to give the parent an opportunity to see the teacher and child interact
> ➢ to provide the teacher with insight into the parent-child relationship and home structure in a non-intimidating way
> ➢ to take unnecessary pressure off of the teacher by focusing on the student and his work samples
> ➢ to increase turn out because parents and students love doing them

When to Hold Student-Led Conferences

For the first conference of the year, the student should generally be nearby in the room but out of earshot (e.g., reading in the library area) so that the parents and teacher can speak privately and involve the child as needed. Typically in the first conference, parents primarily provide background information on the child and the teacher clarifies expectations and progress thus far. Later conferences can then be student-led, as often as once a quarter, with parent-teacher-only conferences as needed.

I use student-led conferences almost exclusively, even in the beginning of the year, because I feel so strongly about my students being actively involved. If I need to speak privately with a parent, I hold a student-led conference and say to the child at the end, "Thank you so much for sharing your thoughts with us! We are so proud of you! Would you please go over to your desk and read or draw just for a little bit so I can speak to your mom alone? We're not saying anything bad about you. We just need to talk about some grown-up things that you don't have to be concerned about."

Preparing for Conferences

Because students take responsibility for these conferences, they require very little work for the teacher. The only thing you need to do is have student work samples available, if you would like to reference them during the conference. One of the most meaningful ways to do this is by setting up a class routine in which students are regularly selecting work for their portfolios. For example, children can select their best work from their stack of graded papers to go home, and write on a sticky note why they chose a particular paper. Or, you could keep various graded assignments (one writing sample, one math activity, one science project, etc.) so that each child has a paper from every subject that can be taken home after the conference. Have students keep their papers in chronological order in a portfolio, which can be stored in a hanging file, manila folder, or even a clean pizza box if you have a lot of 3D or large work samples (ask a pizzeria to donate a class set). The day of the conference, the student pulls her portfolio and, ideally, practices presenting the papers to a buddy, you, or herself.

How the Conferences Work

The child shows her parent(s) her best work from the portfolio and uses the sticky notes she attached to each work sample to help explain why she chose a specific assignment. The child may also initiate or be prompted to discuss how to solve a math problem that was challenging, read a passage to demonstrate a reading strategy, or share a story she wrote and explain the writing process used. This is not as difficult as it sounds, because the child is basically explaining the assignment to the parent. If the selected papers are of a format that you typically use in class, even very young children can explain what was done. Anytime the child is uncertain of what to say, give a prompt such as, "Tell us about what you did here" or "What did you have to do for this assignment?"

The teacher uses the student work as a springboard for discussion during the portfolio sharing and afterwards (however the conversation flows best). As a general rule, you should direct questions to the child first, and follow up with questions for the parent as appropriate.

The ideal interaction is fluid, casual, and focused on all three parties sharing their insights in a positive way. The child typically enjoys being the center of attention and parents appreciate being asked for their opinions. The teacher is able to step down from the responsibility of imparting judgment about a child's abilities and progress, and move into the role of guiding the family towards mutually-drawn conclusions. This is accomplished through carefully selected questioning techniques, conversation, and the sharing of observations. Conferences generally last 10-60 minutes, depending on the level of interaction between the parent and child.

You can use the format shown here to guide your conferences. The sequence of questioning progresses in a natural way and provides an opportunity to discuss nearly every issue of concern: below grade level performance, lack of support at home, interpersonal conflicts, and so on. Each topic is raised through non-intimidating and non-accusatory questions that demonstrate a genuine interest in student and parent viewpoints. You can then respond to the family's ideas appropriately and supportively with your own input, observations, and suggestions.

Sample Questions for Student-Led Conferences		
Topic	**Ask the Child...**	**Ask the Parent...**
Attitude Toward School	How are you feeling about school right now? Do you like coming to school? What do you like about it?	Are those the kind of things you're hearing at home, too?
Strengths	[Review work samples] What do you think is your strongest subject? Why do you think that?	Do you agree? Was this a strength for your child last year, too?
Weaknesses	What subject has been the hardest for you this year? What's most difficult for you?	Do you see that area as being the most difficult for your child?
Areas of Confusion	Is there anything we've been doing in class that is not making sense to you or that you think you need to do better in? How can mom and I help you with that?	Are there any procedures or assignments that you're unsure about or that you don't think are working well for your child right now?
Homework	How has homework been going (amount, type, etc.)? What has been helpful? Has anything felt like busywork that isn't helping you learn? What can we do to make homework really useful practice for you?	What are your feelings about that?
Home Support	What else can we set up for you at home to help you do your best? [Find websites, games, set up a HW routine, determine how you will get books to read at home, find extra practice work, etc.].	Are there any resources or extra practice activities you'd like for me to send home?
Social Development	How are you getting along with the other kids in class? Who are your friends in our room? Is there anything going on between you and the other kids that we need to talk about?	Is this what you've been hearing from your child at home? Does he seem happy with the friends he's made in our class?
Goals	Let's set a goal for this quarter. What is the one thing you would most like to accomplish? Let's make a plan to help you do that.	Is there any specific area that you would like to see your child improve this quarter? What can I do to help support your child and your family?
Follow Up	If you think of anything else you need in order to do well in school, please tell your parents or me. We are here talking *with* you to learn *about* you. We're doing that because we care so much and want you to be successful. We believe you are smart and we want to do everything possible to help you be your very best.	Please call (email, etc.) if you have any questions or concerns about anything. I will be happy to meet with you as often as you like. I'm so glad you came in and we had a chance to talk about all the wonderful things your child is accomplishing this year. When we meet again, let's talk about how well your child has met the goal we set today, and then we'll set another goal for the remainder of the year.

Chapter 32: The Importance of Documentation
Keeping excellent records to protect yourself in an age of accountability

Documentation is a fact of life for most teachers. Many of the suggestions that follow are considered 'unspoken rules' that aren't often communicated properly to new teachers by their school district leaders and administrators. The information in this chapter will help you maintain records that will support your claims when you need to justify the decisions you make in the classroom or prove their effectiveness to a parent or supervisor.

FAQs About Documentation

► **What exactly IS documentation?**

Let's say you have a child who has some behavioral issues and isn't doing well in class. When you bring the issue up to another teacher or your administration, the first thing you are likely to hear is, "Are you keeping documentation?" This essentially means: Are you writing anecdotal records when the child behaves inappropriately, keeping written records of your interventions, filing work samples that support your claim, and maintaining copies of all correspondence with the child's parents and school system employees concerning this child?

► **Is it as complicated as it sounds?**

No, not at all! Once you understand when and how to keep good records, it's fairly easy to set up a system for documentation that requires very little maintenance. It's not a fun thing to think about, but once you get the hang of it, you'll feel a great sense of relief in knowing that you've got yourself covered.

▶ **Why bother? I have so much on my plate right now...**

The purpose of documentation is essentially two-fold: a) it is a key element in getting services for students that you suspect have special needs, and b) to cover yourself in case of a lawsuit, school records audit, or allegation by a parent or administrator that you did not do your job properly.

The main purpose is the first one. No school system that I am aware of will even consider evaluating a student without having substantial documentation from the classroom teacher about the child's behavior, academic progress, interventions attempted, and the results of those interventions. The second purpose is actually a bonus benefit—you don't have to feel stressed when unexpected problems arise, because you've already prepared.

On more than one occasion, a teacher has been accused and later acquitted of wrong-doing in the classroom. If you have a paper trail, you can prove your case against any false allegations against you. Additionally, if a child ever needs to be recommended for special education services or is in danger of being retained, you will have evidence of the modifications you made, what worked, and what didn't.

An example of what can happen with poor documentation records

Teacher takes a phone call with pencil and paper in hand:

"My child told me you took away his recess today!!"
I... think he missed recess, yes, but I didn't have duty today, so I'll have to check with Mrs. Jones.

"But he did all of his homework except reading!"
Let me look through all of the homework papers to see if he had it...

"Well, he said he saw a boy who didn't have his homework and that boy didn't miss recess!"
Who was it? He must not have done his work, if he didn't have recess.

"Well, this is the first time it's ever happened."
I think he was missing a math assignment a couple of weeks ago—I'll get my grade book..."

"I wrote a note so you would know we had football practice late that day and he didn't have time to finish."
What did the note say? I'm not sure I got it.

The parent's overall impression: This teacher is incompetent. She has no idea what my child did and did not do. She's not being fair and treats him differently than the other kids. I'm going to have to check behind her every day to make sure she didn't mess up because I'm clearly the only one with my facts straight.

An example of what can happen with complete documentation records

Teacher takes a phone call with pencil, phone documentation log, and documentation file in hand:

"My child told me you took away his recess today!!"
Yes, I didn't have duty today, but my chart shows he did miss it.

"But he did all of his homework except reading!"
That's correct. At the beginning of the year, we sent home a Third Grade Policies letter explaining that if any portion of a child's homework is missing, that child must miss recess. Each parent and child agreed to that policy and signed it. I can send a copy home if you'd like.

"Well, he said he saw a boy who didn't have his homework and that boy didn't miss recess!"
Yes, the child next to him was absent yesterday. He will need to turn in the assignment by the end of the week or the same consequence will apply.

"Well, this is the first time it's ever happened."
Johnny has done an excellent job turning in his work—I can tell you work very closely with him at home. [Looking over the weekly evaluation form] In fact, this is only the second time he's ever missed an assignment. Two missing assignments certainly won't hurt his homework grade.

"I wrote a note so you would know we had football practice late that day."
[Flips through documentation file to make sure there were no special circumstances with the note] Yes, I have a copy of your note right here. Thanks for letting me know what the problem was. Anytime Johnny will be missing a homework assignment, it would be wonderful if you would continue to write me notes. Johnny's a very conscientious student, so I'm sure this won't be a recurring problem that would affect his grades.

The parent's overall impression: This teacher knows exactly what's going on in her classroom. She is consistent and treats everyone the same. I disagree with the consequence, but I did agree to the homework policy at the beginning of the year. Next time Johnny tells me something unfair happened to him, I'll make sure I know all the facts and the teacher's expectations of him.

► **Do I need to keep documentation on all of my students?**

There are certain things that you should continue to keep all year long for every student:

> ➢ copies of important tests and assignments, preferably signed by parents
> ➢ notes to and from home
> ➢ conference forms
> ➢ progress/interim reports and report cards
> ➢ phone log for all parent contact with brief summaries of each conversation
> ➢ copies of behavior reports or weekly evaluations if you use them

► **When do I need to keep more extensive documentation?**

While you'll need to keep good records for your whole class, it will be necessary to keep more extensive records in particular scenarios when:

♦ **You've had the same semi-serious behavioral problem with a student three or four times.** When this happens, trust your instincts—you'll get a sinking feeling in the pit of your stomach. *These weren't just isolated incidents as the child adjusts to a new class. This is a real problem!*

♦ **A child exhibits symptoms of abuse or neglect.** You might need to document behavioral problems; psychiatric issues (like 'cutting'—intentionally slicing at one's own skin to feel physical pain instead of emotional pain); developmentally inappropriate behaviors (such as masturbating in class—yes, this happens in elementary schools); indications of abuse of any type (wearing turtleneck sweaters in eighty degree weather, scratching in the genital region), etc. Each school system and state has its own system for reporting allegations of abuse—you will probably be trained in this every year by your district so you know what procedures to follow. Keeping good documentation is always a crucial part of the reporting process.

♦ **A child is not making progress in one or more subject areas and/or is in danger of retention.** If October rolls around and one of your students is still making C's, D's, and F's on every math test, you need to be documenting that issue. If a child is improving in math but still can't decode simple four letter words, you need to document. Anytime you suspect a child may need special education services, keep additional records. It's imperative to maintain evidence that you've notified the parent of these problems, as well.

◆ **You have a child whose parent is particularly critical or overly concerned about you, the school, or the child.** Trust your instincts on this one, too—be conscious of parents who:

> ➢ constantly question minor decisions you make in the classroom
> ➢ call frequently to check on their child's academic progress
> ➢ often ask you to intervene in minor disputes between students
> ➢ badmouth a previous teacher, the administration, or another parent
> ➢ are in the middle of a divorce, custody battle, or remarriage
> ➢ are attorneys, teachers, or school system employees
> ➢ are overly protective of their children
> ➢ have extremely anxious temperaments
> ➢ mention a bad experience with a former teacher or school
> ➢ have switched their child(ren) from school to school frequently

These qualities don't necessarily mean that you will have a problem with a parent—they just indicate that you will want to keep especially careful records on his or her child. There is a higher likelihood that you will need documentation to ensure that the child's needs are met and to prove that you have provided every possible accommodation.

Documentation Basics

What to Document

Once you have figured out that you've got a special case on your hands, don't waste any more time. Start documenting anything that seems problematic to you. If the issue is behavioral, talk to your guidance counselor to find out how your administration wants you to handle it. You will probably need evidence of what the child has done, what provoked the behavior, modifications you have made, and at least one conference form documenting that the parents have been notified of the problem. Each school system has its own forms for this, but your anecdotal records are almost always helpful. If the problem is academic, make sure you are keeping copies of tests and key assignments, signed by parents whenever possible.

How to Document

1. Start documentation files for each student. These are different from the kids' cumulative records which are kept on file in the office. I recommend keeping a file of student work that demonstrates evidence of weaknesses and growth, as well as a separate file for parent correspondence and other communication regarding students (see pages 59-61).

2. Keep a copy of ALL notes to and from home. I write informal correspondence on carbon-copy paper and type more formal notes, printing a second copy for my own records. Beware of emailing confidential information! In some school systems, email is considered public domain, so personal information about students is not to be relayed that way even with parents. Check with your administration about the policies in your district.

3. When a parent sends you a note, write your response to the parent at the top of the paper and file it. "Called 3/21- see phone log" or "Sent note home- see attached" and staple a copy of your reply. Never file a parent's note without responding to it if needed and documenting that response.

4. Keep a phone log to document all conversations. This can help remind you of what was said, to who, and when. In some school systems, phone conversations count towards the required number of parent-teacher conferences for the year, so you can fill out a conference form, too.

5. Send home regular notifications about misbehavior and missing or late assignments. A parent cannot legitimately argue that she was not kept informed about these two crucial issues if a form is sent home weekly for her to sign (see Chapter 31, Keeping Parents Informed).

6. Send progress reports home mid-quarter if you suspect a child may receive a "C" or lower in any area, including behavior. Surprises are your worst enemy. Requiring a signature ensures that parents have seen the information and are thereby accountable for it.

I keep the whole class' conference forms and interim reports in one folder. On the inside of the folder, I list all of the students' names and write the date of each conference (in blue ink) and interim report (in black ink). This way I can tell at a glance how many conferences I've had with each parent and who has been notified of their child's progress.

7. Have your principal initial any potentially controversial notes you send home. This keeps her informed, covers you in case a parent responds negatively, and lets the parent know you are to be taken seriously and have backing for your classroom practices. Many administrators require that you gain their approval before sending any notices home, even class newsletters, so this is a good habit to get into.

8. Document each time a child is removed from your classroom. If you send a student to the office, use the referral form provided by your school district. In one particularly troubled school I worked in, teachers would often send children to one another's rooms for a 'time out' if a behavior was disruptive enough to warrant removal but not severe enough to incur administrative action. I created a form to have a record of the incident and provide information to the teacher I sent the child to. I would then photocopy it and send it home for the parent to sign and return (see Chapter 18, The Challenges of High-Poverty Schools).

9. Utilize your guidance counselor's services and keep a copy of information, notes, and resources she provides you. When a social situation seems beyond your scope of expertise, don't be afraid to approach the guidance counselor for advice. Sometimes he can speak with the children and/or the parents on your behalf.

Documentation Assistance from Your Teacher's Union

More than a few of our dedicated colleagues have struggled with accusations of racism, harassment, and negligence. If you have a teacher's union, I STRONGLY advise you to join and utilize its resources. Your union representative can look over your documentation and help you do your job effectively.

Part Eight:
Learning and Adapting to the Realities of Teaching

Chapter 33: The Unwritten Contract
Understanding the realities of public school teaching

There are some truths about teaching in public schools that you won't find in your college textbooks, or outlined in your teaching contract...in fact, you might not be told about them until the day you're responsible for their implementation! This chapter will explain some of the unwritten rules in teaching so that you can be prepared for any situation that arises.

❖ FACT: Your pay scale can be 'frozen'.

Those 'steps' you see on the teacher's pay scale your district provides are not guaranteed in most school systems. The school board can 'freeze' the steps, leaving you on, say, step 3 for several years so that you get paid like a step 3 (3rd year) teacher even if it's your 6th or 7th year. It all comes down to budget cuts. Most school systems have no contractual obligation to move you automatically along to the next step. *BOTTOM LINE: Make financial decisions based on your current, not projected, salary.*

❖ FACT: Pay increases do not necessarily occur each year.

Although most of us have set pay scales, teachers aren't assured of getting cost-of-living raises each year. The school board and union may agree on a 1%-7% pay increase, but you may not get anything in certain years (and 1-2% isn't much in itself). I encourage you to become active in your teacher's union and fight for the top dollar your professional expertise warrants. Sometimes unions will sacrifice pay increases for other benefits (such as lowered health insurance premiums), or will settle for increases that are distributed over the course of several years (such as a 6% increase over a 3 year period, meaning a 2% increase each year).

It's important to be aware of what you're earning and what other teachers in your state are earning, but don't allow it to consume you. We all knew teaching was not a top-paying profession when we entered it, so there's no point in becoming bitter about that fact now. **BOTTOM LINE: *Learn to love your job during the (many) years it takes to reach the top salary.***

❖ FACT: Working conditions vary WIDELY from school to school.

There are teachers who have fully-paid health benefits for their entire families, while others aren't even offered the option to pay for an individual healthcare plan out of pocket. There are teachers making 100K working in beautiful, brand-new schools with more computers in their rooms than students, and some earning 26K to teach forty-five kids who don't speak English in a classroom with no windows and mold creeping up the walls. Some teachers get three hours of planning time a day, others get none whatsoever. Some teachers get several thousand dollars of discretionary funds to spend on their classrooms, others aren't even provided crayons and scissors. These are all American classrooms—I won't even discuss international conditions in which there may be two hundred students in a room with a dirt floor and no textbooks.

My point is, don't be shocked when you find out how much better or worse a teacher in another school has it, even if she teaches just down the road. There's almost always a trade-off: one school might have larger classrooms but less storage and cabinet space; one school district might pay more initially, but offer smaller step increases.

You have to weigh everything involved when deciding where to teach. I took at 12K pay cut and lost my pension in Maryland when I moved to Florida. Spending my afternoons under the palm trees on the beach is truly worth twelve grand to me…but by most people's standards, I was insane. You have to decide where YOU want to be and learn to love where YOU'RE at, and don't be swayed when you hear about how fabulous other schools and systems are. If and when you find something that you really believe is better, go for it, and don't look back. But remember…**BOTTOM LINE: *The grass is always greener.***

❖ FACT: Your planning time is not guaranteed everyday.

Your union contract probably says it is, but it's not uncommon for teachers to have their planning time taken because of practicalities. Many times, there will be meetings and conferences scheduled during your planning time by administration. Or, the special classes themselves may be cancelled. In one school district I worked in, there were no funds to supply substitutes for specials teachers (music, art, etc.), so when the teachers were out, I had to keep the kids during my break. That might mean I had to wait several hours before being able to use the bathroom, and those last minute photocopies or urgent phone calls would just have to be put off. In another school system, the funds were provided, but the school had such a bad reputation that no subs would work there. My current district is the only one I've ever taught in where this is not an issue. If it's a problem in your school, you'll have to get creative: show an educational movie or give an independent assignment during your specials time so you can get your work done, and have a colleague watch your class while you sprint off to the restroom. ***BOTTOM LINE: Don't save critical tasks for planning time that you might not have.***

❖ FACT: Grade books and lesson plan books are collected at the end of the year in most school districts.

Be sure to keep your records up to date, even if no one from your administration has been checking. Theoretically, the school system can be audited, and if you haven't included the things you were supposed to, there can be problems. Make sure you have the required elements (your orientation should explain this—if not, ask your team leader). Know your union contract (or union representative) well because MANY administrators ask teachers to put things in their lesson plans that they are not contractually required to write. ***BOTTOM LINE: Know and follow the expectations for keeping your grade/plan books up to date.***

❖ FACT: Children cannot be 'forced' to say or stand for the Pledge of Allegiance in some states.

You'll have to check your state laws for this, but it's a hot topic in many places. Be cautious if there is a child who does not want to cooperate, either for political/philosophical issues or just out of defiance: the pledge is a risky time to try coercing a child to do what you've asked. **BOTTOM LINE: Make no assumptions: many school traditions are now being questioned and challenged in court.**

❖ **FACT: Most school systems have a *mandatory* reporting act for suspected child abuse.**

Okay, this one actually IS in your contract...but it still comes as a surprise to many teachers. As an educator, you have a professional obligation to alert the proper authorities about any suspicion of child abuse or neglect...and your teaching certification can be revoked if you don't report. Your district will train you to recognize symptoms of abuse and how to follow appropriate protocol. This is an issue that teachers must take seriously, because we HAVE to report our suspicions, even when it's difficult to do. Unfortunately, you will probably have to file a report at least once at some point during your career—it may even be regarding a colleague who is abusive to students. **BOTTOM LINE: Be mentally prepared to do the right thing, even when it's uncomfortable.**

❖ **FACT: Your teaching manuals will not tell you what information your kids actually need to learn.**

That's a simple way of stating that your curriculum is probably not fully aligned with state standards. It means that your teaching manuals will include skills that kids don't need to master at your grade level, and will be lacking concepts that the state mandates for instruction. For example, your math teacher's guide might have an entire chapter on three-digit division, but in your state, students in the grade level you teach might only be responsible for dividing by two-digit numbers.

Who is responsible for identifying the gaps? The school system should (through pacing guides, curriculum outlines, and grade level specifications) but most districts don't do this well, especially since state standards and curricular series change over the years. Ultimately, YOU, the classroom teacher, are responsible for checking your teaching manuals against state standards to make sure you teach everything you're supposed to. Generally, textbooks cover more than what the state requires, so if you teach the whole book, the worst you've done is expose kids to concepts they'll learn in the next grade. But if you know which lessons to skip, you'll have more time to reinforce the skills that your students do need to master. **BOTTOM LINE: Teach the standards, not the textbook.**

❖ FACT: You are not a slave to your teaching manuals.

The majority of us actually have much more control over what goes on in our classrooms than we realize. For instance, most districts have a few "musts" for literacy instruction, but teachers can structure the block any way they see fit for their kids. Post a general schedule which fits district guidelines, but shorten and lengthen the amount of time you actually spend on specific aspects of your instruction in accordance with students' needs. Even if you must do things in a specified order, you can still switch up the materials you use as long as they are approved.

Question the status quo when it stifles your creativity. In general, textbooks are to be used a resource for teaching the state standards—you don't have to read every story in your reading series. And even if you are required to cover each story, you don't have to teach each one the same way—do some on the overhead projector as shared reading, some as read-alouds, some as partner activities...get the idea? You don't have to have kids do each page in all of their workbooks. You may not even have to use workbooks at all! If you do, try sending some pages home, making some into centers, doing a few on dry erase boards in a small group, and so on.

You know your kids best. Stay current on professional research so that you can discover new techniques that are backed by studies proving their effectiveness. Teaching and learning are supposed to be enjoyable and purposeful. **BOTTOM LINE: Think outside the box—you DO have the option to eliminate or restructure what's not working.**

❖ FACT: Your teaching assignment is tentative until after the open enrollment period.

This policy varies slightly by school district, but essentially, here's how it works.

Every school system has a set period of 'open enrollment' (possibly known by another term) which means that the district is monitoring how many kids are in each classroom within each school. This period usually lasts through the 4th-6th week of school. At any time during that period, someone in the school or district administration can determine that your school enrollment is too low, and transfer teachers to other schools with higher-than-predicted enrollment. Teachers with the least amount of tenure (whoever was hired last) are transferred first. Conversely, if your school is overcrowded, the district may send more teachers to you so that your class sizes go down.

More commonly, involuntary transfers happen within schools. If your principal hired you to teach second grade, but the second grade classes are much smaller than anticipated, you can get moved to another grade level. This can and does happen regularly in many places, even AFTER school has begun. Please don't start hyperventilating, but one year, there were a few teachers in my school who were moved to another grade TWICE after school started! They had to move classrooms and begin with new students three times in August. The intra-school transfers have little, if anything, to do with tenure: the principal moves whoever she thinks would be the best fit at the grade level in need of a teacher.

It's important to accept this as a fact of life and not get hung up on what grade you will be teaching. There's a slim chance that you will get moved, so don't get worked up. Just keep the possibility in the back of your mind so you're not caught off guard if the situation does arise. **BOTTOM LINE: Flexibility is always the name of the game in teaching.**

❖ FACT: Your principal can move you around at his discretion.

At the end of the school year, you'll get a tentative teaching assignment. If your administration wants you to be in another classroom even though you've taught in the same room for ten years, guess what, you're moving! If your principal says you're teaching first grade even though you were hired to teach fifth, surprise, you'll be teaching fifth grade next year!

Administrators are supposed to make decisions that benefit the school as a whole, not cater to teacher's individual preferences, although some principals are more cognizant of teacher's desires than others. Some principals rarely move teachers, preferring to keep their staff happy and not rock the boat. Others don't like to let teachers get stuck in a rut and move people around regularly. They don't have to give you a reason and many of them don't. Your choices are to accept it gracefully, politely request to stay in the same grade, or transfer to another school. ***BOTTOM LINE: Be ready to love teaching at any grade level, in any classroom.***

❖ **FACT: The principal has the ultimate say in how your school is run and can often override district and state mandates.**

District employees in my school system are fond of saying, "The buck stops with your principal" as a disclaimer to anything they recommend. School principals generally determine the amount of time you devote to each subject, the teacher dress code, the policy on if you have recess and how long it is, whether teachers are allowed to leave early without being docked pay, pacing and planning guides which outline instruction, etc. I know of MANY situations in which schools do not follow mandates from higher authorities because the principal has overridden them either overtly (because she is allowed to) or covertly (by re-appropriating funds and finding innumerable loopholes in the regulations).

Your response to these types of situations may determine your treatment by administration. For example, I know of a principal who ordered teachers to let kids into the classroom twenty minutes early every morning. Some of the teachers approached the union with their concerns, and the union representative informed the staff and administration that no teacher can be forced to let children in before the first bell. So, several teachers stopped doing it. The principal subtly made those teachers targets for extra scrutiny, e.g., collecting their lesson plans weekly instead of annually and doing more classroom walk-throughs.

Conversely, principal overrides can work in your favor. For example, in my district, all classroom doors are supposed to be locked at all times, even when students are inside, which is a huge hassle. Many principals don't enforce this and teachers can even leave their doors propped open (which is a fire violation). There are thousands of regulations in every school system, all of which were established at different times by different people and are not enforced consistently across the district. ***BOTTOM LINE: Reality within your school may not match higher mandates because school climate is ultimately determined by your administrators. Be prepared to pick your battles.***

❖ FACT: State class size caps are not absolute.

Your state probably mandates how many kids can be assigned to a classroom. There are usually different requirements for different grade levels, with the smallest classes in the lower grades. However, most school districts have found loopholes in the formula and what you get in your classroom may not have anything to do with what you thought was a hard and fast rule. Schools may factor in teacher aides, Title I assistants, and other school employees so that it seems as if the student-teacher ratio is low, but the actual number of kids in the classroom with each teacher is much higher. The No Child Left Behind (NCLB) Act has allowed states to do this for years, although the formula was supposed to have changed during the 2007-2008 school year so that student-teacher ratios could not include other personnel. It's important to remember that NCLB is not fully funding these mandatory class size reductions, so states are left fumbling for a way to comply. ***BOTTOM LINE: If your cap size is 20 kids, expect to have more and be pleasantly surprised if you don't.***

❖ FACT: You may get a new student during the last week of school.

Some schools have very transient populations, meaning that students are constantly transferring in and out. There are teachers who gain and lose students two or three times a month, all year long! Even if your school has a pretty steady enrollment, be prepared for new students to enter even at the end of the year. ***BOTTOM LINE: Always have an extra desk and materials set up for new kids.***

❖ FACT: There are some parents with whom you will not have any contact all year.

This is more common in less affluent areas, but don't be shocked if June rolls around and there are families you have never seen. You'll schedule conferences and they won't show up, you'll telephone them and they won't answer or return your calls, and getting papers signed and returned will be all but impossible. There will also be parents who never check their children's backpacks: you will look inside the bags and see papers from four months ago crumpled up at the bottom. Sometimes it's because parents don't care about their kids' education, but it's important not to jump to that conclusion, because uninvolved parents are usually too busy trying to work through personal and financial problems to tune into their children as much as they would like.

For example, I had a child one year who was working two years below grade level, was constantly in trouble for behavioral issues, and failed the state standardized test. The parents did not respond to a single note home, phone call, email, weekly evaluation, progress report, report card, or conference request. I knew that their electricity was off for weeks at a time because they didn't pay the bills, and they were under a tremendous amount of stress at home. However, on the last day of school, the child walked into the classroom carrying a vase of bent and soiled silk flowers and a card signed by mom thanking me for everything I had done for her child. Even though she didn't respond to my communication, she knew I was working hard with her child, and she appreciated it. ***BOTTOM LINE: Be prepared to keep reaching out to parents even when they don't respond, because most of them really DO care about their kids.***

❖ FACT: New teachers often walk into empty classrooms because the veteran teachers 'loot' everything that isn't nailed down!

This has happened in every school I have ever worked in: a teacher quits or retires in June, and her coworkers swoop in like vultures for extra tables, bookshelves, overhead projectors, desks, manipulatives, and anything else they can grab. For some reason this is considered standard protocol: since the room doesn't belong to anyone at the moment, everything inside is fair game. The unwritten rule seems to be, once the new teacher has begun putting her belongings inside or started setting up the room, things are off limits. In a few schools, teachers will steal things from one another's packed up rooms at the end of the school year (including items people have purchased with their own money), but that's frowned upon by almost everyone: it's like going into someone's home and walking off with whatever you like. Check with other teachers to determine whether there is a problem with teachers taking materials at your school.

Also, ask someone you trust about what items you should have in your room (number of tables, a globe, CD player, etc.), and what you should do to get what you don't have (e.g., ask the principal, ask the person in charge of ordering supplies, or go around to different classrooms to see if teachers have an 'extra' of something). ***BOTTOM LINE: If you're new, expect to have things missing from your room, and be prepared to hunt them down! If you're experienced, make sure you have your name on EVERYTHING!***

❖ **FACT: If your school reimburses you for purchases, you may not be able to keep them if you change schools.**

Keep a detailed account of what you spend. If you transfer to another school, this will help prove that YOU actually purchased each item. You may want to keep a receipt binder or folder with all of your purchases, and write your name on items that belong to you personally. It's also smart to keep a copy of the supply list that you turn into the office each year. If an item such as a stapler gets broken, write that the particular item was 'damaged beyond repair.' This will save you a lot of headache if you must do an exit audit from the school, and could possibly save you from having to pay the school back for items.

It is also important to remember that because you have used an item for years, that does not make it yours. If something was purchased with school funds, you cannot take it with you to another school location (even within the same district). Many principals will also not allow you to remove from the room anything bought with school funds if you change grade levels. This is to help prevent new teachers from having a bare room, and to keep resources divided up equitably. ***BOTTOM LINE: Keep a detailed account of what you spend and what you have been reimbursed for.***

A Final Note

Please don't let this information overwhelm or discourage you! It's meant to be a heads up, not a list of faults within the teaching profession. All of these scenarios may not apply to you, and even if they do, it's not enough to make teaching impossible or even extraordinarily difficult. The idea I want you to walk away with is this: Always expect the unexpected in teaching, so that nothing catches you off guard, and you'll be able to maintain a positive attitude. ☺

Chapter 34: Timesaving Strategies
Discovering how to be a teacher and still have a personal life

Two questions that I hear new teachers ask repeatedly are, "Will I be able to have a personal life once school starts?" and "Is a 40-hour workweek really possible in this field?" The answer to both questions is YES! You do NOT have to work 10, 12, or 14 hour days to ensure that your students are successful. Many excellent teachers have learned how to work within the hours they're paid to put in. Working on the evenings and weekends is not a necessity—there is no point in carrying home a huge bag of work that you are too tired to do.

YOU SHOULD NOT FEEL GUILTY FOR WANTING TO LEAVE AT 3:00! You have a family and friends. You need rest. Teaching is stressful, and it's important to have a break. Don't let anyone imply that if you were truly dedicated to the profession, you would come in early and leave late everyday. It's simply not true. You should work extra hours when you need to, not out of obligation.

Working overtime without pay is almost unheard of in other professions. Think about it: There is always crime to be fought. Are police officers expected to work a few hours after their shift each day, just to get the job done? NO. They do the best they can with the time they are given, and then go home to their families. No one insinuates that if officers worked an extra 20 hours for free every week, the world would be a safer place. People simply don't expect that. We should hold the same expectations for teachers.

Check your teaching contract to find out how many hours per day you are required to work. Depending on the school system, I have been contracted to work from 7.05-7.30 hours a day—that's around 35 hours per week. Because 40 hours is considered 'standard' in most fields, I selected that amount of time as reasonable for me to work each week. That means I can come in about forty-five minutes early each day (or stay late) and still not exceed 40 hours.

A few things to keep in mind as I explain how to prepare yourself and your classroom for a 40-hour workweek:

- **You will have to choose the amount of hours that is reasonable for you**. Forty hours may be too much or too little time, or you may want to vary it by week. There is no magic number for everyone, but I do think it's wise to set a limit for yourself and stick to it so that you don't end up staying at school until sundown every night.

- **It will be very, very difficult to work 40-hour weeks at the beginning (and possibly the end) of the school year.** I always prepare to work as many hours as it takes at first. 70-hour weeks are not atypical for me in August and September (weekends included). I really don't mind, though, because I am confident that it is a temporary sacrifice. The process is similar to teaching classroom procedures—very time consuming and tiring in August, but the pay-offs continue throughout the year.

- **First-year teachers, and teachers who are new to the grade level, school, or school system, will also have a tough time working 40-hour weeks at first.** They might have to settle for alternating 8-hour days and 10-hour days, or spending Sundays working from home. But, if they truly want to stick to a 40-hour workweek, it is possible. One year I was new to my grade level, school, district, *and* state and managed to get to a 40-hour week by October.

So, how is it done? What follows is a list of decisions I have made and methods of structuring my time that have resulted in a fairly consistent 40-hour work week:

☑ **Choose your grade level carefully.**

Any grade above 2nd will require you to spend significantly more time grading papers. The younger the students, the fewer the problems on the workbook page and the shorter the essay and written response. I could grade most of my second graders' papers simply by glancing over them. With third graders, I often have to sit down with a teacher's guide to grade, and must dissect multi-paragraph assignments. There is obviously nothing wrong with teaching older kids; however, you should know that grading papers will typically be a much bigger hassle for you.

☑ **Make your grading system as simple as the school district will allow.**

As discussed in Chapter 24, you don't need to grade every paper, and there's no need for complicated weighting systems. Do whatever is best for your teaching situation, but don't make things harder than they have to be.

☑ **Don't be pressured into serving on any board that you don't want to.**

Most schools require you to be on a set number of committees, such as three, but some people will guilt trip teachers into doing five, six, seven...or more. These committees mean more meetings, less planning time, and additional obligations. If you are the type of person that enjoys serving your school, by all means, go for it! Your contributions are needed and appreciated! But if you are looking for simple ways to reduce the amount of tasks you have at school (especially those that do not directly benefit your students), staying away from the 'extras' is something to think about. You could say, "Since this is my first year here, I just want to focus on my kids and what's going on in my classroom. But it sounds really interesting—if you still need me next year, let me know." When people press the issue, just smile. "Sounds like a great committee. Good luck to you all this year."

☑ **KNOW YOUR CONTRACT, and only attend the number of after-hours activities and planning time meetings that are required.**

I've worked in three school districts: my contract in two of them stipulated that teachers were to stay after hours no more than twice a month for meetings, and the third district did not allow mandatory after-school meetings at all. In each of these districts, teachers could be required to stay for evening activities (such as Open House, PTA meetings, or award assemblies) only twice per year.

Therefore, if the staff is continually asked to do more than that (except in emergencies), we respectfully go to our principal and ask if anything can be done. Only once were we told no, and at that point we approached our union representative and asked him how the staff could address the problem. (In some situations, you may want to go to your union rep first: if you're not sure what the protocol is at your school, ask your mentor or team leader.)

The same goes for incessant during-hours meetings: grade level, IEP, professional development, new teacher workshops, and so on. Your contract should limit these so that the majority of your planning time can actually be spent planning. If it's not, don't be afraid to speak up.

☑ **Spend as much time organizing your room as you need, especially in the beginning of the year.**

Take six hours to reorganize your classroom library. Spent an hour trying to decide where you want your centers to be. Redo your filing system three times until you can find every paper any time you need it. Do whatever it takes to make things go more smoothly for you throughout the year. If you have ever spent twenty minutes looking for a paper you just had and realized it was buried under a pile of 'miscellaneous' stacks, you know how important this is. Make organization a priority and you will never regret it.

☑ **Keep your room neat and clean all day long—don't wait until the end of the day (or later!).**

Straighten the desks, get trash and student belongings off the floor, ensure posters are securely fashioned to the walls and not falling off, put materials away neatly, clear or at least straighten piles of papers on your desk, and so on. Basically, make sure that everyone in the class is picking up after themselves. There are many reasons why straightening up is important: you are modeling cleanliness for the kids, the classroom runs more smoothly, messes don't pile up and become more time-consuming in the long run, and your room is ready to receive visitors at any time. Anyone who pops in during the day will leave with an excellent impression about what you are doing with your kids. *Remember, very few people will ever watch you teach, but dozens and dozens of people will see how you maintain your students' learning environment. Your classroom is a reflection of you and how you teach.*

☑ **Delegate mundane tasks.**

If you don't have parent volunteers or an aide, give coloring, cutting, manipulative-making, center-making, and other simple tasks to a parent to do from home. Even older children can help—many teachers have their own kids come to the school after hours and would be happy to send them to your room to assist you. Or, send the materials home with a teacher who has a teenager in need of community service hours. Keep your eyes open, and you'll find someone who would enjoy doing the tasks that are too time-consuming for you to handle. Many parents who work during the day and therefore can't volunteer in the classroom are very willing to do things at home. Ask them—you WILL be pleasantly surprised with the response!

☑ Don't make a lot of photocopies.

In addition to the arguments for saving paper and avoiding overuse of dittos in instruction, standing at the copier wastes hours and hours of teachers' time. Not to mention the time lost while messing with broken and jammed copy machines...

☑ Multi-task whenever possible.

Grade papers while waiting for meetings to begin, laminate your materials while your copies finish running, or make parent phone calls while sitting at a traffic light on your way to work (use a hands-free device so you can continue to talk while you drive). The only time between 7:30 and 3:00 that I am only doing one thing is lunchtime. I am constantly on the move and never sit idly by. It's tiring, but I am able to go home at a decent hour.

☑ Use your prep time to do miscellaneous tasks that spontaneously arise, rather than depend on that time to do essential tasks.

If your school is perfect, disregard this. But I, for one, have been burned way too many times by leaving something important to be done during my planning time and then finding out my time had to be cancelled. Even if your school always hires substitutes for specialist teachers, you may get a phone call, or get summoned to the principal's office, or get tied up talking to a parent or co-worker in the hall: planning time is short and little things like this quickly eat away at it. So, use your time to return phone calls and emails, straighten up the room, grade papers, and so on.

☑ **When you put in extra hours, try to choose times when few other people are at school.**

I used to come in an hour early so I could remain completely undisturbed for at least forty-five minutes before activity in the hallways began. There's no point in working long hours if someone is constantly coming in and asking you for something or you're tempted to wander next door to 'chat'.

☑ **Indicate in your lesson plans what materials are needed, and gather your supplies each morning.**

In my plans, I underline any materials that I do not already have on hand: copies to be made, special manipulatives, materials I need to make, etc. By gathering the materials first thing in the morning, I know if I need to get anything else and have time to do so.

☑ **Make the most of Morning Work or Bell Work.**

When your kids come in the room, there should be something on the board for them to get started on right away. While they are doing Morning Work, you should be able to: complete attendance; check all homework (if you are grading them on whether the homework is done or not done, this is very quick—put a checkmark on it and give it back to them!); read and respond to parents' notes; and so on. Morning Work, in my classroom, does not stop until I have finished these tasks. I'm just not going to leave a messy pile for myself to deal with later: half-checked homework, a random note from a parent, someone's picture money just lying out, etc. When I am comfortable with beginning our day, we start.

☑ **Structure your daily schedule so that you have 'downtime' when you need it most.**

I have always found it hard to pick up the kids from lunch or specials, bring them in the classroom, and immediately start teaching the next subject. I don't think any of us are ready to focus! So one year, I put our thirty minutes of independent reading time right after lunch. The kids came in, relaxed, and read on their own for a half an hour while I got out the math manipulatives, looked over the lesson, and so on. I used bathroom and drink breaks or class meetings as downtime after specials (right before the exhausting two-hour language arts block began). Even a five-minute warm up can be sufficient. Downtime doesn't mean the kids aren't doing something worthwhile; it just means that you as the teacher are not responsible for instructing at that moment. If you have report cards coming up or some special education documentation that has to be turned in by the end of the day, it's okay to schedule additional downtime for yourself by giving the kids an activity you know they can do independently. With extenuating circumstances, it is perfectly fine to shorten a lesson so that the kids can work on their own while you get things done.

☑ **Write the deadlines for tedious paperwork on a large calendar that you can't miss, then do the work whenever it's convenient.**

I'm not advocating procrastination. But if you have a doctor's appointment tomorrow and you know you'll be sitting in the waiting room for half an hour, why stay late at school today to fill out a child study packet? As long as you are mindful of the deadlines, you can schedule time for these tasks later on.

☑ **Use an organized to-do list.**

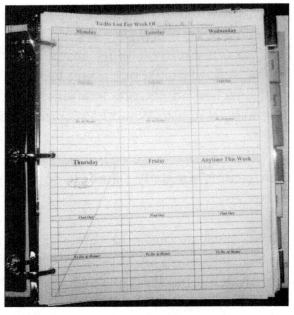

I created a form (available on my website) that has one half column for each day and one for things that could be done at anytime during the week. I write only my most immediate concerns on a particular day's list and make sure everything is crossed off before I go home. There is a separate section in each day's half column for things 'To Find Out', in which I list questions I need to ask or issues to follow up with, and I check that part of the to-do list each time I leave my classroom during the day. Also, there's a section for things to do at home (which is a useful place to make note of anything you want to bring to or from your house, as well).

Chapter 35: Ending the Year on a High Note
Maintaining order and keeping your sanity during the close-out process

Aren't you WORN OUT by June?? Personally, I don't understand where other teachers find the time and energy to do big elaborate projects at the end of the year. I've always got so much paperwork and packing to do that just the thought of organizing a field day, excursion, or picnic exhausts me!

If you're looking for fun and easy-to-implement ideas to make the end of the year special, try the suggestions that follow. Then read on for ways to keep your sanity when you've still got three chapters to teach, a stack of paperwork to complete, the temperature's ninety degrees, and everyone just wants to be at the pool!

How to Keep Kids On-Task When Spring Fever's in the Air

Stay On a Predictable Daily Schedule!!!

One of the most common mistakes teachers make at the end of the year is to get relaxed with their routines and daily schedule. Here's a typical scenario: the teacher is feeling tired and wants to give himself and the kids a break. He decides not to give regular math Morning Work and lets the class do a word search page instead. The kids get excited and forget to follow the rules for staying on-task and completing Morning Work independently. The teacher gets irritated and blames the problem on 'spring fever'.

After that, he figures there's no way the kids will be attentive during the regular vocabulary lesson, so he gives a partner reading assignment instead. The kids become even more wound up and start chattering loudly. The teacher assumes the problem can't be helped and figures the class has been pretty good all year, so he allows students to get noisier than he would normally. The kids realize their teacher is busy doing paperwork and isn't addressing the noise level, so they stop pretending to read altogether. They start calling out to each other, walking around the room, and being silly. The teacher gets totally fed up, yells at the kids, and takes them outside for an early recess so he can get some fresh air. The kids realize that their poor behavior has frustrated the teacher but it's also resulted in extra time outside, so there's no incentive to follow directions when they re-enter the classroom.

This downward spiral can be avoided rather simply: Keep everything the same as much as possible until a week before school ends. Give the same type of tasks in the same order and use a predictable routine in your lessons. Stick to your regular schedule, and when it's interrupted by assemblies and other activities beyond your control, keep the rest of the day as tightly structured as possible.

Many teachers (myself included) like to change instruction and assignments after standardized testing is over for the year and do more creative and hands-on activities. This cannot be done at the expense of having a regular schedule! Determine your new routines and expectations and hold kids to them. Many of your co-workers will not do this and you will be tempted to become lackadaisical. Just remember that teachers who maintain a regular schedule in the classroom have fewer behavioral problems from their students. Kids thrive under predictability. You knew this fact and planned accordingly at the beginning of the year, so don't be fooled into thinking that your kids will suddenly be angels without any structure for the entire month of May.

High-Interest Lessons for the Last Week

It's much harder for kids to stay focused when there's only a handful of days left. Try doing more partner/group work and hands-on activities. You can also give a few high-interest creative projects that will hold students' attention for longer periods of time than regular pencil and paper work. I like to assign Internet research and have kids create presentations for the class on topics they're interested in. Here are some specific activity ideas to use during the last week of school—you can find links for more information on most of these at TheCornerstoneForTeachers.com:

Multi-Day Activities for the Last Week of School

➢ design Super Subject Days—devote each day to one subject area
➢ have a reading celebration with various activities related to books
➢ ask kids to share their skills and knowledge in Teach the Teacher Days
➢ do a beach mini unit or try some ocean-inspired activities
➢ trade classes with your colleagues to do a favorite lesson or activity

Academic and Review Activities

➢ write and illustrate autobiographies
➢ make mini books about favorite activities from each month of the year
➢ write a letter to next year's class
➢ complete creative group research projects
➢ perform in a "What We Know Math Show" or contest
➢ take a nature walk and write poems
➢ enjoy your silent reading time outside
➢ conduct science investigations with bubbles or other fun materials
➢ make kites with acrostics or poems on them and go fly a kite!

Just for the Fun of It

➢ create a word search with the class' names (use a free online resource)
➢ make class tee-shirts as a souvenir for the year
➢ create signed picture frames with a group photo inside
➢ decorate thank-you notes for school staff
➢ design a new bulletin board for next year's class
➢ have a graduation or end-of-year ceremony
➢ give silly or serious end-of-year awards

Keep Procedures and Routines Firmly in Place

If you fill the months of April, May, and June with engaging, appropriate lessons within the structure of a predictable daily schedule, students will have no excuse for not following your procedures. Therefore, don't allow them to get away with behaviors they weren't allowed to exhibit earlier in the year. It's extremely tempting to think, well, there's only a few weeks left, who cares if they're chatty in the hallway and hanging around the pencil sharpeners instead of doing their Morning Work? But I speak from experience when I say that slowly easing up on your expectations will backfire completely. It just adds to the environment of chaos that students are slowly creating and makes it harder to get the class back on track.

Play the Procedures Review game (explained in Chapter 9) to make sure kids have your expectations fresh in their minds, and enforce them consistently. The rules have to be the same every day, all day long. If final report cards are turned in and students are headed to the cafeteria for their last awards assembly, they still have to follow your routines. That means when they play around while lining up, you still say, "Oh, I guess we're not ready to go after all. Everyone walk back to your seats, and we'll try again." If you let it slide, they'll be bouncing off the walls during the entire assembly. Don't get tired or lazy when you're approaching the finish line!

Instead of falling into the negative spiral of punishment for increased misbehavior at the end of the year, try providing more rewards for correct behavior. Tell the kids that you understand how hard it is to still be in school, and that you wish it were summer vacation, too! Explain that you'll be giving extra rewards to students who choose to be self-disciplined and make good choices all the way through the last day of school. Give out beads or tokens (whatever your class behavior system is) more frequently, and acknowledge positive actions as you do so ("You chose to put your papers away neatly in your folder instead of just shoving them in your desk. Thanks for being so responsible!"). Your compliments will reinforce the rules and procedures you expect students to follow at a time when they've likely begun to forget them. You can also randomly give free time passes or other prizes for students who are following directions and getting their work done.

If your class is really and truly 'done' for the year, allow students fifteen minutes at the end of the day to talk, read, or draw with a partner IF they have stayed on-task and you were able to get through all of your lesson plans. If students need a visual reminder for this, write the words 'Free Time' on the board, and erase a letter each time you have to wait for them to follow procedures (or in a positive spin, leave the board blank and write a letter each time the class is attentive and completes their assignments correctly). Each letter can stand for one or two minutes of free time. This is an awesome motivator if used temporarily.

Deconstructing the Room in an Orderly, Structured Way

Keeping the Class Engaged in Meaningful Tasks

The problem with end-of-year room deconstruction and close-out arises when the teacher has things to do but the kids don't. It's tempting to give coloring sheets or other non-academic work, but we all have a lot of curriculum to cover, and it's really not fair to waste kids' time with busy work. Also, children are perceptive—they know when you're just trying to get them out of your hair, and you'll end up spending the whole day trying to keep them on-task.

To keep the class engaged in worthwhile learning activities, I give a special work packet or project during the last week of school. For example, I created a fun ten-page packet in which students research the effects of school uniforms, survey the community for their opinions, graph results, list pros and cons, make decision trees, calculate the costs, identify fact vs. opinion, and so on, culminating in a letter to the PTA arguing for or against a uniform policy for the following school year.

While the kids work, I assist with the parts they need help with and periodically circulate throughout the room to make sure everyone knows what they're doing. However, the work packets free me up to spend most of my time overseeing the students that are assisting with various end-of-the-year tasks.

Jobs for Kids to Do

Children love to help. Unfortunately, sometimes it's more work to train and supervise them than it is to do it all yourself! Here are some jobs that I have had students successfully complete in the past:

- ➢ taking down bulletin board borders and paper
- ➢ taking down posters and student work
- ➢ collecting and trashing staples from bulletin boards
- ➢ putting away chart strips
- ➢ setting up the calendar for next August
- ➢ taking down the word wall
- ➢ taking down the door display

➤ packing books up

➤ recording textbook numbers and stacking texts on shelves

➤ cleaning chalkboards and whiteboards

➤ wiping down shelves, windowsills, cabinets, etc.

➤ labeling everything with masking tape marked with the teacher's name

➤ returning materials to the library, science lab, etc.

➤ reorganizing math manipulatives

➤ straightening the class library

➤ testing out dry erase markers to see which ones need to be thrown away

➤ taking student name labels off of materials

➤ relabeling or sorting materials for next year

➤ taking inventory of center materials that need to be replenished

My suggestion is to have students complete these tasks on the second-to-last day of school. If you do it sooner, it will be very difficult for the kids to concentrate on academic work because the room screams, "School's out!"

I don't allow my kids to ask if there's anything I want them to do because they'll drive me crazy! Instead, I assign interesting, worthwhile tasks for the children to complete and then call them over in pairs to help me. When the helpers finish their assigned tasks, they go back to completing work until I need them again. I rotate through each pair of students as many times as needed until I run out of jobs.

Preparing in Advance

There's lots to be done to prepare your classroom for the summer, but if you plan things out ahead of time, the process can be completed very smoothly. Here are a few ideas for pacing yourself:

A Month Before School Ends

◆ **List the big organizational jobs that need to be done, and assign them to specific weeks.** For example, during your planning or down time during the second week of May, you could clean out your file cabinet; during the third week, clean out the storage closet, containers, and posters; the fourth week reorganize centers and manipulatives; and so on.

♦ **Decide on any special end-of-year activities you would like to do with students**. Notify parents, get administrative permission, and collect materials and supplies.

♦ **Talk to your team leader and colleagues about your school's specific traditions and expectations.** There may be an end-of-year picnic, party, or ceremony that you need to begin preparing for. Also find out whether you'll be getting a checklist with close-out tasks on it, and what typically needs to be done to finish the year.

♦ **Catch up on any organizational tasks you've been meaning to get around to, such as filing.** Try to get your room as clutter-free as possible so you have less to pack and/or put away when school lets out.

Two Weeks Before School Ends

♦ **Begin filling out any close-out paperwork you need to complete.**

♦ **Complete special end-of-year activities you planned.** Do NOT schedule an open house, picnic, trip, or other big event for the last week of school! You'll be frazzled, the kids will be hyper, and the room will be a wreck because you're in the process of deconstructing it. You will definitely not want any parents or visitors in your room when it's half undone. Do the elaborate end-of-year activities early on and the more low-key stuff on the last few days of school.

♦ **Return borrowed materials to their owners.** Over time, you may have accumulated other people's videos, books, teacher resources, staplers, etc.

♦ **Keep yourself from falling behind on grading.** The last thing you want when report cards are due is a huge stack of ungraded papers you've never gotten around to.

♦ **Inventory any materials for which you are required to submit a list.**

- **Complete any necessary paperwork for your students' placement next year.** This may include retention lists and letters, placement cards, and so on.

One Week Before School Ends

- **Slowly begin collecting textbooks and filling out any associated paperwork.**

- **Finish grading all papers and average student grades for the quarter and year.** (Most school districts don't require you to keep taking grades during the last week or two of school.)

- **Complete report cards.** Fill out fourth quarter award certificates if your school does honor roll assemblies.

- **Put together students' cumulative records and files.**

Second-to-Last Day of School:

- **List all of the kid-friendly tasks that need to be done, breaking them down into very small, specific jobs for pairs of students to do.** Examples are listed previously in this chapter. Pair up more responsible students with less responsible students, and call two or three partners at once to complete their jobs. If you call too many at one time, it will be very chaotic—most kids should be sitting down doing their written work, and if they are playing around, they should not be allowed to help. Your main duty during this time is to supervise and facilitate. My class of third graders de-constructed the entire classroom in less than two hours one year using this method.

- **Label all furniture with your name and room number so it does not "disappear" over the summer.**

- **Begin having administration, grade level chairs, specialists, etc., sign off on any inventories you are required to submit.** (Typically, schools provide an end-of-year checklist that must be signed by various people.)

- **Have plastic bags ready for the kids who don't bring their backpacks to school but still need to carry home papers and other belongings.** Some kids (or parents) will assume the children don't need backpacks and won't send them despite your requests. Also, some schools don't allow backpacks on the last day or two of school because children use their backpacks to bring water guns and last-day prank accessories to school, or fill their backpacks with school materials they've stolen. I once taught in a school that didn't allow backpacks at the end of the year because the children had a tradition of bringing large rocks to throw at teacher's cars.

- **Send home all student papers, workbooks, and class work materials.** This way, if you forget to return anything to the kids, you can always send it home on the last day of school. Sending things home in advance also keeps kids from being too weighed down with stuff on the hectic last day.

The Last Day of School

- **Students can do math problems or handwriting practice in shaving cream on their desks.** This gets the top squeaky clean and is lots of fun.

- **Have students completely clean out their desks and scrub them down with sponges and soapy water.** Gather three or four buckets and sponges and demonstrate what to do (and not to do) and what an empty desk looks like. Then call on a volunteer to model as you use reinforcement narration and performance feedback. Ask a few kids at a time to stop doing their independent work and take a turn with the buckets and sponges on their own desks. Take away the privilege of cleaning if they are playing or making a mess.

- **Collect or send home students' school supplies.** Wait until the end of the day when you are sure kids will not need pencils or crayons anymore. You can ask for class donations if you want—lots of my kids give me their old glue, rulers, and so on, since they will all want new supplies for the fall, anyway.

- **Play games and enjoy the kids!** This is the last time you'll all be together. By the afternoon, you should have everything, or most things, done anyway, so relax and spend time talking and playing. We played Four Corners one year and I joined in at the last minute. We had a blast and I wondered to myself, why didn't I do this earlier??

Final Teacher Work Days

♦ **Use any days you are given after the students' last day to finish cleaning and organizing.**

♦ **Always pack up and put away the contents of your desk LAST.** You will be searching for pens, paperclips, and staplers until you walk out the door for the last time, so there's no point in trying to put those items away early.

♦ **Complete all cumulative folders, inventories, and other paperwork.**

♦ **Turn in your grade book and attendance, if required.**

Preparation for the Fall

If you're staying in the same school and grade level, consider using your time in June to make photocopies and do laminating for the following school year. It seems like the machines always break in the fall when everyone has a ton of stuff to put together! You can laminate blank nametags and folders, and also photocopy get-to-know you papers and worksheets for the first units in your course of study. It is always such a joy to come back in August and spend time working on the classroom instead of standing over a copier!

You may also consider planning with your grade level team for the next year. Many teams like to go over the school supply list, behavior modification plan, and recess rules before school lets out. Other teachers would rather do these things in the fall, especially if they know there will be staff turnover.

If there are any projects you want to work on or plan over the summer, take home the materials you think you may need. I like to keep construction paper, poster board, etc., at my house so that I can make things whenever the inspiration hits, even if I don't have access to my classroom.

Chapter 36: Avoiding Burn-Out
Changing your mindset to restore your passion for teaching

Even before the month of August comes to an end, my email inbox is typically bursting with messages from overwhelmed teachers. "Help! I can't do this!", "I feel so inadequate—it's just too much for one person!", and "I don't think I can teach anymore. The kids are so bad—I'm thinking of just quitting." Each person who has contacted me was searching for the same thing: reassurance that their feelings are normal (they are), encouragement that they can handle the responsibilities (they can), and a reason to believe that the rewards of teaching outweigh the costs (they do). That's what this chapter is all about: helping you regain your confidence and avoid burn-out.

The 8 Keys to Enjoying and Growing With Students

What follows are key principles that helped me stay in the teaching profession at times when I didn't think I could take another day. They are based on what I've seen happen in my own life and the lives of other teachers who overcame feelings of hopelessness and frustration and regained their enthusiasm for teaching.

Key #1) Loving your students (even when they're not so loveable!)
Key #2) Seeing the big picture
Key #3) Having a support system
Key #4) Expressing your creativity and yourself in the classroom
Key #5) Learning and growing through professional development in all forms
Key #6) Introspection and recognizing your own needs as a teacher
Key #7) Get a life! Taking time for yourself outside of work
Key #8) Recognizing the need for change and creating new challenges

Key #1) Loving your students (even when they're not so loveable!)

Enjoying and growing with your students is one of the most important ways to combat burn-out. Unfortunately, when you're stressed, it can feel almost impossible to see the kids as the beautiful people that they are. It's really helped me to build times into our daily schedule which force me to step back and remember what's important.

For example, in our daily morning meetings, I set a timer for one minute and the entire class greets one another by name, usually with a handshake of some sort. That's all the time to takes for every student to smile up at me, shake my hand, and say, "Good morning, Ms. Powell!" This act alone sets the tone for the day and reminds me that I'm dealing with kids who have feelings, too.

I also have my students give a 'hug or a handshake' when they leave the classroom each afternoon. This personal acknowledgement gives me another chance to connect with each child and really calms me down at the end of the day when I am feeling stressed. Sometimes I also have 'tickets out the door'—the kids write one thing they learned that day and hand me their paper (the 'ticket') at dismissal. Having a written record that YES, this day was worth getting out of bed for because I did actually get through to the kids, is enough to help me keep going when I'm feeling discouraged.

You can have lunch or snack with your kids as a reward every now and then—an unstructured time to just sit and talk about what's going on in their lives really endears them to you (and vice versa). Having a 'sharing time' in which kids can tell about things they're doing in their personal lives can also help you connect with your kids. We do this during dismissal—each child has a day of the week to share an item or story that he would like the class to know about and takes three questions or comments afterwards. (This is actually a legitimate part of the curriculum, because it addresses the oral language goals in our state standards!)

Another way I connect with my kids is through our class reward system, in which I give beads that the children can exchange at the end of the week for free time. They have to earn ten beads per week, which prompts me to compliment each child individually several times a day. Every time I give a bead, I verbally praise something that the child has done, which helps me to focus on their good qualities and not the things that drive me nuts.

Some school systems train us to think of kids as machines that can be pushed to the limit every minute of the day and perform at 100% of their ability regardless of outside factors, and we have to intentionally do things to remind ourselves that this is not the case. Fortunately, there are an unlimited number of ways to accomplish the goal of seeing students as individual people with feelings and emotions. When kids feel cared for and respected, they will work harder for you and follow your rules, making the day less stressful and more productive for everyone. It's worth taking the time and energy to connect with your kids because the payoffs are ten fold!!

Key #2) Seeing the big picture

It's easy to get caught up in the little things that are so frustrating about being a teacher: repeating directions over and over, dealing with the same behavior problem from the same kid every single day, completing meaningless paperwork, grading a million papers...and if you focus on the small things that drive you crazy, you WILL get burned out. There is a reason you became a teacher—was it to make a difference in a child's life? To express your creativity? To immerse yourself in a subject you love and inspire students to do the same? Reconnect with that part of you. Write out your personal mission statement and post it somewhere in the room where you (and maybe only you) will see it throughout the day. Create goals for yourself that you know you can meet and celebrate your success when you reach them. Don't major in the minors or allow yourself to become discouraged by distractions.

Key #3) Having a support system

I am blessed to have had at least one person in each school I've worked in that I consider a true friend—not just a colleague or associate, but a person that I could call at two a.m. with a flat tire and know that she would pick me up. There were times in my life when I hung out with someone from my job almost every single day, whether it was for something fun like shopping at the mall or hanging out on the beach, or something practical, like running errands together or keeping an eye on her kids while she cooked dinner for us (a good trade, I might add). Knowing that I have someone I can go to with any problem, personal or professional, is the main thing that gets me through the day sometimes—that thought of, *whew, in an hour I can go next door and just vent!*

If you wish you had friends like that in your school, give it time. Because we don't have many opportunities to get to know one another, it usually takes me awhile to get close to my colleagues. Be careful not to prejudge anyone—I often bond with people that I would have never imagined myself relating to! If you aren't making connections with anyone in your current position, you could also consider moving to another grade level or even school where there are teachers that have similar personalities and, ideally, life situations as you. Having a strong support system is just that critical.

Even if you don't have true friends at work—or if you prefer to keep your personal and professional lives separate—it is important to have people you trust and can go to when you're stressed at school. Your spouse, friends, and family do NOT understand what it is like to be a teacher unless they have been educators themselves—what we go through on a daily basis in completely beyond the realm of imagination for the general public. You need to talk to someone who understands the pressure you're under. If you can find one wise person you trust, that might be all you need.

This plays out practically, too. If you just can't tolerate a child's behavior anymore and you have a trusted colleague, you can send the child to him to work for awhile, no questions asked. You have someone to take notes for you at meetings you miss. You have someone to bounce ideas off of when rearranging your classroom or revamping your behavior plan. If you have even a single coworker that you can count on for that, it's going to make a big difference in your energy level and enthusiasm at work.

Key #4) Expressing your creativity and yourself in the classroom

One of the best aspects of being a teacher is that you can typically shut your classroom door and do your thing. YOUR thing. If your head hurts, the kids can do more independent work; if you're feeling energetic, you can teach using a game; if you want to sit down for awhile, you can call the kids to the carpet and teach while relaxing in a rocking chair. We have a tremendous amount of flexibility that we CANNOT overlook. Think about how many people sit at a desk in their office nine hours a day, every day. Hardly anyone gets to change tasks to suit their moods and still be productive—we do, because teaching is as much an art as it is a science, and there are a limitless number of ways to teach effectively.

Before you complain that YOU don't have that kind of flexibility, let me explain that in Florida, third graders are automatically retained if they don't pass the state standardized test, so I and many other teachers are under a tremendous amount of pressure. We have to have our schedules posted and are supposed to adhere to them at all times. Our lesson plans must be planned as a grade level team and followed precisely. And even with these types of restraints, I still maintain a sense of freedom in my classroom. Sure, I need to teach customary measurement between 11:15 and 12:15, but I can teach it any way I want—with the laptop computers, individual dry erase boards, games, manipulatives, group activities, direct instruction, songs...and honestly, I do whatever I feel like that day! I start the lesson, gauge the kids' interest, and adjust accordingly. I don't know of any teachers, other than those who have scripted reading lessons, who are not allowed that sort of freedom, in reality if not technically. Don't lose sight of how awesome it is to structure your day the way you want!

You also have a lot more wiggle room in terms of content than you probably realize. For example, if you need to teach narrative elements or cause/effect, you can use any story you want to introduce your lesson. Pick a favorite book from your childhood or something just published with cool illustrations that you know will catch the kids' attention. And that's just for reading instruction—you've got lots of opportunities to reflect your personality in social studies and science. For example, I love teaching kids about the history of slavery and segregation in America, so I introduce the topic early in the year through various skill-based activities and read-alouds (we are supposed to read daily to the kids but we get to choose the books!). Then in February, when I can justify it because of African-American History Month, we get really in-depth with the subject. Black history is a small part of the state standards, but it IS part of the curriculum, and if I know how to teach it well, I'm going to focus on that.

When they're promoted to the next grade, my kids will almost certainly have a teacher with a different interest in social studies or who is passionate about science, and students will get a deeper understanding of that teacher's favorite topic. As long as you are teaching your state standards, you can emphasize the things you are enthusiastic about and tie those topics in throughout the year.

Of course, everyone has a subject or unit they dread having to teach, and it's important to be aware of that because students normally respond to the teacher's lack of enthusiasm. You may have had a really incredible teacher in your past who loved the subject matter she taught so much that it (almost) made up for the fact that you hated the subject! Conversely, you probably had a teacher that made even your favorite subject seem boring.

The good news is, you can change the way you teach something to change the way students learn it! Use YOUR INTERESTS to improve your teaching in subjects you dislike. Seek out books and Internet resources with interesting tidbits in subjects you are unfamiliar with. For example, I'm not a science person and am totally lost when it comes to the solar system, so I looked up websites with unusual factoids about space. Not only did that increase my interest in the subject matter, but it engaged the kids when I shared what I learned with them, and encouraged them to dig deeper. While planetary formations and orbit paths are still a bit of a mystery to me, I do have some random knowledge that has piqued my interest and helped make the rest of the information more relevant to me—and by extension, to my students.

I also try to use activities that I enjoy doing with the kids to make science instruction less painful for me. For example, we rarely get to 'make things' in third grade, so I look forward to teaching the kids to make a solar system mobile. Using my favorite teaching strategies helps a lot—utilizing computers, doing partner work, and watching exciting videos all make science more fun. There are so many effective teaching techniques—use the ones you like and feed off the excitement you generate in your kids.

Key #5) Learning and growing through professional development in all forms

One of the best energizers is a good teacher workshop...with emphasis on the word GOOD. Unfortunately, you don't always have a choice and the subject matter is not always what you're interested in. But, if you are allowed to give input as to which workshops you take, ask around about what's practical and useful. A good professional development day should leave you dying to get back to your classroom to try out all those new ideas. Seek those opportunities as much as you can.

Professional development can also include informal discussions with coworkers. I was feeling really discouraged one night about how my teaching had become so test-driven and I felt like my kids were giving up and not putting forth their best effort. I called my coworker and we came up with a new approach that helped my kids do a total 180. Seriously. Go out after work for an appetizer with someone on your grade level team and talk about what's working and what's not. You could even do it during school hours—one year I planned for my team to meet during our lunch break every Wednesday to share best practices (we weren't consistent, but hey, it was a good idea!). Find some kind of system for bouncing ideas off each other that works for you.

The fact that you're even reading this book says a tremendous amount about your commitment to the profession and eagerness to learn and grow. Many teachers would never do all of the research you've done, so count yourself as one of the most ambitious, even if you don't feel that way right now! Never discount the value of learning from websites and books—those resources have had a bigger impact on my teaching than anything else, hands down. There are a few teachers whose websites have totally revolutionized the way I teach. They inspire me and keep me excited about going into the classroom.

One word of caution: never compare yourself to any other teacher or allow yourself to become overwhelmed by all of the wonderful things you 'could' be doing! Add a few more activities every year, but don't feel like you're less than anyone else because you don't do all of those fantastic things they do. There are so many teachers who visit my website and say, wow, you must be the best third grade teacher ever! Uh, no. I sit at my desk (gasp!) and grade papers sometimes while the kids do worksheets (yes, worksheets, horror of horrors). What people write about in books and show on websites is never the whole story, and no one is perfect. When I visit someone's website and start to feel inferior and hopeless—and yes, there are several teachers who inadvertently have that effect on me—I leave the site and come back later! I'm doing the best that I can right now, and that's all I can ask of myself.

Key #6) Introspection and recognizing your own needs as a teacher

Teachers are not computers that can be programmed to all teach the same way and all get the same results every time, no matter what school or government officials dictate. You have to respect your own needs because no one else is going to. If you're exhausted, take a sick day, for goodness sake! Leave very simple activities for the kids so your sub plans take ten minutes to do, and sleep in the next day. If you're going through something big emotionally—a divorce, a family member's death—you are not going to be able to teach like nothing is happening. If you're really sad one day, it's okay to show an educational movie related to your unit of study and have the kids write about what they learned while you get yourself together.

You also need to think about your professional goals. Don't take on obligations that aren't furthering what you hope to accomplish in your career or are far removed from the issues you are passionate about. You have to think long and hard about who you are as a person and what you need in order to feel good about what you do. Teaching is NOT an entirely altruistic profession that you should stay in just because you love kids so much. It is your career, and you should pursue it as such. Your needs and interests matter. This might be the first and last time someone tells you that, so don't forget it. It took me years to figure that out on my own.

Key #7) Get a life! Taking time for yourself outside of work

If you're an overachiever like me, you have a tendency to want everything to be perfect and allow teaching to consume your life. The longer you teach, the easier it will become to manage this predisposition, but you have to set limits for yourself, e.g., no staying past 4:00 or only allowing yourself to come in early three days a week. This is important not just because you will burn yourself out, but because someone who works all the time is BORING, and who wants a BORING teacher?

When you're modeling how to respond to a writing prompt, include an anecdote about the movie you saw last weekend. During science, ask the kids if they saw the latest museum exhibit and show the photos you took. Talk about the incredible novel you're reading and how the author uses the best imagery or figurative language, or how you had to use context clues to figure out a word. Play the National Geographic special you saw and recorded for the kids as part of your unit on land formations or world cultures. Recount how you were having coffee with a friend and had a funny misunderstanding because of the homophones 'pair/pear'. Share with the kids how you actually used the term 'parallel' when you were at a football game on Sunday. It's so important to let the kids into your life so they can relate to and bond with you...but that's only possible if you actually HAVE a life to talk about. Be an interesting, well-rounded person. You will be a happier and more effective teacher.

Key #8)   Recognizing the need for change and creating new challenges

I thrive off of change that I initiate and design myself (as opposed to change that is thrust upon me without my input, which naturally I dislike). So, every year I create new challenges for myself. One year it was to run a Reader's Workshop. Another year, my goal was to learn how to teach inquiry science and have more effective parent outreach. Without challenges that I create, I feel stagnant and restless. Not everyone is like that, but if you're reading about burnout, you probably need a self-directed challenge that reflects who you are and who you want to become professionally in order to feel more motivated at work. Become a lifelong learner and always be ready to try something new!

If you just can't shake those feelings of hating what you do, you need to really analyze what you want. Make a list of what your ideal teaching job would be like (hours, class size, extra duties, role of administration, etc). and the characteristics of your ideal job, period. As you compare them, take a look at whether teaching is something you could ever be happy doing—is there enough crossover on the lists? I did this twice when I was ready to leave the field and found that being in the classroom was meeting more of my needs than any other job I could imagine in terms of having fun, flexibility, and lots of time off. Seeing right there in black and white that teaching is an amazing career choice for my personality really boosted my spirits and gave me more enthusiasm to keep going when I was worn out.

If you want to stay in teaching but are unhappy with your current situation, you can switch districts, schools, or grade levels. My move from Head Start to 3rd absolutely saved me—I was so out of patience for cleaning up bathroom accidents and wiping crumbs from tables that I thought I needed to do something else professionally. It turns out I just needed to teach kids who can use the bathroom and feed themselves independently! The longer I teach, the more mature I want my kids to be, and now I would actually consider a move to middle school. I recognize these changes in myself and my preferences, and I allow them to help me create new challenges.

Afterword

The idea of running a classroom can seem overwhelming. After reading this book, you've probably begun thinking about many expectations and procedures that you never realized you needed to consider. You may even be wondering how you're supposed to find the time and energy to focus on academics!

I hope you're absolutely convinced that the cornerstone of effective instruction is classroom management. When you start feeling overwhelmed by all the demands that are on you, stay focused on management and keep a positive outlook. Instruction *will* fall naturally into place. Teaching itself is not that complicated or stressful: managing the classroom is. It's easy for learning to take place once students are motivated to listen, know how to follow along, and stay on-task independently. Your daily routines and predictable schedule create a framework for learning. Filling in that framework is a matter of choosing academic tasks for your students each day.

It doesn't matter how fabulous your lesson is, if your students aren't listening and don't understand how to participate appropriately. It's better to have an average lesson and spectacular management than an incredible lesson in which students are playing around, half-listening, misusing materials, and talking over you. Get your classroom management in place FIRST, and then concentrate on producing and implementing the most effective lessons possible. As you familiarize yourself with your teaching resources and talk to colleagues, you'll pick up new ideas and hone your skills more quickly than you ever thought possible.

Above all, enjoy your job and being with your students. Stay focused on the things you love about being in the classroom. Believe the best about your students, their parents, your colleagues, and your administration, and don't worry about the things you can't control. Live your life in and out of the classroom with passion and zeal.

I hope this book has left you wanting to know more. Please visit TheCornerstoneForTeachers.com to learn about further classroom management strategies, lesson ideas and teaching techniques for every subject area, and most importantly, how to develop a positive mindset and maintain your enthusiasm for one of the highest callings imaginable. May God bless you in all of your pursuits!

Index

CPSIA information can be obtained
at www.ICGtesting.com
Printed in the USA
BVOW09s0735030118
504332BV00001B/23/P